Securing Smart Cities Through Modern Cryptography Technologies

Mishall Al-Zubaidie
https://orcid.org/0000-0002-3149-9129
University of Thi-Qar, Iraq & University of Southern Queensland, Australia

IGI Global
Scientific Publishing
Publishing Tomorrow's Research Today

Vice President of Editorial	Melissa Wagner
Director of Acquisitions	Mikaela Felty
Director of Book Development	Jocelynn Hessler
Production Manager	Mike Brehm
Cover Design	Jose Rosado

Published in the United States of America by
IGI Global Scientific Publishing
701 East Chocolate Avenue
Hershey, PA, 17033, USA
Tel: 717-533-8845 | Fax: 717-533-7115
Website: https://www.igi-global.com E-mail: cust@igi-global.com

Library of Congress Cataloging-in-Publication Data

LCCN: 2025015512 (CIP Data Pending)
ISBN13: 979-8-3373-3326-7
Isbn13Softcover: 979-8-3373-3327-4
EISBN13: 979-8-3373-3328-1
British Cataloguing in Publication Data
A Cataloguing in Publication record for this book is available from the British Library.

Our families, whose steadfast support and encouragement have been a continual source of strength throughout this journey, are deeply appreciated and affectionately dedicated in this book "Securing Smart Cities through Modern Cryptography Technologies".

Our families, whose steadfast support and encouragement have been a continual source of strength throughout this journey, are deeply appreciated and affectionately dedicated in this book.

To my dear father (Hammed)... the ideal man, may God grant him a long life and cure him of all illness... who taught me how to stand firm in the face of challenges.

To my dear mother (Edaa)... the source of goodness, sacrifice, and altruism... my paradise in this world and the hereafter.

To my wife (Hawa)... my companion in struggle and journey, who spared no time or effort to help me... my love, my life, my beating heart, and who filled my life with love, my eternal love that time cannot change or distance erase

To my children (Haider, Mohammed, and Ayoub)... my joy and happiness in times of distress... the light of my eyes

To my brothers and sisters... my support and my strength, the one who shares my joys and sorrows... the example of giving, pride, and sacrifice.

To everyone from whom I have received advice and support

To all my family and friends.

To everyone who has prayed for my well-being

I dedicate this humble book to you...

Mishall Al-Zubaidie

Table of Contents

Detailed Table of Contents

This chapter explores the critical role of advanced cryptographic technologies in securing smart city applications across domains such as e-health, e-commerce, and e-banking. As urban environments become increasingly digitized, safeguarding sensitive data, ensuring transaction integrity, and protecting user privacy emerge as paramount challenges. The chapter explores a spectrum of cryptographic solutions, including blockchain, homomorphic encryption, zero-knowledge proofs, and quantum cryptography, that address these complexities. Through detailed analysis and real-world case studies, it highlights practical implementations and emerging trends that reinforce trust and resilience in smart city infrastructures. Moreover, the chapter discusses the policy and ethical dimensions necessary to balance security with usability and transparency. Finally, it provides a comprehensive framework for integrating cryptographic safeguards into the evolving digital fabric of smart cities, ensuring secure, scalable, and citizen-centric urban services.

As smart cities continue to evolve through the integration of IoT, AI, and big data analytics, the complexity and scale of cybersecurity challenges have intensified. This

it a practical solution for protecting electrical infrastructure in smart cities in the quantum era.

R. Siva Subramanian, RMK College of Engineering and Technology, India
B. Yuvasri, RMK College of Engineering and Technology, India
K. Sudha, RMD Engineering College, India

The rapid development of smart cities has introduced new security challenges, necessitating advanced solutions to ensure trust, resilience, and data integrity. Blockchain technology provides a decentralized and tamper-resistant framework to enhance smart city security, enabling secure identity management, cybersecurity, critical infrastructure protection, and transparent financial transactions. This chapter explores blockchain's role in smart city security, highlighting key applications, challenges, and future research directions. While blockchain enhances security, scalability, interoperability, regulatory concerns, and high implementation costs pose significant challenges. Advancements in quantum-resistant cryptography, AI-driven security models, and decentralized governance are expected to shape the future of blockchain-enabled smart cities. By addressing these challenges, blockchain can provide a secure and transparent foundation for smart city ecosystems, ensuring long-term sustainability and efficiency.

Koduri Sreelakshmi, Department of ECE, GMR Institute of Technology, Rajam, India
Rajesh V. Argiddi, Department of Computer Science and Engineering, Walchand Institute of Technology, Solapur, India
Syeda Meraj Bilfaqih, Department of computer Science, King Khalid University, Gregar, Saudi Arabia
Sanya Yadv, School of Law, Bennett University, Greater Noida, India
D. Ramya, Department of English, Kongu Engineering College, Perundurai, Indonesia
M. Sudha, SaiSriram Engineering College, India

This chapter invites the integration of blockchain technology and cryptographic consensus methods to increase cybersecurity in smart city ecosystems. As the urban environment becomes more and more connected by IoT and data-based infrastructure, the need for safe, transparent, and elastic systems is important. Blockchain provides decentralized trust, tamper-proof records, and strong control, which is important

Foreword

A new era of innovation has been ushered in by the quick developments in smart cities, cryptography, and artificial intelligence, which are changing economies, society, transportation, healthcare, and industries at a never-before-seen rate. Automation, cybersecurity, and decision-making are all being revolutionized by smart cities, but a major obstacle is the growing amount of trustworthy big data that comes with digital transformation and smart decisions. It is therefore crucial to include contemporary encryption methods and practices into computing and information security systems as we head toward a future of highly interconnected digital ecosystems in modern smart cities.

A timely and crucial addition to the conversation about how cybersecurity, artificial intelligence, smart cities, and cryptography performance can all work together to build a safer and ecologically conscious digital future is this book, Securing Smart Cities Through Modern Cryptography Technologies. It combines a wide range of studies, perceptions, and solutions that tackle important issues in computational efficiency, cybersecurity, and cryptography challenges in smart cities.

The book's chapters offer a thorough and multidisciplinary look at how to optimize data security measures in smart cities to safeguard citizens' information, how to use the principles of contemporary cryptography to create secure digital infrastructures, and how innovations like blockchain, quantum computing, encryption, and learning algorithms are influencing the next wave of cyber defense tactics. The book covers a wide range of issues from basic ideas to state-of-the-art technologies, from lowering security concerns to protecting space data and protecting information privacy in e-health, e-transportation, e-commerce, e-banking, and e-governance.

This book's practical usefulness is among its most captivating features. It is now essential to balance performance, efficiency, and security as more companies embrace smart city security systems. This book's talks are not only theoretical investigations; they also provide governments, corporations, researchers, and policymakers with practical road maps for putting safe and environmentally responsible cybersecurity frameworks into place in smart cities.

I applaud the editors and contributors for their creative curation in assembling this enlightening book. By bridging the gap between big data security in smart cities and technical innovation, the book creates a reliable digital ecosystem that may be expanded upon by future generations.

This book, in my opinion, will be a fundamental resource for scholars, researchers, security experts, and decision-makers, helping them to create a future in which big data security and technology coexist. I enthusiastically encourage readers to peruse this volume and set out on a path toward long-term information security in the era of smart cities.

Kuvonchbek Rakhimberdiev

Department of Applied Mathematics and Digital Economy, Tashkent State University of Economics, Tashkent, Uzbekistan

Preface

ABOUT THE BOOK TOPIC

At a pace never before observed at the civilizational level, the Internet of Things (IoT), smart city applications, and artificial intelligence, as we know them, have brought people closer to one another. As a result of this change, some elements reappeared in the shape of less legal activities, such as cybercrime and security breaches, while others were subjected to a series of inadequate corrective actions. In this new era, information represents valuable details, and practically everything represents information, especially personal data, identities, and personal activities and their respective detailed interconnections. Therefore, these are not the only characteristics of a technological society that is fully computerized and where terrestrial borders matter little in limiting the active agents, harmful or not, of this system.

The past ten years have shown that security flaws are, without a doubt, the most difficult problem facing humanity, with civilization being upended by abrupt changes that have significant negative effects on the economy, society, politics, and ecology. Security lapses have a detrimental effect on societies in many different areas. Due to traditional security technological offers, trends, goods, challenges, and solutions, this volatility has serious repercussions for the security of societies and organizations. It also creates a disruption that is currently nearly hard to manage or conceal. Continually, people, businesses, and countries rely on the IoT, the most crucial information highway in a variety of fields, including e-health, e-banking, e-government, e-commerce, etc. It is impossible to separate the IoT from the enormous army of unknown malicious actors who conspire to compromise security in order to gain any sort of advantage in the misuse of information. Cybersecurity vulnerabilities occur through highly technical actions, primarily because people rely on technology but lack the skills necessary to understand its many facets, with security being the most important.

The world needs smart cities, sophisticated, and efficient technology to facilitate quick communication and intelligent decision-making. However, data from smart cities also needs a strong defense against different types of intrusions and breaches. In a time when smart cities, artificial intelligence, and cutting-edge cryptographic technologies are transforming entire industries, the relationship between these technologies and cybersecurity has emerged as a crucial subject for study and development. A thorough attempt to investigate the relationship between cybersecurity and big data, providing insights into their prospects, obstacles, and future directions, is the integration of information security in smart contracts and smart cities.

Researchers, scholars, academics, business professionals, legislators, and students who want to comprehend and use trustworthy security tactics and procedures in the smart cities digital era will find this book to be an invaluable resource. In order to maintain a balance between technological advancement and environmental responsibility, it brings together experts from a variety of fields to present state-of-the-art innovations that combine cryptography technologies like blockchain, quantum, and encryption algorithms with security solutions for smart cities.

THE GOAL

The ever-evolving fields of cybersecurity and information privacy in smart cities make it difficult for information security professionals to keep up with the latest findings in the industry. Because of this, the editors and authors are happy to present the first book edition of Securing Smart Cities Through Modern Cryptography Technologies, a comprehensive standalone edition packed with the best research and references available to give academicians, researchers, and students a solid grasp of the important topics surrounding cybersecurity and information privacy in smart cities. Recurrent investigations and studies included in this book offer both comprehensive and in-depth viewpoints on state-of-the-art theories and advancements in the security of smart cities. In addition to offering insight into new developments and the field's prospects for smart cities, this reference is intended to serve as a single point of reference for conceptual, methodological, technological, and managerial challenges.

ORGANIZATION THE BOOK

This book guide is divided into 10 chapters and was co-authored by authors from multiple organizations across several countries. This substantial involvement allows us to assert a range of perspectives that support the validity of this book.

We acknowledge the outstanding efforts of each and every author. Their extensive expertise in the fields of information privacy and smart city security is shown in this book of research. The book is arranged into sections that cover core principles, modern cryptography technologies, security mechanisms of smart cities, and real-world applications across industries in order to provide a logical and systematic progression of themes.

Chapter 1: Fortifying Smart City Applications: Cryptographic Security in E-Health, E-Commerce, E-Banking, and E-Governance

This chapter explores the critical role of advanced cryptographic technologies in securing smart city applications across domains such as e-health, e-commerce, and e-banking. As urban environments become increasingly digitized, safeguarding sensitive data, ensuring transaction integrity, and protecting user privacy emerge as paramount challenges. The chapter explores a spectrum of cryptographic solutions, including blockchain, homomorphic encryption, zero-knowledge proofs, and quantum cryptography, that address these complexities. Through detailed analysis and real-world case studies, it highlights practical implementations and emerging trends that reinforce trust and resilience in smart city infrastructures. Moreover, the chapter discusses the policy and ethical dimensions necessary to balance security with usability and transparency. Finally, it provides a comprehensive framework for integrating cryptographic safeguards into the evolving digital fabric of smart cities, ensuring secure, scalable, and citizen-centric urban services.

Chapter 2: Cybersecurity in the Smart City Era: Overcoming Challenges with Modern Cryptographic Solutions

As smart cities continue to evolve through the integration of IoT, AI, and big data analytics, the complexity and scale of cybersecurity challenges have intensified. This chapter examines key vulnerabilities ranging from data privacy breaches to cyber-physical system attacks and highlights the critical role of modern cryptographic technologies in addressing these risks. Techniques such as encryption, blockchain, PKI, homomorphic encryption, zero-knowledge proofs, and quantum cryptography are analyzed for their potential to strengthen smart city infrastructures. Drawing on recent case studies and emerging research, we further explore future directions, including post-quantum security and AI-driven cybersecurity frameworks. The findings of this chapter suggest that strategically embedding cryptographic solutions is essential for building secure, resilient, and citizen-centered smart cities capable of withstanding both current and emerging cyber threats.

Chapter 3: Cybersecurity Challenges in Smart City Development

The rapid development of smart cities introduces significant cybersecurity challenges due to the increasing interconnectivity of urban infrastructure, IoT devices, and data-driven systems. This chapter explores the vulnerabilities and security threats that arise in smart city environments, including cyberattacks on critical infrastructure, data privacy risks, and the exploitation of weak encryption protocols. It also examines the role of cryptographic technologies in mitigating these challenges, highlighting encryption methods, blockchain applications, and AI-driven security mechanisms. Additionally, the chapter discusses regulatory frameworks and best practices for enhancing cybersecurity resilience in smart cities. By addressing these concerns, this chapter provides a comprehensive overview of the security landscape in smart city development and proposes strategies to safeguard urban digital ecosystems.

Chapter 4: Cyber Resilient Smart Cities through Big Data and Cryptography

The emergence of smart cities has transformed urban living through the integration of big data and IoT technologies. While these advancements enhance service delivery and infrastructure efficiency in areas like traffic management, healthcare, and public safety, they also raise significant concerns about data security and privacy. This chapter explores the role of cryptographic technologies in securing the vast amounts of sensitive information generated by smart city systems. It discusses encryption, digital signatures, blockchain, and their applications in maintaining data integrity, confidentiality, and access control. Special attention is given to securing IoT devices, which are integral to smart city frameworks but pose unique vulnerabilities. Real-world case studies illustrate the use of blockchain for transparency and end-to-end encryption for personal data protection. The chapter also addresses the growing relevance of quantum-resistant cryptography, proposing a unified security framework for future smart cities to ensure resilience, privacy, and trust.

Chapter 5: Secure IoT Communication in Smart Cities using Cryptographic Techniques

The rapid development of smart cities relies heavily on the Internet of Things (IoT) to enhance urban infrastructure, optimize resource management, and improve citizens' quality of life. However, the increasing interconnectivity of IoT devices raises significant security concerns, including unauthorized access, data breaches, and cyberattacks. Cryptographic techniques play a crucial role in securing IoT communication by ensuring data confidentiality, integrity, and authentication. This chapter explores the application of modern cryptographic solutions such as lightweight encryption algorithms, blockchain-based security models, and post-quantum cryptography in IoT networks. It also discusses key challenges, including computational constraints of IoT devices, scalability, and interoperability, while highlighting potential future research directions for enhancing cryptographic security in smart city IoT infrastructures.

Chapter 6: Tokenization and Micropayments in Smart City Ecosystems

This chapter explores the role of tokenization and micropayments as foundational tools in building scalable and inclusive smart city ecosystems. It examines how blockchain-based tokens can represent digital value and rights, enabling friction-less transactions across diverse urban services such as transportation, energy, and public utilities. The chapter also delves into the mechanisms that support real-time, low-cost micropayments, essential for machine-to-machine (M2M) interactions and citizen engagement in decentralized platforms. Furthermore, it addresses the underlying cryptographic principles, privacy concerns, regulatory challenges, and security implications associated with deploying token-based payment systems in a smart city context. Case studies and emerging use cases are presented to highlight real-world applications, and future directions are proposed to guide policymakers, technologists, and urban planners in leveraging tokenization to build resilient, transparent, and citizen-centric urban environments.

Chapter 7: Quantum Cryptography: The Future of Data Security in Smart Urban Environments

As cities adopt integrated IoT ecosystems and data-driven urban governance, traditional encryption faces the threat of obsolescence by quantum computing attacks. This chapter explores the application of quantum cryptography in protecting smart urban infrastructure, with a focus on quantum key distribution (QKD), post-quantum algorithms, and hybrid systems. Through an examination of deployments in smart grids, traffic management systems, and public health platforms, we illustrate how quantum-resistant protocols reduce threats of data breaches and spoofing attacks. There are special challenges: scaling QKD to millions of IoT devices will need new network architectures, and integrating with legacy systems will need phased "crypto-agility" plans. The chapter presents a model for incorporating quantum-safe practice into urban design, with an emphasis on inter-disciplinary collaboration among cryptographers, policymakers, and city administrators.

Chapter 8: Protecting Data of Power Stations in Smart Cities Using Quantum-Resistant and Zero-Knowledge Proof

The rapid advancement of quantum computing poses significant challenges to conventional cryptography, necessitating the adoption of post-quantum cryptography (PQC) solutions. This chapter proposes a Post-Quantum Lattice Security (PQLS) system for protecting power plant data in smart cities. It integrates Kyber for secure key exchange, Falcon for quantum-resistant digital signatures, ZKP for efficient authentication without revealing sensitive data, and JSON-LD for standardizing the format of data received from different smart meters. To evaluate the security of the proposed framework, we analyze its resistance to various threats, such as side-channel and message recovery attacks. We measured key performance indicators. The results showed an average CPU utilization of 2.4592 MS, memory consumption averaging 1843.899 KB, an execution time of 2.45 MS, and a level averaging 66.27677. This demonstrates that our proposed system offers high security and efficiency, making it a practical solution for protecting electrical infrastructure in smart cities in the quantum era.

Chapter 9: Blockchain Technology as a Foundation for Smart City Security: Enhancing Trust and Resilience

The rapid development of smart cities has introduced new security challenges, necessitating advanced solutions to ensure trust, resilience, and data integrity. Blockchain technology provides a decentralized and tamper-resistant framework to enhance smart city security, enabling secure identity management, cybersecurity, critical infrastructure protection, and transparent financial transactions. This chapter explores blockchain's role in smart city security, highlighting key applications, challenges, and future research directions. While blockchain enhances security, scalability, interoperability, regulatory concerns, and high implementation costs pose significant challenges. Advancements in quantum-resistant cryptography, AI-driven security models, and decentralized governance are expected to shape the future of blockchain-enabled smart cities. By addressing these challenges, blockchain can provide a secure and transparent foundation for smart city ecosystems, ensuring long-term sustainability and efficiency.

Chapter 10: Blockchain-Driven Cybersecurity Architectures for Smart Cities

This chapter invites the integration of blockchain technology and cryptographic consensus methods to increase cybersecurity in smart city ecosystems. As the urban environment becomes more and more connected by IoT and data-based infrastructure, the need for safe, transparent, and elastic systems is important. Blockchain provides decentralized trust, tamper-proof records, and strong control, which is important for protecting complex services such as energy grids, traffic systems, and public safety networks. This chapter evaluates the applicable challenges in cases of various consensus models and smart cities, illuminating the challenges and future directions to protect the urban structures of the upcoming pay general.

A FUTURE PERSPECTIVE

Reliable and effective security solutions are more important than ever as smart cities and cryptographic technologies continue to change the cybersecurity landscape. In order to promote a future where security and performance efficiency coexist, this book attempts to offer a path for integrating smart cities with contemporary cryptography technologies. We would like to express our sincere appreciation to all of the authors, reviewers, and publishing experts who helped make this book possible. Their commitment and knowledge have contributed to the creation of a volume that will motivate academics, scholars, researchers, and industry professionals to advance information security in smart cities. This book is intended to be a first step toward a digital future that is smarter, safer, and more ecologically conscious.

We hope it's helpful to you. Have fun reading!

The Editor,

Mishall Al-Zubaidie

Department of Computer Sciences and Artificial Intelligence, University of Thi-Qar, Nasiriyah, Iraq

Acknowledgment

With great appreciation, we would like to thank everyone who helped us finish this book, Securing Smart Cities through Modern Cryptography Technologies. Without many people's commitment, knowledge, and assistance, this endeavor would not have been accomplished.

First and foremost, we would like to express our sincere gratitude to the staff at IGI Global Publishing for their unwavering support, technical know-how, and direction during this process. Their commitment and professionalism have been crucial to the success of this endeavor. Also, we would like to thank IGI Global for giving us the chance to edit this book and for the great assistance of their team of experts.

Second, we would like to express our sincere gratitude to each chapter's authors and reviewers. Their insightful opinions, thorough criticism, and unwavering dedication have greatly influenced the caliber and depth of this volume. Because of their efforts, this book is now a thorough resource for information security that is sustainable.

Third, we would especially like to express our gratitude to my wife, mother, and father, whose unfailing support, love, and patience have been a continual source of strength. Their assistance has helped us persevere through the difficulties of this project and has been essential to its successful conclusion.

Finally, we want to express our sincere gratitude for the tenacity and fortitude that have allowed us to complete this task. We would like to express our sincere gratitude to everyone who has helped in any form. We sincerely appreciate your efforts and support.

Chapter 1
Fortifying Smart City Applications:
Cryptographic Security in E-Health, E-Commerce, E-Banking, and E-Governance

Md Mehedi Hasan Emon
https://orcid.org/0000-0002-6224-9552
American International University-Bangladesh, Bangladesh

Md. Mazid-Ul-Haque
https://orcid.org/0000-0002-9091-7191
American International University-Bangladesh, Bangladesh

Most. Sharmin Ara Chowdhury
https://orcid.org/0009-0005-1050-8283
Uttara University, Bangladesh

Kh. Mustafizur Rahman
https://orcid.org/0000-0002-9193-2473
World University of Bangladesh, Bangladesh

ABSTRACT

This chapter explores the critical role of advanced cryptographic technologies in securing smart city applications across domains such as e-health, e-commerce, and e-banking. As urban environments become increasingly digitized, safeguarding sensitive data, ensuring transaction integrity, and protecting user privacy emerge as paramount challenges. The chapter explores a spectrum of cryptographic solutions, including blockchain, homomorphic encryption, zero-knowledge proofs, and

DOI: 10.4018/979-8-3373-3326-7.ch001

quantum cryptography, that address these complexities. Through detailed analysis and real-world case studies, it highlights practical implementations and emerging trends that reinforce trust and resilience in smart city infrastructures. Moreover, the chapter discusses the policy and ethical dimensions necessary to balance security with usability and transparency. Finally, it provides a comprehensive framework for integrating cryptographic safeguards into the evolving digital fabric of smart cities, ensuring secure, scalable, and citizen-centric urban services.

INTRODUCTION

The chapter provides an in-depth review of how cryptographic security helps secure and protect the rapidly growing digital services found in smart cities. Since more digital technologies are used in cities for health, trading, banking, governance and agriculture, making data and transactions safer is now very important for both systems and society. Despite the improvements these services have brought to urban environments, they also disclose users and organizations to new cyber threats and data risks. The chapter explores the challenges that current cybersecurity approaches face in smart cities, making it clear that advanced encryption technologies are needed to secure privacy, data safety and authentication. New technologies such as blockchain, homomorphic encryption, zero-knowledge proofs (ZKP), public key infrastructure (PKI) and the fresh area of quantum cryptography are all studied with great attention. Technical advantages are considered, but complexity and potential for large and wide systems are also evaluated. The discussion includes examples of how cryptographic techniques are used in smart city areas. Including numerous studies on national identity, smart hospitals, digital banking and public services, the chapter gives practical examples of the ups and downs of implementation. These cases show the many ways in which innovation, regulation and trust are connected. Moreover, the chapter looks at the wider ethical, legal and policy challenges that arise when cryptographic methods are used in public systems. It supports creating standard guidelines, working together globally and developing regulations that deal with issues on both local and global scales. This chapter concludes by highlighting that cryptographic security should not be treated as a tech solution alone and should instead become a basic requirement for trusted, strong and just smart cities.

THE CRYPTOGRAPHIC IMPERATIVE IN THE AGE OF SMART CITIES

There is a major shift happening in the way cities are structured today. All over the world, cities are switching to smart cities, as these cities use digital technology to make services better, keep resources in check and boost the lives of those living in urban areas. The process of this transformation makes it more obvious that public utilities are dependent on digital technologies. Services like E-Health, E-Commerce, E-Banking and E-Governance are now in the heart of urban development. As more of these services become digital and connected, how to keep them secure has become a top concern for city governments. Thus, cryptography is necessary to ensure the city in cyberspace is safe, confidential and believed in by everyone.

Smart cities are built on the idea of incorporating information and communication technologies (ICT) fully into public services. Cities are becoming better informed and reactive for transformation of Internet of Things devices, cloud computing, big data analysis and artificial intelligence (Ullah et al., 2024). For example, patients can now be monitored online by doctors using devices they wear, there are apps for making digital payments when and where you like and governments can issue legal papers to citizens electronically. The advantages of these innovations are matched by the new risks linked to data exchange over large, complex networks that are susceptible to different types of cyber threats. These threats are real, and they are happening right now. Security breaches such as the row with the 2017 WannaCry ransomware attack on the UK's National Health Service and the 2020 SolarWinds attack on U.S. federal agencies make it clear what can happen due to lax cybersecurity rules (Munk, 2022). This shows that IT security structures designed for standard systems break down in the more dispersed, data-filled and connected world of smart cities.

A combination of firewalls, access controls and intrusion detection systems cannot address the threats now posed by attacking zero-day flaws, phishing using machine learning or encrypting data with quantum computers. Based on all this, cryptographic methods are necessary for guaranteeing digital safety and allowing operations to continue unbroken. The basic function of cryptography is to protect data from being read, to make certain the people involved are legitimate and to ensure that communication remains unchanged. For digital services to run safely, these properties are crucial. Data from E-Health should be encrypted while it is stored and carried across the internet to stop unauthorized use. In addition, both medical devices and software must authenticate before connecting to any other system. Bank transactions are protected from fraud by encryption and thanks to digital signatures, users are confirmed who they say they are.

Cryptography plays a key part in smart cities for uses other than its main, traditional applications. New inventions in cryptography such as homomorphic encryption, blockchain and ZKP have created brand-new secure methods for data handling and checking. The use of homomorphic encryption enables data to be worked on in secret form so that even machines used in health analytics or citizen profiling by companies cannot access private data (Herath et al., 2024). Blockchain technologies give us records that cannot be altered, allowing E-Governance and supply chain experts to work more safely and reliably (Mustafa et al., 2025). There is a lot of risk in E-Banking and digital finance, as just one breach can damage the whole system's trust. Because financial transactions are now handled on mobile, with digital currencies and between peers, proper management and tracking of keys and cryptographic logs is necessary.

The European Central Bank and the U.S. Federal Reserve are looking into how cryptographic frameworks might be used for digital currencies, giving a clear indication that cryptography is now central to future financial designs (Schumacher, 2024). The most advanced step, known as multi-party computation, is being used in blockchain networks today. It supports safe validation of financial contracts without revealing the sensitive details and may play a major role in influencing how regulations and risks are managed around digital finance (Krishna et al., 2025). However, it is not always easy to use cryptography in smart cities. There is still a big problem with scalability in the industry. Operations in cryptography, especially those using homomorphic encryption or ZKPs, can take a lot of computing power and have opened concerns about using them in urgent operations like driving autonomous vehicles or emergency response (Pandey et al., 2024). Furthermore, putting these technologies into old systems, most of which were built without encryption, usually involves a major revision of the system's structure. Solving interoperability challenges is necessary; differing computer and network systems from different places and sectors should exchange data safely. This difficulty is made worse by different national laws about data and encryption, for instance, GDPR in the EU and the CLOUD Act in the U.S.

Quantum computing is set to emerge soon and could disrupt many types of cryptographic systems. Post-quantum cryptography is moving swiftly ahead and NIST is currently working to set standards for quantum-proof algorithms (Khan et al., 2024). Smart cities that do not begin adopting these quantum-resilient systems could become threatened in the short term. Cryptographic technologies must also be used in a fair and clear manner. Technology that maintains privacy can also be used to hide wrongdoing. Blockchain's security means mistakes or deliberate abuse are hard to correct, and the anonymity offered by its technology can be taken advantage of by those who participate in crimes. Clear legal systems, control by civic authorities and firm rules for protecting human rights must be part of any cryptographic use in smart cities. Overall, using cryptographic methods in smart cities is a requirement for technology and a duty for society. Smart cities have larger potential points for attack by cybercriminals. Digital trust, robustness and growth in the industry are built on a foundation of cryptographic security. If there is no smart technology, the main goals of smart cities such as higher efficiency, fairness and a better life, will remain at risk. Cryptographic strength should be a priority for policymakers, engineers, urban planners and scholars at the start of planning digital urban spaces.

Table 1. Cryptographic techniques and their applications in smart city domains

Smart City Domain	Cryptographic Technique	Purpose/Function	Benefits
E-Health	AES, RSA, Homomorphic Encryption	Secure patient data at rest and during transmission; enable encrypted computation	Patient privacy, secure diagnostics
E-Banking	ECC, Blockchain, Digital Signatures	Secure transactions, prevent tampering, authenticate identities	Fraud prevention, transaction integrity
E-Commerce	TLS, Symmetric Encryption, ZKP	Secure payment data, private authentication of users	Customer trust, data confidentiality
E-Governance	PKI, Blockchain	Secure ID systems, ensure document integrity, enable digital voting	Transparency, reduced document fraud
Smart Mobility	Lightweight Encryption, ZKP	Protect vehicle-to-infrastructure communications	Real-time security, reduced spoofing risks
Public Services	Homomorphic Encryption, MPC	Enable secure analytics on citizen data without compromising privacy	Data-driven policy without privacy trade-offs

Table 1 offers a side-by-side look at how different cryptographic methods are being used in smart city services like healthcare, banking, governance, and mobility. Each of these areas has its own kind of data sensitivity and system requirements, so the cryptographic tools aren't always the same. For example, in E-Health, where patient data needs strong protection, techniques like AES and homomorphic encryption are often used. In contrast, the financial side of E-Banking tends to lean on blockchain and ECC to make sure transactions stay secure and unchanged. Privacy-focused methods like ZKPs have also found their place in things like E-Commerce and smart transport systems, mainly for authentication that keeps personal data hidden. Overall, cryptography plays a key role not just in keeping individual info safe, but also in building public trust something smart cities really depend on to run smoothly in today's connected digital world.

CRYPTOGRAPHIC THREATS AND CHALLENGES IN SMART CITY APPLICATIONS

Digital technologies are quickly changing the way urban areas are governed and how citizens take part in government. Artificial intelligence (AI), the Internet of Things (IoT), cloud technology and data help smart city applications increase how well public services are given and how citizens live. Still, the constant growth of attack points on the internet makes the network highly vulnerable to cyber-attacks. A leading risk in these systems is cryptographic security since it is responsible for keeping data confidential, secure and unchanged. The presence of many cryptographic technologies does not undo the various challenges and threats that prevent the safe use of smart city applications and systems for e-health, e-commerce, e-banking and digital administration.

As healthcare moves toward digitization and begins to rely on telemedicine and devices people wear, the threat of unauthorized access is on the rise. Accessing Electronic Health Records (EHRs) puts private data at risk, including information on a person, their health and genetic makeup and insurance. Besides exposing their privacy such breaches can put health at risk by allowing others to alter test or prescription reports in ways that may be unsafe or deadly (Javaid et al., 2023). Even though encryption-at-rest and end-to-end encryption are essential for EHR protection, many health organizations use aging or inadequate protocols because they are too pricey or cannot be used widely (Demirbaga et al., 2024). In addition, adding AI to diagnostics introduces a new kind of risk: encrypted systems might still provide flawed results if someone tricks the underlying algorithms with manipulated or incorrect data.

As banks move financial operations to mobile and digital channels, they are facing a growing variety of threats. Both E-Banking and E-Commerce are often attacked by phishing, MITM and APTs attempting to target cryptographic keys or session tokens (G & Vinothiyalakshmi, 2023). The lack of proper cryptography can let someone change or reuse a transaction, imitate another's identity and ruin the stability and confidence of users. PKI and digital certificates are usually installed as a common solution, but their effectiveness depends upon how securely you handle your keys and certificates, which is still a problem in many instances. Moreover, since increasingly popular contactless and biometric payment methods are used, cryptographic protocols now must handle safe real-time authentication, quick transaction validation and ensure biometric data leakage is prevented, as it cannot be replaced, unlike passwords (Uzun et al., 2021).

In digital governance, cryptographic problems are made even more complicated by having to ensure both openness and privacy. Governments are starting to depend more on systems that use digital ID, online voting systems and digital ways to keep legal records. Because of this, cryptographic systems are needed to confirm identity, approve digital signatures and protect archival. Nevertheless, centralized systems usually favored for managing efficiency leave the network vulnerable to single points of failure. Hacking of Aadhaar revealed the data of more than one billion Indians and supports our point (Sadhya & Sahu, 2024). In decentralized environments, blockchain platforms are not totally safe and may still fall victim to errors in smart contracts and the misuse of their pseudonymity. Metadata collection is still being debated because when authorities can decrypt encrypted data using security mandates, it raises concerns about consent, limiting access and accountability.

Privacy is becoming a major issue everywhere in smart city systems because data is now being collected from everywhere. Large amounts of information about people's actions are regularly collected by surveillance systems, traffic monitoring, digital grids and assistants, usually without the users being aware. Even though differential privacy and ZKP solve the privacy problem during data sharing, people do not use these tools often, as they are both not very efficient and lack a proper implementation plan (Zhou et al., 2024). Because there are no strict guidelines for cryptography in these areas, important user information may easily be revealed, taken advantage of or sold by others with zero consequences, leading to both individual and national privacy issues. There is also a problem with smart city systems because they are not all the same and do not easily connect with each other. A variety of applications, from smart metering to modern courtrooms, collect information using different data formats, protocols and cryptographic methods. The inability of systems to work together prevents data from being exchanged safely between domains and jurisdictions. A protocol made for storing health data in the HL7 format may fail to connect with legal paperwork coded in XML and financial messages that use ISO 20022. Smart city ecosystems may become separated, more exposed to lower security protocols and at risk for attacks across different systems if cryptographic standards are not adopted among all domains (Rizi & Seno, 2022).

A company's ability to grow without limits is another big challenge. Although homomorphic encryption and SMPC help defense against threats, working with them is slower and uses much more computing power than standard encryption methods. When systems are designed to react instantly to emergencies, adjust traffic signals or process millions of trades, the extra time added by cryptographic functions can be too much for such real-time use (Reshma et al., 2025). In addition, fitting this technology into antiquated systems that lack support for cryptography necessitates significant resources and a great deal of architecture restructuring. All these difficulties are complicated further by the coming threat from quantum computing. Although practical quantum computers have not created a threat to cryptographic schemes, research trends imply that the cryptographic systems RSA, DSA and ECC will become useless as Shor's and Grover's quantum algorithms come into use (Kahanda et al., 2023). Classical cryptographic infrastructure alone can leave smart cities exposed to future security dangers if they do not develop post-quantum migration strategies. The NIST is leading work on post-quantum cryptography and has already standardized some quantum-resistant algorithms but using them on a wide scale requires changes in IT security policies and user education as well as their introduction in IT systems (Aydeger et al., 2024).

Cryptographic security continues to be severely affected by potential issues related to people and organizations. In many cases, even if the cryptographic algorithms are sound, poor key practices, insufficient training and lacking crypto rules allow attacks due to human and system errors. Incorrect encryption, preset passwords and outdated certificates are standard security flaws in smart city systems. Hence, it's important to provide security beyond just selecting algorithms by adding auditing, overseeing cryptographic use and teaching users about security.

Figure 1. Cryptographic threat landscape across smart city domains

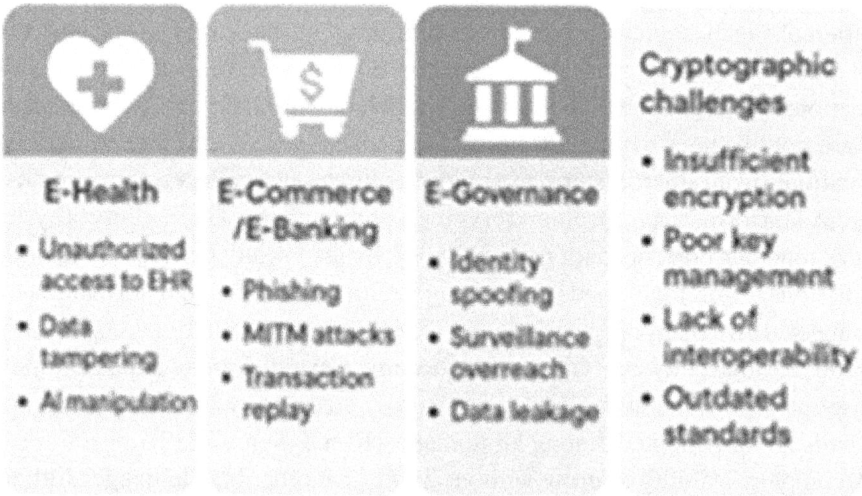

Figure 1 breaks down cryptographic threats that can influence different areas of smart cities. There are three main issues with E-Health; one is unauthorized views of EHRs, another being data manipulation and another using AI to alter things. These sectors are easily targeted by phishing, MITM attacks and attempted transaction repeats. E-Governance must deal with problems such as identity fraud, intense observance and leakage of valuable data. In addition, the figure highlights that cryptography in various sectors lacks sufficient encryption, strong key management, works differently between sectors and relies on using old standards. However, despite cryptographic tools being necessary for protecting smart city applications, their effectiveness is reduced by different technical, organizational and structural challenges. It is important for the future of smart cities that rigorous cryptography, pragmatism, ethical governance and public trust are all worked together.

MODERN CRYPTOGRAPHIC SOLUTIONS FOR SMART CITIES

Modern cryptography plays a key role in protecting smart city infrastructure, dealing with the many difficulties found in E-Health, E-Commerce, E-Banking and digital governance. Since large amounts of sensitive information are constantly made, sent and stored in today's urban centers, guaranteeing that this data is kept private, accurate and valid is a responsibility for society as much as for technology. The progress from old encryption systems to new quantum-resistant ones gives a wide range of tools that can safeguard digital settings from growing risks on the internet.

At the center of cryptography's weapons are symmetric and asymmetric encryption methods. Since data stays saved in most cases, the efficiency and strong guarantees offered by symmetric encryption such as AES, continue to make it the leading choice for protection. In this field, AES encryption is commonly applied to preserve the safety of E-Health Records because, even after storage media are corrupted, the keys are required to read the data (Alkhabet & Ismail, 2023). Protecting data while it is being transferred needs various solutions. Distributed healthcare services such as providers, patients and insurance companies rely on using RSA and ECC to secure their channels of communication. ECC is especially noteworthy as it allows security that is equal to RSA, making keys smaller and cutting down both calculations and network consumption. An end-to-end encrypted platform is used by E-Commerce to secure every bit of sensitive payment and transaction information. Because all data is encrypted on the device of the sender and can only be decrypted along the way by the intended recipient, no other service provider can access it. More frequent financial fraud and data breaches have led to the need for E2EE which provides an important level of privacy that helps restore client trust (Tshuma et al., 2024). Adding encryption to MFA makes it much harder for unwanted access, which matters greatly in the financial sector.

Alongside traditional encryption, blockchain is now being used to ensure greater transparency and higher security for smart city usage. In areas like E-Banking and E-Governance that require great security, important records are stored in unchangeable and verifiable ways using permissioned blockchains. A lack of mutability stops fraud, corruption and tampering, risks present in regular centralized databases (Bodkhe et al., 2020). Blockchain ensures that digital voting systems are reliable, keep voter anonymity and make it easy to check election results, solving fundamental issues faced by democracies (Faruk et al., 2024). Furthermore, using blockchain allows management systems for public assets to clearly monitor ownership, usage and upkeep which improves transparency. In the world of E-Commerce, blockchain plays a key role by letting us track items from when they are produced until they reach the customer. It reduces the risks of fraud and fakes at the same time as helping companies follow ethical standards and match up with rules (Song et al., 2023). Smart contracts take care of compliance without anyone else needing to intervene which reduces opportunity for conflict and fees. Although blockchain tools experience issues, especially relating to scalability and energy, new solutions and mechanisms are helping make them suitable for cities, colleges and schools.

ZKPs offer people a strong cryptographic option to uphold both their privacy and the ability to prove things. Digital identity management systems in smart cities benefit from ZKPs because they allow someone to show they know a piece of information without revealing it. Instead of sharing their full names and birth dates, individuals can confirm their identities to authorities or access the mega site blocked materials by simply presenting their face and other information (Zhou et al., 2024). In e-voting and similar democracy-based applications, protecting both voter anonymity and the honesty of elections is very important. ZKPs make it possible for reports, analysis and laws to be made using shared data, in a way that ensures both clear information and individual privacy remain protected. Homomorphic encryption enables us to complete specific calculations on data that remains encrypted without revealing the data. The new cryptographic discovery could strongly affect the development of smart city analytics. A smart hospital network can look at grouped patient data after encryption to spot patterns in public health, share resources effectively and identify possible disease outbreaks, all without compromising patient privacy (Pandey et al., 2024). Furthermore, towns and cities can use homomorphic encryption in data analytics to guide their work without revealing personal information from their citizens. Although homomorphic encryption has existed for decades, improvements in algorithms and hardware recently improve its chances of being used for practical purposes, but some obstacles such as computational effort, are yet to be resolved (Gong et al., 2024).

Quantum cryptography, mostly QKD, is the forefront of technology that could transform safety in information sharing within cities. Instead of depending on how hard it might be to solve a problem, QKD uses quantum mechanics ideas like superposition and entanglement to detect someone trying to listen in on the communication. This technique helps two estimators generate keys that are safe even against attacks from future quantum computers (Sharma et al., 2021). In Beijing and Geneva, pilot schemes are being carried out with QKD over the metropolitan internet backbone to secure the communications of major city infrastructure. Although still developing and uncommon, true quantum cryptography will soon play a crucial role as threats from new quantum computers put old encryption methods under risk (Vasani et al., 2024). It helps to mention that researchers are always working on developing algorithms that can counterattacks from quantum computers. At present, NIST is closer to finalizing standards for some algorithms, including lattice, hash and code, among others, that cities should now begin to implement to ensure security in the future (Fathalla & Azab, 2024). These new cryptographic standards can be adopted effectively only if everyone in charge coordinates efforts, collaborates across sectors and devotes resources to staff training. Deploying modern cryptographic solutions works best when they are blended with an overall security architecture, not just when they function properly. It is important to use secure software for keys, evaluate all cryptographic programs closely and create frameworks that let security and efficiency work together. Effective training of cybersecurity staff and efforts to educate the public are both needed to avoid problems that might undo the progress made by innovative cryptology methods.

Modern cryptographic solutions are highly effective in shielding the complicated and linked systems found in today's smart cities. AES, ECC and blockchain address several aspects within cities, securing communications, preserving privacy and assuring transparency, together meeting the different needs of digital communication in urban areas. Smart cities will be able to use new technologies such as homomorphic encryption and quantum cryptography to keep the trust and privacy of people safe during the use of new innovations. Cryptography should continue to be seen as the backbone of a smart city's security in the face of new and developing security problems.

Figure 2. Architecture of privacy-preserving data processing using modern cryptography

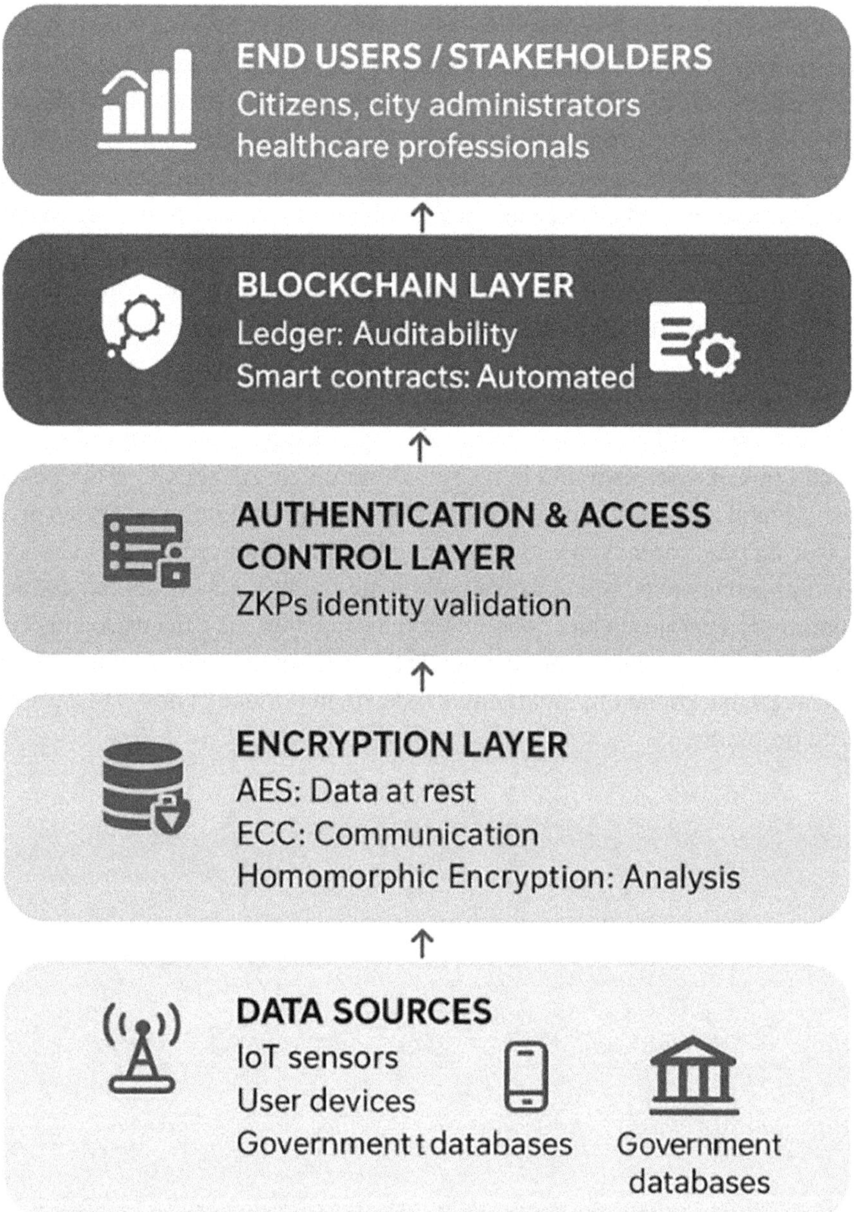

The diagram, called "Architecture of Privacy-Preserving Data Processing Using Modern Cryptography" shows different levels of the smart city's infrastructure. The diagram in Figure 2 represents how various sources of data move to end users, each step being securely protected by advanced cryptography. At the lowest level are Data Sources, composed of IoT sensors, user gadgets and databases the government uses. Encryption security is provided by the Encryption Layer through AES for objects stored in rest, ECC for safe sharing and Homomorphic Encryption for analytics that respect user privacy. At the next layer, Access Authentication & Control, ZKPs are used to prove who someone is and roles are used to limit who can access certain information. Through distributed record keeping (a ledger) and smart contracts, Blockchain Layer helps businesses to verify their actions and automate certain parts of their operations. The upper layer with End Users / Stakeholders features citizens, city officials and service providers getting access to securely managed information. Figure 2 illustrates how today's cryptographic technologies cooperate to ensure that data in smart city networks is safe and transparent.

AI-DRIVEN CRYPTOGRAPHIC SECURITY IN SMART MARKETPLACES

The rise in online marketplaces within smart cities has caused greater worries about fraud, privacy breaches and stealing personal information. Therefore, more advanced cryptographic security frameworks supported by AI are now protecting these digital business environments.

A significant example unites behavior-based anomaly detection with secure multiparty computation (SMPC) to provide better results. SMPC helps multiple people to process joint functions which means their private data remains hidden, even when detecting fraud online (Rahaman et al., 2024). For instance, a marketplace could share and examine all transaction trends jointly to spot irregularities, without revealing main information and make sure that the main information is not accessible to those who are not authorized. Smart blockchain contracts are often used in these systems to enforce compliance, so people are more likely to trust the process and there are fewer conflicts. The partnership between AI and cryptographic security designs a mechanism that can grow to handle new risks, maintain privacy for users and ensure swift operations.

Figure 3. Overview of cryptographic technologies in smart city use cases

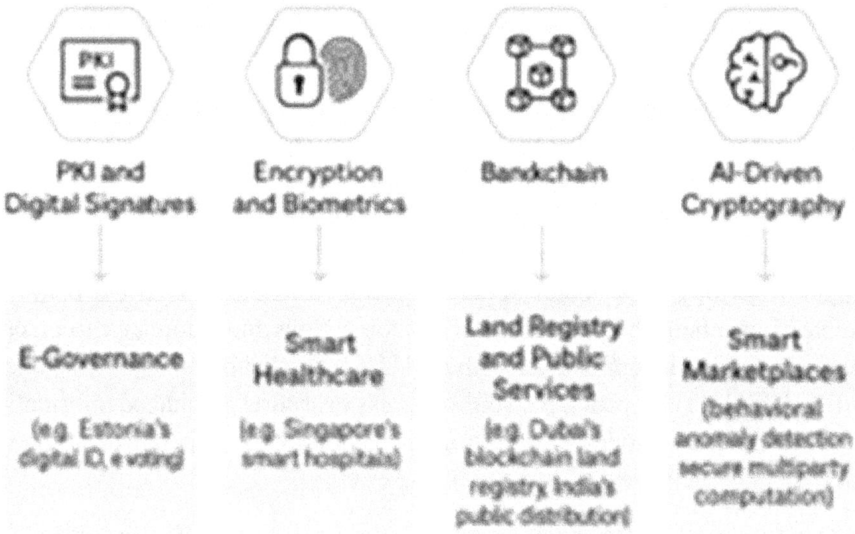

This diagram outlines examples where various cryptographic technologies are found in use in smart cities. Figure 3 represents the key areas in digital security: (1) PKI and digital signatures support online government processes in countries like Estonia, (2) through Encryption and biometrics, smart hospitals secure patient data in Singapore, (3) Land Registry and Public Services benefit from Blockchain in countries such as Dubai and India and (4) Artificial Intelligence is used in cryptography for secure multiparty commerce. It helps visualize each method by matching its use case in modern island infrastructures.

Key Considerations for Cryptographic Deployment in Smart Cities

All these case studies illustrate that the use of cryptographic technologies in smart cities helps protect against a wide variety of cyber-attacks. These findings also highlight things to keep in mind for deployments to take place in the future.

- **Tailored Solutions:** Any cryptography solution should fit the needs of a group, including sector standards, user skills and technical capabilities. IoT devices require lightweight methods for protecting information, but governance platforms often require a strong PKI solution.

- **Interoperability Challenges:** Smart cities often face problems with systems to exchange information across various sectors. For technology to work together without letting security down, we use common cryptographic standards.
- **User-Centric Design:** A user-centric approach to security should be taken so people are inspired to use the solutions. The use of complex keys or passwords may slow down the adoption of security measures among ordinary users.
- **Regulatory Alignment:** It's important for governments to define policies that ensure cryptographic use, privacy of data and cross-border transfers are handled the same.
- **Scalability and Performance:** Homomorphic cryptographic techniques need to improve their performance to handle the information processed in massive smart city networks.

CASE STUDIES AND PRACTICAL IMPLEMENTATIONS

Smart cities can better show how valuable cryptographic technologies are when they are applied in real use. This section reviews real applications that have applied modern cryptography to help make different urban services more secure, private and trustworthy. The case studies include digital governance, healthcare, real estate, public distribution and commerce, proving that cryptographic security is both effective and achievable in operation.

Estonia: Cryptography as the Backbone of E-Governance

Estonia has become an example for the world by applying PKI as an essential security method across its digital government services. Estonia introduced its first e-Residency program and national digital ID in the early 2010s and since then has kept building its cryptographic structure to keep government portals, banking, healthcare and voting systems safe for citizens (Adeodato & Pournouri, 2020). The National ID card in Estonia makes use of public-key infrastructure and is both a way to prove your identity and a device for creating digital signatures. Citizens can now use electronic signatures to securely get online services, so there is no longer a need to visit in person or use physical documents. The cryptographic keys in smart ID cards can only be accessed with your personal PIN, almost preventing anyone from getting in illegally (Troitiño et al., 2024). Estonians have used electronic voting since 2005 which relies on cryptographic security to support public trust. This design uses end-to-end encryption, digital signatures and strong auditing methods to guarantee that votes are secure, votes cannot be traced, and the system can be verified, solving common online voting issues (Llano et al., 2025). The e-Residency programme introduced by Estonia has issued more than 100,000 digital IDs to customers in 176 countries by 2023, so that the numbers of approximately 17 million digital transactions are conducted each year through PKI-grounded authentication and signature infrastructure. The effectiveness of Estonia's cryptographic solution has led other nations to investigate digital democracy, showing that good cryptography supports both transparent and secure forms of administration.

Singapore: Securing Smart Hospitals with Encryption and AI

Cryptographic tools and technologies such as artificial intelligence and biometrics are combined in Singapore's eHealth infrastructure. Urban hospitals use several types of encryptions to secure health information such as EHRs, pictures from imaging tests and patient treatment records. The data that remains stored is secured with AES and ECC is used to secure data exchange between medical gadgets and healthcare workers (Periyasamy et al., 2023). According to data released by the Singapore Ministry of Health, the organization experienced a 93 percent drop in unauthorized EHR access occurrences over a 2-year period, a period that began when multi-factor biometric authentication systems and layered AES/ECC encryption were introduced in local government hospitals (Wong et al., 2025). Biometric authentication uses fingerprint and facial recognition to back up the security provided by encryption and keep out those who do not belong. The combination of biometric data with cryptographic keys boosts the strength of multi-factor authentication efforts and keeps the system safe from identity theft and workers who could attack it (Kannan et al., 2024). Artificial intelligence is also used in Singapore's hospitals for security, as it analyzes cryptographically secure audit logs. Because these logs don't change, businesses can observe current access patterns and so spot cyberattack attempts or anyone breaking the company's policy. By using AI together with cryptography, it's possible for Singapore to guarantee both the privacy of its patients and the accountability of who is accessing the system (Rajawat et al., 2022).

Dubai: Blockchain Transforming Land Registry and Public Services

The use of blockchain technology in government has been driven forward by Dubai's commitment to a smart city. Land registry transactions are one of the most important examples of how blockchain has been applied. Through using a permissioned blockchain to track property ownership, sales and leasing agreements, Dubai has built a record that cannot be altered, making it much harder for fraud to happen and bureaucracy to take time (Quelhas Poças, 2025). The Dubai Department of Land and Property recorded that the average wait time to accomplish property transfers was shortened by 25 percent, from 30 days to 22 days, after introducing a blockchain-based system registration system. Additionally, the department projects projected an estimate of 20 percent decrease in administrative expenses per year (Shuaib et al., 2022). All stakeholders who use the blockchain platform buyers, sellers, real estate agents and government officials have fast access to reliable and consistent information about properties. Automation of transactional conditions by smart contracts improves speed and eliminates the chance for human mistakes or dishonest action (Baroudi & Benghida, 2022). Apart from real estate, Dubai is now using blockchain in business licensing, vehicle registration and public tendering. Blockchain's broad use demonstrates that people now see how its unique cryptographic aspects such as decentralization, immutability and consensus, help increase public trust in digital services (Alam, 2022).

Figure 4. Architecture of blockchain-based land registry system

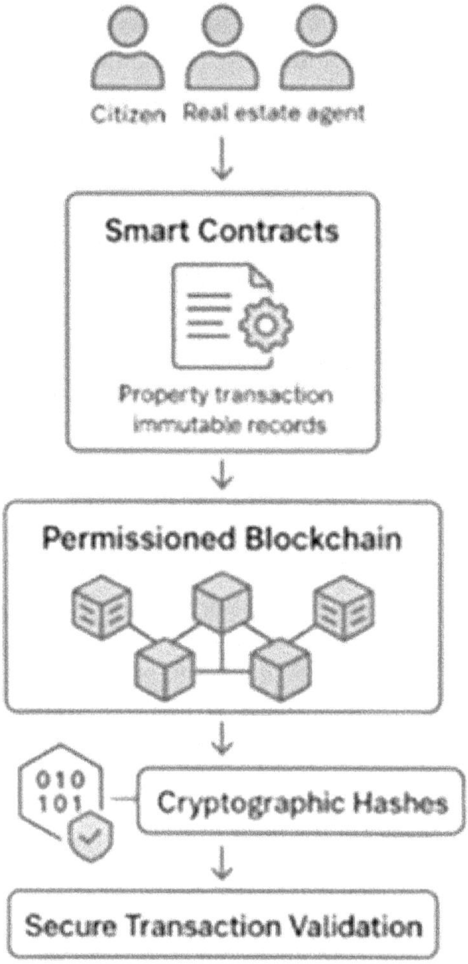

The figure explains how a blockchain-driven land registry system works, taking Dubai as its example. The initial stage of this structure includes people who use the interfaces, including users, agents and officials. The users depend on smart contracts to take care of following property agreement rules and storing the deal records which cannot be manipulated. The contracts are entered into a permissioned blockchain system, where those approved can track and verify all records of who owns the land. Data integrity is protected by using cryptographic hashes which detect when changes are not permitted. A secure transaction validation and consensus mechanism supports the entire system, so that every transaction is checked and accepted by the network participants. The illustration in Figure 4 reveals how blockchain helps build confidence, efficiency and security in current land registry procedures. Therefore, the constant development of cryptocurrencies and the experience of early adopters create a stable and safe ground for smart city services everywhere. The more complex and widespread urban digital systems become, the more important it is for innovation and careful planning of policies to protect both trust and the public good.

India: Blockchain for Transparent Public Distribution Systems

The idea of India's PDS to subsidize food and daily items for many has been frequently tested by problems caused by corruption and leaks. Cryptographic solutions such as blockchain look suitable for making the way subsidies are managed clearer and more accountable. Several Indian states have started using blockchain technology to keep a complete record of the supply chain, including getting, moving and giving out food rations. Since all transactions in the system are organized in a clear, verifiable way, opportunities for stealing goods and making fake claims are significantly cut down (Mishra & Maheshwari, 2021). They also use ZKP to confirm eligibility for beneficiaries without them having to present confidential private information. Pilot programs in Andhra Pradesh and Telangana showed that within less than a year of blockchain adoption, subsidy diversion could be reduced by any significant degree, around 30 percent, and that payments to the targeted population could be increased significantly. These results show that distributed ledger technology holds significant promise in terms of enhancing the social safety net by the government. The privacy-supporting method used in authentication prevents someone else from stealing each person's identity and still guarantees that official entities send subsidies only to the appropriate recipients (Vishnu et al., 2025). Indian blockchain projects are a testament to how cryptographic tools can support massive public programs, mostly in settings with few resources and little government oversight.

EVALUATING THE EFFECTIVENESS OF CRYPTOGRAPHIC INTEGRATION IN SMART CITY ECOSYSTEMS

Cryptographic techniques are vital for maintaining security, secrecy and holiness of data in all domains, especially E-Health, E-Commerce and E-Banking, in smart cities. Because smart city systems are now interlinked, the success of cryptographic solutions is crucial for shielding sensitive data and ensuring people trust them.

Evaluating Cryptographic Performance and Security in Smart Cities

Ensuring cryptographic integration works well requires strong metrics for performance and security. Encryption and decryption rate, ease of managing encryption keys and resistance of the system to various attack types are important indicators. The efficiency of AES and RSA in preventing brute-force attacks and how much computation they require has been examined by experts (Bhat & Giri, 2021). In the field of smart city applications, NIST guidelines offer a structure for looking at cryptography standards. These benchmarks check how strong cryptographic algorithms are which situations they can handle and if they follow international guidelines (Karie et al., 2021). Moreover, researchers are studying how to apply post-quantum cryptography to secure smart city networks from possible threats coming with the development of quantum computing (Mansoor et al., 2025).

Real-World Applications for Cryptographic Technologies in E-Health and E-Banking

The development of cryptographic technology is also closely watched through how people use it, mainly in fields like E-Health and E-Banking. Blockchain technology applied to manage patient information has brought positive outcomes in E-Health. According to research, blockchain is seen to ensure data integrity and protect patient privacy which makes healthcare providers and patients more willing to use it (Masood et al., 2024). E-Banking also depends on using multi-factor authentication and encryption for all its transactions. The addition of easy-to-use ways to authenticate users such as biometrics and mobile tokens has helped more people accept the system. As a result of these efforts, there has been a major fall in fraud and unauthorized access incidents (Khan et al., 2023).

The Role of Encryption in Mitigation of Cyber Risks in Smart City

Smart city ecosystems rely on encryption to limit and control various cyber-related threats. Because encryption is in place, any data on a network stays private and unchanged. Transport Layer Security (TLS) is used in smart transportation systems to shield real-time data from unauthorized access and tampering (Pali et al., 2025). In addition, implementing homomorphic encryption makes sure no sensitive information is exposed during data processing. It becomes very useful when data must be analyzed while protecting privacy such as in smart energy grids and systems used in public health (Munjal & Bhatia, 2023).

Challenges in Maintaining and Evolving Cryptographic Protocols in Smart Cities

There are several problems when it comes to checking, inspecting and upgrading cryptographic protocols in fast-changing urban situations. A major obstacle is that cryptographic techniques need to expand to meet the needs of the constantly increasing number of connected devices in smart cities. The lack of resources in these systems means that using stronger encryption algorithms is usually not possible (Singh et al., 2024). In addition, because cyber threats are changing rapidly, new developments in cryptography are needed all the time. At the same time, it is not easy to update these protocols across a wide network of devices, since it is challenging from both an organizational and technical perspective. It is very important to maintain backward compatibility and keep services functional during updates. Moreover, because cryptographic management isn't standardized in smart cities, there are inconsistencies and chances that something will be missed. Implementing clear and complete policies and guidelines related to cryptography is important to handle these issues properly (Rizi & Seno, 2022).

Cryptographic integration in smart cities should be checked for performance, the number of people using it, the security it provides and its compatibility with modern issues. Although there has been good progress with applying cryptography in many fields, more work is needed to improve scalability, agree on standards and update the systems. Smart cities achieve this by teaming up with relevant parties, focusing on research and development and thus making cyber-attacks less likely and services safer for everyone.

SOCIO-TECHNICAL DIMENSIONS OF CRYPTOGRAPHIC SECURITY IN URBAN SERVICES

Implementing cryptography for security in smart city infrastructure is not only about technology, but also about social issues. There are a lot of factors influencing urban services' use of cryptographic mechanisms such as their efficiency, social standards and the latest technology. It is very important to study this relationship to develop secure, inclusive and strong smart city systems.

Public Trust and Perception of Digital Security

Trust in digital systems from the public is one of the main reasons people use cryptography. Trust forms the basis for accepting any security technology, especially cryptography, as it mostly runs in the background. People need to be sure that their personal information is protected from being accessed or used illegally to fully take part in digital activities. Trust in digital government platforms is now reported to depend a lot on their transparency and whether individuals have experienced data breaches before (Krishna et al., 2025). For instance, places where people highly value transparency, for example in Estonia's e-governance model, tend to use digital identity systems with strong security. In the same way, mistrust can be caused by a lack of knowledge about cryptography or when the system hides how data privacy is ensured. Therefore, many people are hesitant to trust online healthcare or voting, which negatively influences the use and appreciation of strong online platforms. That's why implementing cryptographic technologies must be supported by helping explain how they protect confidential data.

Digital Literacy and Its Influence on Cryptographic Efficacy

The success of cryptocurrency in the financial sector also depends on how well both users and service providers are aware of digital tools. As cryptographic technologies are complex, people need to know some security basics, including what to do with passwords, how to use multi-factor authentication and how to spot phishing scams. According to Javaid et al., (2023), if security is not taught properly, advanced security solutions may not be enough to prevent breaches through tricks or mistakes made by people. Those who provide cryptographic services such as municipal groups and private organizations should be skilled in implementing and running these protocols. A lack of proper skills and training often leads to IT settings being misadjusted and this causes new security problems. Ensuring institutions are prepared and cryptographic tools last long depends on training and ongoing education.

Table 2. Socio-technical influences on public trust and digital literacy in cryptographic urban services

Factor	Description	Impact on Cryptographic Security
Public Trust in Digital Systems	Shaped by transparency, past data breach experience, and institutional reputation	High trust increases user engagement with encrypted platforms
Transparency of Governance	Visibility into how cryptographic protection is applied	Enhances legitimacy and acceptance of cryptographic systems
Digital Literacy	User ability to recognize secure interfaces and manage credentials	Low literacy increases susceptibility to phishing/social engineering
Education and Awareness	Public campaigns and training on privacy and encryption	Improves secure user behaviors and adoption rates
User Interface Complexity	Ease of navigating encrypted or secure portals	Directly affects usability and compliance with secure protocols

Table 2 gives a simplified view of some of the important social and technical factors that affect how much people trust and understand cryptographic systems in smart city environments. Things like how open the government is, how comfortable people are with digital tools, and whether the interface is easy to use all play a big role. These aspects can influence whether people use and trust encrypted systems. While not everything is always under direct control, being aware of these factors can help policymakers and developers shape systems that aren't just secure on paper but also work better for real users. If done right, the solutions will feel both technically solid and more accessible to the public.

Institutional Readiness and Policy Frameworks

It includes all necessary steps for an organization to start and maintain the use of security with cryptography in their daily operations. Before an organization can be ready, it should have well-organized governance, the right technology and supportive government measures. Cryptographic systems are being introduced by urban administrations, but this is hindered by broken policies and financial shortages (Majeed et al., 2021). A good institutional process involves working together between government, technology providers, universities and civil society to make strategies that consider both technology and the community. As seen in Singapore's Smart Nation project, the effort involves involving institutions and citizens together, combining support for blockchain research with campaigns designed to increase trust and understanding of new technology (Almutairi, 2024).

Civic Engagement and Cryptographic Policymaking

People's involvement in politics directly influences cryptographic policy that benefits different urban communities. When policy making is clear and includes opinions from others, people are less worried about electronic surveillance, improper data handling and being overlooked. For instance, when groups like civil society support the process of creating cryptographic policies in public services, the result is often a fair balance between not violating rights and ensuring services are secure (Shneiderman, 2020). In addition, holding public consultations and using participatory design keeps officials accountable and supported by society. Thus, cryptographic security is handled in a way that does not exclude people but becomes a part of smart city administration. A lack of engagement can unintentionally worsen gaps in technology or lessen faith in the government, which often leads to people pulling away.

Equity and Inclusion in Cryptographic Security

There is a major concern in smart cities about making sure protected digital services reach all communities, especially those that need them most. If cryptographic technologies are not implemented by keeping in mind their effect on society, this can cause greater inequality. Cryptographically secure services might be hard for some people to use if they lack easy access to technology, stable internet or online skills. This leads to unequal digital security, leaving groups that are easily attacked by cyber threats or keeping them out of important city services (Abiodun et al., 2021). Also, some biometric-based authentication techniques may accidentally treat specific groups unfairly simply because their features differ or they are not familiar with using new technology (Lucia et al., 2023). It is important that equitable cryptography places more emphasis on ease of use, openness and everyone's inclusion. A few strategies are using simple interfaces, supporting multiple languages, letting users log in without the internet and teaching digital skills through communities. Because of these measures, all urban residents can enjoy the advantages of cryptographic security and not only a small group (Rizi & Seno, 2022).

Table 3. Equity, inclusion, and institutional readiness in cryptographic integration

Dimension	Challenge	Recommended Approach
Institutional Readiness	Limited skilled personnel; outdated infrastructures	Capacity-building programs; inter-agency knowledge sharing
Policy Gaps	Fragmented or outdated cryptographic mandates	Updated, harmonized national/local cryptographic governance frameworks
Socioeconomic Inequality	Unequal access to internet/devices	Offline-compatible services; device subsidy programs
Biometric Discrimination	Inaccuracy for certain groups (e.g., darker skin tones, disabilities)	Multimodal authentication; inclusive testing and audits
Multilingual Populations	Language barriers in secure system use	Multilingual interfaces and support
Accessibility	Visually/physically impaired users unable to interact with security tools	Inclusive UX design; integration with assistive technologies

Table 3 gives a practical look at some of the key structural and social issues that affect how well cryptographic technologies are integrated into smart city systems. It points out common challenges like gaps in institutional readiness, confusing or outdated policies, and difficulties with accessibility. These aren't always easy to solve, but the table includes a few strategies that could help make implementation more inclusive. When these areas are properly addressed, it becomes more likely that cryptographic security will not only be technically strong, but also fair, easier to access, and better suited to the different needs of people living in urban areas. This way, technology doesn't leave certain groups behind and becomes a tool that works for everyone not just the tech-savvy or well-resourced.

The Role of Socio-Technical Research and Interdisciplinary Approaches

The unique qualities of cities also require experts in computer science, social sciences and urban studies continually to work in joint research. A combination of different approaches is required to examine how cryptographic technologies affect social practices, institutions and cultural traditions (Shin & Ibahrine, 2020). It allows for identifying mistakes, challenges end users may face and fresh threats, helping to set strategies for cryptography that are effective and fit well into society. Furthermore, teamwork among scholars, policymakers and practitioners enables the development of new ways for urban cryptographic governance to grow with changing urban requirements. Essentially, cryptographic security in urban services requires us to understand that society and technology cannot be considered apart. Smart cities can only benefit from cryptographic technologies if people trust them, are digitally literate, institutions are up to date, citizens are involved, and the issues of equity are considered. Considering all these aspects together allows for secure, fair, clear and durable digital systems in urban areas.

FUTURE DIRECTIONS AND POLICY IMPLICATIONS

As cryptographic technologies become sorely integrated into smart cities, it will greatly affect how we secure and protect our privacy in cities. However, for this technology to work well, technical standardization, proper regulations, proper ethics and public involvement must all come together. Because of new advances in AI and Internet of Things devices, smart cities are becoming less secure and more complicated. Consequently, both new technologies and public policy should be developed with the future in mind to help cryptographic security remain protective, acceptable, easy to use and globally compatible.

A leading problem for widespread use of cryptography in smart cities is the urgent requirement for standardization among different countries, due in part to quantum computing. The International Organization for Standardization and the National Institute of Standards and Technology have taken important steps toward creating PQC standards. Cryptography experts have made these new algorithms to survive the encryption power of quantum computers which currently endanger our public key infrastructure (Vijayalakshmi et al., 2024). Despite all this, the world's markets are not fully aligned. Adopting cryptography unevenly and using different regulations among nations could divide the cryptographic community, block exchange of data across borders and slow the building of smart cities (Firmansyah & Bansal,

2024). Thus, it is important for policymakers to place value on talking with other countries and cooperating to guarantee standards for cryptography are recognized and applied everywhere they are needed.

It is important that national governments create regulations that require cryptographic protection for important urban services and citizen information. The framework must be planned to fit both tough security needs and how smart cities are run in different ways. Regulations should demand that healthcare, transportation and public administration systems store and send data both safely and securely; while also helping to set up interoperability standards that let different platforms and agencies transfer data securely (Hazra et al., 2024). In addition, governments should build relationships between public and private sectors to inspire the creation and setup of appropriate crypto technologies for their region and avoid using general crypto solutions that might hold back development or ignore minorities.

One of the biggest issues with more people using cryptographic systems is matching tough security measures with ease of access and usage for all users. If cryptographic protocols become too complicated or make devices use too much power, some users might find them difficult to use and choose unsafe alternatives (Singh et al., 2024). For this reason, all cryptographic system development should focus on ease of use, integration with the rest of life and making things uninterrupted for users. The use of password less authentication, biometrics and automated key management appear to be safe ways to make computing more convenient (Uzun et al., 2021). In addition, increasing digital literacy and raising public understanding through campaigns encourages people to accept and apply cryptographic protections in smart city platforms. The future development and implementation of cryptographic security will continue to need consideration of ethical issues. When using cryptography in public elections, it must be done transparently, fairly and accountably to guide public trust and preserve democracy. For instance, technologies designed to preserve user privacy must not be used to bypass legal rules or to prevent investigations of misbehavior. For this reason, well-built governance rules are needed to outline what is allowed when it comes to cryptography and to describe the guidelines for allowing lawful access under conditions (Sultana & Sangeetha, 2022). In addition, tools for cryptographic surveillance used in public services, like monitoring by the police or cities, require oversight and ethics checks to keep them from causing problems or harming any groups. Having independent authorities or ethics groups check cryptographic applications can keep them from violating accepted standards of society and human rights.

In the realm of world urbanization, some global smart city partnerships are already setting the pace of cryptographic administration and innovation. An outstanding one is the European Union Horizon Europe program that funds cross-border development projects based on secure digital infrastructures and privacy-preserving cryptographic methods tailor-made on urban services to be shared among member countries (Jørgensen & Ma, 2025). At the same time, the Japanese Society 5.0 project directly incorporates cryptographic norms into large-scale smart city combat with data protection, increasing a target-oriented strategy to securing the utilization of AI and IoT in the nation (Barrett et al., 2021). In cooperation programs that fall under the UN United for Smart Sustainable Cities (U4SSC) initiative, interoperable security standards and ethical rules are popularized so that the developing states do not feel left behind technologically or institutionally in implementing cryptographic safeguards (Martinez et al., 2024). These international precedents indicate that cryptographic security in smart cities cannot be considered exclusively yet has to coincide with cross-border frameworks uniting technical norms, rules and regulations regimes and ethical values.

In the future, new advancements in cryptography will be needed to fix the unique issues found in smart cities. AI and cryptography coming together will allow security systems to respond to new threats and ways that technology is used. For example, cryptographic protocols with AI improvements could signify changes in normal activities, respond automatically and still hold on to the integrity of the data being protected. In addition, secure and simple cryptography is needed to shield the many resource-limited IoT devices that support smart city functioning. Due to their small capacity and limited battery, these devices use unique and secure cryptographic algorithms to balance safety with saving batteries and processing power. At the same time, with the large amounts of information generated by smart cities, people are worried that scalability will continue to pose a major challenge as they depend on cryptography for protecting their information. Both homomorphic encryption and secure multiparty computation seem to have the promise of handling data safely, yet they are not being used widely because of their computational costs (Kamble et al., 2024). So, further studies should concentrate on improving these advanced methods so they can be used safely and efficiently by cities and large organizations.

Eventually, political policies must adjust quickly to address new technology and related security issues. The introduction of regulatory sandboxes and innovation hubs enables testing chosen cryptographic applications in a controlled setting, leading to repeatable updating based on comments from customers. Consequently, regularly engaging people such as citizens, technologists, legal specialists and members of civil society groups helps bring cryptographic security efforts in line with the changing needs and expectations of the public. The progress of cryptographic security in smart cities is tied to combining innovation, careful regulations, ethical concerns and public contribution. Smart cities can profit from cryptography in technology and make it the basis for safe, fair and strong towns by encouraging collaboration globally, following design principles that value people and strictly uphold open policies.

Figure 5. The cryptographic security ecosystem in smart cities

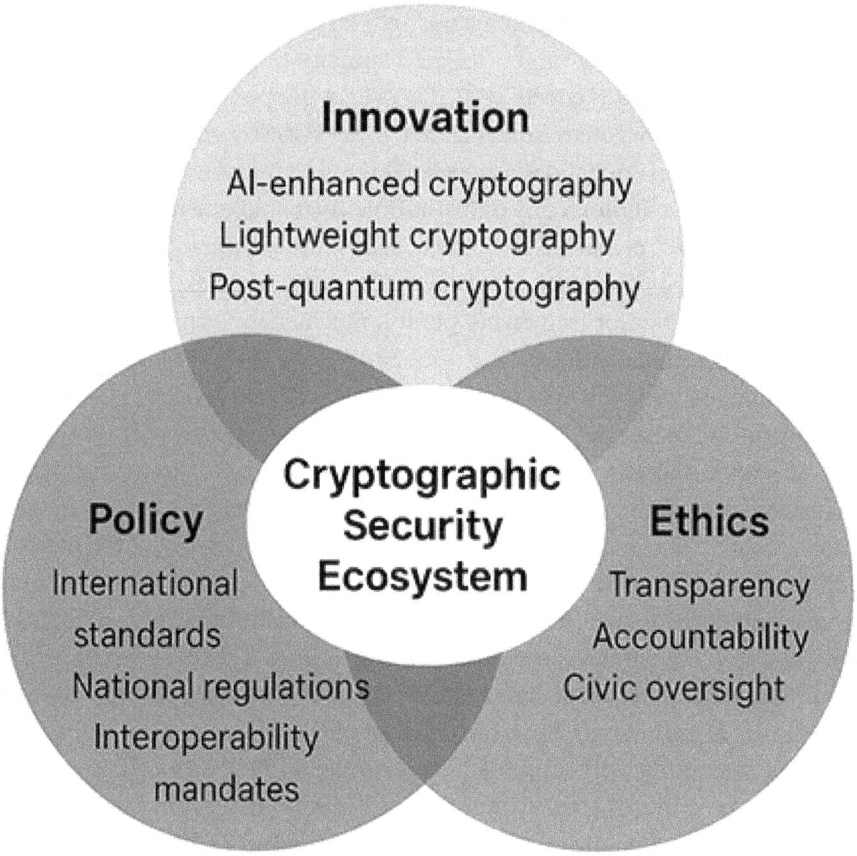

Figure 5 shows a Venn diagram, describing how the elements in the cryptographic security ecosystem are connected in smart cities. It points out the connection between the three main areas: Innovation (AI-based cryptography, lighter encryption and future-ready cryptography), Policy (international rules, local requirements and rules for shared coding) and Ethics (information transparency, accountability and community oversight). The main intersection means the ecosystem must be integrated and tough to support secure and ethical progress in technology for smart cities.

POLICY GAPS AND USABILITY BARRIERS IN CRYPTOGRAPHIC INTEGRATION

Cryptography is often seen as a key part of keeping smart city systems secure. Whether it's protecting electronic health records or keeping online banking transactions safe, these tools are what help people trust digital services in cities. Still, how effective these technologies are isn't just about how strong the math or code is behind them. Two big and connected issues gaps in policy and how easy the systems are to use are holding back the broader and fairer use of cryptographic security in smart urban spaces. These challenges make it harder for cities to adopt these systems in ways that work well for everyone and can last overtime.

Policy Gaps in Cryptographic Governance

The laws and policies around cryptographic technologies in smart cities are still quite scattered and, in many places, not fully developed. Even though international organizations like the ITU, ISO, and NIST have laid out various technical guidelines and best practices, a lot of these don't carry legal weight or get properly implemented into national or local policies (Wang et al., 2023). Because of this, many cities roll out smart technologies without a clear or enforceable cryptographic policy in place. One of the main problems is that there aren't specific rules for how encryption should be used in different public service sectors. Sure, regulations like the GDPR talk about having "appropriate security," but they rarely spell out what kind of encryption strength is enough or how keys should be managed. This vagueness leaves city officials and vendors unsure of what's required, often resulting in patchy implementations or worse, minimal setups just to tick the compliance box (Limniotis, 2021). The enforcement side isn't much better. A lot of cities work with third-party vendors or let individual departments handle digital services, which makes it difficult to apply consistent security standards across the board. In Bangladesh, for instance, some city corporations use encryption in their smart billing or waste management platforms, but there's no shared protocol or standard between them. That lack of uniformity makes it harder to ensure data security or share information smoothly (Joysoyal et al., 2024). Another major issue is that many cities don't really have the capacity to keep cryptographic systems up to date. Encryption standards change quickly take SHA-1, for example, which is now outdated and insecure (Mouha & Celi, 2023). Still, lots of municipal IT teams stick with old algorithms, mainly because they lack the resources, staff, or technical know-how to upgrade. Smaller cities, especially in developing countries, face serious challenges in hiring skilled personnel who can manage complex infrastructures like PKIs or handle certificate renewals (Khan et al., 2022). There's also a big problem with international coordination. As smart city systems and digital services start to cross borders like with e-health data or remittance platforms, differences in cryptographic rules and standards make it tough to keep things interoperable. Without shared guidelines for things like digital signatures or ID verification, the idea of globally connected smart cities starts to fall apart (Toh, 2020).

Usability Barriers and the Human Factor

Technical sophistication by itself doesn't always guarantee that cryptographic protections will be widely adopted or effective. Usability, how easy and accessible a system feels to users, plays a huge role in whether people use these protections or try to bypass them. This problem becomes even more noticeable in public-facing applications, where users come from diverse backgrounds with different levels of education, age, and comfort with digital tools. One of the biggest obstacles is often the complexity of user interfaces. Cryptographic tools like public key exchanges, MFA, or digital signatures often demand users follow unfamiliar steps. Many users struggle with understanding certificate warnings, handling authentication tokens, or simply navigating encrypted portals. Research has shown that when systems feel too complicated, people tend to give up or use less secure options instead (Chalhoub et al., 2021). This is particularly concerning in vital areas like E-Health, where patients might avoid encrypted messaging because they find it too confusing.

Furthermore, these difficult authentication steps tend to hit vulnerable groups the hardest. MFA methods that depend on smartphones or biometric data can exclude older adults, people with disabilities, or those living in lower-income areas without easy access to advanced devices. This raises serious questions about digital fairness and the risk of deepening existing inequalities security shouldn't end up creating new barriers (Robinson et al., 2020). If cryptographic systems ignore the social and technical realities of users, they can become more of a problem than a solution. The lack of digital literacy makes things even tougher. Many people, especially in developing countries, don't fully understand how encryption works or why it's important. Without proper education or guidance, users might distrust encrypted services or fail to follow good security habits like spotting phishing attempts or verifying digital certificates. This "last mile" of cybersecurity, where users interact with secure systems, is often overlooked in smart city planning (Shafik, 2024). It's not just users who face challenges service providers and administrators do too. The backend tools needed to manage cryptographic systems can be complicated. Tasks like key rotation, renewing certificates, and managing identities require special training. In many cities with limited resources, IT staff struggle to keep these systems properly configured, which can lead to mistakes that undermine security (Singun, 2025). Because of all this, designing for usability really needs to be a key focus when deploying cryptographic systems. There are some promising approaches, like "secure-by-design" principles, simpler ways to enroll certificates, and clear visual cues for users, such as security badges. But making these work well means designers, tech experts, and behavioral scientists must work closely together security tools have to be both strong and user-friendly (Mourtzis et al., 2023).

CONCLUSION

As urban populations interact with new technologies in smarter cities, making cryptographic security an essential part of their designs is more important than ever. This chapter highlights that cryptography is fundamental for securing all important parts of a smart city, especially the most sensitive sectors of E-Health, E-Commerce and E-Banking. These technologies can really benefit society in terms of efficiency, access and transparency if the systems they rely on can resist growing cyber-attacks on trust, privacy and how operations are carried out. Encrypting patient data and using secure authentication in E-Health is required not only by technology but also by a strong sense of right and wrong, since data theft can cripple both individual health and the well-being of the public. E-Commerce and E-Banking systems count on cryptographic protocols to guarantee the safety and consistency of transactions which supports the safe and necessary digital economy for today's cities. This chapter presents an analytical discussion of technical, social, and policy aspects of cryptographic security in smart cities, hence a holistic roadmap to the current practitioner and upcoming researchers. It uses specific case studies and empirical insights on performance to conduct present-day state-of play analysis and takes an eye to the future in terms of ethical and regulatory implications. This holistic outlook points to possible orientation towards implementation of cryptographic technologies in intelligent city environments that is feasible and fair. This chapter has clearly shown that a variety of important challenges appear when connecting cryptographic systems to different smart city applications. Because of problems related to scalability, interoperability, privacy and transparency, it's important to approach blockchain technologies by mixing creative ideas with careful policies. The recent advancements in cryptography, including post-quantum methods, ZKP and blockchain, create valuable approaches to make these systems stronger, but they also need firm regulations and uniform standards to make a bigger difference. The success of securing smart city applications depends on participation from society as well as technology. Collaboration between experts, officials, businesspeople and citizens is needed to stop viewing cryptographic protection as an obstacle and instead see it as creating trust and making people stronger. Smart cities can only live up to their promises of resilience, inclusiveness and sustainability when such holistic approaches are used to protect everyone's digital rights.

REFERENCES

Abiodun, O. I., Abiodun, E. O., Alawida, M., Alkhawaldeh, R. S., & Arshad, H. (2021). A Review on the Security of the Internet of Things: Challenges and Solutions. *Wireless Personal Communications*, *119*(3), 2603–2637. DOI: 10.1007/s11277-021-08348-9

Acosta Llano, E., Hurmelinna-Laukkanen, P., & Haapanen, L. (2025). Blockchain for the circular economy, implications for public governance. *International Journal of Public Sector Management*, *38*(1), 30–52. DOI: 10.1108/IJPSM-12-2023-0365

Adeodato, R., & Pournouri, S. (2020). *Secure Implementation of E-Governance: A Case Study About Estonia*., DOI: 10.1007/978-3-030-35746-7_18

Alam, T. (2022). Blockchain cities: The futuristic cities driven by Blockchain, big data and internet of things. *GeoJournal*, *87*(6), 5383–5412. DOI: 10.1007/s10708-021-10508-0

Alkhabet, M. M., & Ismail, M. (2023). Security algorithms for distributed storage system for E-health application over wireless body area network. *Journal of Ambient Intelligence and Humanized Computing*, *14*(12), 15781–15792. DOI: 10.1007/s12652-020-02733-1

Almutairi, B. (2024). *Integrating AI*. Blockchain, and Cloud Computing for Enhanced E-Government Solutions., DOI: 10.4018/979-8-3693-7678-2.ch011

Aydeger, A., Zeydan, E., Yadav, A. K., Hemachandra, K. T., & Liyanage, M. (2024). Towards a Quantum-Resilient Future: Strategies for Transitioning to Post-Quantum Cryptography. *2024 15th International Conference on Network of the Future (NoF)*, 195–203. DOI: 10.1109/NoF62948.2024.10741441

Baroudi, S., & Benghida, S. (2022). Blockchain in Dubai: Toward a Sustainable Digital Future. In *Contemporary Research in Accounting and Finance* (pp. 253–271). Springer Nature Singapore. DOI: 10.1007/978-981-16-8267-4_11

Barrett, B. F. D., DeWit, A., & Yarime, M. (2021). Japanese smart cities and communities: Integrating technological and institutional innovation for Society 5.0. In *Smart Cities for Technological and Social Innovation* (pp. 73–94). Elsevier., DOI: 10.1016/B978-0-12-818886-6.00005-8

Bhat, M. I., & Giri, K. J. (2021). *Impact of Computational Power on Cryptography*., DOI: 10.1007/978-981-15-8711-5_4

Bodkhe, U., Tanwar, S., Parekh, K., Khanpara, P., Tyagi, S., Kumar, N., & Alazab, M. (2020). Blockchain for Industry 4.0: A Comprehensive Review. *IEEE Access : Practical Innovations, Open Solutions*, *8*, 79764–79800. DOI: 10.1109/ACCESS.2020.2988579

Chalhoub, G., Kraemer, M. J., Nthala, N., & Flechais, I. (2021). "It did not give me an option to decline": A Longitudinal Analysis of the User Experience of Security and Privacy in Smart Home Products. *Proceedings of the 2021 CHI Conference on Human Factors in Computing Systems*, 1–16. DOI: 10.1145/3411764.3445691

Demirbaga, Ü., Aujla, G. S., Jindal, A., & Kalyon, O. (2024). Cloud Computing for Big Data Analytics. In *Big Data Analytics* (pp. 43–77). Springer Nature Switzerland., DOI: 10.1007/978-3-031-55639-5_4

Fathalla, E., & Azab, M. (2024). Beyond Classical Cryptography: A Systematic Review of Post-Quantum Hash-Based Signature Schemes, Security, and Optimizations. *IEEE Access : Practical Innovations, Open Solutions*, *12*, 175969–175987. DOI: 10.1109/ACCESS.2024.3485602

Firmansyah, B., & Bansal, R. (2024). *Standardization and Regulatory Challenges in Modern Cryptography*., DOI: 10.4018/979-8-3693-3824-7.ch006

G, V., & Vinothiyalakshmi, P. (2023). Secure Electronic Banking Transaction using Double Sanction Security Algorithm in Cyber Security. *2023 International Conference on Research Methodologies in Knowledge Management, Artificial Intelligence and Telecommunication Engineering (RMKMATE)*, 1–5. DOI: 10.1109/RMKMATE59243.2023.10369665

Gong, Y., Chang, X., Mišić, J., Mišić, V. B., Wang, J., & Zhu, H. (2024). Practical solutions in fully homomorphic encryption: A survey analyzing existing acceleration methods. *Cybersecurity*, *7*(1), 5. DOI: 10.1186/s42400-023-00187-4

Hazra, R., Chatterjee, P., Singh, Y., Podder, G., & Das, T. (2024). *Data Encryption and Secure Communication Protocols*., DOI: 10.4018/979-8-3693-6557-1.ch022

Herath, H. M. S. S., Herath, H. M. K. K. M. B., Madhusanka, B. G. D. A., & Guruge, L. G. P. K. (2024). Data Protection Challenges in the Processing of Sensitive Data. In *Data Protection* (pp. 155–179). Springer Nature Switzerland., DOI: 10.1007/978-3-031-76473-8_8

Hossain Faruk, M. J., Alam, F., Islam, M., & Rahman, A. (2024). Transforming online voting: A novel system utilizing blockchain and biometric verification for enhanced security, privacy, and transparency. *Cluster Computing*, *27*(4), 4015–4034. DOI: 10.1007/s10586-023-04261-x

Javaid, M., Haleem, A., Singh, R. P., & Suman, R. (2023). Towards insighting cybersecurity for healthcare domains: A comprehensive review of recent practices and trends. *Cyber Security and Applications*, *1*, 100016. DOI: 10.1016/j.csa.2023.100016

Jørgensen, B. N., & Ma, Z. G. (2025). Digital Twin of the European Electricity Grid: A Review of Regulatory Barriers, Technological Challenges, and Economic Opportunities. *Applied Sciences (Basel, Switzerland)*, *15*(12), 6475. DOI: 10.3390/app15126475

Joysoyal, R., Uddin, S. S., Islam, T., Sarker, S. K., Li, L., Ahsan, F., Bhatti, U. A., & Zafir, E. I. (2024). Blockchain for sustainable city transformation: A review on Bangladesh. *Engineering Reports*, *6*(9), e12948. Advance online publication. DOI: 10.1002/eng2.12948

Kahanda, G., Patel, V., Parikh, M., Ippolito, M., Solanki, M., & Ahmed, S. (2023). *The Future Era of Quantum Computing*., DOI: 10.1007/978-3-031-20160-8_27

Kamble, A., Jiet, M. M., & Puri, C. (2024). Homomorphic Encryption and its Applications in Multi-Cloud Security. *2024 International Conference on Inventive Computation Technologies (ICICT)*, 1493–1499. DOI: 10.1109/ICICT60155.2024.10544773

Kannan, N., Sundar, R., Rammorthy, M., Haleem, S. L. A., & Manikandan, R. (2024). *Healthcare Data Encryption Based on Secure AI Model with Computational Analysis Using Machine Learning Algorithms*., DOI: 10.1007/978-3-031-75771-6_29

Karie, N. M., Sahri, N. M., Yang, W., Valli, C., & Kebande, V. R. (2021). A Review of Security Standards and Frameworks for IoT-Based Smart Environments. *IEEE Access : Practical Innovations, Open Solutions*, *9*, 121975–121995. DOI: 10.1109/ACCESS.2021.3109886

Khan, H. U., Sohail, M., Nazir, S., Hussain, T., Shah, B., & Ali, F. (2023). Role of authentication factors in Fin-tech mobile transaction security. *Journal of Big Data*, *10*(1), 138. DOI: 10.1186/s40537-023-00807-3

Khan, M. A., Javaid, S., Mohsan, S. A. H., Tanveer, M., & Ullah, I. (2024). Future-Proofing Security for UAVs With Post-Quantum Cryptography: A Review. *IEEE Open Journal of the Communications Society*, *5*, 6849–6871. DOI: 10.1109/OJCOMS.2024.3486649

Khan, S., Luo, F., Zhang, Z., Rahim, M. A., Ahmad, M., & Wu, K. (2022). Survey on Issues and Recent Advances in Vehicular Public-Key Infrastructure (VPKI). *IEEE Communications Surveys and Tutorials*, *24*(3), 1574–1601. DOI: 10.1109/COMST.2022.3178081

Krishna, B., Krishnan, S., & Sebastian, M. P. (2025). Understanding the process of building institutional trust among digital payment users through national cybersecurity commitment trustworthiness cues: A critical realist perspective. *Information Technology & People*, *38*(2), 714–756. DOI: 10.1108/ITP-05-2023-0434

Limniotis, K. (2021). Cryptography as the Means to Protect Fundamental Human Rights. *Cryptography*, *5*(4), 34. DOI: 10.3390/cryptography5040034

Lucia, C., Zhiwei, G., & Michele, N. (2023). Biometrics for Industry 4.0: A survey of recent applications. *Journal of Ambient Intelligence and Humanized Computing*, *14*(8), 11239–11261. DOI: 10.1007/s12652-023-04632-7

Majeed, U., Khan, L. U., Yaqoob, I., Kazmi, S. M. A., Salah, K., & Hong, C. S. (2021). Blockchain for IoT-based smart cities: Recent advances, requirements, and future challenges. *Journal of Network and Computer Applications*, *181*, 103007. DOI: 10.1016/j.jnca.2021.103007

Mansoor, K., Afzal, M., Iqbal, W., & Abbas, Y. (2025). Securing the future: Exploring post-quantum cryptography for authentication and user privacy in IoT devices. *Cluster Computing*, *28*(2), 93. DOI: 10.1007/s10586-024-04799-4

Martinez, C., Bueti, C., Brékine, A., Grimm, C., & Ziegler, S. (2024). *IoT for SDGs*., DOI: 10.1007/978-3-031-39650-2_31

Masood, I., Daud, A., Wang, Y., Banjar, A., & Alharbey, R. (2024). A blockchain-based system for patient data privacy and security. *Multimedia Tools and Applications*, *83*(21), 60443–60467. DOI: 10.1007/s11042-023-17941-y

Mishra, H., & Maheshwari, P. (2021). Blockchain in Indian Public Distribution System: A conceptual framework to prevent leakage of the supplies and its enablers and disablers. *Journal of Global Operations and Strategic Sourcing*, *14*(2), 312–335. DOI: 10.1108/JGOSS-07-2020-0044

Mouha, N., & Celi, C. (2023). *A Vulnerability in Implementations of SHA-3, SHAKE, EdDSA, and Other NIST-Approved Algorithms* (pp. 3–28). DOI: 10.1007/978-3-031-30872-7_1

Mourtzis, D., Angelopoulos, J., & Panopoulos, N. (2023). The Future of the Human–Machine Interface (HMI) in Society 5.0. *Future Internet*, *15*(5), 162. DOI: 10.3390/fi15050162

Munjal, K., & Bhatia, R. (2023). A systematic review of homomorphic encryption and its contributions in healthcare industry. *Complex & Intelligent Systems*, *9*(4), 3759–3786. DOI: 10.1007/s40747-022-00756-z

Munk, T. (2022). *The Rise of Politically Motivated Cyber Attacks*. Routledge., DOI: 10.4324/9781003126676

Mustafa, G., Rafiq, W., Jhamat, N., Arshad, Z., & Rana, F. A. (2025). Blockchain-based governance models in e-government: A comprehensive framework for legal, technical, ethical and security considerations. *International Journal of Law and Management*, *67*(1), 37–55. DOI: 10.1108/IJLMA-08-2023-0172

Pali, P., Pandey, D., & Yadav, M. (2025). *Enhancing Smart Transportation System: Blockchain Based Integrating Cloud Database Management System* (pp. 603–617). DOI: 10.1007/978-3-031-72617-0_31

Panahi Rizi, M. H., & Hosseini Seno, S. A. (2022). A systematic review of technologies and solutions to improve security and privacy protection of citizens in the smart city. *Internet of Things : Engineering Cyber Physical Human Systems*, *20*, 100584. DOI: 10.1016/j.iot.2022.100584

Pandey, S., Bhushan, B., & Hameed, A. A. (2024). Securing Healthcare 5.0: Zero-Knowledge Proof (ZKP) and Post Quantum Cryptography (PQC) Solutions for Medical Data Security. In *Soft Computing in Industry 5.0 for Sustainability* (pp. 339–355). Springer Nature Switzerland. DOI: 10.1007/978-3-031-69336-6_15

Periyasamy, G., Rangaswamy, E., & Nawaz, N. (2023). *Big Data Systems Architecture and Data Security Fundamentals—Case Study Approach for a Hospital in Singapore* (pp. 277–287). DOI: 10.1007/978-3-031-17746-0_23

Quelhas Poças, M. (2025). *Public Sector Blockchain Use Cases for Societal Development*., DOI: 10.1007/978-3-031-85936-6_6

Rahaman, M., Arya, V., Orozco, S. M., & Pappachan, P. (2024). *Secure Multi-Party Computation (SMPC)*. Protocols and Privacy., DOI: 10.4018/979-8-3693-5330-1.ch008

Rajawat, A. S., Bedi, P., Goyal, S. B., Shaw, R. N., Ghosh, A., & Aggarwal, S. (2022). *AI and Blockchain for Healthcare Data Security in Smart Cities*., DOI: 10.1007/978-981-16-7498-3_12

Reshma, S., Goyal, V., Kokila, R., Vibha, K., & Indirani, S. (2025). AI Tools for the Software Development of Real-Time Communication Systems. In *Modern Insights on Smart and Secure Software Development* (pp. 139–172). IGI Global., DOI: 10.4018/979-8-3693-9851-7.ch005

Robinson, L., Ragnedda, M., & Schulz, J. (2020). Digital inequalities: Contextualizing problems and solutions. *Journal of Information. Communication and Ethics in Society*, *18*(3), 323–327. DOI: 10.1108/JICES-05-2020-0064

Sadhya, D., & Sahu, T. (2024). A critical survey of the security and privacy aspects of the Aadhaar framework. *Computers & Security*, *140*, 103782. DOI: 10.1016/j.cose.2024.103782

Schumacher, L. V. (2024). Central Bank Digital Currencies (CBDCs): Exploring Characteristics, Risks and Benefits. In *Decoding Digital Assets* (pp. 81–157). Springer Nature Switzerland. DOI: 10.1007/978-3-031-54601-3_12

Shafik, W. (2024). *Shaping the Next Generation Smart City Ecosystem: An Investigation on the Requirements*. Applications, Architecture, Security and Privacy, and Open Research Questions., DOI: 10.1007/978-3-031-59846-3_1

Sharma, P., Agrawal, A., Bhatia, V., Prakash, S., & Mishra, A. K. (2021). Quantum Key Distribution Secured Optical Networks: A Survey. *IEEE Open Journal of the Communications Society*, *2*, 2049–2083. DOI: 10.1109/OJCOMS.2021.3106659

Shin, D., & Ibahrine, M. (2020). The socio-technical assemblages of blockchain system: How blockchains are framed and how the framing reflects societal contexts. *Digital Policy. Regulation & Governance*, *22*(3), 245–263. DOI: 10.1108/DPRG-11-2019-0095

Shneiderman, B. (2020). Bridging the Gap Between Ethics and Practice. *ACM Transactions on Interactive Intelligent Systems*, *10*(4), 1–31. DOI: 10.1145/3419764

Shuaib, M., Alam, S., Ahmed, R., Qamar, S., Nasir, M. S., & Alam, M. S. (2022). Current Status, Requirements, and Challenges of Blockchain Application in Land Registry. *International Journal of Information Retrieval Research*, *12*(2), 1–20. DOI: 10.4018/IJIRR.299934

Singh, S., Sharma, P. K., Moon, S. Y., & Park, J. H. (2024). Advanced lightweight encryption algorithms for IoT devices: Survey, challenges and solutions. *Journal of Ambient Intelligence and Humanized Computing*, *15*(2), 1625–1642. DOI: 10.1007/s12652-017-0494-4

Singun, A. (2025). Unveiling the barriers to digital transformation in higher education institutions: A systematic literature review. *Discover Education*, *4*(1), 37. DOI: 10.1007/s44217-025-00430-9

Song, Y., Liu, J., Zhang, W., & Li, J. (2023). Blockchain's role in e-commerce sellers' decision-making on information disclosure under competition. *Annals of Operations Research*, *329*(1–2), 1009–1048. DOI: 10.1007/s10479-021-04276-w

Sultana, S. S., & Sangeetha, J. (2022). *Internet of Things: Security Mechanisms* (pp. 581–595). DOI: 10.1007/978-981-16-8862-1_38

Toh, C. K. (2020). Security for smart cities. *IET Smart Cities*, *2*(2), 95–104. DOI: 10.1049/iet-smc.2020.0001

Troitiño, D. R., Mazur, V., & Kerikmäe, T. (2024). E-governance and integration in the European union. *Internet of Things : Engineering Cyber Physical Human Systems*, *27*, 101321. DOI: 10.1016/j.iot.2024.101321

Tshuma, S., Masengu, R., & Dube, M. (2024). *Security and Privacy Challenges in Digital Marketing*., DOI: 10.4018/979-8-3693-2165-2.ch018

Ullah, A., Anwar, S. M., Li, J., Nadeem, L., Mahmood, T., Rehman, A., & Saba, T. (2024). Smart cities: The role of Internet of Things and machine learning in realizing a data-centric smart environment. *Complex & Intelligent Systems*, *10*(1), 1607–1637. DOI: 10.1007/s40747-023-01175-4

Uzun, E., Yagemann, C., Chung, S., Kolesnikov, V., & Lee, W. (2021). Cryptographic Key Derivation from Biometric Inferences for Remote Authentication. *Proceedings of the 2021 ACM Asia Conference on Computer and Communications Security*, 629–643. DOI: 10.1145/3433210.3437512

Vasani, V., Prateek, K., Amin, R., Maity, S., & Dwivedi, A. D. (2024). Embracing the quantum frontier: Investigating quantum communication, cryptography, applications and future directions. *Journal of Industrial Information Integration*, *39*, 100594. DOI: 10.1016/j.jii.2024.100594

Vijayalakshmi, D., Krithiga, S., Gangisetty, T., Dayana, R., & Vadivukkarasi, K. (2024). *Encryption Protocols and Security for 5G* (pp. 78–112). DOI: 10.4018/979-8-3693-2786-9.ch004

Vishnu, C. R., Chatterjee, P., Maddali, S. P., & Akenroye, T. O. (2025). Characterizing the critical success factors influencing blockchain technology adoption in Indian public distribution system: An exploratory approach. *Benchmarking*, *32*(4), 1410–1433. DOI: 10.1108/BIJ-07-2023-0466

Wang, H., Kang, X., Li, T., Lei, Z., Chu, C.-K., & Wang, H. (2023). An Overview of Trust Standards for Communication Networks and Future Digital World. *IEEE Access : Practical Innovations, Open Solutions*, *11*, 42991–42998. DOI: 10.1109/ACCESS.2023.3270042

Wong, B. K. M., Voon, M. L., & Law, F. L. (2025). Preparing digital citizens for smart healthcare in the Asia-Pacific: Strategies, challenges, and opportunities. In *Digital Healthcare, Digital Transformation and Citizen Empowerment in Asia-Pacific and Europe for a Healthier Society* (pp. 539–560). Elsevier., DOI: 10.1016/B978-0-443-30168-1.00008-6

Zhou, L., Diro, A., Saini, A., Kaisar, S., & Hiep, P. C. (2024). Leveraging zero knowledge proofs for blockchain-based identity sharing: A survey of advancements, challenges and opportunities. *Journal of Information Security and Applications*, *80*, 103678. DOI: 10.1016/j.jisa.2023.103678

KEY TERMS AND DEFINITIONS

Quantum Cryptography: This area of cryptography draws on the quirky behavior of quantum mechanics like superposition, entanglement, and the no-cloning principle—to try and create communication channels that can't be broken, at least in theory. Unlike regular cryptographic systems, quantum cryptography can detect if someone is eavesdropping because measuring a quantum system tends to mess with it.

Shor's Algorithm: Back in 1994, Peter Shor came up with a quantum algorithm that can factor large numbers way faster than classical ones. This is a big deal because current encryption systems like RSA and ECC rely on the fact that factoring is hard. If large-scale quantum computers become real, these systems could be broken easily with Shor's method.

Grover's Algorithm: Developed by Lov Grover in 1996, this quantum search technique speeds up the time it takes to find something in an unsorted database. In terms of cryptography, it means symmetric algorithms like AES might not be as safe as we thought they'd still work, but we'd need longer keys to keep things secure against quantum attacks.

Post-Quantum Cryptography (PQC): This branch of cryptography is focused on building algorithms that can stand up to quantum computing threats. It includes a mix of approaches like lattice-based, code-based, and hash-based methods and it's currently being evaluated by NIST as part of its global standardization efforts.

Smart City: A city that uses ICT together with IoT to become more efficient and improve life for citizens

Cryptography: The technique and understanding of methods for securing both messages and data by encryption, to achieve confidentiality, integrity, authentication and ensure that no one can deny receiving them

Blockchain: A decentralized system that keeps track of transactions on multiple machines, making everything easier to see, more secure and trusted without any central body in control

Zero-Knowledge Proof (ZKP): A cryptographic technique that allows someone to show another person a statement is valid without revealing anything more

Homomorphic Encryption: An encryption scheme makes it possible to carry out computations on encrypted information, with privacy intact during the whole process

Quantum Cryptography: A technique that makes use of quantum rules so that the encryption approach is theoretically unbreakable through quantum key distribution

Public Key Infrastructure (PKI): A method for creating, handling and sending digital certificates that relate public keys to entities for safe electronic communication

E-Health: The delivery of health services using digital tools and electronic messages which cover all aspects of health data, telemedicine and health monitoring

Quantum Key Distribution (QKD): QKD lets two parties share encryption keys in a super secure way by using quantum bits (or qubits). The most well-known method, BB84, uses photons and relies on the idea that if someone tries to listen in, the act of measuring the quantum state will reveal the intrusion.

RSA (Rivest–Shamir–Adleman): RSA is a public-key encryption system that's been widely used since the late 20th century. It's based on the difficulty of factoring big numbers, but unfortunately, it wouldn't hold up against quantum attacks especially from Shor's algorithm. That's why researchers are looking for alternatives.

Elliptic Curve Cryptography (ECC): ECC offers high security using smaller key sizes by applying math from elliptic curves. While it's efficient and widely adopted, ECC also becomes vulnerable in the face of quantum computing. Once again, Shor's algorithm could be its downfall.

Symmetric Key Cryptography: This is the kind of cryptography where the same key is used to both encrypt and decrypt data. AES is a popular example. Even though it's more resistant to quantum threats than public-key systems, Grover's algorithm means we'll probably need to use longer keys moving forward.

Quantum Supremacy: This term refers to the point when a quantum computer can solve a problem way faster than the best classical computer ever could. Although it's still mostly experimental, once quantum supremacy becomes common, it could shake up a lot of existing encryption systems.

Lattice-Based Cryptography: This approach uses math problems based on lattices (think grids in multiple dimensions) that are tough for both classical and quantum machines to solve. Algorithms like Learning with Errors (LWE) are part of this category, and they're currently among the top candidates for post-quantum security standards.

Chapter 2
Cybersecurity in the Smart City Era:
Overcoming Challenges With Modern Cryptographic Solutions

Md Mehedi Hasan Emon
https://orcid.org/0000-0002-6224-9552
American International University-Bangladesh, Bangladesh

ABSTRACT

As smart cities continue to evolve through the integration of IoT, AI, and big data analytics, the complexity and scale of cybersecurity challenges have intensified. This chapter examines key vulnerabilities ranging from data privacy breaches to cyber-physical system attacks and highlights the critical role of modern cryptographic technologies in addressing these risks. Techniques such as encryption, blockchain, PKI, homomorphic encryption, zero-knowledge proofs, and quantum cryptography are analyzed for their potential to strengthen smart city infrastructures. Drawing on recent case studies and emerging research, we further explore future directions, including post-quantum security and AI-driven cybersecurity frameworks. The findings of this chapter suggest that strategically embedding cryptographic solutions is essential for building secure, resilient, and citizen-centered smart cities capable of withstanding both current and emerging cyber threats.

INTRODUCTION

This chapter, titled "*Cybersecurity in the Smart City Era: Overcoming Challenges with Modern Cryptographic Solutions*" offers a comprehensive exploration of the critical cybersecurity dimensions that will characterize the future of the smart city.

DOI: 10.4018/979-8-3373-3326-7.ch002

Spatially speaking, the focus on navigating the cybersecurity landscape of smart cities starts with observing how the vehicles of IoT, AI and big data have never occurred in such possibilities and complexities at once, making them as many opportunities as they are vulnerabilities. This is in preparation for the growing need to understand the role of robust security frameworks in all cities that are becoming more and more digitalized and linked. The second section, Cybersecurity Challenges in Smart Cities, discusses the leading threats to smart infrastructures. Data privacy, confidentiality breaches, vulnerabilities of IoT and networked devices, bridging the interoperability gap and standardization gap, as well as cyber-physical security risk issues are carefully looked through. The challenges are contextualized around recent events with each being presented in a timely and realistic picture of the cyber threat environment. Next, Cryptographic Technologies for Smart City is presented and where modern cryptographic solutions are detailed in detail. For their contributions in securing them, techniques of symmetric and asymmetric encryption, blockchain, public key infrastructure (PKI), homomorphic encryption, zero knowledge proofs (ZKP), quantum cryptography are analyzed.

In the fourth part Case Studies on Cryptography Applications in Smart Cities the theory is applied to practice by real world examples. They are including blockchain based digital identity systems in Estonia, homomorphic encryption applications in health care, PKI based IoT communication in Singapore and the development of quantum resistant cryptographic system that was initiated by U.S. National Institute of Standards and Technology (NIST). These cases demonstrate the use of cryptography to protect digital ecosystems maintained by leading city and institution. It then moves on to Future Trends and Recommendations, which looks at important new breakthroughs like post quantum cryptography, AI and machine learning use in systems security enhancement, a requirement for a seamlessly thought-out policy and regulatory framework, as well as ethical aspects of implementing cryptography. By providing such a forward-looking perspective of building resilient adaptive and ethically sound smart city infrastructures, these insights are provided. The chapter concludes with the idea of Strengthening Smart Cities with Cryptographic Security and with a summary of the key insights and an emphasis on how they require proactive cryptography driven security to secure the future of urban life.

It makes several important contributions in this chapter. It then starts to systematically identify and categorize the evolving cybersecurity threats regarding smart cities. Second, it connects theoretical advances in cryptography that cannot be put into practice globally with practical applications through global cases studies. Third, it communicates about the strategies for future proofing including post quantum ready and AI ready. Second, it highlights two additional technical concerns in the design of the smart city infrastructures: how to incorporate different actors' needs, desires, and values within the very complex city infrastructure system, and how to use statistical modeling to safeguard citizen privacy. Finally, the chapter provides actionable recommendations and ethical guidelines for researchers, policymakers, and technology developers to consider when designing secure, resilient and citizen centric smart city infrastructures.

NAVIGATING THE CYBERSECURITY LANDSCAPE IN SMART CITIES

The surge of smart cities has completely revolutionized the infrastructure of cities by the fusion of technologies like IoT, AI and big data analytics. They have greatly improved urban efficiency, sustainability and the quality of citizens' services, creating living environments hosting dynamic ecosystems where data in real time is required for taking decisions. Nevertheless, it has also added significant issues to cybersecurity as this growing dependence on digital and networked technologies. With the growing of smart cities, they are confronted by greater risks, such as data breaching, unauthorized access and sophisticated cyberattacks against fundamental facilities (Demertzi et al., 2023).

There are serious problems regarding these cybersecurity problems. The fact that smart city ecosystems are founded on a level of secrecy, integrity and availability is essential for their own sustainability and security. A cyberattack that destroys a layer in the city's digital infrastructure like power grid and transportation system could interrupt a large portion of life, endangering public safety while eroding confidence in a digital infrastructure being provided by the city (K. Ahmad et al., 2022; Khan et al., 2020). Smart cities as a result are characterized by their high data collecting intensity, which entails a lot of privacy problems: sensitive information about residents and companies is being continuously created and stored. If there are no strong security mechanisms, this data is a very tempting target for the malicious minded, who have to use their weaknesses for monetary or political gain (Djenna et al., 2021).

In this perspective, contemporary cryptographic technologies are used to be an integral part of cybersecurity in smart cities. One of the most critical functions of these technologies is to offer secure communication for transmitting data and preserving data integrity as well as advanced means of authentication. Various cryptographic methods of encryption, blockchain, homomorphic encryption, ZKP and quantum cryptography can create strong security schemes to fight off the great cyber challenges. Justice is found using blockchain technology in the fact that transactions are immutable and tamper proof with homomorphically encrypted data allowing it to be processed without revealing any sensitive information (Zafir et al., 2024).

Figure 1. Smart city cybersecurity ecosystem overview

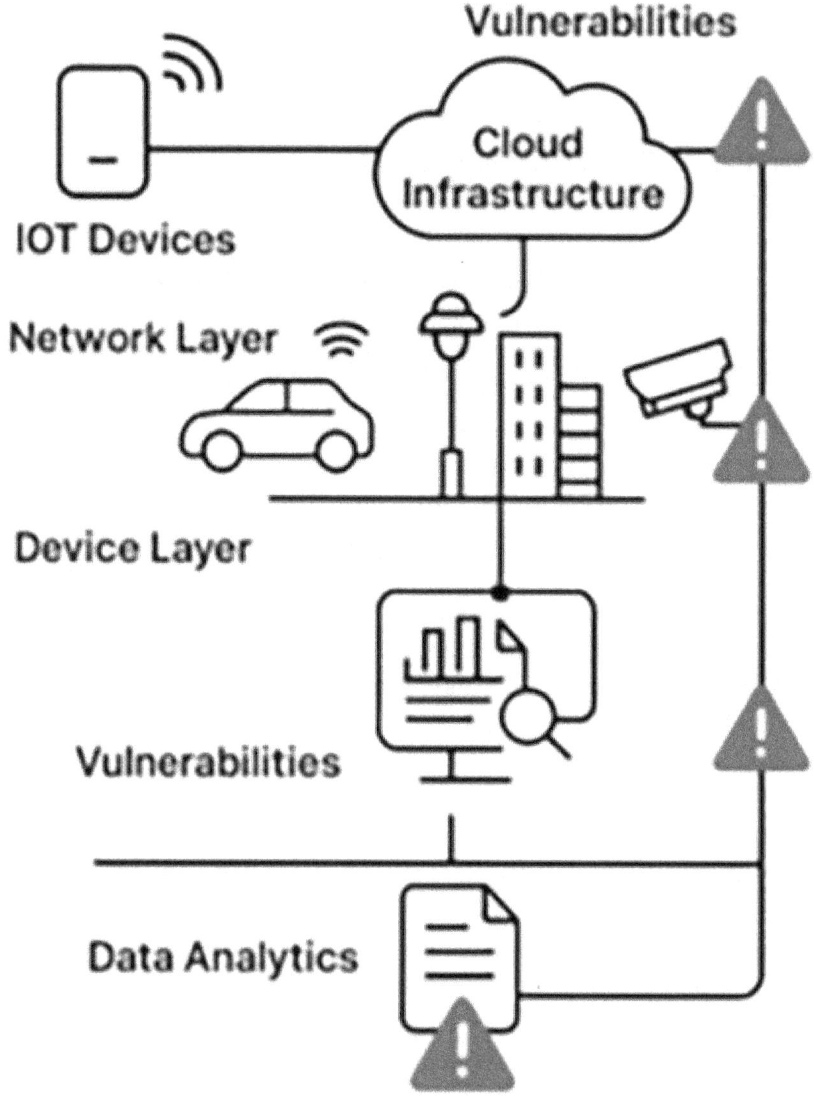

Figure 1 shows a detailed picture of cybersecurity in smart cities, highlighting the many risks found in their infrastructure. The figure shows how IoT devices, the network layer, the device layer and the data analytics layer, all interact with cloud infrastructure. Smart devices like sensors, meters and surveillance tools use the network layer to exchange information with urban system infrastructure. Because of these interactions, the cloud and device layers get the information they need for real-time processing and everyday work. The final stage is for data analytics engines to examine huge amounts of collected data, supporting planning and automation. The figure also makes it clear that different risks can target each layer of the system. Many insecure endpoints, misconfigured cloud systems, vulnerable devices and unprotected analytical tools combine to make the overall attack surface larger. By using red warning symbols, the document highlights the places where cryptographic and security efforts should be particularly advanced. This diagram reveals that using cryptography at all stages is vital in making cities safer from cyberattacks.

CYBERSECURITY CHALLENGES IN SMART CITIES

With the development and integration of modern technology into smart cities, they present several cybersecurity threats that affect the conception, integrity, confidentiality of digital infrastructures. Then, this section studies the most crucial cybersecurity challenges that smart cities face, including data privacy and confidentiality concerns, threats to IoT and networked devices, interoperability and standardization flaws as well as cyber-physical security risk.

Data Privacy and Confidentiality Issues

Smart cities aggregate and analyze huge volumes of personal and operational data resulted from different stakeholders, including their citizens, governmental structures, and the enterprises. The data can be sensitive around infrastructure management and urban services and might also include personal identifiable information (PII). Sensitive information's can be used for nefarious objectives and may lead to privacy disengagements or identity theft; and to avoid this, unauthorized access to sensitive information can be very detrimental (Shafik, 2025).

The volume and variety of data come with a major difficulty of securing privacy: a lot of data is involved, and it comes from a lot of sources. Data from many platforms combine in smart city systems and are even more vulnerable to exposure. These linking personal data from smart health devices, traffic monitoring systems, and so on may form a detailed picture of people that can be compromised if being infiltrated. However, strong data governance systems are necessary to address privacy issues efficiently when the interrelation between the different data sources is required (Rasool et al., 2022).

Smart cities need to operate with E2E encryption and a strong access control procedure, just to ensure data confidentiality. With end to end encryption, the data received at origin is encrypted and may only be depended by the designated receiver on destination thus ensuring that while in transmission, the data is inaccessible to any party except to the receivers (Hazra et al., 2024). Additionally, the risky cases of illegal access to sensitive information can be minimized at any level through employing strong access control mechanisms, such as MFA, etc. However, such security features are at odds with realities about how different companies and division within the city have varying degrees of maturity in terms of cybersecurity (Suleski et al., 2023). Additionally, data privacy poses another regulatory aspect in its management. Because of this, smart cities need to carefully navigate through their data protection law framework consisting of such legislation as the GDPR in Europe and the CCPA in the United States (Nanayakkara et al., 2024).

Threats to IoT and Networked Devices

Smart city infrastructure is fundamentally tied into the IoT as it allows for real time collecting and analysis of data for many applications stemming from the smart grid, intelligent transportation systems and automated surveillance (Sarker, 2022). IoT devices present a great deal of threats to cybersecurity with their expansion. IoT devices are filled with lots of devices, the majority of which have not been designed with proper security measures and are designed as perfect targets for fraudsters. All these weaken the vulnerabilities because of the inadequate default passwords, lack of firmware upgrades and lack of security procedures (Sharma et al., 2025).

The DDoS attack is a common threat to such devices. A DDoS attack involves so many hacked devices to inundate a target system with traffic which stops its functionality. Such assaults may affect essential functions of smart cities, whether traffic control or emergency response services. IoT vulnerabilities had such significant consequences in 2016, when a Mirai botnet attack demonstrated the ability to exploit unprotected IoT devices, and cause significant disruptions is key internet services (Xenofontos et al., 2022). Additionally, malware implants can corrupt the core of the IoT devices to allow attackers to obtain unauthorized access to the network and adjust critical systems. Such a system of smart traffic signal would also bring about considerable hazards for public safety if it were hacked: traffic interruptions and accidents may suffer greatly (Demertzi et al., 2023).

Interoperability and Standardization Challenges

Interoperability issues arise in the amalgamation of smart cities based on many technologies from different smart city manufacturers. Security of multiple systems is driven by a lack of uniform standards. This may leave each vendor to adopt its own security protocols, which might be different and attacker exploitable (Abdelkader et al., 2024). A city that tries to be smart can be filled with many IoT devices of various manufacturers who each use different communication protocols and security requirements. In the absence of consistency, there is no basis or form to develop a coherent security architecture that would prevent vulnerabilities of one system from breaking the whole infrastructure (Ahmad & Mir, 2021). Furthermore, since there are no defined security protocols, risk assessments and audits cannot be conducted with completeness.

To protect the smart city infrastructure, it is very important to formulate universally recognized cryptographic standards. Standardized security protocols may help promote interoperability amongst systems, with safe flow of data and communication throughout the devices. For this reasons, entities such as the Internet Engineering Task Force (IETF) and the ISO play an important role in drafting and supporting these standards. Interoperability problems are best tackled through collaboration among the stakeholders, also including government entities, private sector organizations, and academic institutions. The cultivation of partnerships would enable smart cities to create cohesive security strategy that includes best practices and an interoperable technology development (Ismagilova et al., 2022).

Cyber-Physical Security Risks

Integrated cyber-physical systems that include the most critical infrastructure, such as smart energy grids, intelligent traffic management, and so forth, are what make up a smart city. Although these technologies deliver higher efficiency and service, they are fraught with high cybersecurity threats. And cyber-attacks against these systems can be very catastrophic such as those causes' power outages, transportation breakdowns and interruption to the systems that might be needed in the event of an emergency. An attack on a smart grid could lead to significant blackouts that impact consumers both in their homes and the most important serving functions, including hospitals and emergency response centers. Smart transportation systems could compromise, therefore they could alter the traffic patterns and decrease to accidents as well as congestion (Elassy et al., 2024). The ramifications of such assaults on cyber physical systems become avoidable and motivate the protection of them.

CRYPTOGRAPHIC TECHNOLOGIES FOR SMART CITIES

Since smart cities are emerging and making use of the latest technology, safety of the data and communication infrastructure is necessary. To solve the cybersecurity problems associated with the smart city infrastructures which are based on the networked systems, cryptographic technologies are vital. This section discusses many cryptograph technologies relevant to smart cities such as encryption methods, blockchain, PKI, homomorphic encryption, ZKP, and quantum cryptography.

Figure 2. Comparison of cryptographic technologies

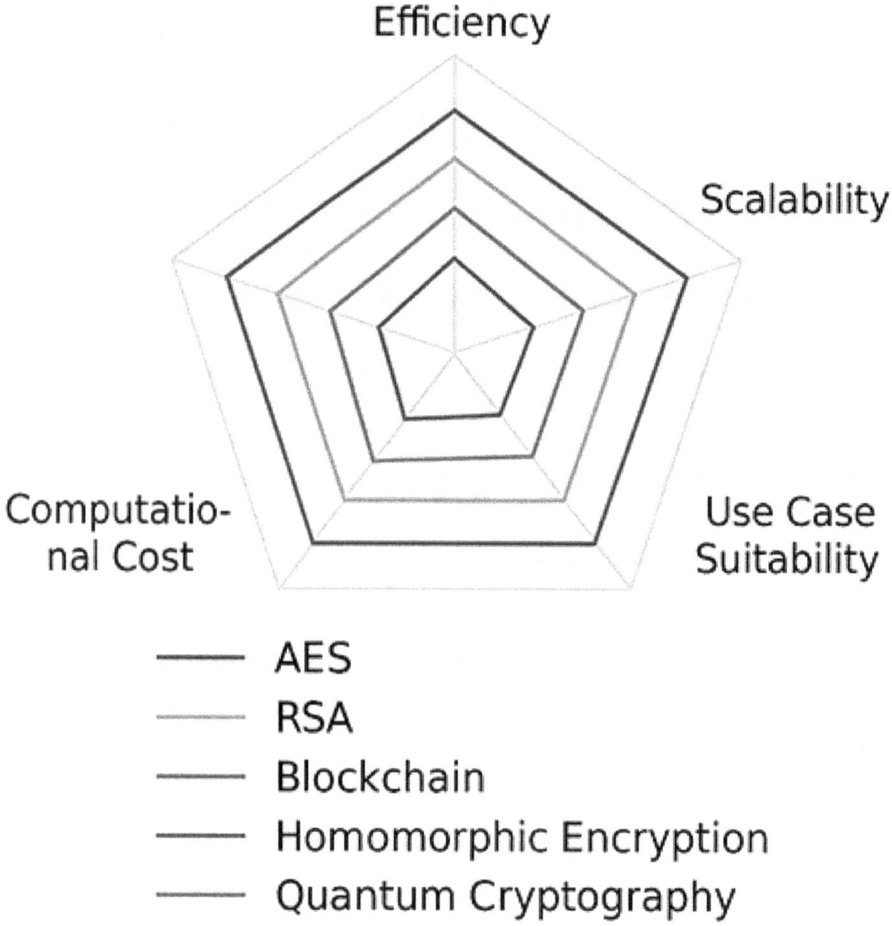

Using a radar chart, Figure 2 compares the main features of five cryptographic technologies: AES, RSA, Blockchain, Homomorphic Encryption and Quantum Cryptography along the parameters of efficiency, scalability, suitability for various tasks, computing requirements and security. AES is suitable for real-time smart city use because it performs well on all measures, showing a high level of efficiency, scalability and keeps computational costs low. Although RSA is secure, it takes a lot of resources to use which is a problem when large numbers of people need it. Blockchain technologies are ideal for both scalability and matching use cases in areas such as decentralized identification and maintaining data accuracy in smart cities. Still, they may not work efficiently in situations where everything relies on speed because of how their consensus works. This type of encryption provides an advantage by letting you work on encrypted data which improves privacy in analytics. As a result, it is more expensive to run and not as efficient, so it is more often used for things like handling sensitive health or citizens' data. Quantum Cryptography is still being developed, but it seems promising for the future's safety needs. In the current stage, it does not achieve many people using it or affordability, due to its experimental nature and support structure. Figure 3 allows smart city planners and cybersecurity professionals to compare each technology and choose the correct cryptography solution for their situation.

Encryption Techniques: Symmetric vs. Asymmetric Encryption

A smart city must encrypt sensitive information to preserve the secrecy of the data being stored in it because conversion of information into an unreadable (encrypted) form to be accessed by only the authorized individuals (decoders) is necessary. Symmetric and asymmetric encryption methods are primarily the encryption methods. In Symmetric encryption the same key is applied both in the encryption as well as the decryption process. This is the right way to impact that large datasets are protected with little overhead and quick processing which suits smart city applications that need to pump the data fast (K. Ahmad et al., 2022; Osman, 2019). Symmetric encryption, amongst others, is the AES, a well-known, robust and fast. AES works on fixed size blocks size of 128, 192 or 256 bits to provide different security levels using keys of size 128, 192 or 256 bits (Alenezi et al., 2024).

Symmetric encryption has the strong advantage of speed and efficiency, especially in dealing with large amounts of data flowing out of smart city sensors and devices. However, a significant impediment is safe dissemination of encryption keys. An adversary may then easily decode what turns out to be confidential information if a symmetric key is compromised during transmission (Banoth & Regar, 2023). Hence, in order to support smart cities, secure key management protocols should involve use of secure communication channels for key exchange and frequent key rotation are required. Asymmetric encryption, or public-key cryptography, employs two keys: a public key for encryption and a private key for decryption. However, this method serves the purpose for conducting safe key exchange and authentication necessary for communication in smart cities (Banoth & Regar, 2023). RSA and ECC are two well-known notables of asymmetric encryption methods. Subsequently, ECC is based on the algebra of elliptic curves over finite fields as opposed to the mathematical challenge of factoring large prime numbers, which current RSA encryption is based on; again, offering the same level of security with smaller key sizes (Ugbedeojo et al., 2024). In symmetric encryption the key distribution issue is resolved but in asymmetric encryption this issue is not resolved. Smart cities can disperse public keys widely across the town without divulging the private keys, thus permitting secure communication without direct secret key exchange. This is a very useful Attribute for applications that must have secure communication across a diverse set of IoT devices and systems. While higher in computational burden, higher in time taken than symmetric encryption, asymmetric encryption does offer some extra benefit. Generally, they use a hybrid technique which uses symmetric encryption for bulk data encryption and asymmetric encryption for key exchange and authentication (Halak et al., 2022).

Blockchain for Security: Decentralized Identity Verification and Secure Transactions

Decentralized identity management and tamper-proof data storage are amongst the most solid instruments brought about by blockchain technology for securing the smart cities. Many of its applications, however, are more secure transactions, maintaining public records or automated services, which are suitable for distinctive characteristics of blockchain, such as immutability and transparency. As conventional identity verification solutions mostly rely on centralized databases that might get breached or exploited, it is recommended to use Decentralized Identity Management. A blockchain provides a decentralized platform for users to safely keep track of their digital identities. Decentralized data governance is permitted on a blockchain by storing identification information that will allow smart cities to mitigate the risk of identity theft and fraud (Tyagi & Seranmadevi, 2024).

Blockchain technology gives rise to peer-to-peer trade or trading among unrelated parties where the transfer of funds requires no specific corporate network. It means that these self-executing contracts make it, so these middlemen are no longer necessary, that there is a reduction in transaction costs and increase in efficiency. For smart city application, blockchain can be used to send smart utility service invoicing automatically and securely between suppliers and customers (Majeed et al., 2021).

PKI: Managing Digital Identities and Secure Authentication

A smart city is a place where PKI maintains secure communication and it helps to manage the digital identity. Hardware, software, rules and standards that can be integrated are brought together to produce, distribute, and maintain the digital certificates (digital identities) that require to prove the identities and the security of data (Höglund et al., 2020).

Digital Certificates: Digital certificates are electronic credentials that indicate the association between a public and a private key on behalf of a person (or their business), organization or another device. PKI use certificates to authenticate digital identities for the security of smart cities communication among users and devices.

For instance, PKI can guarantee IoT devices connected to the smart grid are authorized before accessing the network (Prateek et al., 2023).

Secure Authentication: PKI based systems offer strong and relatively foolproof authentication methods, i.e. digital signatures and certificate-based authentication. Digital signature offers integrity and authenticity as the sender is able to print their message with their private key and receiver can also verify that if they use the sender public key (Hemminghaus et al., 2021). Moreover, because secure access management is important to protect sensitive data and key infrastructure in smart city applications, this procedure applies in such scenarios.

Homomorphic Encryption: Privacy-Preserving Data Analytics

Homomorphic encryption is a complex cryptographical technique that allows you to process encrypted data while not cracking it. This capability ensures data analysis and processing with anonymity, which is very crucial in smart cities where such data cannot handle it securely (Munjal & Bhatia, 2023).

Privacy-Preserving Data Analytics: As big data analytics is widely used in smart cities, analysis of such information should be conducted, but at the same time they should be kept confidential. According to homomorphic encryption, data analysts can calculate on encrypted data while preserving the secrecy of the original data. However, patient data can be examined by healthcare institutions to benefit public health without compromising individual privacy (Murdoch, 2021).

Applications in Smart Cities: Homomorphic encryption can be used in very different applications in smart cities such as finance, public government and healthcare. But financial organizations may look at transaction data in order to spot any fraud while remaining safe from information from their client. Depending on the source, data from many sources can be consolidated by public organizations to extract insights about urban development patterns while protecting sensitive citizen information. Although homomorphic encryption promises a great deal, it is an emerging technology, and could have lower performance, in terms of computation, compared to traditional encryption techniques. Research in this area is trying to improve homomorphic encryption algorithms so that they could be implemented more practically (Gonzalez et al., 2022).

ZKP: Enhancing Authentication without Exposing Sensitive Data

Cryptography called ZKP allows one party to prove being able to know some specific information to another party without showing what the information is. Secure identity verification of sensitive information, and negotiation of authentication procedures in smart cities becomes more feasible using this method (Zhou et al., 2024).

Authentication Use Cases: ZKP can bring a number of smart city applications, such as identity verification and safe access management. To show the eligibility for public service access, a citizen would not reveal their identify or any personal information to the authorities (Zhou et al., 2024). This privacy preserving function is most suitable if some personal information can attract privacy infringements or discrimination if released.

Advantages of ZKP: ZKP may prove to be an implementable approach to bolstering the security of authentication systems in the smart cities and reduce the chances of data breaches. This decreases the probability of illegal access to personal information by far in the authentication procedure because of the lack of sensitive information. In addition, ZKP acts as an additional support for users to trust digital services, a type of system that will encourage users to interact with it. While ZKP integration in smart city applications may require additional computation resources, performance and efficiency of ZKP protocols keep getting improved (Aggarwal et al., 2024).

Figure 3. Workflow of ZKP in smart city authentication

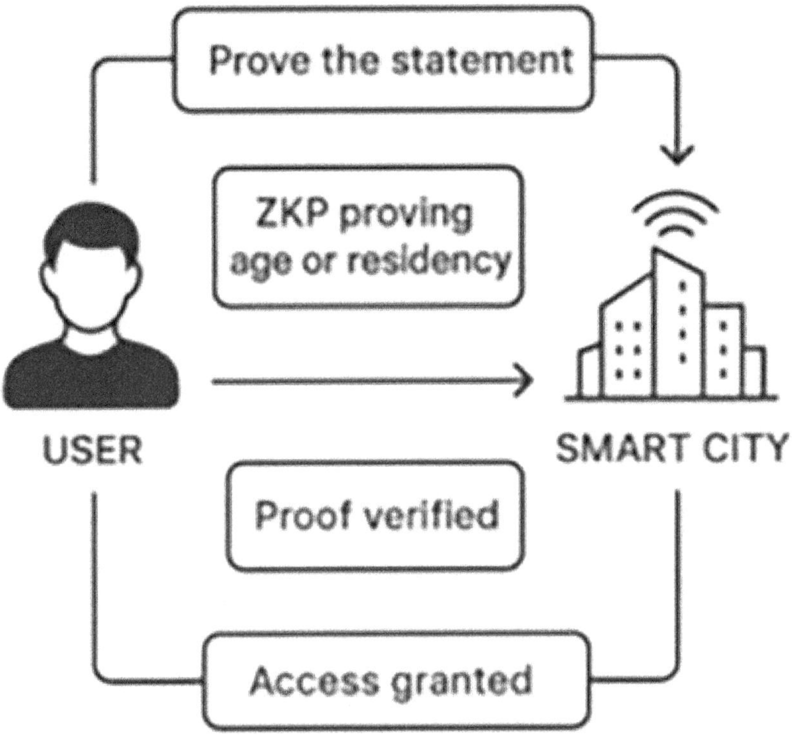

Figure 3 demonstrates the stages by which ZKP technology is used in smart cities to ensure secure and private user authentication. The purpose of this framework is to let a user demonstrate a characteristic such as age or where they live but not expose any underlying data. The first step is for the user to produce proof of a claim they make. Its validity is proven using zero-knowledge algorithms which allow you to confirm the truth without revealing what's hidden. Following the transmission of the ZKP to the city's system, it is compared with rules that were set in advance. After a successful result, access opens to the necessary smart service. This method secures your data and guarantees user privacy. It is essential for making smart city services follow modern cryptographic rules.

Quantum Cryptography: Securing Smart Cities against Quantum Computing Threats

Since the progress of quantum computing technologies, the whole of the classical cryptography has certain problems. Therefore, smart city infrastructures are at the risk of being dismantled by prevalent cryptographic methods such as RSA and ECC with the ability of quantum computers (Biswas et al., 2024). This difficulty is apparently solved by quantum cryptography such as QKD.

Quantum Key Distribution (QKD): It is the technology that allows two parties to produce and exchange a safe encryption key based on the laws of quantum physics. QKD is different from traditional key distribution techniques in that each effort of eavesdropping during the key exchange is detected by the communication parties (Sharma et al., 2021). When it comes to smart cities, this attribute ensures secrecy and integrity of the encryption keys that are used to safeguard communications.

Future-Proofing Smart City Security: It is necessary for the use of quantum cryptography in smart cities to guarantee the resilience of their security architecture. Since the advent of quantum computers, this includes QKD within smart city security practices to ameliorate the dangers that existed from quantum attacks (Biswas et al., 2024).

CASE STUDIES ON CRYPTOGRAPHY APPLICATIONS IN SMART CITIES

With the new technology being used with smart cities, the need to have stringent security measures is more critical. Cryptography is the necessity of the importance that any sensitive information and secure communication amongst linked systems. Then this section discusses several case studies that give examples of the practical use of different cryptographic technologies in smart cities: blockchain based identity management system, homomorphic encryption in healthcare, secure communication between IoT devices via PKI, etc., and solutions that provide quantum resistance cryptographic.

Blockchain-Based Smart City Identity Management Systems

Estonia's digital identification system is the most important example of the application of blockchain technology in identity management in smart cities. By using blockchain, Estonia has innovated the use of it for safe digital IDs where residents can use a system to easily access government services while at the same time making identity theft less dangerous (Adeodato & Pournouri, 2020).

Estonia's Digital Identity Framework: Estonia's e-identity system allows Estonian residents to verify their identity and use different services online, including electronically voting, healthcare, banking, etc. and public records management. By recording the digital identity on a blockchain it is guaranteed that personal data cannot be changed and is freely accessible by authorized users alone. In addition to securing the information, this method is also decentralized allowing residents to own their personal information and a trust is developed among the residents (Bandara et al., 2021).

Identity Verification Process: In Estonia the identity verification is possible with a digital ID card with secure chip, which contains a public key of the user. This allows citizens to securely authenticate themselves with their digital ID during government services interactions over the internet. Every transaction is stored on the blockchain, and these are marked as transparent and unalterable audit trail. It is important for openness in order to keep accountability and trust in public services (Johri et al., 2022).

Minimizing Identity Theft: Blockchain technology has a significant impact in decreasing the chances for the occurrence of identity theft. Conventional identification systems are usually centralized and hence open to information breach and unnatural access. On the other hand, Estonia's methodology for its blockchain based method disperses the identification data over several nodes, which is very difficult to breach for the adversaries. As a result, the public trust in digital services in Estonia has significantly increased and identity-related fraud has been significantly reduced (Adeodato & Pournouri, 2020).

Impact on Public Service Delivery: Public service delivery in Estonia utilizes blockchain based identity management. Services can be used by citizens in a quick and convenient manner without the need to be physically presented with physical papers or going to government offices. As a matter of fact, the procedure has improved public satisfaction, notably cutting down governmental administrative costs (Sung & Park, 2021).

Homomorphic Encryption in Healthcare and Public Data Sharing

A new cryptographic technique known as homomorphic encryption permits calculations on an encrypted quantity, without the need to decrypt. The ability to perform such functionality is especially important in healthcare where such information needs to be protected but also enable data analysis and transfer. The use of homomorphic encryption has started in numerous healthcare organizations and smart city projects to mitigate privacy issues in public health surveillance and cooperative research.

Use Case in Healthcare Data Analysis: A practical application of homomorphic encryption is a variant of this where healthcare institutions in the United States partner to process patient data in order to evaluate the information for health research purposes. Without getting critical patient information revealed, researchers may analyze encrypted medical records using homomorphic encryption. This method ensures recognition of health trends and results while ensuring strict observance of all kinds of rules like the Health Insurance Portability and Accountability Act (HIPAA) in protecting patient confidentiality (Munjal & Bhatia, 2023).

Public Health Monitoring: Homomorphic encryption may be used in smart city initiatives aimed towards public health monitoring. For example, city authorities may take health data from a range of sources like hospitals, clinics and wearable devices to monitor the transmission of infectious illnesses or even monitor the effectiveness of public health efforts. With homomorphic encryption, public health professionals remain able to get insight from data while always maintaining privacy of individuals (Munjal & Bhatia, 2023).

Collaboration Among Healthcare Institutions: The fact that Homomorphic encryption allows healthcare organizations to help solve research problems while concurrently protecting patient data, is intriguing. As an example, hospitals may collect and aggregate data from multiple hospitals to study the effectiveness of a particular therapy in which each Quantum medical institution on the actual feedback sends its encrypted data to a centralized platform for analysis. That is, without decryption of the data the analysis may be carried out, thus protecting sensitive patient info (Wu et al., 2022).

Challenges and Limitations: Due to significant benefits of homomorphic encryption, its uses in health care and the smart city are limited by performance issues. Homomorphic encryption methods may be computationally expensive, one of which being slowing data processing speed. The current research is interested in improving the efficiency and feasibility of the homomorphic encryption algorithms for real world applications (Munjal & Bhatia, 2023).

Secure IoT Communication through PKI and TLS Protocols

The service of the smart cities has been enhanced due to the use of IoT devices, which has also brought the operational efficiency through IoT devices. These devices are crucial to the security of, and data that is being delivered with, the devices. PKI and Transport Layer Security (TLS) protocols have been used by Singapore's smart city projects to secure IoT connectivity; data could be sent with the assurance of confidentiality and integrity.

PKI for Device Authentication: PKI is used in Singapore's smart city projects to provide digital identities and authenticate IoT devices. Then a unique digital certificate is assigned to every device, which relates its identification to a public key. It's produced by a reputable CA and intended to authenticate the device prior to its network connection. PKI enables the use of Singapore to only give certain critical infrastructure and services to authorized devices (Garba et al., 2021).

TLS for Secure Data Transmission: Data pick up and transmission are all backed by TLS protocols in Singapore's smart city initiatives. Data in transit between the IoT devices and the cloud is protected from interception and alteration with TLS. The data obtained from smart meters or traffic sensors is sent securely to the central computers for processing and analysis. It encrypts worthy information like energy use and traffic patterns so only those who have access to it can know (Sun et al., 2021).

Enhancing IoT Security Posture: The PKI and TLS protocols help greatly integrate and improve the security framework of IoT systems in smart cities. A couple of these solutions are aimed at reducing the risks associated with unauthorized device access and data breaches by authentically connecting them, so to speak. Also, digital certificates as well as encryption algorithms will be continuously upgraded, making it harder for future threats to breach security safeguards (Diaz-Sanchez et al., 2019).

Real-World Impact: PKI and TLS enhanced the confidence that residents have in the security of an IoT device or service in Singapore's smart city effort. However, as the confidence of the inhabitants in data privacy grows, this leads to an increasing engagement with smart city technology by inhabitants, which results in a greater efficiency for the use of urban services realized through the smart city technology (Ismagilova et al., 2022).

Quantum-Resistant Cryptographic Solutions for Long-Term Security

Conventional cryptography approaches have some flaws with advancement of quantum computing technologies. Encrypted smart city infrastructures rely on RSA and ECC, which are now in danger of being compromised by very powerful computers, quantum computers. To that burgeoning danger, smart cities are a very engaged field, in which our services will ensure the enduring security of smart cities, as is done by entities such as the U.S. NIST, defining quantum resistant cryptographic algorithms.

NIST's Post-Quantum Cryptography Initiative: NIST has recently launched a standardization initiative of the Post-Quantum Cryptography (PQC) to offer cryptographic algorithms resistant to attacks by quantum computers. The goal of this program is to evaluate and choose quantum resistant algorithms for addition to current security frameworks. Smart cities will be furnished with the capabilities essential in combating quantum attacks on their data and communications by the algorithms chosen here (Aydeger et al., 2024).

Case Study in Smart Cities: Now several smart city efforts are inquiring into using quantum resistant algorithms. The advent of novel encryption methodology using lattice-based cryptography, hash-based signatures, multivariant polynomial equations has been attained by research done by academic institutes and technology firms. Withstood the attack from conventional as well as quantum computers and thus are appropriate for securing smart city applications, these algorithms (Fathalla & Azab, 2024).

Long-Term Security Planning: Smart cities must implement quantum resistant cryptography solutions in order to secure the infrastructures of the future time threats. Cities proactively put these algorithms to use to avoid the perils associated with breakthroughs in quantum computing as well as protect their critical data. For the shift to quantum resistant encryption it will necessarily involve a cooperation between governmental bodies, industry executives and academics defining standards and guidelines for implementation (Nanayakkara et al., 2024).

Challenges and Considerations: Although problems arise with the implementation of quantum resistant algorithms. Switching from ordinary to quantum resistant methods may require a massive number of investments in infrastructure, training and regulatory updates. Furthermore, such algorithms must be cleared for efficacy that they meet the operational demands of smart city applications (Aydeger et al., 2024). With the need to face future security threats in smart cities, it has been evident that endless efforts are being carried out to develop quantum resistant cryptographic solutions. These sophisticated algorithms can be implemented to strengthen the resistance of the urban areas against the rising threats, protecting the key infrastructure and citizen data.

DISCUSSION: CRITICAL INSIGHTS INTO CRYPTOGRAPHY AND CYBERSECURITY IN SMART CITIES

Modern cryptographic solutions become an opportunity to introduce them to solutions of smart city infrastructure. While this chapter has studied the technologies, the applications and the future directions separately, comprehensive coverage is necessary as to be able to summarize findings, critically analyze trade-offs and offer subtler perspectives in the field of policy, technology, and research

Comparative Analysis of Cryptographic Technologies

In Table 1 that comparing cryptographic solutions is not sufficient to identify the only best one, leaving much to be desired in smart city ecosystems. While the work is computationally efficient, it lacks convenient key distribution across large networks. RSA and ECC are asymmetric encryption whose key management deals but comes at extra computation overhead (Adeodato & Pournouri, 2020). Unlike blockchain technology, though, blockchain technology comes with immutability and transparency but lacks scalability and energy consumption limits that make it unavailable for live or real time applications like traffic (Bandara et al., 2021). Homomorphic encryption and ZKP offer revolutionary privacy-preserving capabilities. Yet, they have high computational complexity and do not have standardized implementations (Johri et al., 2022). However, the high costs of quantum cryptography infrastructure mean that it cannot be adopted as a key part of protecting against threats from the possibility of quantum computing in developing cities, yet quantum cryptography becomes a long-term necessity (Adeodato & Pournouri, 2020). Therefore, the most pragmatic way to move forward is to have a layered cryptographic architecture whereby the light encryption for IoT, blockchain for identity management and quantum resistant algorithms for the core infrastructures are combined.

Table 1. Comparative analysis of cryptographic technologies for smart cities

Cryptographic Technology	*Key Features*	*Strengths*	*Limitations*	*Smart City Applications*
Symmetric Encryption (AES)	Single key for encryption/decryption	Fast for large data sets	Key distribution is challenging	Securing sensor data in IoT networks
Asymmetric Encryption (RSA, ECC)	Public and private key pair	Secure key exchange, digital signatures	Slower encryption process	Authentication of devices and citizens
Blockchain	Decentralized, immutable ledger	Tamper resistance, transparent auditing	Scalability and energy consumption	Identity management, transaction validation
Public Key Infrastructure (PKI)	Trusted digital certificates	Strong authentication and encryption	Complex management at large scales	IoT device authentication, secure communication
Homomorphic Encryption	Computation on encrypted data	Preserves data privacy in processing	High computational cost	Healthcare data analytics, public administration
Zero-Knowledge Proofs (ZKP)	Verify information without revealing data	Strong privacy preservation	Implementation complexity	Secure voting, financial transactions
Quantum Cryptography (QKD)	Quantum key distribution	Resistant to quantum computing attacks	High infrastructure cost	Future-pro

Addressing Smart Cybersecurity Challenges

It is important to observe that the most immediate threats concerning cybersecurity are the IoT vulnerabilities and data privacy breaches (summarized in Table

2). They further reinforce that PKI and TLS protocols represent the first layers of defense, but they are to be integrated into a dynamic threat detection system using AI and ML (Rasool et al., 2022). However, there are still interoperability challenges on the systemic level. Different vendors managing different security machines do not have a common framework. Thus, there are many separate attack surfaces. Such globally recognized cryptographic protocols for smart city ecosystem are of imperative need, as pointed out in this analysis. In addition, smart cities expose us to cyber physical risks attacks on energy grids and autonomous transportation and cyber physical security cannot be a silo, it must be threaded through the best digital design principles with physical security considerations, as under a true cyber physical resilience framework.

Table 2. Summary of cybersecurity challenges and cryptographic solutions in smart cities

Cybersecurity Challenge	*Description*	*Recommended Cryptographic Solution*
Data Privacy and Confidentiality Issues	Risk of unauthorized access and data leakage	End-to-end Encryption, Homomorphic Encryption
Threats to IoT and Networked Devices	Vulnerable endpoints and weak security configs	PKI, TLS Protocols, Lightweight Encryption
Interoperability and Standardization Challenges	Diverse systems lacking unified security standards	Blockchain, PKI frameworks
Cyber-Physical Security Risks	Potential attacks on critical infrastructures	Quantum Cryptography, Blockchain for resilience

This section covers an extensive exploration to show that security in a smart city is now not just a technical matter but much more than a socio technical challenge, in particular, an economic and political issue. Secure infrastructures are built on cryptographic technologies but depend as much upon governance, cooperation of the public domain and the private sector, and the trust of citizens. Therefore, both technological invention and adaptive governance models, ethical foresight and global interoperability standards are necessary for successful, inclusive and 'smart' cities that are resilient.

FUTURE TRENDS AND RECOMMENDATIONS

The adoption of cryptographic technology in protecting digital infrastructures and saving people's sensitive information will play a great role in the development of smart cities. Even the growing reliance on networked systems, artificial intelligence, and the IoT have potential, but equally provide security issues. The ensuing factors should be tackled by forthcoming trends in cryptographic innovations to ensure continual sustainability of smart cities in terms of the evolving threats of cyber risks, regulatory and ethical compliances. In this section we discuss some important future trajectories such as progress in post quantum cryptograph, AI accelerating cyberspace defense, the legislation design, etc. and their ethical problems in cryptographic applications.

Advancements in Post-Quantum Cryptography

Traditionally, conventional encryption methods have been unable to withstand the threat that quantum computing is posing. It is the case that modern encryption theories like RSA (Rivest-Shamir-Adleman) and ECC (Elliptic Curve Cryptography) rely on mathematical problems which quantum computers may solve in polynomial time using algorithms such as Shor's. This advancement compromises the security of the smart city infrastructure which unfortunately depends on cryptographic methods for protection of communication networks, digital identities and financial transactions (Sahoo et al., 2024).

Transition to Post-Quantum Cryptography

In order to fight against the threats brought by quantum computing, the academia is developing PQC algorithms to resist quantum attacks. In support of its effort to standardize quantum resistant cryptographic algorithms, the NIST was looking at lattice based, hash based and multivariate polynomial cryptographic schemes (Fathalla & Azab, 2024).

1. **Lattice-Based Cryptography:** Quantum resistance systems based on lattices, like Kyber and Dilithium, result in very high security and a good amount of computational efficiency. Likewise, these methods are only as strong as other problems, such as the Learning with Errors (LWE) problem, for which both improvements and quantum progress tend to be in vain (Ravi et al., 2024).
2. **Hash-Based Cryptography:** Systems of digital signatures using the cryptographic hash function are hash-based signature systems like XMSS (Extended Merkle Signature Scheme) as well as SPHINCS+ (Strongly Consistent Hashing of N thieves Plus). As a post-quantum option, then, these systems are robust security assurances that depend on number theoretic assumptions, but that can be provided independently of number theoretic assumptions (Ananda Mohan, 2023).

3. **Multivariate Polynomial Cryptography:** Encryption mechanisms provided by multivariate cryptography techniques are obtained from the use of nonlinear polynomial equations in the finite fields. But these are computationally expensive methods that offer resilient security framework that fails with quantum attacks (Dey & Dutta, 2023).

Challenges and Adoption Considerations

The adoption of post-quantum cryptographic algorithms presents several challenges:

- **Performance Overhead:** Traditionally, quantum resistant algorithms often require more computation resources, which complicates them from deploying with resource limited IoT devices.
- **Migration Complexity:** Modification in software, hardware, and network protocols is required in smart city infrastructures based on classical cryptography to transform from classical to post -quantum cryptography.
- **Interoperability Issues:** Smooth integration therefore requires that current security systems are capable to work interoperable with post-quantum cryptography technologies.

Since quantum computing is progressing, communities will need to take the lead to embed the PQC guidelines into their cybersecurity when implemented.

Integration of AI and Machine Learning for Adaptive Cybersecurity

Proactive threat identification, while actively defending the systems becomes the new trend with exaggeration with technologies like AI and ML. AI driven cybersecurity solutions based on AI mechanisms to find the weakness of the cryptographic systems, detect the abnormal situation, and responding to attacks in real time could be strengthen the resilience of cryptographic systems in a smart city.

AI-Driven Threat Detection

Current security models work from a rule-based approach and are unable to manage the cyber space which is continuously evolving to struggle on cyber threat. AI driven systems are capable of efficiently scanning the large network data to identify and address the problems.

1. **Anomaly Detection with ML Algorithms:** Intrusion detection systems based on deep learning may identify atypical patterns in the network traffic, that may indicate future intrusions. Paying for this is, for example, intelligence in urban traffic management systems, which apply machine learn induced anomaly detection to keep off denial of service (DoS) assaults on the transportation infrastructure.
2. **Automated Incident Response:** Depending on your threat response requirements, the Security Information and Event Management (SIEM) system driven by AI might be able to handle the automation of threat response by isolating the infected devices and reducing the attack vectors before the attack is able to spread across the network.
3. **Behavioral Analytics for Fraud Prevention:** Behavioral analytics (BA) instruments based on AI-driven analysis of the user behavior patterns are used to find fraudulent methods of action, so as to enhance the security of payment systems of the smart town and the platforms of e-governance.

Challenges in AI-Driven Cybersecurity

Despite its advantages, AI-integrated cybersecurity solutions face several challenges:

- **Adversarial AI Attacks:** False data injection during the attack on the AI model results in an incorrect threat assessment.
- **Computational Demands:** Deploying AI based security solution in low power IoT devices is very challenging due to the fact that AI requires significant amount of processing power.
- **Data Privacy Concerns:** To not peacefully violate ethical and regulatory standards, AI driven monitoring systems must have the ability to balance security with privacy.

In order to comprehensively use AI in cybersecurity, it should be linked with sophisticated cryptographic methods to strengthen smart city security schemes.

Policy and Regulatory Frameworks for Cryptographic Adoption

For cryptography technology to be deployed securely in smart cities, governments and regulatory agencies play a crucial role. For maintaining cybersecurity in sustainable form and protecting people's digital rights, it is critical to establish robust policy framework and to formulate compliance requirement.

Regulatory Standards and Compliance

Several global security standards guide the adoption of cryptographic measures:

- **General Data Protection Regulation (GDPR):** Stringent encryption rules to protect personal data of the citizens in smart city apps are imposed.
- **NIST Cybersecurity Framework:** It recommends how cryptographic measures may be used to protect essential infrastructures.
- **ISO/IEC 27001:** It establishes some optimal methods of information security management using encryption techniques.

Legislation for Secure Data Governance

Governments must implement data governance regulations to oversee the use of cryptography technology in smart cities. Essential factors to consider are:

- **Mandating Encryption for Sensitive Data:** All personal and financial data processing carried out by smart city services must make use of very good encryption techniques.
- **Secure Key Management Policies:** Define rules for storing and keeping cryptographic keys that would prevent unauthorized access.
- **Cross-Border Data Transfer Regulations:** According to international security legislation, regulations need to be established for the exchange of data between many countries.

Ethical Considerations in Cryptographic Implementations

Using cryptography solutions in smart cities requires adherence since they must be sensitive to ethical considerations to safeguard residents' rights and avoid misuse. The integrity of security solutions must not be contradicted by any means to privacy and real freedoms as well as transparency, which is the main instance that ethical problems must be taken into consideration.

Balancing Security and Privacy

Even though encryption protects data from cyber-attacks, and cryptographers take precautions not to let this data leak to third parties, it can be used for illegitimate purposes like spying. It is a guarantee that governments and technology providers will ensure private rights are upheld in encryption and remain within the bounds of the law.

1. **Avoiding Mass Surveillance:** Cryptographic techniques may not be used for unjustified monitoring of people. The transparent encryption rules must ensure visibility of types of data, criteria, and conditions under which they can be accessed and only allow the access to the data by the authorized individuals with accountability.
2. **Transparency in Encryption Algorithms:** The confidence is fostered by open-source cryptography algorithms through independent validation of the security protocol. Yet, where proprietary encryption solutions are available, it may be the case that they contain invisible flaws that compromise security.
3. **Ethical AI in Cryptographic Decision-Making:** In the event of biased decision making or discriminatory access to trusted services, AI driven encrypted management systems need to take into consideration ethical criteria.

Post quantum encryption needs to become the future of cryptography in smart cities, also AI cyber security should solve that, as well as Robust Legislative Framework and Ethical Governance. With increasing sophistication of cyber threats, smart cities need to adopt adaptive cryptography as part of the solutions and keep the international security requirements as that while respecting resident's rights in the digital world. Resilience requires socially accountable, narrowly targeted technology development where the decision on the level of technology within a city is based on systems and application rather than linking individual components of technology.

CONCLUSION: STRENGTHENING SMART CITIES WITH CRYPTOGRAPHIC SECURITY

Smart cities development is both fast and raises a bunch of cybersecurity problems including data privacy, IoT vulnerabilities, interoperability, and cyber physical security threats. Digital infrastructure is highly dependent upon networks through which urban settings are situated, and these strategies for secure communications, protecting sensitive data, and coping with cyber risks are powerful cryptographic ones. The methods to achieve encryption, such as encryption techniques, blockchain security, PKI, homomorphic encryption, zero knowledge proof, and quantum cryptography are many and are discussed in this chapter. These technologies create the basis for improved security in smart city applications, namely in identity management, secure IoT connection and if necessary, in privacy preserving data analytics. Practical implementations of cryptographic technologies are demonstrated through case studies such as Estonia's blockchain based identity management system, Homomorphic encryption for healthcare data exchange, and Singapore's deployment of PKI to secure IoT devices. The relevance of cryptographic techniques to shield smart city systems from cyberattacks are implicitly demonstrated by these occurrences. It also discusses the coming of age of quantum resistant cryptographic solutions that will be necessary for dealing with the security issues that arise with future developments in the quantum computing landscape.

There are significant prospects of using AI and machine learning to the cybersecurity methods for real time threat detection, automated incident response and fraud prevention. Due to computing efficiency, migration complexity and interoperability problems, going to post quantum cryptography system is not an easy task and calls for diligence on part of the governments, regulatory agencies and technology vendors to work collaboratively. To ensure compliance with such global security standards as GDPR, NIST and ISO 27001, a set of policy and regulatory frameworks should have to be developed to enforce cryptographic best practices. The issue of cryptography is critical for handling ethical issues in smart cities, because to balance security and privacy, openness is important. In the judicious use of cryptographic technology, there needs to be a way to prevent mass monitoring, use open-source security solutions and to guarantee that AI driven encryption uses ethical decision-making principles. Addressing these fundamental questions smart cities can secure and resilient digital environment, promote innovation and protect the citizen rights. Given the importance, the future of cryptographic security within smart cities will hinge on proactive developments of encryption, standardization of regulatory and ethical governance. The response to the creation of smart cities that are intelligent and secure is going to be a multidisciplinary effort in bringing a technology innovation perspective up with regulatory enforcement and ethical oversight.

REFERENCES

Abdelkader, S., Amissah, J., Kinga, S., Mugerwa, G., Emmanuel, E., Mansour, D.-E. A., Bajaj, M., Blazek, V., & Prokop, L. (2024). Securing modern power systems: Implementing comprehensive strategies to enhance resilience and reliability against cyber-attacks. *Results in Engineering*, *23*, 102647. DOI: 10.1016/j.rineng.2024.102647

Adeodato, R., & Pournouri, S. (2020). *Secure Implementation of E-Governance: A Case Study About Estonia*., DOI: 10.1007/978-3-030-35746-7_18

Aggarwal, T., Kumar, S., Singh, S. K., Gupta, B. B., Nedjah, N., & Castiglione, A. (2024). *Zero Knowledge Proofs and Their Applications in Cryptography*., DOI: 10.4018/979-8-3693-5330-1.ch003

Ahmad, K., Maabreh, M., Ghaly, M., Khan, K., Qadir, J., & Al-Fuqaha, A. (2022). Developing future human-centered smart cities: Critical analysis of smart city security, Data management, and Ethical challenges. *Computer Science Review*, *43*, 100452. DOI: 10.1016/j.cosrev.2021.100452

Ahmad, S., & Mir, A. H. (2021). Scalability, Consistency, Reliability and Security in SDN Controllers: A Survey of Diverse SDN Controllers. *Journal of Network and Systems Management*, *29*(1), 9. DOI: 10.1007/s10922-020-09575-4

Alenezi, M. N., Alabdulrazzaq, H., Alhatlani, H. M., & Alobaid, F. A. (2024). On the performance of AES algorithm variants. *International Journal of Information and Computer Security*, *23*(3), 322–337. DOI: 10.1504/IJICS.2024.138494

Ananda Mohan, P. V. (2023). Hash-based Digital Signatures- A tutorial review. *2023 IEEE International Conference on Public Key Infrastructure and Its Applications (PKIA)*, 1–8. DOI: 10.1109/PKIA58446.2023.10262777

Aydeger, A., Zeydan, E., Yadav, A. K., Hemachandra, K. T., & Liyanage, M. (2024). Towards a Quantum-Resilient Future: Strategies for Transitioning to Post-Quantum Cryptography. *2024 15th International Conference on Network of the Future (NoF)*, 195–203. DOI: 10.1109/NoF62948.2024.10741441

Bandara, E., Liang, X., Foytik, P., Shetty, S., Hall, C., Bowden, D., Ranasinghe, N., & De Zoysa, K. (2021). A blockchain empowered and privacy preserving digital contact tracing platform. *Information Processing & Management*, *58*(4), 102572. DOI: 10.1016/j.ipm.2021.102572

Banoth, R., & Regar, R. (2023). Asymmetric Key Cryptography. In *Classical and Modern Cryptography for Beginners* (pp. 109–165). Springer Nature Switzerland., DOI: 10.1007/978-3-031-32959-3_4

Biswas, S., Goswami, R. S., & Reddy, K. H. K. (2024). Advancing quantum steganography: A secure IoT communication with reversible decoding and customized encryption technique for smart cities. *Cluster Computing*, *27*(7), 9395–9414. DOI: 10.1007/s10586-024-04429-z

Demertzi, V., Demertzis, S., & Demertzis, K. (2023). An Overview of Cyber Threats, Attacks and Countermeasures on the Primary Domains of Smart Cities. *Applied Sciences (Basel, Switzerland)*, *13*(2), 790. DOI: 10.3390/app13020790

Dey, J., & Dutta, R. (2023). Progress in Multivariate Cryptography: Systematic Review, Challenges, and Research Directions. *ACM Computing Surveys*, *55*(12), 1–34. DOI: 10.1145/3571071

Diaz-Sanchez, D., Marin-Lopez, A., Mendoza, F. A., Cabarcos, P. A., & Sherratt, R. S. (2019). TLS/PKI Challenges and Certificate Pinning Techniques for IoT and M2M Secure Communications. *IEEE Communications Surveys and Tutorials*, *21*(4), 3502–3531. DOI: 10.1109/COMST.2019.2914453

Djenna, A., Harous, S., & Saidouni, D. E. (2021). Internet of Things Meet Internet of Threats: New Concern Cyber Security Issues of Critical Cyber Infrastructure. *Applied Sciences (Basel, Switzerland)*, *11*(10), 4580. DOI: 10.3390/app11104580

Elassy, M., Al-Hattab, M., Takruri, M., & Badawi, S. (2024). Intelligent transportation systems for sustainable smart cities. *Transportation Engineering*, *16*, 100252. DOI: 10.1016/j.treng.2024.100252

Fathalla, E., & Azab, M. (2024). Beyond Classical Cryptography: A Systematic Review of Post-Quantum Hash-Based Signature Schemes, Security, and Optimizations. *IEEE Access : Practical Innovations, Open Solutions*, *12*, 175969–175987. DOI: 10.1109/ACCESS.2024.3485602

Garba, A., Chen, Z., Guan, Z., & Srivastava, G. (2021). LightLedger: A Novel Blockchain-Based Domain Certificate Authentication and Validation Scheme. *IEEE Transactions on Network Science and Engineering*, *8*(2), 1698–1710. DOI: 10.1109/TNSE.2021.3069128

Halak, B., Yilmaz, Y., & Shiu, D. (2022). Comparative Analysis of Energy Costs of Asymmetric vs Symmetric Encryption-Based Security Applications. *IEEE Access : Practical Innovations, Open Solutions*, *10*, 76707–76719. DOI: 10.1109/ACCESS.2022.3192970

Hazra, R., Chatterjee, P., Singh, Y., Podder, G., & Das, T. (2024). *Data Encryption and Secure Communication Protocols.*, DOI: 10.4018/979-8-3693-6557-1.ch022

Hemminghaus, C., Bauer, J., & Wolsing, K. (2021). SIGMAR: Ensuring Integrity and Authenticity of Maritime Systems using Digital Signatures. *2021 International Symposium on Networks, Computers and Communications (ISNCC)*, 1–6. DOI: 10.1109/ISNCC52172.2021.9615738

Höglund, J., Lindemer, S., Furuhed, M., & Raza, S. (2020). PKI4IoT: Towards public key infrastructure for the Internet of Things. *Computers & Security*, *89*, 101658. DOI: 10.1016/j.cose.2019.101658

Ismagilova, E., Hughes, L., Rana, N. P., & Dwivedi, Y. K. (2022). Security, Privacy and Risks Within Smart Cities: Literature Review and Development of a Smart City Interaction Framework. *Information Systems Frontiers*, *24*(2), 393–414. DOI: 10.1007/s10796-020-10044-1

Johri, S., Mehta, K. J. S., Shukla, P. K., Podile, V., & Singh, D. P. (2022). The Impact of Block Chain in Accounting and Auditing Domain - A Critical Approach for Enhanced Efficiency and Transparency. *2022 2nd International Conference on Advance Computing and Innovative Technologies in Engineering (ICACITE)*, 1628–1632. DOI: 10.1109/ICACITE53722.2022.9823420

Khan, T., Rahman, S. M., & Hasan, M. M. (2020). Barriers to Growth of Renewable Energy Technology in Bangladesh. *Proceedings of the International Conference on Computing Advancements*, 1–6. DOI: 10.1145/3377049.3377086

Majeed, U., Khan, L. U., Yaqoob, I., Kazmi, S. M. A., Salah, K., & Hong, C. S. (2021). Blockchain for IoT-based smart cities: Recent advances, requirements, and future challenges. *Journal of Network and Computer Applications*, *181*, 103007. DOI: 10.1016/j.jnca.2021.103007

Munjal, K., & Bhatia, R. (2023). A systematic review of homomorphic encryption and its contributions in healthcare industry. *Complex & Intelligent Systems*, *9*(4), 3759–3786. DOI: 10.1007/s40747-022-00756-z

Murdoch, B. (2021). Privacy and artificial intelligence: Challenges for protecting health information in a new era. *BMC Medical Ethics*, *22*(1), 122. DOI: 10.1186/s12910-021-00687-3

Nanayakkara, N. D. G. T., Nanayakkara, G. A. S. Y., Karunanayaka, K. M. C. M., Kumara, C. P. T. K., & Karunanayake, N. (2024). Smart Cities, Secure Data: Navigating the Evolving Landscape of Data Protection Challenges. In *Data Protection* (pp. 251–285). Springer Nature Switzerland. DOI: 10.1007/978-3-031-76473-8_11

Osman, A. M. S. (2019). A novel big data analytics framework for smart cities. *Future Generation Computer Systems, 91*, 620–633. DOI: 10.1016/j.future.2018.06.046

Prateek, K., Maity, S., & Amin, R. (2023). An Unconditionally Secured Privacy-Preserving Authentication Scheme for Smart Metering Infrastructure in Smart Grid. *IEEE Transactions on Network Science and Engineering, 10*(2), 1085–1095. DOI: 10.1109/TNSE.2022.3226902

Rasool, R. U., Ahmad, H. F., Rafique, W., Qayyum, A., & Qadir, J. (2022). Security and privacy of internet of medical things: A contemporary review in the age of surveillance, botnets, and adversarial ML. *Journal of Network and Computer Applications, 201*, 103332. DOI: 10.1016/j.jnca.2022.103332

Ravi, P., Chattopadhyay, A., D'Anvers, J. P., & Baksi, A. (2024). Side-channel and Fault-injection attacks over Lattice-based Post-quantum Schemes (Kyber, Dilithium): Survey and New Results. *ACM Transactions on Embedded Computing Systems, 23*(2), 1–54. DOI: 10.1145/3603170

Sahoo, A. K, I. K. A., & Rajagopal, S. M. (2024). Comparative Study of Cryptographic Algorithms in Post Quantum Computing Landscape. *2024 5th International Conference on Data Intelligence and Cognitive Informatics (ICDICI)*, 36–40. DOI: 10.1109/ICDICI62993.2024.10810828

Sarker, I. H. (2022). Smart City Data Science: Towards data-driven smart cities with open research issues. *Internet of Things : Engineering Cyber Physical Human Systems, 19*, 100528. DOI: 10.1016/j.iot.2022.100528

Shafik, W. (2025). *Generative Adversarial Networks: Security*. Privacy, and Ethical Considerations., DOI: 10.1007/978-3-031-76710-4_5

Sharma, H., Kumar, P., & Sharma, K. (2025). Advanced Security for IoT and Smart Devices. In *Emerging Threats and Countermeasures in Cybersecurity* (pp. 191–216). Wiley., DOI: 10.1002/9781394230600.ch10

Sharma, P., Agrawal, A., Bhatia, V., Prakash, S., & Mishra, A. K. (2021). Quantum Key Distribution Secured Optical Networks: A Survey. *IEEE Open Journal of the Communications Society, 2*, 2049–2083. DOI: 10.1109/OJCOMS.2021.3106659

Suleski, T., Ahmed, M., Yang, W., & Wang, E. (2023). A review of multi-factor authentication in the Internet of Healthcare Things. *Digital Health, 9*, 20552076231177144. Advance online publication. DOI: 10.1177/20552076231177144

Sun, C.-C., Sebastian Cardenas, D. J., Hahn, A., & Liu, C.-C. (2021). Intrusion Detection for Cybersecurity of Smart Meters. *IEEE Transactions on Smart Grid, 12*(1), 612–622. DOI: 10.1109/TSG.2020.3010230

Sung, C. S., & Park, J. Y. (2021). Understanding of blockchain-based identity management system adoption in the public sector. *Journal of Enterprise Information Management, 34*(5), 1481–1505. DOI: 10.1108/JEIM-12-2020-0532

Tyagi, A. K., & Seranmadevi, R. (2024). Blockchain for Enhancing Security and Privacy in the Smart Healthcare. In *Digital Twin and Blockchain for Smart Cities* (pp. 343–370). Wiley., DOI: 10.1002/9781394303564.ch16

Ugbedeojo, M., Adebiyi, M. O., Aroba, O. J., & Adebiyi, A. A. (2024). RSA and Elliptic Curve Encryption System. *International Journal of Information Security and Privacy, 18*(1), 1–27. DOI: 10.4018/IJISP.340728

Wu, Z., Xuan, S., Xie, J., Lin, C., & Lu, C. (2022). How to ensure the confidentiality of electronic medical records on the cloud: A technical perspective. *Computers in Biology and Medicine, 147*, 105726. DOI: 10.1016/j.compbiomed.2022.105726

Xenofontos, C., Zografopoulos, I., Konstantinou, C., Jolfaei, A., Khan, M. K., & Choo, K.-K. R. (2022). Consumer, Commercial, and Industrial IoT (In)Security: Attack Taxonomy and Case Studies. *IEEE Internet of Things Journal, 9*(1), 199–221. DOI: 10.1109/JIOT.2021.3079916

Zafir, E. I., Akter, A., Islam, M. N., Hasib, S. A., Islam, T., Sarker, S. K., & Muyeen, S. M. (2024). Enhancing security of Internet of Robotic Things: A review of recent trends, practices, and recommendations with encryption and blockchain techniques. *Internet of Things : Engineering Cyber Physical Human Systems, 28*, 101357. DOI: 10.1016/j.iot.2024.101357

Zhou, L., Diro, A., Saini, A., Kaisar, S., & Hiep, P. C. (2024). Leveraging zero knowledge proofs for blockchain-based identity sharing: A survey of advancements, challenges and opportunities. *Journal of Information Security and Applications, 80*, 103678. DOI: 10.1016/j.jisa.2023.103678

KEY TERMS AND DEFINITIONS

Smart Cities: – Urban settings that leverage complicated technologies such as IoT, AI, and big data to elevate infrastructure, management, greenery, and citizen other services to benefit general efficiency and protection.

Cybersecurity: Maintaining confidentiality, integrity and availability of digital systems, networks and data from cyber threat, such as hacking, data breaches and unauthorized access.

Encryption: A process to encrypt the data in a format which is unintelligible to the one who is not authorized to access the sensitive information, using symmetric (e.g. AES) or asymmetric (e.g. RSA or ECC) techniques.

Blockchain: Decentralized and tamper-proof digital ledger system which provides better security with safe transaction, identity management, and data integrity without the dependency of the central authority.

Homomorphic Encryption: A sophisticated cryptographic technique that can calculate cryptographically on encrypted data, but without decrypting, to preserve privacy in e.g. secure data analytics and healthcare information processing.

Zero-Knowledge Proofs (ZKP): A cryptographic mechanism which augments privacy in authentication and safe transactions, that is, one party can prove that he knows certain information without revealing the actual data.

Quantum Cryptography: It presents a security framework based on principles of quantum physics (such as quantum key distribution, or QKD) that can provide encryption techniques which do not provide as an attack from quantum computers.

Public Key Infrastructure (PKI): A framework which manages the use of digital keys and certificates allowing safe authentication, communication and identity verifications, and helps mitigate the cyber impersonation and fraud within the smart city ecosystems.

Chapter 3
Cybersecurity Challenges in Smart City Development

Binastya Anggara Sekti
https://orcid.org/0000-0001-5489-4888
Universitas Esa Unggul, Indonesia

ABSTRACT

The rapid development of smart cities introduces significant cybersecurity challenges due to the increasing interconnectivity of urban infrastructure, IoT devices, and data-driven systems. This chapter explores the vulnerabilities and security threats that arise in smart city environments, including cyberattacks on critical infrastructure, data privacy risks, and the exploitation of weak encryption protocols. It also examines the role of cryptographic technologies in mitigating these challenges, highlighting encryption methods, blockchain applications, and AI-driven security mechanisms. Additionally, the chapter discusses regulatory frameworks and best practices for enhancing cybersecurity resilience in smart cities. By addressing these concerns, this chapter provides a comprehensive overview of the security landscape in smart city development and proposes strategies to safeguard urban digital ecosystems.

INTRODUCTION

The Evolution of Smart Cities

In recent decades, the world has witnessed a very rapid rate of urbanization. Major cities in various parts of the world, from New York, Tokyo, to Jakarta and Mumbai, are experiencing tremendous population growth (Almihat & Munda, 2025;

DOI: 10.4018/979-8-3373-3326-7.ch003

Sanada & Zappa, 2025). This flow of urbanization is driven by various factors, such as economic opportunities, access to education, and better health facilities in urban areas. However, this urbanization growth brings new challenges that must be anticipated immediately. Rural and urban development in Indonesia has become a prioritized national development agenda (Susilowati et al., 2025).

As the city's population grows, the needs of urban people increase drastically. Demand for energy, clean water, transportation infrastructure, housing, and other public services has seen a significant surge. Unfortunately, the growth of this need has not always been matched by increased capacity and quality of services, leading to various social and economic pressures in urban environments. Based on these conditions, the need for a more comfortable and reliable living space is also increasingly needed in urban cities. The paradigm of a smart city is expected to provide smarter solutions to the needs and problems of residents and ensure sustainable living (Cengiz et al., 2025). Due to the imbalance between population growth and the availability of resources, various crises began to emerge. The energy crisis, food crisis, lack of housing, traffic congestion, and increased carbon emissions are real challenges faced by big cities. In addition, environmental problems such as air pollution, land degradation, and urban waste also exacerbate existing conditions, threatening people's quality of life and the sustainability of urban ecosystems. Increasing global energy demand and increasing impacts of the climate crisis have led to an increase in CO_2 emissions. For example, Turkey has committed to achieving net-zero carbon emissions by 2053 in line with the Paris Agreement, emphasizing the important role of energy transition strategies (Ertane et al., 2025).

The complexity of the problems caused by urban areas encourages the creation of a new approach that not only focuses on economic growth, but also requires attention to the social problems caused, and the aspects of environmental damage that need to be maintained so that the sustainability of the city can meet the needs of the community without sacrificing the younger generation to prepare for the presence of the next or future generation. Based on the results of previous studies, recognizing urban technology is carried out static. The current technological developments and the dynamic nature of smart cities are not good enough to use static classification (Cao et al., 2025). Some of the complexities and challenges of smart cities encourage the development of IoT technology that can support the creation of further developments in IoT technology itself. IoT can create traffic management, energy management, and digital health services, etc. If all digital devices are on the city network, it can create a sound system in a smart city that is desperately needed by the community. IoT can support the creation of traffic management in smart cities, which can help provide real-time information on the availability of vehicle parking slots inside or outside buildings for visitors (Alkhudhayr, 2025).

The development of advanced technology that is increasingly sophisticated today, encourages the concept of a smart city as a strategic solution in solving various city problems. The massive use of IoT in smart cities has resulted in efficiency in all aspects, improved the quality of public services, reduced pollution and other environmental impacts, and strengthened community resilience to various crises. Smart cities are the hope to be able to build resilient and sustainable cities in the future. The development of the smart city concept is in line with the implementation of the smart city concept by every leader in the world in making maximum use of various digital technologies that are constantly developing such as AI, IoT, Big Data, and BlockChain. Based on data from the United Nations in 2022, more than 56% of the world's population lives in cities. This number will continue to increase to more than 68% in 2050. This increase in the population will cause the need for smart infrastructure to increase in terms of handling urbanization, energy shortages, and environmental problems (UN, 2022). The rapid development of urbanization has been a major factor in the transformation of cities in the world. In the last decade, the rate of urbanization has increased significantly. The United Nations estimates that by 2050, more than six billion people, or about 70% of the global population, will live in urban areas (UN, 2025). With the increasing population density in large cities, innovative approaches are needed to ensure that cities can continue to function as ecosystems that support economic, social, and environmental well-being. Therefore, smart city development is a strategic solution in facing future challenges and realizing a safer, more efficient, and sustainable urban ecosystem.

Based on the above picture, smart cities can represent the future of urban development, blending technology with essential infrastructure to improve efficiency and quality of life. However, this massive interconnectivity can expose cities to increased cybersecurity risks. This chapter presents an overview of cybersecurity challenges specific to smart city environments and proposes strategies to mitigate risk through modern cryptography technologies.

Chapter Objectives

The objectives of this chapter discussion are:

- Identify and categorize critical cybersecurity threats in smart cities.
- Evaluate the effectiveness of cryptographic solutions in mitigating these threats.
- Propose a conceptual cybersecurity framework tailored for smart city deployment.

KES TECHNOLOGIES IN SMART CITIES

A smart city certainly uses the support of advanced technology to improve the quality of public services, time efficiency, reduce energy waste by sharing resources, and always try to prevent environmental damage such as air pollution and others. The following are the key technologies for the development of a smart city.

IoT (Internet of Things)

The Internet of Things is the idea that different intelligent devices can join with one another and talk to each other through a network of the Internet. All attached equipment can gather, send, and get information right away, making a very active digital environment. In the setting of wise cities, IoT acts as a spine that aids many city areas beginning from travel and energy going to surroundings control. With this ability, IOT turns into a key base in enhancing how well public services work making the best use of resources, and bettering the quality of life for city dwellers (Alkhudhayr, 2025; Cengiz et al., 2025).

One of the most important applications of IoT in smart cities is traffic management. IoT sensors in traffic lights, highways, and traffic signals directly measure traffic density. This data is then processed using artificial intelligence (AI) to automatically adjust traffic light cycles, thereby reducing congestion and travel times. The implementation of this system not only improves traffic efficiency, but also reduces exhaust emissions, thus supporting the city's goal of creating a cleaner and healthier environment. Traffic monitoring systems can integrate real-time image processing and IoT-based data transmission for mobility assessment (Bakirci, 2025). In the energy distribution sector, IoT plays an important role through the development of smart grids. These smart grids are able to monitor energy consumption in real time and automatically adjust to improve efficiency. For example, the use of smart meters can help residents better manage their electricity consumption, detect energy waste early, and promote more sustainable energy consumption. Smart grids can also integrate renewable energy sources such as solar and wind power into urban energy distribution systems. Incorporating sustainable cybersecurity measures in smart cities, sustainable digital protection strategies, the use of blockchain for cybersecurity in smart networks, and cybersecurity solutions that minimize resource consumption are all important factors. (Achuthan et al., 2025).

Waste management has also become more efficient thanks to IoT technology. Sensors on public waste bins monitor their capacity in real time and transmit data to the city management center. This information is used to plan more efficient waste collection routes, thereby reducing fuel consumption and operating time of waste transport vehicles. In addition, historical data from these systems can be used to plan the placement of new waste bins in areas where they are needed, as well as to support recycling programs and sustainable waste management. Waste management is one of the core tasks of smart cities. The Internet of Things (IoT) is a promising technology that offers a potential solution for the transformation of traditional systems. An example of modern technology is an IoT-based smart waste bin that provides real-time information on the charging status to the cleaning department (Kim et al., 2025). Overall, IoT provides rich and in-depth data that is very useful for city managers to improve services and operational efficiency (Ma & Peng, 2024). Through the application of IoT, cities can become more responsive to the needs of their citizens, anticipate problems before they become crises, and carry out various city functions smarter and more resource-efficiently. The role of IoT technology in the development of smart cities is inevitable and even more needed as the needs for smart cities increase in the future.

AI and Machine Learning

Artificial Intelligence and Machine Learning are the two key supporting data-driven decision-making factors for smart cities. The two combined have the ability to analyze huge volumes of data and find patterns previously not visible- enabling cities to operate more effectively, efficiently, and responsively to the needs of citizens. AI and ML will not only assist in enhancing public service performance but also in generating accurate predictions for resource management, traffic management, and security enhancement. Integration of AI and ML can do well in regulating the transportation modes about carbon emission by different road transport modes (Matura et al., 2025; Tameemi et al., 2025).

In the planning of movement and flow of vehicles, AI helps forecast where there will be slowdowns and find the best paths for public transport. Using information from many places like road detectors, security cameras, and citizen alerts, AI figures which spots often get crowded and suggests different ways right away. An up-to-date example of this use is the current traffic calculation tool offered by Google Maps; it uses AI info to give better guesses for how long a trip will take and to suggest the quickest way. When certain rules exist, Google Maps can also arrange for the system to send vehicles on different paths that are safer so that it can lessen both crowding on roads as well as crashes (Vignesh et al., 2025). In the contribution to public safety, AI and ML help consolidate municipal surveillance systems. For instance, an AI-based facial recognition system which marks unusual individuals in public places and also identifies their unusual behavior which may be linked to imminent security threats will improve the feeling of safety among the public since situations can be managed well before they happen (Kuvonchbek et al., 2024). Another advantage is that AI-based video analytics will give a security officer better capability to monitor crowd situations like a protest or even when there is fire outburst, providing an opportunity to respond quickly. Video classification models detect garbage disposal by both vehicles and people; those who are responsible can be identified through facial as well as vehicle plate recognition (Alharbi et al., 2025).

Energy optimization is also one of the key areas where AI contributes to the development of smart cities. Using predictive algorithms, AI can analyze energy consumption patterns in smart buildings and automatically adjust the use of electricity, lighting, and cooling systems according to actual needs. For example, a building that adopts AI to control lighting and room temperature can significantly reduce energy consumption by using only electricity when needed and in optimal amounts. This approach can save on electricity consumption costs. AI can also perform real-time adjustments to specific colored lighting conditions (e.g., orange for motivation and purple for cognitive engagement), proven to improve students' attention, impulse control, creativity, and skills (Quiles-Rodriguez et al., 2025). Overall, the integration of AI and ML in various smart city infrastructures provides tremendous added value. Cities can become more adaptive, proactive in overcoming challenges, and more oriented towards improving the quality of life of their residents. With the continued development of this technology, in the future, the role of AI and ML in creating more sustainable and intelligent cities is expected to become increasingly real and dominant.

By utilizing AI and machine learning, smart cities can improve responsiveness to various urban challenges (Ahmed et al., 2022; Dwivedi et al., 2021; Fei et al., 2022; Hwang et al., 2020; Russell & Norvig, 2020). The Internet of Things (IoT) and Machine Learning (ML) are key enablers for data-driven smart environments. For example, a smart city uses technology and information to not only enhance citizens' quality of life but also to improve the efficiency of urban services. In this sense, IoT and ML have come to constitute the backbone smart city solutions as they enable them to realize big data acquisition, analytics, and wise decision-making (Ullah et al., 2024). The implementation of AI and ML within the infrastructure of smart cities offers great added value. Smart cities may become more adaptive, more proactive in dealing with challenges, and more focused on enhancing the quality of life for citizens. With further development in this field, eventually, the role of AI and ML in creating cities that are smarter and more sustainable will be much more leading.

Blockchain

Blockchain is a disruptive technology that provides transaction recording facilities securely and transparently without the need for a central authority. In a smart city environment, blockchain has joined other technologies such as the Internet of Things (IoT) and cloud computing to open up new horizons in security, operational scalability, and operational efficiency. Blockchain is a decentralized ledger system without interruption, many of the traditional weak points in data management in urban infrastructure can be overcome with blockchain (Bourbon & Murimi, 2024; Sefati et al., 2024).

One of the main applications of blockchain in smart cities is through healthcare systems. All kinds of real-time health information such as pulse, sugar levels, and other vital parameters can be captured by wearable IoT devices. This data is processed first at the cloud computing layer for faster response; and then sent securely to the cloud. Blockchain ensures the permanence and transparency of patients' health records; this means that once the data is entered, it cannot be changed without the consensus of the network participants which means an additional layer of trust for sensitive medical data. In addition, smart contracts can improve these systems by automating data access permissions so that only authorized people have access to or can change patient information (Kaniadakis & Foster, 2024; Kumaran et al., 2025; Li et al., 2025; Rahouti et al., 2025; Ren et al., 2025; Shang & Deng, 2025; Tan et al., 2024). In addition to healthcare, blockchain manages digital identities in smart cities. With blockchain-powered identity systems, citizens can securely manage their identities and leverage them to access various public services. This significantly lowers the risks associated with identity theft and fraud. The e-Residency program is a prime example of how blockchain can transform the management of citizens' identities by providing secure access to a wide range of government and private services.

Blockchain will also be able to help automate business transactions and government services. In smart cities, for example, this can be applied to scenarios where you pay taxes or utility bills (electricity, water, etc.) are automated. Even property ownership can be transferred securely in the same arrangement. Real estate transactions can be expedited even further with better security using self-executable contracts that will automatically transfer ownership once payment terms are met—no intermediaries accepted and far less bureaucracy. Blockchain can guarantee increased transparency and trust in municipal governance. This can happen when cities adopt blockchain-based e-voting systems that guarantee a hassle-free election process thus building more public trust in democratic procedures. It is a decentralized and transparent technology that is well-suited for monitoring how public funds are allocated, procurement is conducted, and all other government operations. The fact that modern cities face many challenges in Blockchain itself has technology that might be able to solve them. Reducing bureaucracy, improving security levels, automating services, and increasing transparency will increase public trust as it will increase operational efficiency which makes it a cornerstone technology for sustainable urban development.

Cloud Computing

Cloud is simply put as the internet, and computing means process. The model for technolog y that enables the delivery of computing services over the internet, without the user needing to own or manage physical infrastructure directly, is known as cloud computing. This, therefore, implies that cloud computing could be described as an internet-based model for computing since, most times, people represent the internet as a cloud within any network diagram. That supports connectivity between various devices and computers allows resource sharing to become very efficient and flexible. Some services acros s these clouds involve a wide range key functions such as data storage data processing and intelligence-based computing capabilities. The categories of these three main in services are shown in Figure 1 (Bharany et al., 2022; Sanaj & Joe Prathap, 2020).

Figure 1. Cloud computing

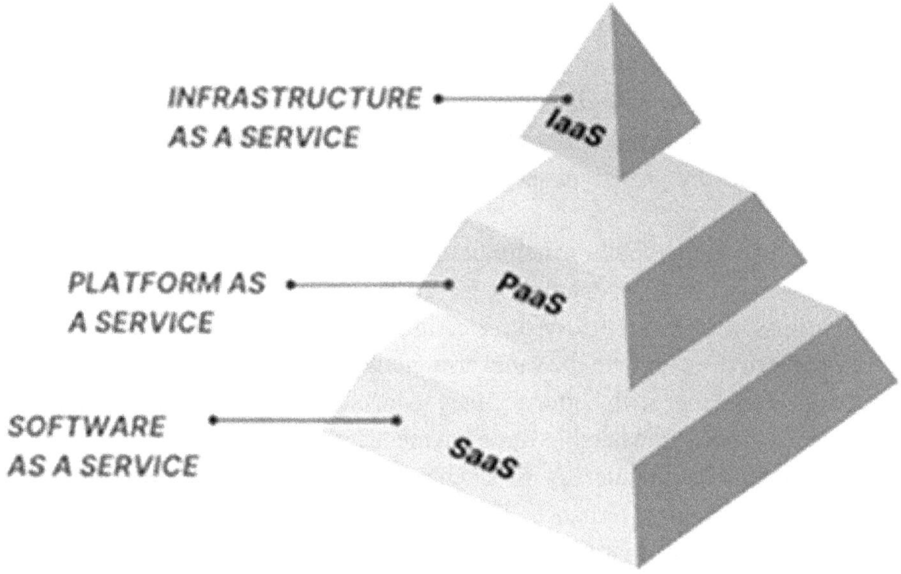

Cloud computing supports smart city data infrastructure with convenient and scalable storage and the easy availability of a wide range of public and private services. As there has been a huge increase in the data generated by IoT devices, smart networks, security systems, and more, cities need robust ways to store, handle, and use this information quickly. Cloud computing helps cities solve problems with the old way of storing data by providing flexible resources that can change with various needs immediately. The main use of cloud computing in smart cities is to enable data sharing among various government departments. These departments have been highly compartmentalized, for example, health services, transportation, and public safety; therefore, there are many inefficiencies with some duplication of data. Therefore, through the cloud platform, data sharing will be easy to do among hospitals, clinics, and public health authorities for better coordination in patient care as well as how quickly they can respond to any emergency related to the health status of the population. For example, a cloud-based health information system that shares patient information across multiple healthcare delivery locations with adequate security measures in place to ensure privacy.

Cloud computing helps support the environment by monitoring environmental conditions in real-time, which is critical for urban sustainability management as well as public health management. In these cities, for example, where they use IoT sensors to monitor air quality, water pollution, and noise levels, it stores all the data that goes into the cloud database. Then the information is processed and analyzed with a cloud-based analytics platform. In such a way, anomalies can be detected very quickly and then pollution points can be identified so that mitigation strategies can be implemented. All these major cities have taken advantage of cloud platforms that focus their efforts on monitoring air quality can now inform in real-time and also make decisions.

Cloud computing is also important in the evolution of cloud-based public services. Through cloud platforms, governments can provide various e-government applications such as online tax reporting, business registration, social service applications, and sometimes virtual town halls. This service substantially improves convenience for citizens as it eliminates the need to physically visit government offices; therefore it saves time and reduces administrative costs. Cloud computing can also improve service availability and disaster recovery—public services must remain functional during unexpected outages. In this way, in addition to better managing large amounts of data, it also significantly improves the accessibility and quality of public services. Cloud computing platforms provide flexibility, scalability, and security in supporting the construction of smart city infrastructure that is modern, resistant to cyber disturbances, highly responsive, and trustworthy by citizens, and can adapt to the needs of cities, increasing population that continues to increase over time.

General Risks in Smart Cities

The concept of a smart city brings many benefits to its citizens, such as improvements in public services, efficiency in various sectors of life, availability of basic needs, and sustainable improvement of quality of life. But because digital infrastructure is the main part, there are various very serious cyber security security threats, which should not be ignored. With the integration of millions of digital devices—from IoT sensors, and blockchains to cloud computing platforms—a new surface has emerged that has created vulnerability. Cybercriminals can infiltrate from anywhere because every device will be connected to a smart city system that is an access point that cybercriminals use, in other words, the risk of cyberattacks will continue to increase as smart cities grow.

Data privacy is an essential aspect that must be protected. Smart city collects huge volumes of personal data from various sources like surveillance cameras, environmental sensors, and traffic systems as well as from city service databases. If there is any unauthorized access to this sensitive data, serious privacy violations, identity theft or even targeted attacks on individuals or groups could happen. Without strong encryption and strict access controls, the private information used to improve the quality of life in a city can become a security threat that needs to be safeguarded. However, critical infrastructure in smart cities also provides an attractive target for cyber threats. The network that manages everything from electricity distribution, water supply, public transportation, and emergency services is becoming more digital and remotely accessible. A successful attack on one of those systems leads to large-scale service disruptions, economic losses, and even a risk to public safety. A faulty smart grid can result in extensive power outages, while a faulty traffic management system can result in fatal traffic accidents or halt emergency response efforts to unusual emergency situations.

Ransomware is one of the big problems in cyberspace, it will also attack smart city infrastructure. The disruption caused by ransomware has been felt in many cities around the world by locking public service applications under the pretext of asking for a large amount of money to unlock them. This can lead to financial losses and lower the level of public trust. The nature of smart cities is highly dependent on digital infrastructure, so systems to be able to detect and prevent ransomware are indispensable to protect smart city infrastructure. Given that ransomware risk is a critical issue, the discussion of cyber security will be important in this chapter. Various understandings and efforts to deal with cyber threats are expected to encourage the progress of smart cities that are safe and always maintain public trust. Table 1 explains the various challenges and solutions related to various cyber-attack threats in cyberspace.

Table 1. Challenges and possible solutions

Challenge	Description	Possible Solution
Data Breaches	Unauthorized access to personal and municipal data	Strong encryption, access control
IoT Vulnerabilities	Weak security in interconnected devices	Secure firmware updates, authentication protocols
Ransomware	Attackers encrypt critical city infrastructure	Regular backups, incident response plans
Infrastructure Sabotage	Cyberattacks on essential services	AI-based monitoring, multi-layer security

The Data Authorization Center (DAC) applies advanced cryptographic techniques in managing all access to the system and secure data control with these cryptographic techniques (Sefati et al., 2024). Figure 2 shows the conceptual framework of IoT in a Smart City.

Figure 2. Conceptual diagram of IoT in smart city.

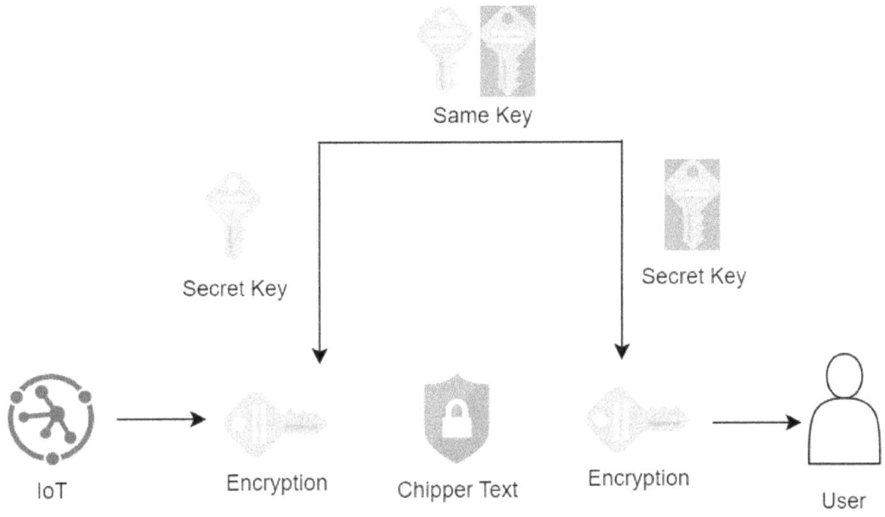

CYBERSECURITY THREATS IN SMART CITIES

Smart cities can integrate advanced technologies such as the Internet of Things, artificial intelligence, and cloud computing to improve urban management, optimize citizen services, and promote sustainable development. These innovations bring many benefits, but also bring new cybersecurity challenges that may have a profound impact on public privacy and safety. As society becomes more and more dependent on digital systems, smart cities are becoming an increasingly attractive target for cyberattacks. Therefore, it is important to identify and address the most important cybersecurity threats in this connected city ecosystem. The Internet of Things enables connectivity that connects many services and objects. However, this also makes it vulnerable to cyberattacks (Ragab et al., 2025). This section discusses some of the main cybersecurity threats facing smart cities, focusing on data and privacy breaches, critical infrastructure intrusions, ransomware attacks, and emerging threats related to AI and IoT vulnerabilities.

Data Breaches and Privacy Violations

In smart city infrastructure, there is a large collection of people's personal data and sensitive operational data obtained from IoT devices, CCTV, various public service application platforms, and other shared applications. All of this data and information, if not properly protected, can cause enormous and detrimental risks. Cybercriminals can freely exploit vulnerabilities to obtain sensitive information that is used to gain access to systems in unauthorized ways, which can lead to large-scale losses and dangerous privacy breaches (Ragab et al., 2025). The risk of data breaches is very high in smart cities due to the proliferation of interconnected digital systems or devices that have not received enough attention from users so that it can be said that the system is open from cyber-attacks. According to a study on cyber-security, more than 30% of breaches in smart cities come from IoT devices that are not sufficiently protected, such as insecure sensors, and public Wi-Fi networks that can be hacked. As a result of these breaches, these IoT devices are used to commit confidential identity theft; and financial fraud that users are not aware of, so that it can ultimately lower the level of trust of individuals and the public.

The following is an example of a case of this problem. According to various sources, in 2020, a European smart city experienced a cyberattack that exposed the personal information of more than 200,000 residents, including names, addresses, and medical records. The breach occurred due to vulnerabilities in the city's IoT infrastructure, highlighting the importance of securing all endpoints. Another incident involved intercepting unencrypted data transmission from smart meters, allowing attackers to manipulate energy consumption records and lead to billing fraud. In the UK, the lowest level of total cyberattacks in the last six months was 61 cybersecurity incidents disclosed. In comparison, 2019 saw an average of nearly 80 data breaches and cyberattacks per month. However, it is not all good news. Several major incidents occurred in January 2020, increasing the total number of records broken to a substantial 1,505,372,820 (ITGovernanceUK, 2020). Table 2 below summarizes some of the major smart city data breaches that occurred in the past five years, illustrating the common causes and extent of the damage:

Table 2: Major smart city data breaches in the last five years

Year	City	Data Compromised	Cause of Breach
2019	Singapore	1.5M healthcare records	Unsecured cloud storage
2021	Barcelona	CCTV footage leaked	IoT device vulnerability
2022	New York	500K smart grid user data	Phishing attack

IoT Device Vulnerabilities

Internet of Things (IoT) devices are the backbone of the smart city ecosystem, the presence of these devices enables real-time monitoring, automation, and intelligent decision-making across a wide range of sectors, from transportation and energy management to public safety and healthcare. However, despite their important role, in general, IoT devices are used with little attention to cybersecurity. This surveillance makes them highly vulnerable to exploitation by malicious actors.

A significant issue with IoT device security is the widespread use of default credentials. Many manufacturers ship devices with pre-set usernames and passwords, which users often overlook to change during installation. An attacker can easily gain access rights by splitting the default configuration. It should also be noted that most IoT devices do not have built-in encryption protocols, which without an encryption protocol will make data transmission vulnerable to intrusion and manipulation during data communication between IoT devices and central systems. The critical point on most IoT devices is the lack of security features. Most IoT devices are designed as a durable device without the support of after-sales service. So that the absence of security updates will certainly give rise to new vulnerabilities that are used by cybercriminals. This vulnerability will become more and more open over time, making it an easy target for cybercriminals.

An incident of attacks on IoT devices has occurred known as the Mirai botnet. This attack successfully infected thousands of IoT devices with malware, so devices such as IP cameras and routers in homes were compromised. The purpose of this intrusion is to carry out a massive Distributed Denial-of-Service (DDoS) attack that will shut down most internet services. Another example that occurred in 2021, an attacker infiltrated a traffic management system that allowed hackers to manipulate traffic light signals, resulting in traffic light blurring. This attack is very dangerous to human lives. Based on the examples above, security should be a priority in a smart city. Encryption technology, security updates, and firmware updates are important things to do in reducing the occurrence of risks. The advancements in Internet of Things (IoT) technology and the increasing demand for data transmission highlight the critical need for seamless integration between communication networks and IoT to improve efficiency (Ullah et al., 2024). Figure 3 below is an example of several IoT in Smart Cities that have the opportunity to be unsuccessful and must be secured.

Figure 3. IoT in smart cities

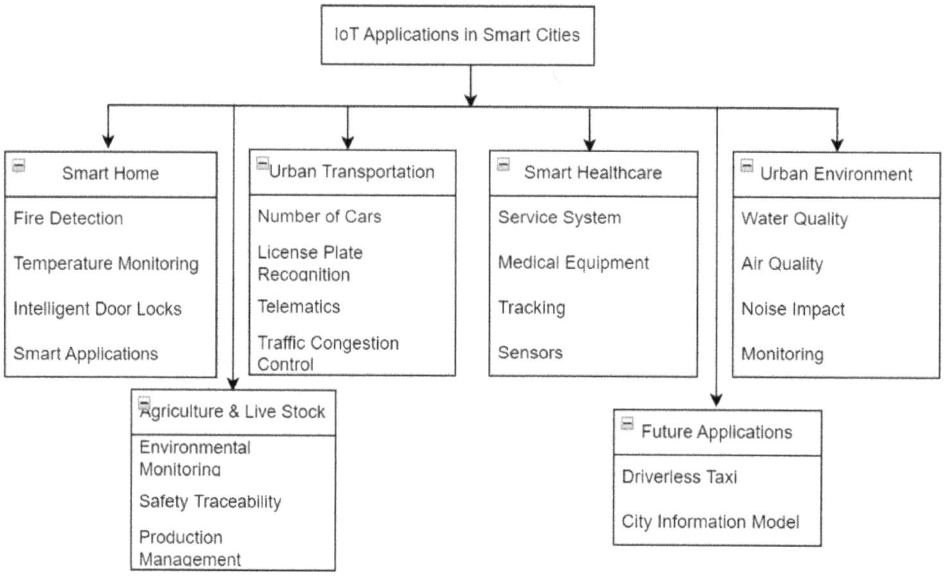

Ransomware Attacks

In the era of smart cities, city governments have become an increasingly attractive target for ransomware attacks. Ransomware is a form of malicious software that encrypts important data and systems, making it inaccessible until a ransom is paid to the attacker. Because smart cities rely heavily on digital infrastructure to manage public services, transportation, utilities, and emergency response, the consequences of such attacks can be severe and easily widespread, impacting operational efficiency and citizen safety. The interconnected nature of smart city systems, while enabling improved service delivery, also creates a wider attack surface. Cybercriminals exploit vulnerabilities in network infrastructure, and usually carry out phishing attacks to gain access to the system, once they manage to infiltrate the system, they then commit malicious acts by encrypting databases and operational software, which has an impact on the paralysis of municipal services. In most cases, affected cities are faced with a difficult decision: pay a ransom determined by criminals or endure prolonged system outages while trying to make recovery efforts.

Several incidents of ransomware attacks have occurred in the United States. In an article in the journal Lohrmann Cybersecurity entitled "Ransomware: Who Is to Blame or Not to Blame in the Baltimore Attack?", it is known that there was an incident in the Baltimore city smart city system where ransomware attacked the public service system, namely property transactions for several weeks. This caused considerable financial losses. Another note that occurred in Atlanta in 2018, there was a ransomware attack that paralyzed the main activities of utility billing and court scheduling systems, this can be seen from an article on the Ransomware Breach media entitled "Atlanta Ransomware Attack Recovery Costs: $17 Million Total?". The loss to the system recovery cost amounted to $17 million. Table 3 shows the Financial Impact of Ransomware Attacks on Smart Cities.

Table 3. Financial impact of ransomware attacks on smart cities

City	Year	Ransom Demanded	Recovery Cost
Atlanta	2018	$51,000	$17 million
Baltimore	2020	$100,000	$18 million
Dallas	2023	$1 million	$25 million

Infrastructure Sabotage

Smart cities' reliance on digital systems connected to various public services provides opportunities for sabotage. Interconnected public services such as transportation systems, energy network systems, drinking water supply systems, and various rapid service units are very attractive targets for sabotage by cybercriminals because they can have a big impact on society and cause a stir.

Terrorist groups in cyberspace that are widely circulated have caused discomfort are destructive to the system and even threaten lives. In addition, cybercrime actors can also be politically motivated, which can create chaos and political instability that is very detrimental to legitimate government authorities. Some of the incidents that have occurred are as follows. In 2020 there was a coordinated cyberattack that crippled the power grid in a country in Europe that led to a total and widespread power outage affecting at least 230,000 people. The attacker's way is to infiltrate the energy control system, by shutting down the substation so that there is a prolonged power outage in winter. In winter, heating is very vital for survival. This shows that cyber-attacks on national vital infrastructure are a humanitarian crisis. Another example that caused a widespread crisis was in 2018 in the United States where there was an attack on a smart water installation. The criminals managed to infiltrate the control system and almost succeeded in changing the chemical composition of the drinking water mixture. However, if it is not detected, this will certainly have an impact on endangering thousands of residents who consume drinking water. This incident illustrates the importance of implementing cybersecurity protocols on vital state installations. From several cases that occur, the high frequency of sabotage of vital infrastructure in smart cities, it is necessary to apply security principles to every smart city design. Risk assessment activities need to be carried out comprehensively, in addition to conducting trainings on information security awareness to the entire community while helping to prevent threats that can harm all parties.

Lack of Standardized Security Protocols

As with the development of an enterprise system, the development of the smart city concept always involves many parties and focuses on system operations, so that concerns about security systems are often forgotten. Without a good security system framework, new vulnerabilities will arise in the system that will be targeted by cybercriminals.

Challenges Due to Lack of Standards:

- Different IoT manufacturers use varying encryption methods, creating compatibility issues.
- Municipal governments struggle to implement uniform cybersecurity policies across all smart city systems.

Recommendations:

- Adoption of global security standards such as ISO 27001 for smart cities.
- Implementation of zero-trust security models to minimize risks.
- Regular penetration testing and vulnerability assessments.

Smart cities are the same concept of city development as previous city innovations, as the concept of smart cities combines various technologies that focus on efficiency and effectiveness, as well as reducing adverse environmental impacts. The technologies in smart cities are encryption, cryptography, blockchain, cloud computing, etc., which are used to deal with various cyberattacks. With the combination of these technologies, it will make the development of the city sustainable.

MITIGATION STRATEGIES

As smart cities continue to develop, measures in cyber security must continue to be improved. In addition, a mitigation strategy has also been developed that can ensure the resilience, security and sustainability of all activities in the smart city ecosystem.

Cryptographic Security Measures

Very good encryption methods with cryptography techniques such as AES-256 and TLS 1.3 have been able to protect some devices. This protocol guarantees confidentiality, and data integrity, and prevents various unauthorized access attempts. The End-to-end encryption system applied in the communication network is a system that guarantees the security of cyber communications very well. The use of this encryption system is a secure step in good access rights management activities. Table 4 shows some cryptographic security techniques in smart cities.

Table 4. Cryptographic security technique

Cryptographic Security Technique	Description	Use Case in Smart Cities
AES-256	Advanced encryption standard with 256-bit key	Securing IoT device communications
TLS 1.3	Transport Layer Security for encrypted data transmission	Secure data exchange between city services
Homomorphic Encryption	Allows computations on encrypted data without decryption	Privacy-preserving smart healthcare systems
Zero-Knowledge Proofs	Verifies identity without revealing private data	Secure authentication for public services

Blockchain for Secure Transactions

Blockchain technology is a technology used for increased security by providing centralized transaction records in a highly secure manner. In smart cities, this technology can be used for community identity management, for voting, and providing facilities for smart contracts. Transaction records on the blockchain that cannot be changed will help prevent unauthorized data change activities. Blockchain can be expanded by consensus, combining public and private chains, but still maintaining security well. Table 5 shows some examples of blockchain technology applications for smart cities.

Table 5. Blockchain applications in smart cities

Blockchain Application	Benefits	Implementation in Smart Cities
Identity Management	Secure and verifiable identity records	National digital ID systems
Smart Contracts	Automated and self-executing contracts	Efficient public service transactions
Supply Chain Security	Transparency in logistics	Monitoring infrastructure material sourcing
Secure Voting Systems	Fraud-resistant elections	Digital municipal voting platforms

AI-Based Threat Detection

AI-based cyber security devices have been able to help deal with various cyber threats well and in real time. With machine learning in AI-based cyber security devices, security devices can learn unusual activities and can become potential cyberattacks. AI can also detect anomalies in IoT devices and conduct analysis in carrying out IT risk management. In addition, Depp Learning can also conduct an in-depth analysis of the early symptoms of cyber threats, analyzing the behavior of objects that lead to attacks that can paralyze cyber-attacks that are detrimental to data integrity. Table 6 is showing AI-based security features in smart cities.

Table 6. AI-based security features in smart cities.

AI-Based Security Feature	Function	Application in Smart Cities
Anomaly Detection	Identifies irregularities in data patterns	Detecting unauthorized network intrusions
Behavioral Analysis	Monitors user activity for suspicious behavior	Preventing insider threats in government agencies
Predictive Analytics	Forecasts potential cyber threats	Early risk detection for city infrastructure
Automated Threat Intelligence	Gathers and processes cybersecurity insights	Real-time security updates for public services

Public Awareness and Training

Educating all residents about cyber security is very necessary. Socialization about security awareness, and cyber security training need to be carried out to prevent losses from adverse cases such as phishing, the importance of containing passwords that are difficult to guess, and not forgetting the principle of prudence in their activities in cyberspace. The principle of prudence is very important to maintain security in online activities.

Regulatory Compliance and Standards

NIST is a framework in cybersecurity that is highly relevant to be implemented in smart cities. Compliance with cyber security policies in smart cities will be able to increase various adverse risks, slow handling of incidents, and the sustainability of information security. Policies such as the General Data Protection Regulation (GDPR) created and implemented will help to create a robust and accountable data protection system. Table 7 shows the Regulatory Standards in Smart Cities.

Table 7. Regulatory standard in smart cities

Regulatory Standard	Purpose	Implementation in Smart Cities
NIST Cybersecurity Framework	Guides organizations in managing cybersecurity risks	Developing secure city infrastructure
ISO 27001	Information security management standard	Ensuring data protection compliance
GDPR	Data privacy regulation	Protecting citizen information
Local Cybersecurity Laws	Mandates on digital security and infrastructure protection	Legal enforcement of cybersecurity practices

In protecting complex smart city infrastructure from various types of cyber threats, it is very effective to implement multi-layered security systems such as the application of cryptography, AI-based cyber threat detection, the use of blockchain technology, and the implementation of compliance with security policies.

CASE STUDIES

Singapore's Smart Nation Initiative

Singapore has very strong cyber security technology, including AI-based cyber security systems. Singapore's cyber security agency is tasked with national security, ensuring all smart city devices such as IoT, public services and all digital transactions can be protected by the state. Singapore's smart nation sensor devices can integrate data collection and analysis for its country's operations well. Singapore also employs digital identity verification through the National Digital Identity (NDI) system, ensuring secure access to online government services. Singapore is ranked 5th out of the world's smart cities (StraitsTimes, 2024). Table 8 shows key security features and their impact.

Table 8. Key security feature

Key Security Feature	Description	Impact
AI-Based Monitoring	Uses AI for real-time security analysis	Early detection of cyber threats
Blockchain for Identity	Decentralized identity verification system	Enhanced security for public services
Cybersecurity Regulations	Strict legal frameworks for digital security	Improved national cyber resilience
Smart Sensor Networks	Monitors environmental and infrastructure conditions	Proactive maintenance and risk mitigation

Barcelona's Secure Smart Infrastructure

Barcelona integrates IoT security protocols and AI-driven threat detection in its smart city initiatives. The city employs a decentralized data architecture with strong encryption measures to protect citizen data. Barcelona's smart lighting and traffic management systems incorporate real-time security monitoring to prevent cyber intrusions, ensuring uninterrupted service delivery. The city also uses a data sovereignty model, giving citizens control over their personal data through encrypted digital identity management. Table 9 shows security iImplementation and it benefits.

Table 9. Security implementation and its benefits

Security Implementation	Description	Benefits
Decentralized Data Architecture	Secure data storage across multiple nodes	Reduces single points of failure
IoT Security Protocols	Encrypts communication between smart devices	Prevents unauthorized access
AI-Driven Threat Detection	Uses machine learning to monitor city infrastructure	Rapid threat identification and response
Data Sovereignty Model	Allows citizens to manage personal data access	Enhances privacy and trust

Both Singapore and Barcelona serve as leading examples of how cities can implement cutting-edge cybersecurity solutions to protect digital infrastructure while maintaining efficiency and privacy in smart city initiatives (Ward et al., 2025).

FUTURE DIRECTIONS

The future of smart city security will be shaped by the continuous evolution of technology and the increasing sophistication of cyber threats. To ensure resilience and trust, smart cities must adopt cutting-edge innovations such as quantum cryptography (Widodo et al., 2024), AI-based security systems, and dynamic regulatory policies. In addition, international collaboration will be crucial in the protection of globally interconnected urban ecosystems.

Advancements in Quantum Cryptography

Quantum cryptography technologies such as Quantum Key Distribution (QKD) technology have succeeded in providing a huge leap in improving security in data communication networks. This technology has covered the loopholes in traditional cryptographic methods that can be solved by quantum computers. QKD uses the principles of quantum mechanics in its task to detect when there are abnormal symptoms in the communication network and at the same time prevent damage. The longer quantum technology becomes easily accessible to everyone, the need for a quantum-resistant system to protect all devices in smart cities. Some of these QKD pilot projects can be found in the cities of Tokyo and Geneva, namely how to protect communication devices from quantum attacks with quantum devices as well. The success of this project is certainly important for the future of smart cities across the country (Widodo et al., 2024).

AI-Driven Automated Security

The application of artificial intelligence (AI) in cybersecurity technology has grown significantly to date. In the future, smart cities will depend on and rely on the presence of AI-based security systems. Some machine learning algorithms will be able to recognize abnormal behavior patterns, look for vulnerabilities, detect and neutralize various threats that come. With this adaptive AI-based security system, it will be able to reduce human involvement so that it is faster and more appropriate in the security actions of various devices in the smart city. This development will continue to evolve until it produces a security system that is real-time, accurate, and can be used in various sectors.

Evolving Regulatory Frameworks

As technological capabilities advance, regulatory frameworks continue to evolve in parallel to effectively address emerging cybersecurity threats. Policymakers need to draft regulations that are flexible enough to accommodate innovation while ensuring strong security and privacy protections. The new framework is expected to drive the adoption of standards for data protection, incident reporting, and critical infrastructure defense. In addition, regulations must address ethical considerations in technology such as facial recognition and big data analytics to be able to maintain public trust. The GDPR on the European Union has set a strong precedent, but additional global and national efforts will be needed to support the growth of secure smart cities.

Cross-Border Cybersecurity Collaboration

As described earlier, the nature of smart cities is interconnected, so cybersecurity cannot be approached only within national boundaries. International cooperation will be essential to counter various transnational cyber threats. Cross-border initiatives should focus on sharing information, standardizing cybersecurity protocols, conducting joint cyber threat simulations, and promoting collaborative research. Forums such as the Global Forum on Cyber Expertise (GFCE) and the cybersecurity task force under the United Nations are examples of how countries can collectively address challenges. A coordinated global response will be able to significantly improve the cyber resilience of smart cities in the future.

CONCLUSION

In smart cities, all human life activities rely heavily on and depend on interconnected digital devices where everything can happen due to the existence of IoT technology to unite lifters and cloud computing to store data. This condition is very important to pay serious attention to cyber security for the sustainability of the smart city. The cyber security system needs to be supported by cryptographic techniques, AI-based security detection, blockchain-based centralized storage, and a governance compliance framework that can affect the sustainability of smart cities, namely to prevent adverse conditions such as viruses, ransomware, abuse of access rights, and various kinds of cyber sabotage.

Most IoT devices as the backbone of smart cities are vulnerable devices as an entry point to cyber threats because they are generally not well configured, and they also have minimal security features. This needs to be handled further with the implementation of a layered security system to improve security on IoT devices. In addition, training for all residents about security awareness in cyberspace is also still needed as an effort to prevent threats that can come at any time. A need for cooperation with all parties, including government agencies and private companies as sponsors, to continuously innovate in building a cyber security system in strengthen cyber security in urban areas. Another important thing is to create a culture of security awareness among all citizens to use all the facilities in the smart city. Further development of quantum cryptography techniques and AI-based smart security systems also needs to be continuously developed to turn off the sustainability and resilience of smart cities in the long term. Thus, realizing a safe smart city requires a comprehensive strategy by utilizing the latest technologies, improving the quality of various policies, and the active involvement of all elements of society. Because the key to the success of the realization of a smart city and its sustainability is greatly influenced by trust and security in every transaction activity carried out.

REFERENCES

Achuthan, K., Sankaran, S., Roy, S., & Raman, R. (2025). Integrating sustainability into cybersecurity: Insights from machine learning based topic modeling. *Discover Sustainability*, *6*(1), 44. DOI: 10.1007/s43621-024-00754-w

Ahmed, S., Alshater, M. M., El Ammari, A., & Hammami, H. (2022). Artificial intelligence and machine learning in finance: A bibliometric review. *Research in International Business and Finance*, *61*, 101646. DOI: 10.1016/j.ribaf.2022.101646

Alharbi, E., Alsulami, G., Aljohani, S., Alharbi, W., & Albaradei, S. (2025). Real-time detection and monitoring of public littering behavior using deep learning for a sustainable environment. *Scientific Reports*, *15*(1), 3000. DOI: 10.1038/s41598-024-77118-x

Alkhudhayr, H. (2025). Internet of things based parking slot detection and occupancy classification for smart city traffic management. *Engineering Applications of Artificial Intelligence*, *152*, 110802. DOI: 10.1016/j.engappai.2025.110802

Almihat, M. G. M., & Munda, J. L. (2025). The Role of Smart Grid Technologies in Urban and Sustainable Energy Planning. *Energies*, *18*(7), 1618. DOI: 10.3390/en18071618

Bakirci, M. (2025). Internet of Things-enabled unmanned aerial vehicles for real-time traffic mobility analysis in smart cities. *Computers & Electrical Engineering*, *123*, 110313. DOI: 10.1016/j.compeleceng.2025.110313

Bharany, S., Kaur, K., Badotra, S., Rani, S., Kavita, , Wozniak, M., Shafi, J., & Ijaz, M. F. (2022). Efficient middleware for the portability of paas services consuming applications among heterogeneous clouds. *Sensors (Basel)*, *22*(13), 5013. DOI: 10.3390/s22135013

Bourbon, B., & Murimi, R. (2024). Decentralization, blockchains, and the development of smart communities in economically challenging environments. *Ledger*, *9*, 30–50. DOI: 10.5195/ledger.2024.302

Cao, J., Wang, X., Chen, G., Tu, W., Shen, X., Zhao, T., & Li, Q. (2025). Disentangling the hourly dynamics of mixed urban function: A multimodal fusion perspective using dynamic graphs. *Information Fusion*, *117*, 102832. DOI: 10.1016/j.inffus.2024.102832

Cengiz, B., Adam, I. Y., Ozdem, M., & Das, R. (2025). A survey on data fusion approaches in IoT-based smart cities: Smart applications, taxonomies, challenges, and future research directions. *Information Fusion*, *121*, 103102. DOI: 10.1016/j.inffus.2025.103102

Dwivedi, Y. K., Hughes, L., Ismagilova, E., Aarts, G., Coombs, C., Crick, T., & Williams, M. D. (2021). Artificial Intelligence (AI): Multidisciplinary perspectives on emerging challenges, opportunities, and agenda for research, practice and policy. *International Journal of Information Management*, *57*, 101994. DOI: 10.1016/j.ijinfomgt.2019.08.002

Ertane Baş, E., Emeç, Ş., & Yiğit, V. (2025). Simulation of Renewable Energy Systems with Alternative Energy Scenarios in Turkey's Electrical Energy Planning. *Sustainability (Basel)*, *17*(6), 2665. DOI: 10.3390/su17062665

Fei, N., Lu, Z., Gao, Y., Yang, G., Huo, Y., Wen, J., & Wen, J. R. (2022). Towards artificial general intelligence via a multimodal foundation model. *Nature Communications*, *13*(1), 3094. DOI: 10.1038/s41467-022-30761-2

Hwang, G. J., Xie, H., Wah, B. W., & Gašević, D. (2020). Vision, challenges, roles and research issues of Artificial Intelligence in Education. *Computers and Education: Artificial Intelligence*, *1*, 100001. DOI: 10.1016/j.caeai.2020.100001

ITGovernanceUK. (2020). List of data breaches and cyber attacks in January 2020. *ITGovernanceUK*. Retrieved from https://www.itgovernance.co.uk/blog/list-of-data-breaches-and-cyber-attacks-in-january-2020-1-5-billion-records-breached

Kaniadakis, A., & Foster, P. (2024). The role of fintech startups and big banks in shaping trust expectations from blockchain use in mainstream financial markets. *Technological Forecasting and Social Change*, *203*, 123376. DOI: 10.1016/j.techfore.2024.123376

Kim, J., Manna, A., Roy, A., & Moon, I. (2025). Clustered vehicle routing problem for waste collection with smart operational management approaches. *International Transactions in Operational Research*, *32*(2), 863–887. DOI: 10.1111/itor.13282

Kumaran, K. S., Khekare, G., Thanu Athitya, M., & Arulmozhivarman, A. (2025). Integrating blockchain, internet of things, and cloud for secure healthcare. *Indonesian Journal of Electrical Engineering and Computer Science*, *37*(2), 928–936. DOI: 10.11591/ijeecs.v37.i2.pp928-936

Kuvonchbek, R., Azamzade, A. K., Makhmudov, S., Bekzod, T., & Sarvar, M. (2024, December). Ensuring the Security of Transactions in Financial Information Networks Based on Modern Symmetric Cryptosystems in the Digital Economy. *In Conference on Internet of Things and Smart Spaces* (pp. 145-162). Cham: Springer Nature Switzerland. DOI: 10.1007/978-3-031-95299-9_13

Li, S., Niu, K., & Wu, B. (2025). A blockchain-based secure data sharing scheme with efficient attribute revocation. *Journal of Systems Architecture*, *159*, 103309. DOI: 10.1016/j.sysarc.2024.103309

Ma, Y., & Peng, Y. (2024). Design of Intelligent City Communication Network Based on Internet of Things. *Applied Mathematics and Nonlinear Sciences*, *9*(1), 1–15. DOI: 10.2478/amns-2024-1509

Matura, A., Singh, R. K., & Kumar, R. (2025). Decarbonizing road transport: A systematic literature review based on use case analysis. *Case Studies on Transport Policy*, *101416*, 101416. Advance online publication. DOI: 10.1016/j.cstp.2025.101416

Quiles-Rodriguez, J., Palau, R., & Mateo-Sanz, J. M. (2025). How Artificial Intelligence-Assisted Colour Lighting Can Improve Learning: Evidence from Recent Classrooms Studies. *Applied Sciences (Basel, Switzerland)*, *15*(7), 3657. Advance online publication. DOI: 10.3390/app15073657

Ragab, M., Ashary, E. B., Alghamdi, B. M., Aboalela, R., Alsaadi, N., Maghrabi, L. A., & Allehaibi, K. H. (2025). Advanced artificial intelligence with federated learning framework for privacy-preserving cyberthreat detection in IoT-assisted sustainable smart cities. *Scientific Reports*, *15*(1), 4470. DOI: 10.1038/s41598-025-88843-2

Rahouti, M., Drid, H., Hamouid, K., Massmi, K., & Mehenna, S. E. (2025). Brave-sdn: Blockchain-reliant authentication for versatile east–west bound in distributed sdns. *International Journal of Information Security*, *24*(1), 1–15. DOI: 10.1007/s10207-024-00962-5

Ren, Y., Chen, L., Bai, Y., Ye, J., & Zhao, Y. (2025). Blockchain-based cross-domain query integrity verification mechanism for outsourced database. *Computer Standards & Interfaces*, *92*, 103926. DOI: 10.1016/j.csi.2024.103926

Russell, S., & Norvig, P. (2020). Artificial Intelligence: A Modern Approach. *Pearson*. ISBN 10: 1-292-40113-3. Available in http://lib.ysu.am/disciplines_bk/efdd4d1d4c2087fe1cbe03d9ced67f34.pdf

Sanada, K., & Zappa, M. (2025). Japan's international cooperation on smart city development in Asia: International effort beneath the smart rhetoric in India and in Thailand. *Research in Globalization*, *10*, 100270. DOI: 10.1016/j.resglo.2025.100270

Sanaj, M. S., & Prathap, P. J. (2020). Nature inspired chaotic squirrel search algorithm (CSSA) for multi objective task scheduling in an IAAS cloud computing atmosphere. *Engineering Science and Technology, an International Journal*, *23*(4), 891–902. DOI: 10.1016/j.jestch.2019.11.002

Sefati, S. S., Craciunescu, R., Arasteh, B., Halunga, S., Fratu, O., & Tal, I. (2024). Cybersecurity in a scalable smart city framework using blockchain and federated learning for internet of things (IoT). *Smart Cities*, *7*(5), 2802–2841. DOI: 10.3390/smartcities7050109

Shang, F., & Deng, X. (2025). A data sharing scheme based on blockchain for privacy protection certification of Internet of Vehicles. *Vehicular Communications*, *51*, 100864. DOI: 10.1016/j.vehcom.2024.100864

StraitsTimes. (2024). Singapore is world's 5th smartest city. Retrieved April 3, 2025, from https://www.straitstimes.com/singapore/singapore-is-5th-smartest-city-in-the-world-top-in-asia-global-index

Susilowati, A. P. E., Rachmawati, R., & Rijanta, R. (2025). Smart village concept in Indonesia: ICT as determining factor. *Heliyon*, *11*(1), e41657. Advance online publication. DOI: 10.1016/j.heliyon.2025.e41657

Tameemi, H. A., Shayea, G. G., Khaleel, Y. L., Habeeb, M. A., Hussein, N. A. H. K., & Albahri, A. S. (2025). A Systematic review of metaverse cybersecurity: Frameworks, challenges, and strategic approaches in a quantum-driven era. *Mesopotamian Journal of CyberSecurity*, *5*(2), 770–803. DOI: 10.58496/MJCS/2025/045

Tan, T. M., Salo, J., Alejandro, T. G. B., Tan, G. W. H., Ooi, K. B., & Dwivedi, Y. K. (2024). Guest editorial: A blockchain-based approach to marketing in the sharing economy. *Journal of Business Research*, *177*, 114639. DOI: 10.1016/j.jbusres.2024.114639

Ullah, A., Anwar, S. M., Li, J., Nadeem, L., Mahmood, T., Rehman, A., & Saba, T. (2024). Smart cities: The role of Internet of Things and machine learning in realizing a data-centric smart environment. *Complex & Intelligent Systems*, *10*(1), 1607–1637. DOI: 10.1007/s40747-023-01175-4

UN. (2022). World Population Prospects 2022: Summary of Results. Retrieved April 3, 2025, from https://www.un.org/development/desa/pd/content/World-Population-Prospects-2022

UN. (2025). Adapting Humanitarian Action to an Urban World. Retrieved from https://unhabitat.org/sites/default/files/download-manager-files/Global Alliance for Urban Crises WHS Brief - Final.pdf

Vignesh, R., Pabitha, C., Shamritha, V., & Prathija, A. (2025, January). Integrated Road Safety System for Real-Time Waterlogging Detection and Traffic Management Using Google Maps API. *In 2025 International Conference on Multi-Agent Systems for Collaborative Intelligence (ICMSCI)* (pp. 1165-1170). IEEE. DOI: 10.1109/ICMSCI62561.2025.10894697

Ward, K., Abbruzzese, T., Bunnell, T., Cardullo, P., Chang, I. C. C., Miller, B., & Woods, O. (2025). A comparison of comparisons: Evidence from an international comparative study of 'smart cities'. *Environment and Planning C. Politics and Space, 23996544251320261*(7), 1217–1239. Advance online publication. DOI: 10.1177/23996544251320261

Widodo, A. M., Pappachan, P., Sekti, B. A., Anwar, N., Widayanti, R., Rahaman, M., & Bansal, R. (2024). Quantum-resistant cryptography. In *Innovations in Modern Cryptography* (pp. 100–130). IGI Global., DOI: 10.4018/979-8-3693-5330-1.ch005

KEY TERMS AND DEFINITIONS

Smart City: An area or city whose citizens have used IoT-based technology in their activities for efficiency in many ways to provide an improvement in the quality of life for all residents.

Cybersecurity: A security system that aims to protect data and system from various cyber-attacks.

IoT (Internet of Things): A technology that can connect various devices over the internet so that it can exchange data and communicate over long distances.

Cryptography: A system that implements an algorithm designed to hide data so that it is safe from unwanted third-party interference.

Threat Model: A structured model that can compromise information security.

Homomorphic Encryption: An encryption method that can process data without the need to perform a description process.

Governance: A framework that ensures the security and availability of information.

Chapter 4
Cyber Resilient Smart Cities Through Big Data and Cryptography

R. N. Ravikumar
https://orcid.org/0009-0009-3705-1681
Marwadi University, Rajkot, India

S. Aarthi
https://orcid.org/0009-0006-9064-2091
Marwadi University, Rajkot, India

Anorgul Ashirova
Mamun University, Khiva, Uzbekistan

Gularam Masharipova
Alfraganus University, Tashkent, Uzbekistan

Zokir Mamadiyarov
Termez University of Economics and Service, Termez, Uzbekistan

Lal Tlan Sang
https://orcid.org/0009-0003-3320-8377
TODA PVC Co., Ltd., Samut Sakhon, Thailand

ABSTRACT

The emergence of smart cities has transformed urban living through the integration of big data and IoT technologies. While these advancements enhance service delivery and infrastructure efficiency in areas like traffic management, healthcare, and public safety, they also raise significant concerns about data security and privacy. This chapter explores the role of cryptographic technologies in securing the vast amounts of sensitive information generated by smart city systems. It discusses encryption, digital signatures, blockchain, and their applications in maintaining data integrity, confidentiality, and access control. Special attention is given to securing IoT devices, which are integral to smart city frameworks but pose unique vulnerabilities. Real-world case studies illustrate the use of blockchain for transparency and

DOI: 10.4018/979-8-3373-3326-7.ch004

end-to-end encryption for personal data protection. The chapter also addresses the growing relevance of quantum-resistant cryptography, proposing a unified security framework for future smart cities to ensure resilience, privacy, and trust.

INTRODUCTION

The 21st century is a revolutionary period in the development of the city, the phenomenon of smart cities with the use of innovative technologies in both tangible and intangible infrastructure to streamline services and ensure a high level of life quality. To keep all aspects of the city in order, such urban ecosystems are using high connectivity with closely linked systems, such as the Internet of Things (IoT) devices, AI, Big Data Analytics, Cloud Computing, etc. The core of such transformation is the accumulation and analysis of enormous amounts of data, due to which it becomes possible to make real-time decisions and proactive governance (Al-Badi et al., 2020). Nonetheless, the hyper-connectivity presents an immense danger to cybersecurity and privacy risks. The interdependence of the distributed networks, large streams, and edge devices with limited resources lead to an increasing number of attack opportunities in terms of data leaks, uncontrolled access, and compromise of systems. Hence, it is important to guarantee the integrity of data, confidentiality, and resiliency of the system (Das & Das, 2023). Cryptography finds its way to be a key element in protecting smart city infrastructure, ensuring safe transfer of data, authentication of identities, access control and the trustworthiness of the system. The cross-road of big data and cryptography with smart cities, the underlying core methods of cryptography, their applications to urban systems, and the upcoming issues including the quantum threat are offered in this research work (Bibri & Krogstie, 2020). It provides an overview to technologists, policy-makers and urban planners of how to architect secure, privacy-respecting, resilient digital cities.

Definition and Vision of Smart Cities

A smart city can be defined as an urban area that applies digital technologies, data analytics, and interconnected infrastructure to the enhancement of the quality, performance, and interactivity of urban services, while at the same time minimizing resource consumption and adverse environmental impact. Essentially, a smart city incorporates Information and Communications Technology (ICT), Artificial Intelligence (AI), IoT, and Big Data systems to solve urban challenges in real time. A smart city collects heterogeneous data from traffic lights, energy meters, public transit systems, surveillance, and healthcare institutions for good. This combined data is utilized to make choices that improve traffic, energy consumption, security, trash management, and emergency response. The notion of a smart city goes beyond efficient operations. Its goals include citizen-centricity, digital inclusion, environmental sustainability, and participatory government (Fang et al., 2021). A liveable, efficient, and resilient urban place where technology can empower people, promote good health, boost economic development, and make public services accessible, safe, and responsive is the objective. As urbanization rises rapidly, the smart-city paradigm is being touted as a sustainable solution to global city dilution. Cryptography technologies are essential to smart-city frameworks because data integrity, privacy, and security are crucial to achieving this objective.

Role of Big Data and IoT in Urban Transformation

The city has evolved quickly, making big data and the Internet of Things crucial. Today's urban environment is digitalized via IoT and big data. Thus, cities become more efficient, adapt to new requirements, and provide customized services. Smart meters, linked cars, environmental sensors, wearable health monitors, and public surveillance create real-time data from around the city. Data is pooled, processed, and analysed using big data analytics systems for actionable insights. Traffic congestion, energy needs, and emergency incidents may be predicted using predictive analytics to help municipal administrators adapt services in real time. Big data and IoT technologies change governance from reactive to proactive (Khan et al., 2022). Dynamic routing optimizes public transit, real-time symptom reporting helps health systems track outbreaks, and real-time consumption data balances grids. Thus, saving time, boosting sustainability, and improving urban life. However, its true advantage hinders proper data management and effective cybersecurity and privacy-preserving systems. The above Figure 1 illustrates the flow of real-time data from devices like smart meters into a big data system, where it is processed through predictive analytics to optimize urban services such as traffic control and energy usage.

Figure 1. Role of IoT and big data in smart city predictive analytics

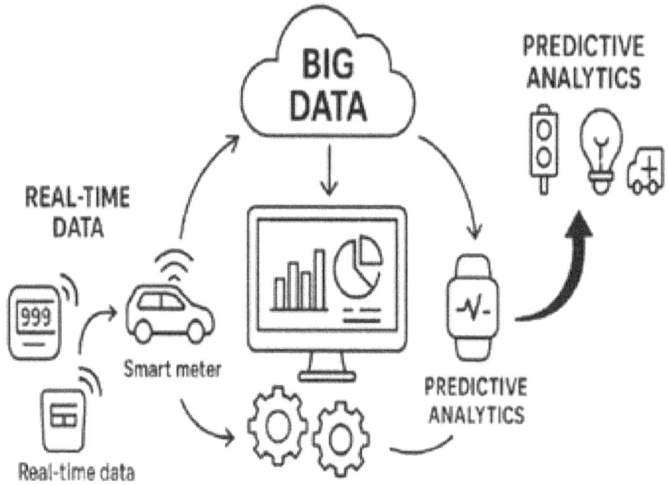

Literature Review

Since smart cities have been rapidly developing, the amount of big data collected and used is now very large, and considerable cyber-security systems are needed to handle such sensitive information in a safe way. It is observed that a couple of studies highlighted how real-time analytics can be used to enhance urban activities, including transportation, the distribution of energy, and healthcare, and the challenges of interoperability and data integrity (Patel et al., 2024). Conventional cryptographic protocols like Advanced Encryption Standard (AES), Rivest-Shamir-Adleman (RSA), and Elliptic Curve Cryptography (ECC) continue to constitute the foundation of safe data transfer over IoT nodes and clever structures (Sharma & Shrestha, 2024). Moreover, Privacy-Preserving Analytics New privacy-enhancing cryptographic methods, homomorphic encryption and differential privacy, have been developed and can be used to perform calculations on encrypted data and aggregate information without invading the privacy of individual users (Zhang et al., 2019). Blockchain has also become a revolutionary technology in the improved management of a city. It has been commonly recognised that its application in clear land registry systems, e-voting and irreversible transactional records will enhance accountability and minimise corruption (Kshetri, 2018). Implementing such systems to include smart contracts and decentralized consensus functions also enhances their properties because it allows them to be tamper-proof, and have an automated decision-making process (Zhuk, 2025). Nevertheless, with the emergence of quantum computing, traditional cryptographic algorithms are endangered, whereas scientists encourage the creation of quantum-safe protocols to protect the urban security system in the long run (Mosca, 2018). In addition, the literature underlines the role of international standards like ISO 27001 and National Institute of Standards and Technology (NIST) Cybersecurity Framework in the promotion of globally unified security practices in smart city ecosystems. Although considerable efforts have already been realized, the current research findings suggest that the further inclusion of lightweight, scalable, and post-quantum cryptographic tools that fit with the resource-limited urban settings are still required.

Importance of Cybersecurity and Data Privacy

This becomes really bad for smart cities because smart cities work on data driven-decisions, therefore leaving a larger vulnerability to cyber security and privacy issues. Integration of myriad IoT devices, interlocking systems and open data platforms balloons the attack surface and exposes organisations to cyber threats, including unauthorized data access, identity fraud, ransomware and critical infrastructure interruptions (Al-Badi et al., 2020). In addition, PII, geolocation data, health records, behavioural patterns and other information about individuals are present in smart city data, which give rise to serious ethical and legal issues regarding individual privacy. A compromise of such systems may not only result in denial of service, but also affect public confidence and slander reputation in the long run.

Thus, cybersecurity is not only a technical need but a strategic need for building resilient urban communities. Data encryption, secure authentication, network partitioning, intrusion detection, and strict access control are some of the essential elements that should be included to maintain the integrity, confidentiality, and availability of the data in smart city. Modern cryptographic techniques are the essential enablers here (Li et al., 2015). They foundational stool in standards to secure data and ensure its authenticity, and to protect user privacy. By infusing these techniques at all layers of the smart city, including edge devices to cloud platforms, cities build cyber-resilient infrastructures that are innovative and trusted.

Objectives of the Chapter

The main aim of the chapter is to investigate how cryptograph and big data analytics can be combined in building safe, transparent, and resilient smart cities. It will seek to examine the protection of citizen information and solution of urban systems, using methods of highly sophisticated cryptography, Including End-To-End Encryption, Blockchain, Homomorphic Encryption, and Quantum-Resistant

Algorithms. The Research work also considers real-world applications, governance systems, and multiplayer systems to give an in-depth picture of how security, data privacy, and data-deduced knowledge can be presented conveniently in smart city environments.

THE ROLE OF BIG DATA IN SMART CITY ECOSYSTEMS

Smart cities are increasingly predicated on connectivity, intelligence, and automation to all of which big data collection, analysis, and utilization contribute. Big data such as big data is the term referring to data sets (i.e., large data) that are developed at high speed, and are in different formats (Al-Badi et al., 2020). In a smart city, and particularly in a connected one, such data is harvested from myriad devices, systems and from human interaction to offer real-time intelligence that helps cities become more liveable, responsive and citizen-centric.

Sources and Types of Big Data in Smart Cities

Smart cities produce large amounts of information in different forms that can be used to make real-time and wise decisions and manage cities. Important examples are the IoT devices like smart traffic lights, air quality night, and water meters, as well as surveillance systems that constantly produce structured data. Smart systems, such as infrastructure, power grids, waste management, and public transport, generate data used in the operational findings and analysis of current performance (Li et al., 2015). Location-based and biometric data are provided by mobile and wearable devices whereas governmental services provide administration-related records such as permits, health and education data. Also, there are sentiment and behavioural data that are disorganized in platforms of citizen engagement and social media platforms. The received data have different forms: it is structured (sensor logs), partly structured (app-generated JSON/XML), and unstructured (images, videos, texts). Such heterogeneity mandates elaborate storage, processing and analysis systems. Collectively, such sources constitute a digital ecosystem, which enables the application of predictive analytics, policymaking, and service optimization in the realm of smart cities, seizing, at the same time, important questions related to data quality, interoperability, and privacy.

Key Applications of Big Data in Smart Cities

Big data can significantly transform the capability of informed, proactive and automated decision-making in the major urban sectors. In transportation and mobility, cities use real-time data to manage congestion, count and clear bottlenecks and change the status of traffic signals. The data are provided automatically by Global Positioning System (GPS) enabled cars, traffic cameras and sensors, and ride shares. Intelligent mobility apps provide individuals with the best routes and schedules to work and enhance mobility in the city (Ismail et al., 2025). To monitor the environment, sensors that monitor the air and water quality are useful in detecting trends of pollution, some ensure the law gets enforced on the environment and even predict some events like floods or heatwaves. Hospitals and authorities can access big data and use it in targeting the disease outbreak, resource utilization, and enhanced outcome in the field of public health and disaster management. Analytics are also helpful in contact tracing and strategies to distribute vaccines in case of crisis such as pandemic.

At the energy and utility management level, smart grids would be used through the real-time consumption data to balance on the supply-demand, sense the faults, mitigate the emissions, and streamline the water and waste utilities (Riki et al., 2020). Finally, historical and live data help in the planning and establishment of the land-use, infrastructure, and zoning in urban areas. The process makes cities more sustainable, resilient and responsive to the challenges of rapid urbanization. Figure 2 illustrates the core domains where big data enables intelligent decision-making in smart cities. It highlights applications in transportation and mobility, environmental monitoring, public health and disaster management, energy and utility optimization, and urban planning. Each sector leverages real-time and historical data to improve service efficiency, sustainability, and citizen well-being through predictive analytics, automation, and system-wide coordination.

Figure 2. Key applications of big data in smart cities

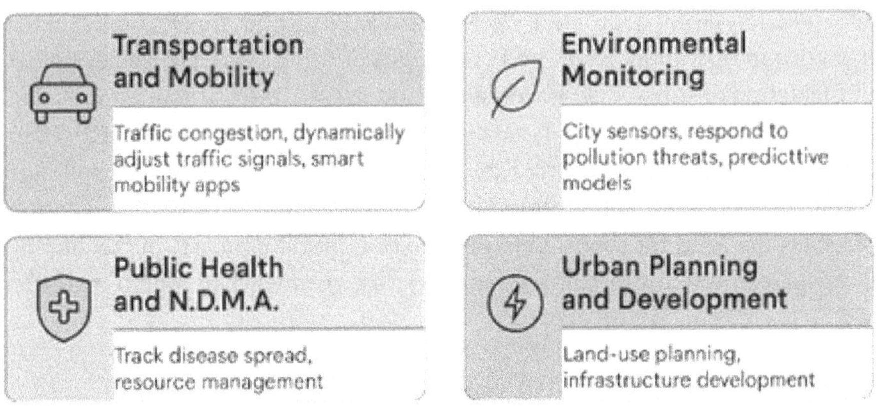

Benefits of Big Data in Urban Governance Strategic Benefits

Big data has considerable strategic value to urban governance as it can facilitate data-driven policymaking and increase the productivity of the state administration. It will enable managers of cities to provide individual services, rationalize material resources and enhance working processes. In open data platforms, the civic engagement and the trust between the citizens and the government institutions are created by transparency (Wang et al., 2021). Moreover, real-time analytics allows proactive decision-making, which helps in the decreased response to becoming responses to urban challenges. Big data is also very instrumental in the achievement of sustainability through monitoring of environmental impacts and organization of applicable eco-friendly policies. All of these advantages come together in making the urban environments smarter, more responsive, and citizen-centric.

Key Challenges in Urban Data Utilization

There are a number of key issues with regard to the use of walled data in smart cities that may complicate efficient governing such places and service delivery. Data siloing and interoperability is one of the main problems because the data is usually divided by departments and decision-making is not integrated. The quality of data becomes another issue, once relevant, well-presented and accurate data is not presented, the results of analytics and planning become unreliable. Bad data may lead to loss of trust among citizens when a decision that will yield negative results is taken based on corrupted insight (Oliha et al., 2024). Continuous gathering of sensitive personal information, location, health, and behavior also results in the issues of privacy and ethical implications, which require closer compliance with the principles of consent and transparency. Besides, cyber-security risk is escalating as networked systems continue to have more exposure to attacks, data theft, and interference of operation. Risks and challenges of this nature have necessitated the implementation of strong data governance models, safe infrastructure, uniform data policies and citizen-friendly policies that guarantee trust, efficiency, and inclusivity in urban digital communities. Table 1 outlines key cybersecurity challenges in smart city data utilization, highlighting their impact and corresponding solutions. It emphasizes the need for robust data governance, privacy-preserving technologies, and transparent systems to build secure and trustworthy urban digital ecosystems.

Table 1. Cybersecurity risks and solutions in urban data utilization

Cybersecurity Challenge	Description	Proposed Solution
Data Silos & Interoperability	Fragmented data across city departments	Open data standards, centralized platforms
Data Quality & Governance	Inaccurate or outdated data impacts decisions	Implement robust data governance frameworks
Privacy Violations	Persistent collection of personal data	Consent-based systems, privacy-preserving analytics (e.g., differential privacy)
Cybersecurity Risks	Increased attack surface due to interconnected systems	Encryption, multi-factor authentication, intrusion detection systems
Public Mistrust due to "Bad Data"	Misleading or false data undermines trust in city services	Transparent and validated data sharing mechanisms

CRYPTOGRAPHIC FOUNDATIONS FOR SMART CITY SECURITY

With smart cities evolving into orchestrate digital ecosystem capturing most data generated by sensors, devices and systems at scale; securing data is top priority. Cryptography (the discipline of securing information) is a cornerstone essential to protect the confidentiality, integrity and authenticity of data in the highly complex and integrated deployment of a smart city. Here, we will discuss the cryptographic algorithms on which smart city data and system security is built in this section (Das & Das, 2023) . Figure 3 illustrates core components of cryptographic security, including encryption, authentication, digital signatures, and key management.

Figure 3. Core components of cryptographic security in smart cities

A Brief of Cryptographic Techniques

Cryptography is the process of protecting data in storage or in transit as well as performing processing. Mechanisms which guarantee that only participants with authorization can read, modify or transmit the information. Therefore, the general cryptographic techniques that are used in smart cities (Das & Das, 2023). Encryption is the transformation from readable data (plain text) to unreadable format (cipher text) using a mathematical function and a key. Figure 4 represents symmetric key encryption, where the same secret key is used for both encryption and decryption of plain text into cipher text and vice versa.

Figure 4. Cryptography types

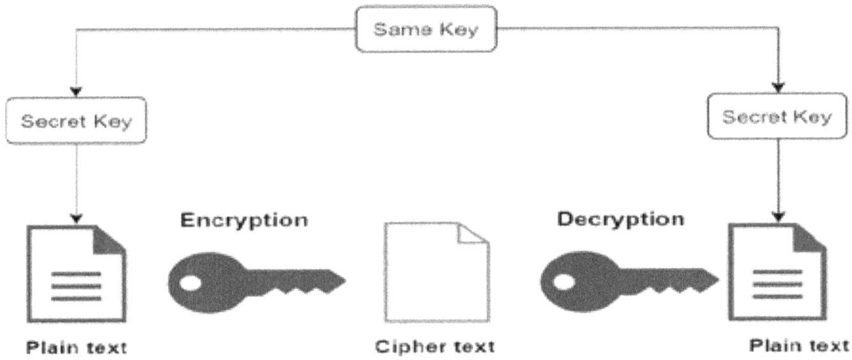

Symmetric Encryption

Symmetric encryption refers to a cryptographic method of data encryption and decryption in that the identical secret key is employed in encrypting or decrypting data. It encrypts plain text that can be read into randomly-looking cipher text by means of a mathematical algorithm and a secret key, providing secrecy in transportation or conservation. Key distribution is a crucial dilemma since both the sender and the receiver have to realize a shared common key (Das & Das, 2023). Symmetric encryption is very effective and appropriate where large amount of data is to be encrypted. Popular algorithms are AES, (Advanced Encryption Standard) and DSS, (Data Encryption Standard). It is superior in speed and easiness which makes it suitable in real-time applications such as IoT and network security.

Asymmetric Encryption

The asymmetric one, also referred to as public-key cryptography, employs two keys; one public and one secret to transmit data in a secure way. Data is encrypted with the help of the public key, but only its matching private key can be used to decrypt it, and thus confidentiality is provided even in the case of untrusted channels. There is no necessity in sharing a common key, unlike in symmetric encryption, hence, it is more secure as far as key distribution is concerned. This method is common in digital signatures, secure email, Secure Sockets Layer (SSL) and Transport Layer Security (TLS). It gives stronger authentication and non-repudiation than symmetric methods although it is computationally slower. Popular algorithms are Rivest, Shamir, Adleman (RSA), Elliptic Curve Cryptography (ECC) and Diffie-Hellman key exchange.

It is better suited for smart city high volume data encryption (e.g., communication between IoT devices) as it is faster and imperative. Symmetric algorithms such as Advanced Encryption Standard (AES) this as smart cities transition from orchestrating a complex number of digital elements capturing large scale sensor, devices & systems led data is of highest priority to protect data. Cryptography (the field dedicated to securing information) is at the nucleus of importance to securely data confidentiality, integrity and authenticity in such an elaborate and interlinked implementation on which a smart city function (Das & Das, 2023). In this section, we will describe the cryptographic algorithms used to secure smart city data and system. Table 2 summarizes key cryptographic techniques used in smart cities, highlighting their type, common algorithms, and practical applications. These methods collectively ensure data confidentiality, integrity, privacy, and secure communication across urban digital infrastructure.

Table 2. Key cryptographic techniques used in smart cities

Technique	Type	Examples	Use in Smart Cities
Symmetric Encryption	Encryption	AES, DES	Fast encryption of large data volumes (e.g., traffic or energy usage data)
Asymmetric Encryption	Encryption	RSA, ECC	Secure key exchange, device authentication
Digital Signatures	Authentication	RSA, DSA	Validating data authenticity and integrity
Hashing	Integrity	SHA-256, SHA-3	Ensuring data is not tampered during transmission
Homomorphic Encryption	Privacy	Paillier, BGV	Computation on encrypted data without decrypting
Differential Privacy	Privacy	Laplace, Exponential Mechanisms	Aggregate insights while preserving individual data privacy

Cryptographic Protocols in Smart City Ecosystems

The key pillar of safe communication and data management in the smart city environments involves cryptographic protocols. These protocols enable data exchanged between the IoT devices, sensors, control systems, and the cloud infrastructures to be confidential, with integrity, and data is authenticated (Anthony Jnr et al., 2021). Symmetric encryption algorithms such as Advanced Encryption Standard (AES) are common in performing data protection on the real-time because they are efficient in the protection of the high throughput situations like the traffic or energy grid. Asymmetric schemes, such as RSA and ECC, enable easy and safe exchange of keys as well as authentication of device which is very important in heterogeneous and open networks. Also, the authenticity and integrity of data is also ensured using digital signatures and hashing methods which eliminate the use of tampering data in transit. Security protocols homomorphic encryption and Secure Multi-Party Computation (SMCP) enable the computation of encrypted information without the release of confidential details (Anthony Jnr et al., 2021). The combination of these cryptographic methods enables smart cities to develop a trusted digital infrastructure, securely manage the digitally recorded information, avail their services in a verifiably secure manner, and maintain regulatory compliance of such services within the hyper-connected urban environment.

Cryptography in the Context of Privacy Protection

Smart cities produce large volumes of big personal data like countries of residence, health histories and usage habits. It is imperative that this sensitive information be guarded to keep the trust of its citizens. In solving these issues, cryptographic techniques have been advanced and are considered as the developing privacy solutions of big data. The theory of differential privacy enables cities to do aggregated data analysis without revealing any information about individuals so that it will provide knowledge about user identity at the same time (Figueiredo et al., 2022). Homomorphic encryption facilitates operations to be executed on an encrypted information, and it avoids decryption of the information hence maintaining confidentiality of the information during execution of the operations. Also, Secure Multi-Party Computation (SMPC) involves jointly calculating a shared result whilst maintaining a privacy of their individual inputs, when parties come together in order to perform a joint analysis. All these cryptographic mechanisms help able smart cities to use the data in a responsible manner that respects the right to privacy of the citizen.

Ensuring Security for Future Challenges

Quantum computing is one of the new forms of technology that are potentially disruptive to the main cryptography systems that include RSA and ECC as cryptographies because they can easily be cracked using Shor algorithm, among other quantum algorithms. To overcome these threats, scientists have been making quantum-resistant cryptographic algorithms based on lattice problem, hash-based signatures and code-based encryption (Oliha et al., 2024). Such future-proof solutions will protect the smart city infrastructure against sophisticated cyber-attacks. Also, practices that encourage constant innovation of encryption, digital signatures and key management systems are essential in order to secure data, guarantee system integrity and continued confidence by citizens. To have long-term cyber-resilience in an urban ecosystem, there should be proactiveness in adopting post-quantum cryptography.

SECURING SMART CITY INFRASTRUCTURE

The successful implementation of smart cities demands the use of cryptographic technologies which protect the security and privacy of massive data exchanges between systems, devices and citizens. Under assured protection, ICT (Information and Communication Technology) needs to integrate cryptographic solutions into its physical and digital layers to defend sensitive information while critically securing critical infrastructures (Riki et al., 2020). This section is based on a detailed investigation of the use of cryptography throughout the machinery of smart cities. Figure 5 illustrates how cryptographic security enables secure data flow, processing, and control within smart city infrastructures like traffic systems, energy grids, and smart buildings.

Figure 5. Integrating cryptography in smart city infrastructure

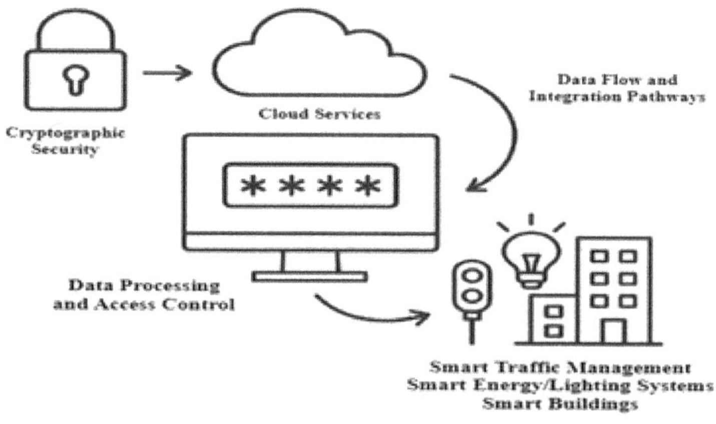

Integration of Cryptographic Solutions in IoT Infrastructures

The IoT is the foundation of the technology used in smart cities because it has the potential to integrate real-time data transmission of equipment such as smart meters, traffic sensors, air and water quality monitors. Since the devices have limited resources, and under a limited bandwidth environment, security mechanisms should be efficient and lightweight (Vempati, 2024a). The activities that are critical in terms of security of IoT ecosystems include device authentication and secure communication. Using Public Key Infrastructure (PKI), devices have the capability to create and maintain digital certificates, public/private key pairs whose identities can be verified and can determine secure channels.

The data is also protected in a device-to-system type of conversation using TLS and Datagram Transport Layer Security (DTLS) protocol that protects against eavesdropping and man-in-the-middle attack. Lightweight cryptographic algorithms like ECC and AES are generally the algorithm of choice due to their speed and efficiency because of lack of computing power (Vempati, 2024b). Also, the preserving of data integrity and authentication is very important. Digital signatures enable devices to sort information by using the private keys and the recipients identify authenticity by using the associated public keys. Such hashing algorithms as SHA, check changes during the transmission process by creating the unique hash results. Collectively, these cryptographic tools will make IoT systems of the smart cities secure, credible, and hardened to cyber threats.

Cryptographic Integration in Smart City Data Centres

A smart city data centres are the core facilities where a lot of information produced by the city systems is collected, processed and stored. Such centres have to provide effective data protection that should be in accordance with privacy rules and security policies. Consecutive encryption in storing and transmitting information is among one important measure (Riki et al., 2020). End-to-End Encryption (E2EE) is being used to make sure that information sent by and between IoT devices are held in encrypted form both in transit and storage, to avoid eavesdropping or wrongful modification. Encryption of the database can protect sensitive data like personal identifiers, medical reports and traffic data making it immune to any possible disruptions. As a way to safely store encryption keys and obtain secure access to keys, Key Management Systems (KMS) are implemented to store the keys securely, grant access, and can automate key rotation, which consequently increases security.

Access control and authentication are the means of controlling who (or by which system) has access and to which portions of data and system capabilities (Popov & Semyachkov, 2020). Role-Based Access Control (RBAC) uses system and data access privileges granted to users based on system roles, users with system access will have access to configuration data, and simply users will be limited to service-level information only. Multi-Factor Authentication (MFA) further holds access by necessitating a sequence of passwords, biometrics or something like a piece of equipment-based token. Furthermore, transparency and reliability come with the blockchain application in the data centres of smart cities. Blockchain uses principles of cryptography through digital signature, hash functions, and consensus algorithms to guarantee traceable and tamper-proofed storage of data. This is particularly useful in the provision of various services to the people and fraud control where transactional accounting records can play an important role to record accountability in the service provision as well as in money following (Lawelai et al., 2025). Corruption in other spheres like voting and resources allocation are no exceptions to blockchain protection. Moreover, services are automatically delivered using smart contracts whose provision depends on the conditions predetermined in it, where it has digital signatures and cryptographic hashes. Examples of applications that take advantage of these self-executing contracts are fare collection or smart transportation routing as they provide transparent, secure and automated transactions. On the whole, the promotion of cryptography and blockchain in smart city data centres contributes to a better data security level, trust, and efficiency of operations.

Cryptography on us Citizen's Right to Privacy and Data Security

The main problem is based on the fact that in smart cities, personal data are constantly created by citizens, including location, health history, and financial transactions privacy. To counter these, encryption measures play a vital role in the protection of individual data and safe handling of data on the digitalized infrastructure (Fang et al., 2021). E2EE encrypts personal data at the initial sending point as well as in the storage place, with the only ones who are authorized to decrypt and read the information being the individuals at the other end on its reception. Such an approach will guarantee that, even in a situation where one intercepts data, it will be unreadable and tamper-proof. Additionally, there is the concept of the differential privacy and privacy-preserving analytics which enable a secure data analysis. The difference privacy mechanism adds statistical noise or noise to the data sets; thus, it is not possible to extract all individual information even when using fine grain analysis (Bibri & Krogstie, 2020). Additionally, cryptographic algorithms enable operations over an encrypted data; the data does not have to be decrypted and the level of security is sustained. These practices combined will respect the rights of citizens to protect privacy and enable smart cities to work productively when using the data in planning and health care delivery without interfering with confidentiality.

Ensuring Security in the Face of Future Challenges

With the development of quantum computing, there will be an issue to existing cryptographic standards, specifically RSA and ECC, which the quantum algorithm (i.e. Shor) will attack. Subsequently, scientists are coming up with quantum-resistant cryptographic algorithms that can store data even in the face of quantum attacks. These entail hash-based signature, lattice-based algorithms and code-based encryption techniques, which are hold up to the massive amount of computation by quantum machines. In the case of smart cities, the crucial factor to ensuring data confidentiality, integrity, and trust is introducing these advanced cryptographic technologies at all the levels, including IoT devices, cloud layers, and infrastructure (Alzahrani & Alfouzan, 2022). Cryptography, digital signatures, and blockchain mechanisms have to be advanced and remain resistant to any new threats and support user privacy and practical communications. At the moment when cities turn to next-generation technologies, post quantum cryptography becomes vital to establish secure digital infrastructures. Such a proactive strategy will help smart cities remain safe and functional and will take care of their technological infrastructure as well as the privacy of their citizens even when in an increasingly digitalized world.

Novel Techniques in Big Data and Cryptography Implementation

The inter-connectivity of big data and cryptographic innovation has given rise to some new methods that have boosted data security, privacy and use in smart cities. Of these, homomorphic encryption has become an innovative technique that enables calculations to be made on encrypted data directly, and therefore, keeps confidentiality throughout processing streams (Rajabpour Sanati et al., 2024). This is especially applicable in sensitive analysis in the healthcare or traffic monitoring systems. Differential privacy combined with federated analytics is another state-of-the-art, which allows learning about the city using distributed datasets at scale, but without learning about individuals in the data. This assures citizens confidentiality in terms of behavioural patterns analysis or mobility patterns. It is considering using Zero-Knowledge Proofs (ZKPs) blockchain to make transactions, or identity verifications secure but without revealing the data they represent. This can be used in voting smart contracts, in allocation of subsidies or land registry. Moreover, the systems of AI-driven cryptographic key management use machine learning to optimize the processes of cryptographic key life cycle management, detect anomalies, and perform dynamic access control instantly. Lastly, quantum resistant cryptography, including lattice-based encryption and hash-based signatures is also gaining momentum as a secure method against the threat of quantum computing in the future. The new implementations do not only enhance data protection but also make people trust them and achieve more intelligent and safer city administration.

BLOCKCHAIN FOR URBAN TRANSPARENCY AND TRUST

Blockchain principles enabled urban transparency and trust-based management. Decentralization, immutability, and transparency may help cities construct efficient, accountable systems. Blockchain technology verifies property ownership to avoid land registry disputes and fraud. Positive avatars provide civil society members full control over their information and secure services with decentralized management (Wang et al., 2021). Blockchain standardises product tracking via municipal records and ensures product legitimacy to facilitate sustainable city procurement. This reduces corruption and record manipulation by eliminating dependence on centralized government organizations. The system's unalterable nature enables legitimate entities to constantly recognize sensitive information changes while boosting accountability. Open Blockchain ledgers allow individuals to monitor government activity, boosting public trust in leaders (Alva et al., 2023). This article showed that block chain technology underpins urban territory digital avowal, providing transparency and smart citizen-oriented government.

Overview of Blockchain Principles

Blockchain is a distributed database specialising in the decentralised management and protection of data, which is dispersed across several computer networks. Figure 6 illustrates the core components of blockchain technologies like Smart Contracts, Consensus Mechanisms, Transparency, Immutability, and Decentralization forming a continuous cycle of trust and security.

Figure 6. Core principles of blockchain

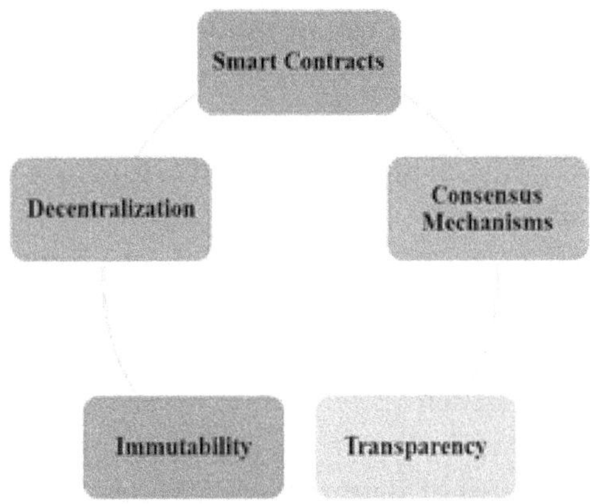

There are five major principles on which blockchain technology works that renders it extremely trustworthy in the smart cities. The data is distributed with a variety of nodes, and due to decentralisation, there is no entity having control over it (Balogun & Olorunmade, 2023). Immutability ensures that data cannot be tampered with as it ensures that what has been documented cannot be erased or changed. Transparency enables stakeholders to view every transaction on either of the two types of ledgers which can either be permissioned or a public ledger and this encourages accountability. The safe transactions are verified through consensus systems, such as Proof of Work (PoW), Proof of Stake (PoS) and PBFT. Finally, smart contracts are automated procedures that are performed under standardized terms and conditions following a trustful partnership in digital interactions of urban systems (Kálmán, 2024).

Real-World Applications of Blockchain in Land Records, Identity, and Urban Supply Chains

Smart cities are warming up to the use of blockchain technology in order to create greater transparency in smart cities, guarantee solidity in data management in dread city areas and diminish the amount of embarkation. In land records management, one of the ground breaking uses is its application. In such cities as Dubai, Andhra Pradesh (India), blockchain has been used to build the land registries in a digital form that cannot be altered. Besides excluding document falsification and unjust ownership claims, it also helps the citizens with safe access to ownership evidences, minimizing land conflicts and bureaucracies (Akhmetbek & Špaček,

2021). Estonia has presented an excellent role model in identity management, as all citizens possess a digital identity document that is secured by blockchain, which allows them to access health care, voting, financing and governmental services. Decentralized Identity (DID) platforms enable citizens with access to their personal data and reduce opportunities to equate and treat information about identity theft and information abuse. This model enhances the trust between citizens and the government institutions.

Blockchain is also relevant to the point of supply chains in cities mainly in logistics, food safety, and pharmaceutical tracking. Blockchain enables cities and logistics companies to note every supply step of the journey: origin to delivery, and all that in time-stamped records that can be verified. This assists in proving the authenticity of goods, monitoring carbon footprints, and ensuring sustainability principles. As an illustration, Food Trust of International Business Machines (IBM) has also been introduced in partnership with suppliers and Walmart to provide traceability of food. The comparative adoption of blockchain in these three areas as shown in Figure 7 below is shown in relation to pilot implementation of blockchain in smart cities projects. The most adopted land records are because of high demands of transparency, and in this area, there are the identity systems and supply chains (Asha et al., 2025). Urban application of the blockchain technology will only gain momentum as this urban infrastructure technology further matures; it will provide scalable, secure services and solutions that increase efficiency, trust, and resilience in the modern governance of the city.

Figure 7. Blockchain adoption in key urban use cases

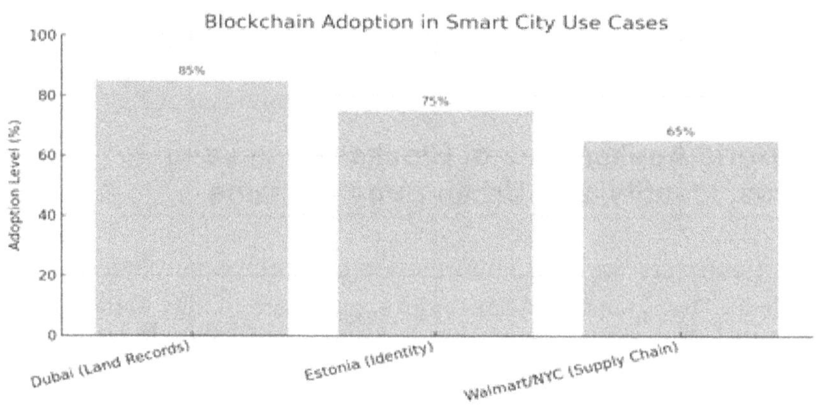

CASE STUDIES OF CRYPTOGRAPHY IN SMART CITIES

Smart cities with fully linked networks need cryptography technology for security and development. The Union of Information Technology and Communications offers Estonia with a Public Key Infrastructure (PKI) for secure service identification, digital voting, electronic healthcare, and tax filing. Barcelona's smart-grid and IoT networks encrypt citizen data. Dubai uses blockchain for visa applications, utility bill payments, and property registration to verify data and prevent fraud. Quayside developers in Toronto examined existing encryption mechanisms for sensitive urban data from sensor and AI deployment (Bibri & Krogstie, 2020). These cities use Blockchain to clarify processes, smart contracts, and restricted data. Since end-to-end encryption protects all documents, including health information, only authorized access is allowed. These examples demonstrate how cryptographic technologies build confidence and business continuity in hazardous metropolitan environments.

Case Study: Estonia – A Global Leader in Cryptography-Based Smart Governance

The Republic of Estonia is also a world-leading expert in cryptographic technologies that enable creating a solid and fully digital system of governance. As a part of its national program e-Estonia, the country has also installed strong Public Key Infrastructure (PKI) and digital signatures and end-to-end encryption in most of its public services (Krishna Pasupuleti, 2024). Thoroughly cryptographically protected digital ID cards, citizens can legally and reliably access e-Voting, e-Tax, e-Banking, e-Health and e-Residency services with authentication and legal-grade digital signatures. These services are meant to be efficient, transparent and tamper-proof. For example, blockchain is used in the systems of government where the integrity and traceability of data is guaranteed to discourage unauthorized changes. It is the safe digital environment that has made the level of current adoption high achieving over 95 percent of citizens who file their tax using it, and those who use e-Banking, and those who can access encrypted health records digitally reaching 90 percent and 88 percent respectively (Wang et al., 2021). One of the good examples of how well-designed cryptographic systems raise citizen trust, privacy protection and provide effective services is Estonia, and so it is a model that can be replicated in bigger and better smart cities in the future across the world. Figure 8 illustrates the adoption rates of Estonia's major cryptography-based digital services, including e-Tax, e-Health, and e-Banking. The X-axis lists the services, while the Y-axis shows their respective adoption percentages. It highlights Estonia's leadership in implementing secure, citizen-focused digital governance using cryptographic technologies.

Figure 8. Adoption of cryptography-based digital services in Estonia

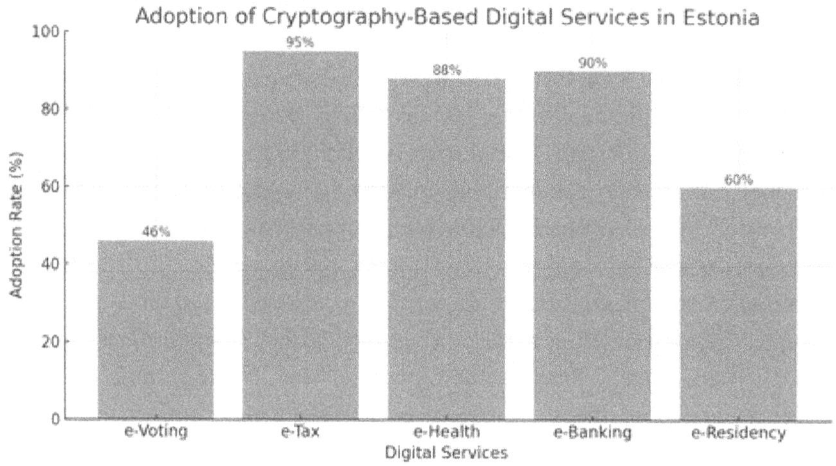

Blockchain Adoption for Public Services

Urban governance is getting transparency through Blockchain technology by using cryptographic hashing mechanisms and digital signatures to achieve a cleaner government by reducing corruption in the public services sector (Parenti et al., 2022). By the year 2030, Dubai intends to convert all the government paper into blockchains that will execute safe smart contracts, digital identities, and real estate transactions. To make citizen involvement in issues concerning policymaking at the local level tamper-proof, Seoul employs blockchain in its e- voting system. Switzerland, a state known as the Crypto Valley, uses blockchain technology to document the housing operations, the digital identity, and payment of taxes in a form of cryptocurrency. Such real-life implementations improve operational sanity, inspire trust and inculcate transparent and tamper-free systems in all the government services at the city levels.

End-to-End Encryption for Citizen Data Protection

End-to-End Encryption (E2EE) is crucial in protecting the citizen information in the smart cities as information transmitted and stored can only be read by authorized individuals. Sidewalk Labs promised to employ E2EE to protect personal data and sensor data in Quayside smart city of Toronto. The Linking New York Together (LinkNYC) Wi-Fi network of New York City has already implemented E2EE to ensure the privacy of communication between the citizens, as well as San Diego is experiencing the benefits of E2EE to ensure that data communicated between traffic control systems and self-driving vehicles is not maliciously exploited (Fang et al., 2021). According to the privacy framework such as the General Data Protection Regulation (GDPR), E2EE will not allow intrusion and will ensure data secrecy at any stage of its life in smart cities.

RESULTS AND DISCUSSION

Technological innovations to use cryptographic practices and big data analytics in the infrastructures of smart cities have shown quantifiable results in various areas of urban programs. As is confirmed by case studies of Estonia e-Governance, blockchain strategy in Dubai, encrypted metropolis in Toronto, cryptographic implementations lead too much improvement in the aspects of trust, data protection, and efficiency of services. Better citizen confidence and fewer data breaches cases are seen through End-to-End Encryption (E2EE) of the public networks in the city of LinkNYC, and blockchain in the city of Zug that provides open and transparent land records. Immutability and accountability are guaranteed with the use of blockchain whose applications are prominent in the delivery of public services, registration of land and voting.

Moreover, pilot program outcomes suggest that homomorphic encryption and differential privacy can fulfil advanced analytics with no privacy loss to individuals; a notable characteristic of population sized urban applications. Some challenges that are yet to be solved also emerge in the discussion: interoperability between departments, international standards, and overhead on computation in the application of advanced cryptographic systems. Furthermore, in a new era of quantum computing, the city has to invest in quantum-solvent cryptography systems so as to maintain long-term security. Finally, big data and its intersection with cryptography build up the safe, transparent and citizen-driven state of governance. This does not only enhance technical resilience but also citizens' confidencc and policy acceptability, consolidating the pillar of long-running smart city development. Figure 9 highlights the effectiveness of cryptographic and data-driven technologies in enhancing trust, privacy, and operational efficiency across selected smart city projects. It visualizes comparative impact scores from real-world implementations like Estonia's e-Governance and New York's LinkNYC.

Figure 9. Impact of cryptographic and big data integration in smart city case studies

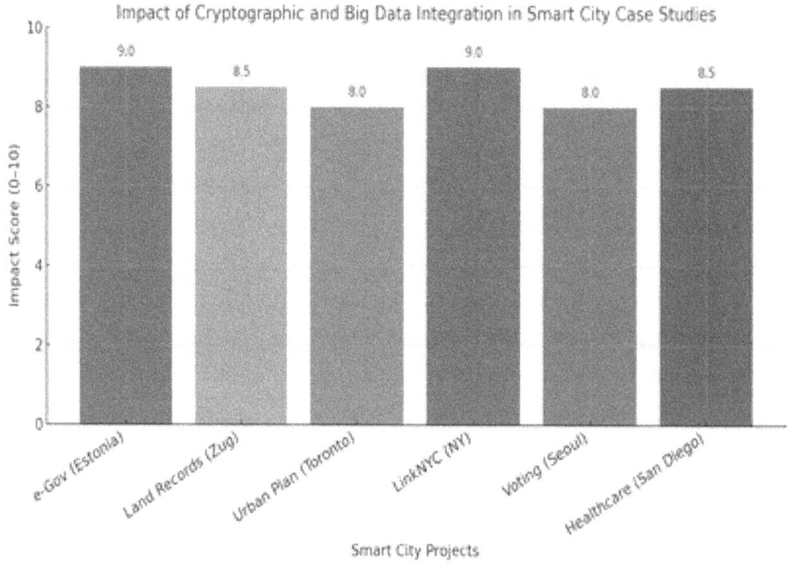

FUTURE TRENDS AND CHALLENGES

Smart city initiatives raise cryptography issues and seek better solutions. However, Shor's algorithm and other quantum algorithms may readily break established public-key cryptography systems, making quantum computing a huge threat to encryption. At this point of development, quantum-resistant algorithms are needed to secure urban digital infrastructure from future attacks (Dziundziuk & Dziundziuk, 2025). Global policymaking and standards are prioritized. Currently, NIST and ISO are defining worldwide cryptographic principles to improve trust and compatibility across global cities and nations. AI was included to enhance key management and perform Anomaly Detection and Context-adaptive Encryption. New cryptographic solutions bring new data abuse concerns, and as the regulatory process improves, ethical questions may arise about cryptographic instruments (Oliha et al., 2024). To address developing concerns, governments, technologists, and civil society groups must work together to build resilient infrastructure for future cities.

Rise of Quantum Computing and Need for Quantum-Resistant Algorithms

Current cryptographic systems are defective in security especially in cases where quantum computers are considered since they tend to bring about drastic changes to the computational power. RSA and ECC are used as the foundation for building smart city, but they are easily attacked by Shor's and Grover's quantum algorithms (Minbaleev & Evsikov, 2023). The quantum computing advancement calls for the development of new cryptographic algorithms for use when faced with a quantum computer attack. Cryptography is at the moment aimed at creating security techniques that are derived from lattice problem, in addition to the use of hash-based signatures combined with that of multivariate polynomial. The forecast of such future smart city's data as well as structures and services call for the implementation of preventive measures to protect digital urban systems.

Policy and Standardization Efforts

As the field of cryptography and its utilization advances quickly, emerging unadjusted polity and global normative to ensure accurate system compatibility in smart cities (Min, 2023). There are professional associations like National Institute of Standards and Technology (NIST) alongside International Organization for Standardization (ISO) in the establishment of official standards for regression methods and data protection protocols as well as quantum-secure protocols. In all, well-designed policies must achieve three aims that include those for security/privacy, as well as those for defining advancement through a framework that tackles matters on surveillance and citizens' rights and cross-border data transfers the application of smart cities requires high support for development of new standards to build trustful relationships between governments and private and citizens sectors.

The Role of AI in Enhancing Cryptographic Applications

Cryptography now has its best line of defense in the AI technology. Smart cities utilize AI in cryptographic security through threat detection and perform an efficient key management system, as well as intelligent encryption operational system (Al-Badi et al., 2020). Recent machine learning techniques can recognize security threats at a faster rate than the conventional security systems while the artificial intelligence systems are able to warrant security slight variations depending of the risk rates. AI testing also brings benefits in the world of cryptology, where it allows the usage of cryptanalysis for testing complex cryptographic algorithms. Introducing AI changes the processes within systems as it happens with combining AI in systems because

AI brings inherent bias in the algorithms and asks for explanation of the operations while at the same time needing supervision for avoiding hacking attacks.

COLLABORATION FOR CYBER-RESILIENT SMART CITIES

This therefore emphasizes the criticality of the establishment of cyber-resilience in smart cities whereby government institutions and academic institutions need to collaborate with industrial organisations (Alzahrani & Alfouzan, 2022). Through their power, governments create laws, and the academic institutions, which are often supported by funding, work on security and fund cybersecurity as a course of studying for future personnel. This industry present basic and requisite features related to security and technology necessary for deployment. Organizational protocols that are standardized in nature and interwork becomes possible through the requisition of global protocols and benchmarks that cities embrace (Sindhuja et al., 2024). Formal academic and professional training programs, as well as public awareness and involvement drives serve as the basic for nurturing competent professionals in the field of cybersecurity as well as thinking citizens of society. These measures unite comprehensive solutions for the security of smart city that strengthens its support tools and protects people from new threats in the digital world.

Government, Academia, and Industry Partnerships

Successful and safe implementation of smart cities needs robust and continuous partnerships within the government, universities, and businesses. Governments have an important role in facilitating the process of developing laws, regulations, and financial resources that would help to promote the projects in cybersecurity (Lykidis et al., 2021). College and universities will play the role of conducting innovative research in the sphere of cybersecurity, algorithms development, and risk analysis. At that, they will help educate the new generation of experts. Technology firms provide expertise and assets required to apply cybersecurity at big scale, which assist in carrying out operations within the city system. The collaboration in three sectors is more innovative, policy friendly, and has the ability to create robust smart city infrastructures fast (Wang et al., 2021). Combined forces of scholars or policy-makers and of private companies allow revealing the weaknesses of the system and preventing them, building a solid basis in the field of trust, security, and long-term digitalization of the urban surfaces.

Creating Global Frameworks and Best Practice

With the works of smart cities rising in every corner of the world, the emergence of globalized security patterns and international best practices gain a new level of urgency. Such constructs guarantee standardised cybersecurity measures without interfering with the local laws and regulations. International agencies like the United Nations (UN), World Economic Forum (WEF), and the International Telecommunication Union (ITU) have played a huge role in advising cities to transform securely digitally (Jnr. et al., 2023). They also have efforts to facilitate multilateral policymaking and encourage cross-national policing to fight cross-border cybercrime. Also, some of the practices that will be of great use in the securing of the urban infrastructures include sticking to cybersecurity certification including ISO 27001, and NIST Cybersecurity Framework. The implementation of them on a tactical and operational level will ensure better preparedness of cities against the presence of nationwide cyber threats and service disturbances. Interoperability of smart cities in the form of standardized practices also allows safer data transmissions and threat intelligence sharing. On the whole, international structures and international best practices are key to the establishment of strong, safe and reliable smart city ecosystems across the different global set-ups.

Capacity Building and Citizen Awareness

The process of the cyber-resilience of smart cities consists of two purposes: professional expertise and increased awareness of the general population. Capacity building means training the staff that can be able to develop and implement protective effect against the critical infrastructure like transportation and healthcare (Figueiredo et al., 2022). Collaboration is needed between governments and educational institutions to develop they ways of certification programs, designing special courses and assisting in non-stop developing the work force. This will guarantee a talent pool of experienced personalities ready to solve emerging online risks. Awareness among citizens also is very crucial because the residents ought to be enlightened on safe data usage and on threats detection. Public awareness and online literacy initiatives provide people with knowledge about danger threats like phishing, identity theft, and information leaks. Educated people are the initial vanguard system of a cybersecurity infrastructure of a smart city (Zhuang et al., 2024). The combination of talented experts and knowledgeable citizens makes up a strong source of cyber-resilience. This interconnected solution is enhanced when international standards are backed and synchronized policy platforms to put a city in a stronger position to defend and recover against digital attacks.

CONCLUSION

Urban environment is being transformed by evolution of smart cities by incorporating digital technologies like IoT, Big Data and Artificial Intelligence. Although these innovations make it possible to conduct efficient, citizen-oriented, and sustainable governance, there are considerable challenges that come with the innovations, i.e., linked to cybersecurity and data privacy. This chapter has indicated key importance of cryptography and big data analytics in the security, integrity and credibility of smart city infrastructures. Important tools in urban systems protection are cryptographic tools, including symmetric and asymmetric techniques, as well as special techniques, Homomorphic Encryption, Differential Privacy, and Blockchain. Using Encryption Protocols, Digital Signature, Secure Key Management Systems play a crucial role in the protection of secret data about the citizens and preservation of privacy of messages exchanged between inter-connected gadgets. Moreover, blockchain has been able to revolutionize by providing transparency, accountability, and resistance to fraud in the provision of public services related to land records, identity verification and urban supply chain.

An example of the effects of the implementation of cryptographic and data-driven solutions is presented by case studies of such countries as Estonia, Dubai, and Toronto, which shows how the abovementioned solutions can contribute to an augmentation of the trust of its citizens, efficiency of its operations, and security of its digital footprint. The chapter also points to the necessity of future-proofing the digital urban infrastructure by utilizing quantum-resistant cryptography in preparation against quantum computing, an increasingly common threat. Secure smart cities can also be achieved because of the dynamic partnership between governments, academia, and industry. This partnership should be taken to the international standards and development of capacity, and creation of public awareness to develop resilient digital ecologies. To create an inclusive and trust-based environment in the urban context with the help of technology, ethical considerations, compliance to international laws, and cross-border data sharing has to be resolved. To conclude, smart cities are sustainable only when they are constructed with the basis of security and transparency along with citizen-oriented governance. Future cities have the potential to accomplish the optimal ratio between innovation and privacy through responsible determination of cryptographic solutions and big data analytics as current cities lacked the same ratio.

REFERENCES

Akhmetbek, Y., & Špaček, D. (2021). Opportunities and barriers of using blockchain in public administration: The case of real estate registration in Kazakhstan. NISP. *J. Public Adm. Policy*, *14*(2), 41–64. DOI: 10.2478/nispa-2021-0014

Al-Badi, A., Sharma, S. K., Jain, V., & Khan, A. I. (2020). Investigating emerging technologies role in smart cities' solutions. In *IFIP Advances in Information and Communication Technology* (pp. 230–241). Springer International Publishing.

Alva, P., Mosteiro-Romero, M., Pei, W., Bartolini, A., Yuan, C., & Stouffs, R. (2023). Bottom-up approach for creating an urban digital twin platform and use cases. CAADRIA Proceedings. DOI: 10.52842/conf.caadria.2023.1.605

Alzahrani, N. M., & Alfouzan, F. A. (2022). Augmented Reality (AR) and cyber-security for smart cities-A systematic literature review. *Sensors (Basel)*, *22*(7), 2792. DOI: 10.3390/s22072792 PMID: 35408406

Anthony Jnr, B., Abbas Petersen, S., Helfert, M., & Guo, H. (2021). Digital transformation with enterprise architecture for smarter cities: A qualitative research approach. *Digit. Pol. Regul. Gov.*, *23*(4), 355–376. DOI: 10.1108/DPRG-04-2020-0044

Asha, S., Baddur, K., & Jaya Singh Dhas, L. (2025). High speed wireless communication technologies including 5G and beyond for reliable smart city IoT networks. In IoT Architectures and AI-Enabled Smart City Solutions for Sustainable Urban Development (pp. 102–132). RADemics Research Institute.

Balogun, A. A., & Olorunmade, G. (2023). Blockchain technology adoption against corruption in emerging economies. In Advances in Finance, Accounting, and Economics (pp. 22–36). IGI Global. DOI: 10.4018/979-8-3693-0770-0.ch002

Bibri, S. E., & Krogstie, J. (2020). The emerging data–driven Smart City and its innovative applied solutions for sustainability: The cases of London and Barcelona. *Energy Informatics*, *3*(1), 5. DOI: 10.1186/s42162-020-00108-6

Das, S., & Das, A. (2023). Future perspective of quantum cryptography for smart cities of the 21st century. In Advances in Systems Analysis, Software Engineering, and High Performance Computing (pp. 326–342). IGI Global.

Dziundziuk, B., & Dziundziuk, V. (2025). Methodology for integrating blockchain into digital governance systems: Analysis of challenges, benefits, and opportunities for society. *Science & Public Policy*, scaf022. DOI: 10.1093/scipol/scaf022

Fang, Y., Shan, Z., & Wang, W. (2021). Modeling and key technologies of a data-driven smart city system. *IEEE Access : Practical Innovations, Open Solutions*, *9*, 91244–91258. DOI: 10.1109/ACCESS.2021.3091716

Figueiredo, B. J. R. Costa Rogério Lu\'\is de C and Santos, L., & Rabadão, C. (2022). Cybersecurity and privacy in smart cities for citizen welfare. In Smart Cities, Citizen Welfare, and the Implementation of Sustainable Development Goals (pp. 197–221). IGI Global.

Ismail, A. I., Ismail, M. A. H., & Johari, S. (2025). Smart cities implementing IoT applications for security technologies and future recommendations. *Ijirss*, *8*(3), 1376–1387. DOI: 10.53894/ijirss.v8i3.6802

Jnr., B. A., Sylva, W., & Watat Josue Kuika and Misra, S. (2023). A framework for standardization of distributed ledger technologies for interoperable data integration and alignment in sustainable smart cities. J. Knowl. Econ., 15(3), 12053–12096.

Kálmán, M. (2024). Mosaics from the legal regulation of blockchain technology. In *Collection Regional Law Review* (pp. 215–223). Institute of Comparative Law. DOI: 10.56461/iup_rlrc.2024.5.ch17

Khan, M. A., Siddiqui, M. S., Rahmani, M. K. I., & Husain, S. (2022). Investigation of big data analytics for sustainable smart city development: An emerging country. *IEEE Access : Practical Innovations, Open Solutions*, *10*, 16028–16036. DOI: 10.1109/ACCESS.2021.3115987

Krishna Pasupuleti, M. (2024). Blockchain for Transparent Governance: Securing Public Services in the digital era. In Blockchain in Government: Tools for Transparent Governance and Secure Public Services (pp. 146–173). National Education Services.

Kshetri, N. (2018). 1 Blockchain's roles in meeting key supply chain management objectives. *International Journal of Information Management*, *39*, 80–89. https://doi.org/https://doi.org/10.1016/j.ijinfomgt.2017.12.005. DOI: 10.1016/j.ijinfomgt.2017.12.005

Lawelai, H., Purnomo, E. P., Nurmandi, A., Jovita, H., & Baulete, E. M. (2025). Cybersecurity policy on smart city infrastructure: a mapping of new threats and protections. J. Sci. Technol. Policy Manag.

Li, D., Cao, J., & Yao, Y. (2015). Big data in smart cities. *Science China. Information Sciences*, *58*(10), 1–12.

Lykidis, I., Drosatos, G., & Rantos, K. (2021). The use of blockchain technology in e-government services. *Computers*, *10*(12), 168. DOI: 10.3390/computers10120168

Min, K. S. (2023). An exploratory research of anti-corruption policy using blockchain. *Korea Assoc Corruption Stud*, *28*(3), 5–26. DOI: 10.52663/kcsr.2023.28.3.5

Minbaleev, A. V, & Evsikov, K. S. (2023). Regulation of quantum communications in the ``smart city'' information system. E3S Web Conf., 419, 1006.

Mosca, M. (2018). Cybersecurity in an Era with Quantum Computers: Will We Be Ready? *IEEE Security and Privacy*, *16*(5), 38–41. DOI: 10.1109/MSP.2018.3761723

Oliha, J. S., Biu, P. W., & Obi, O. C. (2024). Securing the smart city: A review of cybersecurity challenges and strategies. Eng. Sci. Technol. j., 5(2), 496–506.

Parenti, C., Noori, N., & Janssen, M. (2022). A Smart Governance diffusion model for blockchain as an anti-corruption tool in Smart Cities. *Journal of Smart Cities and Society*, *1*(1), 71–92. DOI: 10.3233/SCS-210122

Patel, V., Department of Computer Engineering Silver Oak College of Engineering & Technology, S. O. U. and D. D. J. A., Khara, D. S., & Tivari, G. D. (2024). Examining the integration of responsible AI principles in Social Media Marketing for Digital Health: A theoretical analysis. INTERANTIONAL JOURNAL OF SCIENTIFIC RESEARCH IN ENGINEERING AND, 08(07), 1–13.

Popov, E., & Semyachkov, K. (2020). 7I-model for smart city development. *Archives of Business Research*, *8*(7), 143–157. DOI: 10.14738/abr.87.8615

Rajabpour Sanati, S., Zebardast, M., Jamshidi, R., & Sadeghi, M. E. (2024). Designing and localizing a novel cybersecurity model according to smart city digital infrastructure components (A Case Study of GreenWeb Co.). International Journal of Innovation in Management. *Economics and Social Sciences*, *4*(3), 1–18.

Riki, R., Widyarto, S., Kahar, S., & Hariyanto, S. (2020). Smart city comprehension in community development. Proceedings of the Proceedings of the Third Workshop on Multidisciplinary and Its Applications, WMA-3 2019, 11-14 December 2019, Medan, Indonesia. DOI: 10.4108/eai.11-12-2019.2290864

Sharma, S., & Shrestha, S. (2024). Integrating HCI principles in AI: A review of human-Centered Artificial Intelligence applications and challenges. *J. Fut. Artif. Intell. Tech.*, *1*(3), 309–317. DOI: 10.62411/faith.3048-3719-47

Sindhuja, M., Alice, K., Nancy, A. M., & Vinoth, N. A. S. (2024). Cybersecurity Strategies for Smart Cities. In Advances in Geospatial Technologies (pp. 77–98). IGI Global. DOI: 10.4018/979-8-3693-8104-5.ch004

Vempati, S. (2024a). Securing smart cities: A cybersecurity perspective on integrating IoT, AI, and Machine Learning for digital twin creation. *J. Electr. Syst.*, *20*(3), 1420–1429. DOI: 10.52783/jes.3548

Vempati, S. (2024b). Securing smart cities: A cybersecurity perspective on integrating IoT, AI, and Machine Learning for digital twin creation. *J. Electr. Syst.*, *20*(5s), 2817–2827. DOI: 10.52783/jes.3052

Wang, J., Nguyen, D. Q., Bonkalo, T., & Grebennikov, O. (2021). Smart governance of urban data. E3S Web Conf., 301, 5005.

Zhang, R., Xue, R., & Liu, L. (2019). Security and Privacy on Blockchain. *ACM Computing Surveys*, *52*(3), 1–34. Advance online publication. DOI: 10.1145/3316481

Zhuang, Y., Cenci, J., & Zhang, J. (2024). Review of big data implementation and expectations in smart cities. *Buildings (Basel, Switzerland)*, *14*(12), 3717. DOI: 10.3390/buildings14123717

Zhuk, A. (2025). Beyond the blockchain hype: Addressing legal and regulatory challenges. *SN Social Sciences*, *5*(2), 11. DOI: 10.1007/s43545-024-01044-y

KEY TERMS AND DEFINITIONS

Smart City: An urban area that uses digital technologies, data analytics, and interconnected infrastructure to enhance urban services, minimize resource consumption, and improve quality of life.

Big Data: Extremely large data sets that are analyzed computationally to reveal patterns, trends, and associations, especially relating to human behavior and interactions.

Internet of Things (IoT): A system of interrelated devices that collect and exchange data over a network without requiring human-to-human or human-to-computer interaction.

Cryptography: The practice and study of securing communication and data through encoding techniques to ensure confidentiality, integrity, and authentication.

Symmetric Encryption: A cryptographic method where the same key is used for both encryption and decryption (e.g., AES, DES). Fast but key distribution is a challenge.

Asymmetric Encryption: Uses a public key for encryption and a private key for decryption (e.g., RSA, ECC), enabling secure data transmission over untrusted networks.

Digital Signature: A cryptographic value derived from a message and a secret key, used to verify the authenticity and integrity of a digital message or document.

Hashing: A technique to convert data into a fixed-size string (hash) that represents the original input, used to verify data integrity (e.g., SHA-256).

Homomorphic Encryption: Enables computation on encrypted data without decrypting it, preserving confidentiality throughout processing.

Differential Privacy: A system for publicly sharing information about a dataset by describing patterns of groups while withholding information about individuals.

Public Key Infrastructure (PKI): A framework that enables secure, encrypted communication and identity verification through the use of digital certificates.

Blockchain: A decentralized, distributed ledger that records transactions across many computers, ensuring transparency, immutability, and traceability.

Smart Contract: Self-executing digital contracts with the terms of the agreement directly written into code, enabled via blockchain.

Quantum Computing: An emerging computing paradigm that uses quantum bits and principles to perform complex calculations faster than classical computers, threatening traditional cryptographic methods.

Quantum-Resistant Cryptography: Cryptographic algorithms that are secure against both classical and quantum computer attacks (e.g., lattice-based, hash-based algorithms).

Zero-Knowledge Proof (ZKP): A cryptographic method where one party proves to another that they know a value without revealing the actual value.

End-to-End Encryption (E2EE): Ensures that only communicating users can read the messages, protecting data during transmission and storage.

Role-Based Access Control (RBAC): A method of restricting system access to authorized users based on their role within an organization.

Multi-Factor Authentication (MFA): An authentication method that requires multiple credentials (e.g., password + OTP or biometrics) for user verification.

Secure Multi-Party Computation (SMPC): A cryptographic protocol enabling multiple parties to jointly compute a function over their inputs while keeping those inputs private.

Chapter 5
Secure IoT Communication in Smart Cities Using Cryptographic Techniques

K. Ganesh Kumar
https://orcid.org/0000-0002-5719-6193
Velalar College of Engineering and Technology, India

M. Rajalakshmi
https://orcid.org/0000-0003-4768-1029
Dr. N.G.P. Institute of Technology, India

N. V. Keerthana
https://orcid.org/0000-0001-8878-2083
Velalar College of Engineering and Technology, India

ABSTRACT

The rapid development of smart cities relies heavily on the Internet of Things (IoT) to enhance urban infrastructure, optimize resource management, and improve citizens' quality of life. However, the increasing interconnectivity of IoT devices raises significant security concerns, including unauthorized access, data breaches, and cyberattacks. Cryptographic techniques play a crucial role in securing IoT communication by ensuring data confidentiality, integrity, and authentication. This chapter explores the application of modern cryptographic solutions such as lightweight encryption algorithms, blockchain-based security models, and post-

DOI: 10.4018/979-8-3373-3326-7.ch005

quantum cryptography in IoT networks. It also discusses key challenges, including computational constraints of IoT devices, scalability, and interoperability, while highlighting potential future research directions for enhancing cryptographic security in smart city IoT infrastructures.

INTRODUCTION

As cities worldwide expand and update, they're becoming more than just concrete and asphalt filled with people and objects—they are intelligent, dynamic entities that are fuelled by technology. At the heart of this upheaval is the Internet of Things (IoT), a sprawling, ever-expanding ecosystem of devices, sensors, and systems that gather and share vast amounts of data across the globe, in real time. From traffic lights that respond to conditions, to energy grids that respond to use, to wearable health devices that broadcast real-time data to medical staff, IoT systems are redefining what it means to be a city. These technologies go beyond automation—they enable the delivery of better public services and enable decision-makers to react more quickly to evolving patterns of demand in urban populations. Yet risks are growing as long as more things are connected. Every linked-up gadget is a possible conduit for cyberattacks. From surveillance cameras and public Wi-Fi to smart streetlights and environmental monitors, each node on the network processes data, some of it highly sensitive. One hacked device could be used as a gateway for hackers, who could gain access to intrusive levels of personal information, cut off key services, or cause mass digital disruption.

Cities are turning to cryptography, one of the pillars of digital security, as a defence. Cryptography is the science of using mathematics to encrypt and decrypt data and to secure computers. It guarantees that the data is kept secret and not modified at the time of transmission, and it is accessed by those to whom it is intended. For smart cities in particular, it's an essential line of defence for a disparate set of systems from parking kiosks to energy grids. However, such cryptographic techniques in IoT-based smart cities come with challenges. A large majority of IoT devices are made small in size, cost, and energy consumption. These devices lack the same memory, processing power, and battery life as laptops or smartphones. Legacy encryption mechanisms such as Rivest Shamir Adleman (RSA) or Advanced Encryption Standard (AES) may be too overhead-demanding for such low-resource threats despite being secure (Rasha and Hammed, 2024). To solve that problem, researchers are looking to lightweight cryptography—a family of encryption schemes designed to efficiently protect less powerful devices. Among the lightweight encryption algorithms, PRESENT, SIMON, and HIGHT provide strong encryption with low energy consumption and reduced memory requirements. Such techniques are also currently being applied for some smart city applications such as smart metering, air quality monitoring, and wearable health devices.

In addition to lightweight cryptography, blockchain is being considered in many urban sciences as a solution for more secure urban data systems. On the Blockchain's immutable ledger, stored information cannot be manipulated, which thereby ensures the authenticity and traceability of transactions. But even with encryption or blockchain, we always need good authentication and access controls (Jebbar et al., 2024). Multi-Factor Authentication (MFA), digital certificates, biometric identification, and role-based access systems make sure that only an authenticated user and device can interact with the sensitive city infrastructure.

LITERATURE REVIEW

The security of IoT-based smart town structures has attracted considerable research attention in recent years, because the proliferation of related devices introduces new vectors for cyber threats. Several studies emphasize the critical role of cryptographic mechanisms in ensuring the confidentiality, integrity, and authenticity of data traversing smart city environments. Khan et al. (2024) spotlight the mixing of blockchain distributed ledger technology in remote sensing for smart cities, demonstrating stronger information integrity and transparency in real-time programs. This aligns with the growing fashion of leveraging blockchain to establish stable communication and garage infrastructures, mainly in decentralized environments where agreement is difficult to set up. Javed et al. (2024) propose a multi-hop IoT communication model that strengthens transmission security, even as addressing puts off troubles in smart city deployments. Their paintings show that routing protocols, whilst combined with encryption mechanisms, can appreciably improve the resilience of records change towards interception and loss.

Similarly, Ahuja et al. (2023) introduce a chaos-mapping gadget for stable transmission of visual statistics, utilizing lightweight encryption to address the constraints of facet IoT gadgets. This displays the need for using resource-efficient algorithms, which include PRESENT, HIGHT, or SPECK in environments with restricted processing energy and memory. Other researchers have explored post-quantum cryptography (Sharma et al., 2023) as a future-evidence approach to securing clever town infrastructure. These strategies are in particular designed to face up to quantum computing attacks, which threaten to compromise present-day uneven encryption protocols like RSA and Elliptic Curve Cryptography (ECC). The role of AI in improving IoT security is likewise gaining traction. Muniswamy and Rathi (2024) provide an overview of using machine learning models to locate anomalies and expect protection breaches in IoT networks, advocating for the combination of AI-pushed risk detection structures into existing cryptographic frameworks.

Moreover, the importance of standardized communication protocols together with Transport Layer Security (TLS), Datagram Transport Layer Security (DTLS), Message Queuing Telemetry Transport (MQTT), and Constrained Application Protocol (CoAP) is nicely highlighted within the literature. These protocols are often adapted to fit the necessities of low-strength, extensive-vicinity IoT networks, providing encrypted communication channels even for lightweight devices. While lots of progress has been made, several authors agree that key management remains one of the most urgent challenges. Managing cryptographic keys at scale, mainly in heterogeneous smart metropolis environments, demands robust and scalable Public Key Infrastructure (PKI) solutions and automatic key rotation structures. Collectively, these studies underscore the multidimensional nature of secure IoT verbal exchange in smart cities. They factor into an evolving panorama where cryptographic innovation ought to keep pace with increasing tool connectivity and the emerging threats of a digitized city future.

ROLE OF IOT IN SMART CITIES

Modernity is moving into an era: cities are rapidly becoming "smart cities"—urban ecosystems augmented with technology to enhance infrastructure, services, and quality of life, as mentioned in Figure 1 (Khan et al., 2024). Central to this revolution is the IoT—a constellation of interconnected devices that collect, share, and interpret data in real-time. By infusing intelligence into transportation, utilities, healthcare, and other critical components, IoT helps cities adapt and evolve into more responsive, efficient, and environmentally friendly. IoT can be dubbed as the nervous system (Khan et al., 2024). The smart city collects data from sensors installed all over the urban context. These devices range from air quality monitors to surveillance cameras, Global Positioning System (GPS) -enabled buses, and smart electricity meters. They interact with centralised platforms and mobile apps to enable informed decision-making and automated responses. Smart waste bins, for example, can tell sanitation departments when they are full (Saleem et al., 2024). Smart traffic systems can alter signal timings based on congestion data. This transfer of information enables city leaders to better run roads, sewers, streetlights, and other urban operations, possibly enabling them to tackle challenges more effectively. But with smart cities increasingly dependent on real-time data, data security and privacy are also major issues. The sensitive nature of the data being collected—from citizen movements to energy usage patterns—means any breach may have serious implications. Hence, protecting communication and supporting trust is an essential part of smart city infrastructure, and cryptographic techniques are fundamental for this purpose.

The heterogeneous nature of smart city IoT systems is one of the greatest challenges they possess. Devices differ in size, processing capabilities, memory, and power limitations. From low-powered sensors to edge servers dealing with video data, these devices still need to talk to each other reliably and across secure channels. But conventional cryptographic techniques (Ahuja, & Gupta, 2023) are often resource-intensive and thus ill-suited to many IoT components. That is where lightweight cryptography comes in — and it is essential. The other algorithms, i.e., PRESENT, HIGHT, SIMON, and SPECK, are oriented towards providing a very strong security with a small power and memory footprint and are targeted towards constrained IoT devices that will be used in applications such as smart lighting, smart parking, and healthcare wearables, etc.

Cryptography (Ahuja et al., 2023) has various roles in IoT-based smart cities. It keeps data confidential by encrypting it, maintains data integrity by detecting unauthorized changes, and provides authentication by ensuring that devices and users are properly identified. That's because without these safeguards, malevolent actors could compromise systems, resulting in potentially catastrophic consequences. In the future, smart traffic lights (Saleem et al., 2024) or electricity metres could be hacked and cause accidents or service disruptions.

Cryptographic approaches are generally of two types: Symmetric and asymmetric. Symmetric algorithms, such as AES, are speedier and more efficient, thus perfect for time-critical applications. Yet both parties have to have a shared secret key, which is hard to manage at the scale of millions of devices. This restriction is solved with the help of asymmetric Cryptography that implements public and private keys for communication between two unknown parties. Asymmetric methods, and in particular, the ECC algorithm, have become a trend in IoT contexts since the required key size is much smaller than that of RSA, providing a secure design with relatively low computational costs. Figure 1 shows the various smart city applications that use IoT to address societal problems.

Figure 1. Smart city IoT applications

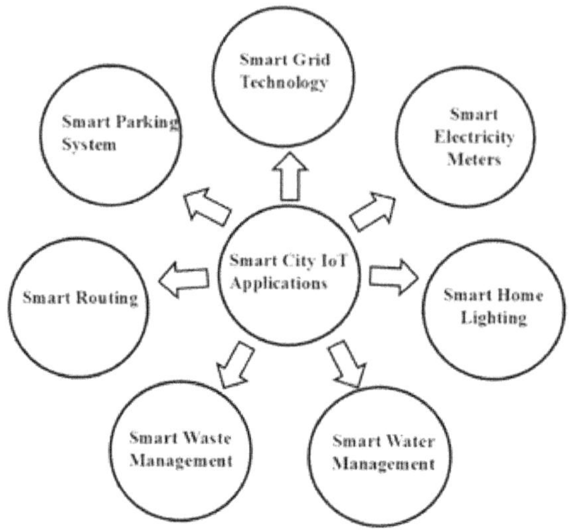

Blockchain technology, alongside traditional cryptography, is emerging as a powerful tool for securing IoT communications in smart cities. Blockchain (Padma & Ramaiah, 2024) is a decentralized, tamper-evident way of writing down data and transactions. Its cryptographic underpinnings make it impossible to change what has been added without discovery. This is especially applicable in use cases such as Peer-to-Peer (P2P) energy trading, ride-sharing, and digital identity. Blockchain is also already being implemented in smart city projects in places like Dubai, various European countries, and North America, with the technology already being used for secure storage of citizen data and even electric vehicle charging.

Authentication access control (Padma & Ramaiah, 2024) is another critical factor in IoT security for smart cities. Authenticated devices are only validated, ensuring authorized access to the network. To validate identities, digital certificates, biometric data, or cryptographic signatures are used. Access control models — role-based or attribute-based access — limit access to data and systems to authorized users only, a critical consideration in industries like healthcare, in which confidentiality of patient data is paramount. Standard protocols for secure communication have been adapted to work for IoTs. Different protocols for different use cases have been optimized, e.g., Transport Layer Security (TLS), Datagram Transport Layer Security (DTLS), Message Queuing Telemetry Transport (MQTT), Constrained Application Protocol (CoAP), etc. CoAP is suited for constrained devices in home automation, while MQTT allows for real-time messaging in logistics and industrial IoT, as examples.

Many smart cities across the globe (Padma & Ramaiah, 2024) have already deployed secure IoT systems. It uses robust PKI to manage its digital certificates and encrypt (Javed et al., 2024) its data for transport and environmental monitoring. Barcelona uses lightweight encryption in its smart lighting systems to securely communicate with control centers. As the asymmetric cryptography and blockchain are combined, it secures the system parking and increases the public trust. New York City's Cyber Command watches over its critical infrastructure 24/7, using cryptographic tools and AI to find and react to threats.

Though progress has been made, challenges still exist. One of the biggest is key management, finding a way to generate, distribute, and rotate cryptographic keys in a secure way at scale. Moreover, the multitude of manufacturers and standards creates interoperability problems. Moreover, the threat landscape is always changing, and what is secure today could be exposed tomorrow.

Post-quantum cryptography techniques to make them viable on quantum computers should be vetted by developers and administrators ahead of time to future-proof smart cities. Another step forward is integrating (Khan et al., 2024). AI and machine learning for threat detection and a dynamic response. Most importantly, security should never be an afterthought — that is, designing in cryptographic protections from the outset must be a governing principle. IoT security has a human element as well. Everyone — developers, city planners, policymakers, and citizens — needs to understand the implications of cybersecurity on the smart city. Systems will be secure, interoperable, and cost-effective on account of public awareness, training, and international commonality on the standards.

SECURITY CHALLENGES IN IOT COMMUNICATION

As smart cities continue to grow, the dependence on the IoT for real-time data gathering and communication poses unique security challenges. These cities use thousands — if not millions — of devices and connect them to manage public services, infrastructure, and safety systems. Although this level of interconnectedness is critical for efficiency and automation, it also dramatically increases the attack surface, exposing IoT devices (Ahmad et al., 2024). Networks are exposed to many threats. The details become one of the main problems of limited resources in most IoT devices. These devices are designed to be low-cost and energy-efficient, focusing on low processing power, memory, and storage. As a result, they are typically unable to support conventional, strong security features such as advanced encryption or multi-factor authentication. That makes enforcing strong security without overloading the devices or draining their batteries difficult.

To make matters worse, there are no universal standards across the IoT space. The real issue is that there is no single framework that can guarantee consistent security practices across all devices and platforms due to the continuously evolving nature of IoT development, which is most often vendor-driven and involves proprietary technologies. There is less ability to manage and secure devices across the spectrum in a standardized way, which leads to all kinds of security holes (Joshi & Sulaiman, 2024) and integration challenges. The 4th Industrial Revolution is underway with the rapid rise of smart cities and the increasing wealth of data exchanged between devices. From mobile devices and changing topologies to massive amounts of data, IoT networks need to deal with all of these while preserving confidentiality, integrity, and availability. Figure 2 indicates the various security challenges in data management and distribution techniques used in smart city applications.

Figure 2. Security and data management

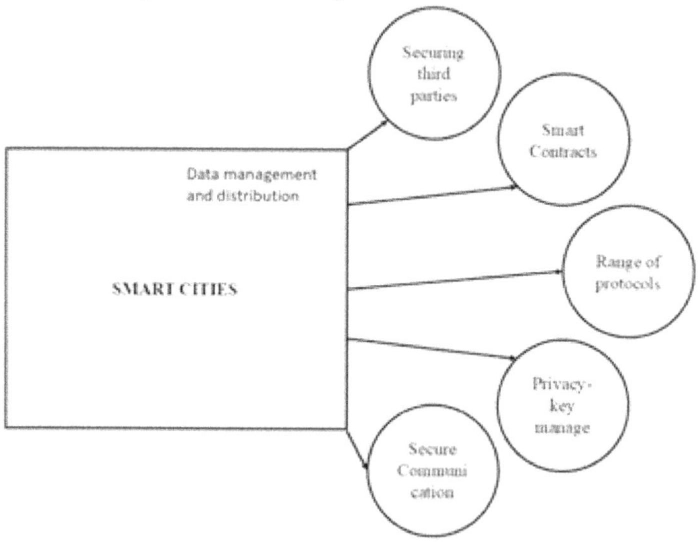

Administrators have a colossal challenge configuring and managing device identities, authenticating users and sensors, and updating access credentials across a large, decentralized network.

Privacy is another major issue. Devices within a smart city ecosystem (Muniswamy & Rathi, 2024) often collect sensitive information, from personal identifiers and location data to video feeds and health metrics. If this data is not encrypted and access-controlled, it can be intercepted or accessed by unauthorized parties. The implications of such violations are not merely technical but social, and they can erode citizen trust, cause reputational harm, and, in case the data is misused, lead to physical damage. Then, ensuring the communication is authentic and not fake is just as important. With the potential to spoof a valid device, an attacker could intervene with record streams to modify the statistics or introduce potentially dangerous instructions to the machine. This type of spoofing or tampering can be very critical, specifically if it involves important infrastructure, such as visitors' lights, energy grids, or emergency services.

There is also a physical security challenge. Many IoT (Muniswamy & Rathi, 2024) Devices are deployed outdoors or in remote locations, such as streetlights, traffic poles, or waste bins, and hence are prone to tampering, theft, or physical damage. When compromised, attackers can extract credentials or inject malicious firmware, making the device a potential attack point against the entire network. Aside from targeted attacks, denial-of-service (DoS) and distributed denial-of-service (DDoS) attacks can render IoT systems unresponsive. These attacks can inundate devices or networks with traffic, distracting them from anything else. Indeed, these types of botnets made up exclusively of hacked IoT devices have already been deployed to carry out some of the most disruptive DDoS attacks in history. With the sheer scale and prominence of IoT in smart cities, the opportunities for large-scale disruption are a tangible threat. Another vulnerability that is often overlooked is that of the communication protocols themselves. Many of them use lightweight protocols — like MQTT or CoAP — which optimize for efficiency rather than security. Examples include protocols that are not supported or shunned, such as Witty or MEG (Message Later), these are ineffective without a strong cryptographic layer and can be exploited or eavesdropped on by those who wish to listen in on your devices (Double bass, Message Replay).

The last long-term challenge is managing the lifecycle of IoT devices. Devices can stay in use for long periods, but might not get ongoing maintenance or software upgrades. Without patches, known vulnerabilities become exploit code, which translates to persistent backdoors that can work their way through even a smart city network (Rishiwal et al., 2024). Outdated firmware and unsupported hardware become the weakest links in otherwise secure systems in many cases. Verily, the security challenges with which IoT communication in smart cities is confronted are multiple and complex, and emerge as an inherent property of the architecture of current systems. Whether its motherboard components that can't find anything but ConnectX or host DevSecOps that can't get their real-time network data, we are constantly fighting the uphill battle of getting secure communication between devices. To overcome these challenges, not only are technology solutions needed, but also cooperation between various governments, manufacturers, and researchers is needed to come up with scalable, standardized, and future-proof security practices.

CRYPTOGRAPHIC TECHNIQUES FOR SECURE COMMUNICATION

Cryptography (Ahuja et al., 2023) of multiple types, the most elementary form is symmetric encryption. This method employs the same cryptographic key to encrypt and decrypt the data, as shown in Figure 3. Its key advantage is speed and efficiency, suitable in situations in which both parties already trust each other and have confidence in the key exchange method. Common symmetric encryption algorithms include the Advanced Encryption Standard (AES) and Blowfish. They are widely used in Virtual Private Networks (VPNs), file encryption systems, and secure video conferencing platforms, as shown in Figure 4.

By contrast, asymmetric encryption (or public-key cryptography) uses a two-key system: a public key that is made available to anyone to use and a private key that only its owner knows. If a party wants to send a secret message, it can do so using the other party's public key to encrypt it. The message may only be decrypted by the receiver with their associated private key. This kind of encryption exists at the base layer of secure email, digital identity verification, and site security (the little padlock you see in your web browser). RSA and ECC are among the most well-known asymmetric encryption techniques. In addition to shielding the confidentiality of messages, cryptography also protects the integrity of facts — that is, it allows structures and customers to verify the authenticity of records. This is where the cryptographic hash functions come in. A hash function produces a unique fixed-length fingerprint for a specific dataset. Any change in the data, even with a single character, will provide a vastly different hash value, making tampering obvious. While it is not possible to run a reverse hash to get back to the data we already had, we can still do this, or check that their data has not been tampered with. SHA-256 is a commonly used example of a one-way function that is critical for blockchain technology (Rishiwal et al., 2024) and password protection.

One more powerful cryptographic tool is the digital signature. That is an online stamp of authenticity. By signing a document digitally, someone is using their private key to verify their identity and signal that the material has not been modified since it was signed.

The recipient can then verify the signature with the sender's public key. Digital signatures (Irshad et al., 2023) are key components in many modern digital applications, such as electronic contracts, secure software updates, and cryptocurrency transactions. A big challenge in secure communication is key exchange (how to share the cryptographic keys), especially in cases where the parties do not meet physically. This is tackled by key exchange algorithms. Diffie–Hellman key exchange: One of the first and most widely known approaches, the Diffie–Hellman key exchange. This protocol allows two parties to agree upon a secret key in a way that is resistant to eavesdropping. A more optimized and secure version of Ephemeral Diffie-Hellman (DHE) is called Elliptic-Curve Diffie–Hellman (ECDH), which offers enhanced performance and is widely used by secure messaging applications and Virtual Private Network (VPN) services. Figure 3 shows the cryptographic techniques involved in the secure communication process.

Figure 3. Cryptographic techniques for secure communication

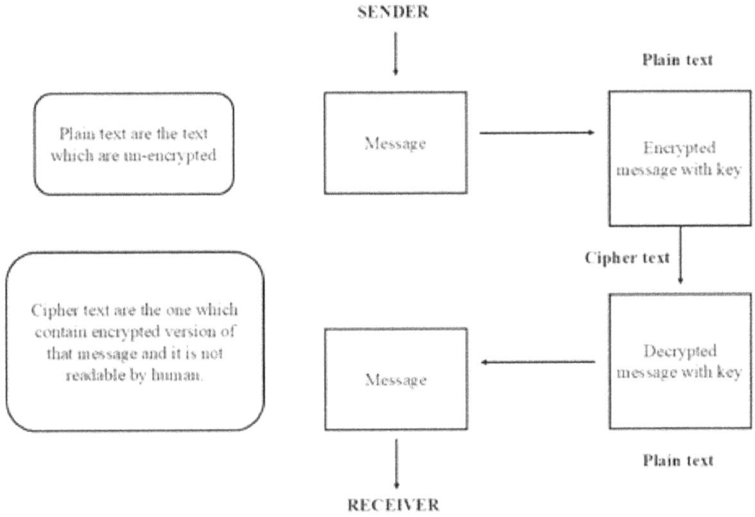

Transport Layer Security (TLS) (Padma & Ramaiah, 2024) Works in the background to keep everyday activities on the web secure. If a website address starts with "https://," that means TLS is enabled. It authenticates the website, encrypts the communication, and blocks eavesdropping. TLS is an integral part of securing online banking, e-commerce transactions, and general web browsing. The Public Key Infrastructure (PKI) is the basis of much of online trust. PKI is built upon trusted entities — Certificate Authorities (CAs). These organizations provide digital certificates to websites and services to prove their legitimacy. Your web browser looks up these certificates to decide whether a site is trustworthy. If something seems suspicious, the browser displays a warning message like "This connection isn't private.

As strong as these cryptographic technologies are, there are still weaknesses in the system. One of the major issues is key management — that is, the secure generation, distribution, and storage of encryption (Ahuja et al., 2023) keys. Furthermore, human fallibility continues to be a primary weakness. Even the best encryption systems can be negated by poor password habits, open to phishing attacks, and mis-configured systems. In terms of the future, quantum computing presents a major threat to current cryptographic standards. The faster calculations performed by these quantum machines would have the ability to break encryption that classical computers would take millennia to decrypt. To combat this impending threat, scientists are already creating post-quantum cryptographic methods; lattice cryptography, hash-based signature schemes, and more exist. These new technologies are designed to be resilient in a future in which quantum computers are practical to use. Figure 4 indicates the various cryptographic techniques used to provide security in IoT devices.

Figure 4. Cryptographic security in IoT device

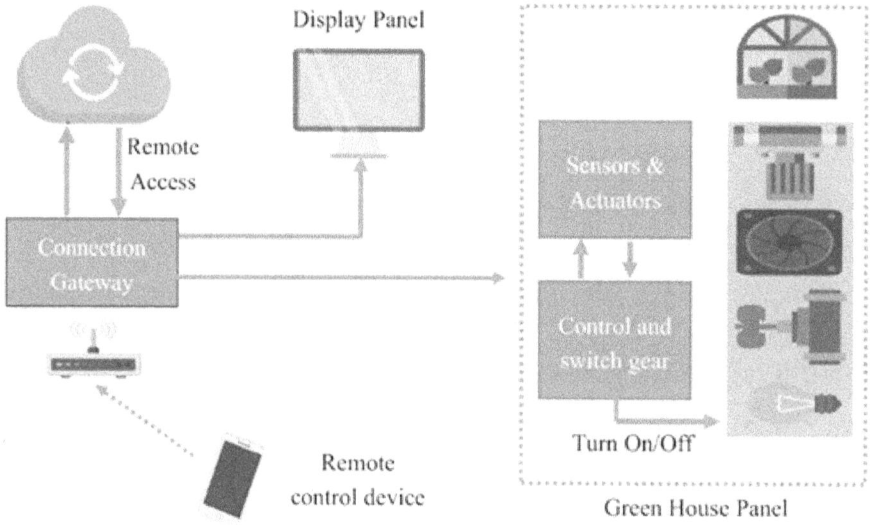

All in all, cryptography is an omnipresent but often hidden force standing between us and an irreversible rupture of fundamental rights. Whether it's shielding your private messages and online banking transactions or verifying that an update for your software, or a digital report, is certainly coming from who you observed it's far, cryptography is an important part of our modern digital infrastructure. In an era wherein the era is unexpectedly evolving and cyber threats have become more and more state-of-the-art, cryptography should also evolve, safeguarding the integrity, confidentiality, and authenticity of virtual communication for generations to come.

CRYPTOGRAPHIC PROTOCOLS IN IOT COMMUNICATION

Blockchain (Khan et al., 2024) and DLT has revolutionized the very notion of trust, transparency, and security in digital systems. Blockchain was first defined in 2008 because of the era at the advent of Bitcoin, but it is unexpectedly evolving into a ubiquitous era with potential use far beyond simply cryptocurrency. Both blockchain and other forms of DLT provide decentralized, tamper-evident, and transparent strategies for recording transactions and handling information. That approach has made way for solutions in different industries such as finance, healthcare, supply chains, and even government services, as shown in Figure 5.

At a fundamental level, a blockchain is a form of distributed ledger in which data is combined into blocks. Each block consists of a chain of records or transactions, linked to the previous block through cryptography (Habib, & Chishti, 2023). Methods that ensure a continuous or unbroken chain. Once a block is appended to the chain, it's virtually impossible to revise that block without changing every block after it, which requires the consensus of most participants of the network. This immutability is not only built-in, but it also makes blockchain highly secure against tampering or fraud. Unlike this block structure, distributed ledger technologies do not always use this. They address a wider variety of decentralized data-sharing technologies as shown in Table 1. It is precisely because the data is shared across many nodes in all DLT systems that consensus algorithms are leveraged to ensure updates are validated and agreement is reached on what the state of the system is. Alternative data structures and consensus models are used by some, like Internet of Things Application (IoTA's) Tangle, Hedera Hashgraph, but are still targeted towards similar goals of decentralization and trust.

One of the most groundbreaking concepts that blockchain (Saleem et al., 2024) brought to us was the ability to create "trustless" systems, that is, when two or more parties can conduct transactions, or trust each other's data, without needing a third-party authority such as a bank or a notary. This is done via smart contracts, self-running programs coded directly onto the blockchain. Such contracts enforce the terms of an agreement as soon as the specified conditions are fulfilled. Automation eliminates human errors, guarantees faster transactions, and reduces costs by cutting out intermediaries. In economic services, this concept is the inspiration for Decentralized Finance (DeFi), which is taking bigger strides. DeFi structures provide on-chain offerings along with loans, financial savings, bills, trading, and yield farming, which can be available across the clock and worldwide. These systems are built to be transparent and inclusive, probably increasing get right of entry to thousands and thousands who have confined get right of entry to bank offerings. Beyond finance, blockchain and Distributed Ledger Technology (DLTs) are also reworking sectors, inclusive of supply chain management. These gears, which enable stakeholders to follow items' trips from uncooked material to final delivery in real-time, in the end foster authenticity and decrease opportunities for fraud. This potential is specifically important in sectors where best practices and traceability are vital, consisting of prescription drugs, food safety, and comfort goods. Each time a product modification is made, this transaction is recorded in the ledger. Thus, both companies and purchasers can believe that the product is ethically sourced and legitimate. Figure 5 depicts the various cryptographic protocols used in the IoT Communication to provide better security.

Figure 5. Cryptographic protocol in IoT communication

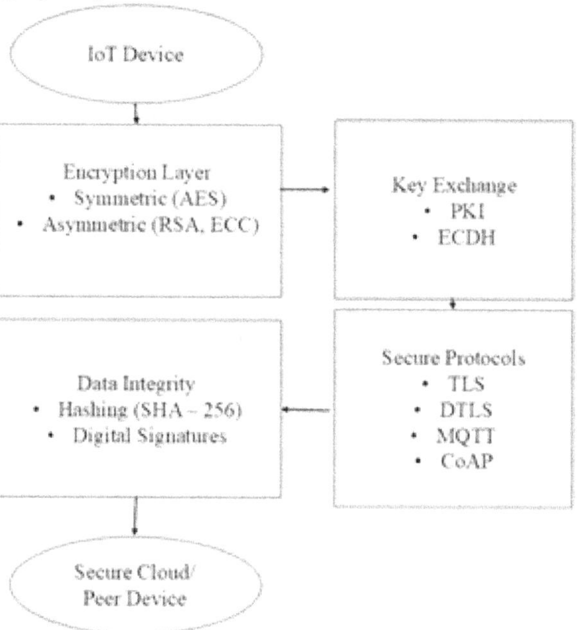

The healthcare area is also leveraging the generation to save and manipulate records securely. Using allotted ledger technology, clinical information may be encrypted and accessed only through approved customers, maintaining each's confidentiality and facilitating statistical sharing among medical caregivers. This may also bring about advanced diagnoses, simplified remedies, and less administrative overhead. Another promising use of blockchain is for drug traceability—ensuring that pharmaceutical products remain authentic all along their supply chain to combat counterfeit medications. And worldwide governments are starting to look into blockchain for a range of public sector purposes. Blockchain (Rishiwal et al., 2024)-primarily based virtual identification answers empower people with ownership and manipulate of their private data, permitting them to use a steady and streamlined approach to authentication than cutting-edge ID schemes. Blockchain-primarily based systems hold promise for reinforcing the transparency and security of balloting strategies, thereby minimizing election fraud and boosting public believe. Likewise, land registries stored on a blockchain are tamper-proof and defend against corruption or dispute by ensuring possession facts are correct and transparent.

Although blockchain (Rishiwal et al., 2024) and DLTs bring lots of advantages, but they also have their challenges and issues to consider. Scalability is a significant challenge, particularly for public block-chains utilizing Proof of Work (PoW) mechanisms for consensus-building. Layer 2 protocols, sharding, and recent consensus protocols — also called the Proof of Stake (PoS) and Delegated Proof of Stake (DPoS) protocols — are coming together to address this challenge and improve performance without compromising security.

Energy consumption is also a concern, especially with PoW systems like Bitcoin that need huge amounts of computing power and energy to function. This dovetailed with environmental impact, spurring interest in more sustainable alternatives. PoS, for example, greatly reduces energy consumption by eliminating mining in favor of a mechanism in which validators are selected according to how many tokens they hold and are prepared to "stake" as a deposit. Interoperability is another key area of focus. As such, we see a growing number of blockchain platforms (Rishiwal et al., 2024), and with this, a pressing need for cross-chain communication. Examples of these interoperability mysteries, the tasks that can be hidden under the hood of a decentralized network, like a car engine. Table 1 show the comparison of various metrics and its range considered for the performance evaluation of the proposed system.

Table 1. Comparison of component metrics and range

Component	Metric	Typical Value / Range
AES	Encryption Time (128-bit block)	< 1 ms on constrained MCU
ECC	Key Length	256 bits (equivalent to 3072-bit RSA)
RSA-2048	Key Generation Time	~500 ms (on low-power device)
MQTT	Bandwidth Consumption	~10–30 bytes per message
CoAP	Payload Size	~4–10 bytes (UDP-based)
DLT (IoTA)	Confirmation Time	< 10 sec

Another serious hurdle is regulatory uncertainty. World governments are still figuring out how to classify and regulate blockchain-based assets and systems. In many jurisdictions, questions about taxation, compliance, and client protection cross unresolved. A coherent and cohesive criminal framework is vital to ensure the continuing increase and mainstream attractiveness of blockchain technologies. As of October 2023, pick governments have begun issuing chapters and policies to determine whether or not to make changes in these areas greater deeply, but international consensus is still in development. While those issues are extensive, they do not diminish the capability that blockchain and DLTs have to fundamentally change the manner in wherein we store, process, and confirm records. These technologies are consequently setting up the principles for an extra decentralized, obvious, and stable digital international. Be it improving financial inclusion, protecting the integrity of the supply chain, or computer guarding the interests of users, blockchain and DLTs are set to create an extensive and enduring impact.

USE CASES IN SMART CITIES

Urban life is being reshaped by smart cities. To advance these goals, they leverage digital technologies and data-driven approaches to enhance citizens' quality of life, improve efficiencies across city services, and support sustainable long-term growth. At the heart of these intelligent systems lies the new wave of innovations disrupting industries, including the IoT, the power of (Khan et al., 2024) Artificial Intelligence (AI), data analytics, blockchain, and Distributed Ledger Technologies (DLT). These are just small puzzle pieces fitting into one another and forming an intelligent ecosystem that reacts based on the data received. These things, in turn, optimize the working of the cities in the present world. The transportation and traffic management domain are the most prominent smart city technology application. It employs IoT-based sensors embedded in roads, vehicles, and traffic signals to monitor vehicle flow, optimize signal timings and reduce congestion. By analyzing traffic patterns, AI-enabled tools assist urban planners in making proactive decisions. Intelligent parking systems are among them, and aid drivers in real time with finding free parking spaces, thereby reducing the time spent searching for a parking space and lessening carbon emissions. Better route planning and on-time arrival have just become easier with real-time tracking, while digital ticketing adds more flexibility for the passengers, improving the overall commuting experience.

Another area where smart cities (Khan et al., 2024) are contributing a lot is energy management. Smart grids with sensors and artificial intelligence allow them to track the production and consumption of electricity more effectively. It can also adapt quickly to changes in energy demand and facilitates the integration of renewable energy sources, such as solar and wind power. Retail smart meters or smart meters at the consumer's place provide real-time information, and with many households with smart meters, the ability to conserve energy and improve your electricity bill is also possible. Even street lighting, a no-brainer, is becoming smart, as LEDs, the kind that can adjust to the time of day or foot traffic, can save dramatically on energy and operating costs. The waste management – Smart technologies have also transformed. Sensors atop trash bins can sense just how full they are and alert services when to come collect. That helps garbage trucks route more effectively, reducing unnecessary trips and fuel use. It also makes streets cleaner. Another application is recycling, where AI-powered systems can sort materials automatically and more accurately than a human worker, thus increasing recycling and reducing landfill waste.

Smart city (Javed et al., 2024) technologies also provide useful tools for another key area: water management. Sensors embedded throughout the water infrastructure measure pressure, flow rate, and water quality. It allows cities to detect leaks or inefficiencies and respond in real time, thereby helping conserve water and reduce the cost of maintenance. And entrees and other green spaces are receiving smart irrigation systems that provide optimal watering schedules based on data and soil moisture readings. The result is more landscape, less water waste. The foundation for every city's success is safety and security, and intelligent cities use (Khan et al., 2024) AI-enabled surveillance systems, emergency response coordination platforms, and predictive policing tools to increase public safety. Advanced video analytics specifically, can detect abnormal behavior, enabling law enforcement to respond faster to threats. Emergency response systems are integrated so that fire departments, medical teams, and police can coordinate locally more effectively. Forecasting tools provide an early warning signal to agencies about high-risk areas or crimes that have not yet been committed, which mitigates potential crimes.

In the realm of governance, blockchain-based digital identity prevents fraud while providing seamless access to public services through e-governance platforms. Residents can pay their taxes, file documents, and even vote online using a single digital ID. They improve accessibility to government services with less bureaucracy and more transparency. Blockchain (Saleem et al., 2024) can also assist land management by establishing immutable property records that protect citizens from fraud and facilitate property transfers.

All these activities also support the idea of sensor-based monitoring, that one of the important aspects that smart cities aim for is environmental sustainability. For instance, they can collect real-time data on air quality, noise pollution, temperature, and humidity. This is crucial information enforcement of environmental regulations and exposure management in public health. These AI systems (Khan et al., 2024) can detect pollution trends and advise them on measures they can take to reduce pollution, resulting in a healthier urban environment. These smart cities are getting smarter and also making advances in healthcare. Citizens can also make the delivery of medical care more convenient by using tools such as wearable health trackers, AI diagnostics, and video telemedicine platforms. They also help enable remote patient monitoring to limit inpatient visits and help with chronic conditions. This would enable emergency services to respond to medical incidents more rapidly, employing GPS and real-time location data to arrive on-scene sooner, which can be a matter of life and death.

The other domain upended via technology is education. Online classrooms, customized learning platforms, and digital resources are transforming education to be more flexible and accessible. AI tools can customize content to an individual student's learning style, increasing engagement and outcomes. To ensure that school students from all strata can participate in the digital learning revolution, smart cities are also creating infrastructural connectivity. Smart cities, though, at their core are about how technology can help create better communities — more sustainable, more efficient, and more responsive to constituent needs. Applications that can take advantage of smart cities are various, from reduced road congestion, energy consumption, and user safety, to life and education improvement. As the planet continues to urbanize, as we face complex challenges: climate change, scarcity of resources, etc., the role of technology in determining the design of resilient, livable urban environments will be even more critical.

CRYPTOGRAPHIC SOLUTIONS FOR SECURE IOT COMMUNICATION IN SMART CITIES: GLOBAL CASE STUDIES

As cities worldwide become increasingly connected with technology, ensuring that all that data stays safe is more important than ever. Cryptography — the science of securing information — is no longer just an idea for researchers or cybersecurity experts. It's out there being used in smart cities to make urban life safer, more efficient, and more trustworthy.

Take Singapore, for example. A lot of you have probably heard of the Singapore Smart Nation initiative, where Singapore deployed huge IoT networks across public infrastructure The St. Louis city deploys cryptographic tools to secure data (Sharma, & Saleem, 2023). For everything from public transit and surveillance systems to environmental monitoring. A way to verify devices (PKI: Public Key Infrastructure), to ensure only 'trusted' devices can send and receive information. To safeguard the real information sent over, the system is utilizing end-to-end encryption with AES, one of the most reliable encryption standards. And in areas like waste management and logistics, blockchain is keeping records secure and tamper-proof.

In Barcelona, the city has looked to smart lighting systems to enhance energy usage and public safety. But these systems also need protection." As many IoT devices have limited processing capabilities, lightweight encryption techniques such as the PRESENT algorithm are used. Streetlight-to-control center communications are encrypted using DTLS, so hackers can't interject themselves into the system or snoop on the data. And it is a nice codicil to show how the right cryptographic tools can protect even small devices.

Amsterdam is getting crafty with its parking scheme. This is done via encrypted digital tokens for cars to access previously reserved parking spots, instead of the most common ways. Every transaction is safely logged onto a blockchain, and asymmetric encryption ensures that all communication between vehicles and infrastructure is secure. It's a high-tech method of reducing fraud and keeping things going.

In New York City, that security takes a more urgent form. The emergency services and surveillance networks process sensitive data like live video and emergency communications, so encryption (Ahuja et al., 2023) is essential. RSA and ECC are used by the city to protect this critical information. Moreover, centralized key management systems help provide access fast at the times it is most needed, but also keep everything secure. This allows emergency teams to respond more quickly while protecting data from potential cyberattacks.

On the other hand, in Dubai, smart hospitals are transforming the system of healthcare. Wearable IoT devices track patients' vital signs in real time and send the data to securely encrypted cloud systems based on a concept called homomorphic encryption. That's particularly powerful because the data can be processed without needing to be decrypted, ensuring patient information remains private even during analysis. Throw in biometric authentication for staff access, and you have a system that respects both privacy and efficiency in health care.

These examples highlight the role that cryptography (Ahuja et al., 2023). Already plays in how our cities run. There are, of course, challenges. It can get a bit complex to manage all these cryptographic keys that are needed for these systems. Devices can't always overcome hardware limits inside their boxes, and getting everything to collaborate over disparate networks and standards isn't easy. Cities are, however, working around these menaces, customizing their security tactics as per their distinct necessities.

One of the big lessons learned from these real-world applications is that no one cryptographic approach alone is sufficient. Instead, a combination of approaches tends to be more effective. While symmetric encryption performs much faster, asymmetric methods are used more for securely sharing keys. Blockchain can be beneficial for maintaining transparent records, and lightweight encryption creates a system where even low-power devices can be kept secure. While the role may seem understated, ultimately, cryptography is the quiet backbone behind how modern smart cities can run. By keeping data secure, protecting privacy, and ensuring that only the right people and devices can access sensitive systems, cryptographic tools are helping cities build trust and use their resources more efficiently in a connected environment.

FUTURE DIRECTIONS AND RECOMMENDATIONS

As we move further forward into the 21st century, it is becoming painfully clear that we have made great strides in technology and innovation, as well as policy, but the road ahead is a long and arduous one. The challenges we face today — from social inequality to climate change — insist that we not only have to act, we have to think differently. The way we broaden our perspective, use technology wisely, redefine leadership, and center people and the planet in development is how we shall determine the future.

Much of the advancement in research and policy has developed under restrictively narrow lenses. In the future, not only must we include more voices, particularly the voices of those who were previously excluded, but also a wider variety of types of knowledge, including lived experience, cultural knowledge, and wisdom. Instead of championing short-term victories, we need to prioritize long-term impact and draw lessons from successes and failures around the world.

Blockchain Technology (Ahmad et al., 2024) is a powerful tool, but its potential for good or bad depends on how it's wielded. The future demands a more intelligent relationship with technology — one focused on leveraging artificial intelligence and big data to address the real problems people face, and ensuring that this technology is accessible to everyone. This is how information should be shared: safely and more equitably. But the most urgent thing we need to do in technology is to bake in privacy, fairness, and consider the unintended consequences as we build things.

Equally important is leadership and policy reform, which were apparent. Councils of participation should be fluid, multidisciplinary, and based on evidence and lived experience. Communities shouldn't just be invited to help shape the policies that affect them after decisions have already been made; they need to be brought in at the starting line. Cross-sector collaboration — between governments, businesses, nonprofits, and citizens — is key to making meaningful, just change.

At the heart of all progress are people. It is important to invest in education, leadership development, health, and well-being. We need to see a school system that moves beyond rote memorization and "teaching to the test," focusing instead on fostering creativity and emotional intelligence alongside problem-solving skills. Upskilling is certainly important, particularly during a time of rapid technological change, to make sure that workers are empowered and future generations are ready and confident. It will create a society that is more resilient and resourceful. Supporting mental health and holistic well-being will lead to a more resilient company and society.

Things like sustainability should not be an afterthought; It needs to become a guiding tenet of public policy, economic planning, and technological innovation. We should see circular economies that reduce waste and favor reuse become the standard.

Investing in green infrastructure, clean energy, and climate-resilient communities is essential if we want to be able to leave the planet intact for future generations.

Measurement is another key area. Without the right metrics and tracking systems in place, improvement can be hard to measure. Data collection that is reliable and real-time, transparency, and community access to data are needed. That visa information enables accountability and better decision-making. Some call it data, but it can tell a story and help make a difference when numbers count.

These should be non-negotiable pillars of future planning — fairness and inclusion. It is imperative to recognize and tear down systemic barriers, make technology more inclusive, and ensure that leadership and decision-making bodies mirror the diversity of the people they serve. Equity cannot just be a buzzword; it must be baked into action and policy. Finally, the way we communicate these ideas will ultimately determine how well they are accepted and put into practice. You have to distil complex ideas and communicate them in relatable ways. Ideas can come to life with storytelling, visuals, and digital tools, driving engagement. And the best way to improve is to create spaces — both online and offline — for people to be able to share their ideas, to ask questions, and to learn from one another.

Thus, the future is a mixture of opportunities and challenges. If we commit to education, collaboration, listening, and prioritizing inclusivity and sustainability then we truly can be the change the world needs and create a better world for everyone.

COMPARATIVE ANALYSIS OF CRYPTOGRAPHIC APPROACHES

Within modern digital infrastructure, cryptography has turned out to be an essential aspect of its structure. Building on this narrative, cryptography (Khan et al., 2024) has constantly been a game-changer in securing data; from defensive emails and online banking transactions to stopping categorized authorities' communications from reaching the wrong hands, cryptographic systems allow information integrity, confidentiality, and authenticity. Over the years, specific cryptographic methods have emerged and feature their benefits and disadvantages. As we delve into the comparative evaluation of cryptographic systems, we can discuss the 3 leading kinds of cryptosystems—symmetric key cryptography, asymmetric key cryptography, and hash capabilities—and explore rising technologies like quantum cryptography and homomorphic encryption.

Symmetric encryption (Ahuja et al., 2023) is one of the most widely used and oldest techniques of cryptography. It employs a common key for encryption and decryption. Some commonly used algorithms are Advanced Encryption Standard, DES (Data Encryption Standard), and Blowfish. One of the strengths of symmetric encryption is its speed and efficiency, making it perfect for encrypting large quantities of information. But there are critical barriers to symmetric cryptography. The key distribution is the largest assignment both parties need to get right of entry to an identical mystery key, but one that couldn't be discovered by a 3rd party. However, in the context of big systems, in which many people exist, dealing with and exchanging these keys securely will become complex and dangerous. Once a key is compromised, all records encrypted with that secret are no longer secure.

Asymmetric encryption (Ahuja et al., 2023), additionally called public-key cryptography, solves the important aspect of distribution hassle through the use of key pairs: one key (the public key) is used to encrypt information, and the alternative (the private key) is used to decrypt it. The maximum well-known asymmetric algorithms are RSA, ECC, and DSA. This approach strengthens protection, in particular for verbal exchange through insecure channels, which include the internet. It also offers wireless signature capabilities, providing an added layer of verification for both identities and the integrity of the message. Asymmetric encryption is slower and more computationally expensive compared to symmetric encryption, thus, it is not ideal for encrypting huge amounts of data. Comparison Table of different cryptographic methods is shown below in Table 2.

Table 2. Comparison of different cryptographic methods

Method	Key Size (bits)	Speed	Security Level
Symmetric	128/ 192/256	Very Fast	High
Asymmetric	2048/ 3072	Slow	High (with >2048-bit)
Hash	256	Fast	High
Quantum	Quantum bits (qbits)	Experimental	Theoretical Max
Homomorphic	2048+ (varies)	Very Slow	High

Hash functions belong to a different group of cryptographic elements that use no encryption or decryption. Instead, they accept an input and return a fixed-length output, nicknamed a hash or digest. Examples of hash functions include Secure Hash Algorithm-2 (SHA-2), Secure Hash Algorithm-3 (SHA-3), and Message-Digest Algorithm 5 (MD5). The cryptographic hash functions are commonly used for ensuring data integrity, storing passwords securely, as well as in digital signatures. A good hash function must not be reverse-engineered (producing the original input from the hash) nor allow collisions (producing the same hash for different inputs). Yet if a hash algorithm is open to collisions, which could mean the systems built on top of it are vulnerable.

Quantum computing is still emerging as a field. Progress, however, is unpredictable, and threats to traditional cryptographic systems loom. It is based on two fundamental principles of cryptography, namely the factoring of large integers and the problem of discrete logarithms, which underlie RSA and ECC, respectively. That's where quantum cryptography comes in. Quantum Key Distribution (QKD) is one of the well-known techniques that leverages the principles of quantum mechanics for secure key distribution. The most famous of these QKD protocols is the Bennett-Brassard 1984 protocol (BB84), which ensures that when an eavesdropper tries to intercept the communication, it changes the quantum state and alerts the communicating entities. Although quantum cryptography is extremely secure in theory, it is still in its early days, practically speaking. For it to go mainstream, then scalability, cost, and environmental stability issues need to be solved.

Homomorphic encryption is an emerging technology that facilitates computations on encrypted data without decrypting it. It is especially useful in applications such as secure cloud computing and privacy-preserving data analysis. There are kinds of homomorphic encryption—partially, somewhat, and fully homomorphic encryption—all with functionality and performance to a greater or lesser degree. Fully Homomorphic Encryption (FHE) allows for unlimited operations over ciphertexts, but it is still impractical for even the most real-world applications based on this approach due to the high computational cost. Comparison Table of examples of Different Cryptographic Methods is shown in Table 3.

Table 3. Comparison table of examples of different cryptographic methods

Method	Example	Pros	Cons
Symmetric	AES, DES, Blowfish	Fast, Good for large data	Hard to share keys, risk if the key is leaked
Asymmetric	RSA, ECC, DSA	Safer key sharing supports digital signatures.	Slower, uses more power
Hash Functions	SHA-2, SHA-3, MD5	Checks data integrity, stores passwords.	No encryption can have collisions.
Quantum	QKD (e.g., BB84 protocol)	Very secure, detects spying	Expensive, not ready for wide use
Homomorphic	Partially, Somewhat, Fully HE	Can compute on encrypted data	Very slow, not practical yet

Every cryptographic method has its specific use case, benefits, and drawbacks. Symmetric cryptography is fast and efficient, but has difficulties in key distribution. Asymmetric encryption eliminates the key distribution problem and enables two parties to digitally sign a message, but it is slow and computationally expensive. Hash functions provide good integrity verification and are suitable for password storage, however, they are vulnerable to collision attacks if not updated. Quantum cryptography promises theoretically unbreakable security, but so far has not produced widely deployable systems. Homomorphic encryption allows for computations on encrypted data, but is limited in performance and complexity.

As the digital world keeps changing, no single approach to cryptography will ever be perfect for everything. Instead, security systems typically use a variety of techniques; it's a trade-off between speed, scalability, and security. Ongoing research and development in cryptography will therefore continue to be critical as new threats materialize, especially due to the rise of quantum computing. However, the right cryptographic approach ultimately depends on the specific needs of each application and requires a deep understanding of each method's strengths and weaknesses to make informed security decisions.

CONCLUSION

The IoT is essential to smart towns, allowing real-time data exchange throughout structures like visitors, power, and healthcare. However, this connectivity introduces the maximum crucial protection risks. Encryption remains the centre of safety, but due to restricted resources in many gadgets, lightweight cryptographic strategies are critical. Encryption remains the centre of protection; however, due to restricted resources in many devices, lightweight cryptographic strategies are essential. Hybrid models—the usage of public-key cryptography for key exchange and symmetric encryption for information—offer a balance of security and performance. Blockchain enhances accept as true with through supplying transparent, tamper-proof records sharing, already utilized in cities like Dubai. Homomorphic and post-quantum encryption are paving the way for destiny-proof facts privacy. Secure get right of entry is similarly strengthened with the aid of multifactor authentication, virtual certificate, and protocols like TLS and MQTT. Cities like Singapore, Barcelona, and New York are already imposing these answers. Challenges like device range and key management stay, requiring scalable encryption, AI-driven hazard detection, and schooling. Cryptography is the muse of steady, privacy-first, smart cities.

REFERENCES

Ahmad, A. Y. A. B., Verma, N., Sarhan, N. M., Awwad, E. M., Arora, A., & Nyangaresi, V. O. (2024). An IoT and blockchain-based secure and transparent supply chain management framework in smart cities using an optimal queue model. *IEEE Access : Practical Innovations, Open Solutions*, *12*, 51752–51771. DOI: 10.1109/ACCESS.2024.3376605

Ahuja, B., Doriya, R., Salunke, S., Hashmi, M. F., & Gupta, A. (2023). IoT-Based Multi-Dimensional Chaos Mapping System for Secure and Fast Transmission of Visual Data in Smart Cities. *IEEE Access : Practical Innovations, Open Solutions*, *11*, 104930–104945. DOI: 10.1109/ACCESS.2023.3318014

Habib, M. Y., Qureshi, H. A., Khan, S. A., Mansoor, Z., & Chishti, A. R. (2023). *Cybersecurity and Smart Cities: Current Status and Future*. Chapter presented at the 2023 IEEE International Conference on Emerging Trends in Engineering, Sciences and Technology (ICES&T). DOI: 10.1109/ICEST56843.2023.10138843

Irshad, R. R., Hussain, S., Hussain, I., Ahmad, I., Yousif, A., Alwayle, I. M., & Badr, M. M. (2023). An intelligent buffalo-based secure edge-enabled computing platform for heterogeneous IoT network in smart cities. *IEEE Access : Practical Innovations, Open Solutions*, *11*, 69282–69294. DOI: 10.1109/ACCESS.2023.3288815

Javed, M. A., Alkhathami, M., AlMohimeed, A., & Almujalli, A. (2024). Secure Multi-hop assisted IoT communications in Smart cities. *IEEE Access : Practical Innovations, Open Solutions*.

Jebbar, W., Razzaq, R., & Tahayur, D. (2024). Blockchain and cryptography framework of e-apps with big data. *Journal of Education for Pure Science*, *14*(3).

Joshi, H. P., & Sulaiman, S. A. (2024). Revolutionizing Smart City Communication: A Secure Framework Using Modern Security Technologies. *Asian American Research Letters Journal*, *1*(10), 48–64.

Khan, A. A., Laghari, A. A., Alroobaea, R., Baqasah, A. M., Alsafyani, M., Bacarra, R., & Alsayaydeh, J. A. J. (2024). Secure remote sensing data with blockchain distributed ledger technology: A solution for smart cities. *IEEE Access : Practical Innovations, Open Solutions*, *12*, 69383–69396. DOI: 10.1109/ACCESS.2024.3401591

Muniswamy, A., & Rathi, R. (2024). A detailed review on enhancing the security in Internet of Things-Based Smart City Environment using Machine learning algorithms. *IEEE Access : Practical Innovations, Open Solutions*, *12*, 120389–120413. DOI: 10.1109/ACCESS.2024.3450180

Padma, A., & Ramaiah, M. (2024). Blockchain based an efficient and secure privacy preserved framework for smart cities. *IEEE Access : Practical Innovations, Open Solutions*, *12*, 21985–22002. DOI: 10.1109/ACCESS.2024.3364078

Rasha, R., & Hammed, A. (2024). Maintaining security of patient data by employing private blockchain and fog computing technologies based on internet of medical things. *Informatica (Vilnius)*, *48*(12).

Rishiwal, V., Agarwal, U., Alotaibi, A., Tanwar, S., Yadav, P., & Yadav, M. (2024). Exploring secure V2X communication networks for human-Centric security and privacy in Smart cities. *IEEE Access : Practical Innovations, Open Solutions*, *12*, 138763–138788. DOI: 10.1109/ACCESS.2024.3467002

Saleem, M., Farooq, M. S., Shahzad, T., Hassan, A., Abbas, S., Ali, T., & Khan, M. A. (2024). Secure and transparent mobility in smart cities: Revolutionizing AVNs to predict traffic congestion using MapReduce, Private Blockchain and XAI. *IEEE Access : Practical Innovations, Open Solutions*, *12*, 131541–131555. DOI: 10.1109/ACCESS.2024.3458983

Sharma, T., Kumar, M. R., Kaushal, S., Chaudhary, D., & Saleem, K. (2023). Privacy aware post quantum secure ant colony optimization ad hoc on-demand distance vector routing in intent based internet of vehicles for 5G smart cities. *IEEE Access : Practical Innovations, Open Solutions*, *11*, 110391–110399. DOI: 10.1109/ACCESS.2023.3311515

KEY TERMS AND DEFINITIONS

Asymmetric Encryption: Asymmetric encryption, also known as public-key encryption, is a cryptographic technique that uses two mathematically related keys: a public key for encryption and a private key for decryption.

Blockchain Technology: Blockchain is a decentralized, digital ledger that records transactions in a secure and transparent manner.

Cryptography: Cryptography is the practice of securing information through the use of coded algorithms and techniques.

DoS Attack: A denial-of-service (DoS) attack is a type of cyberattack that aims to make a website or service unavailable to its intended users by overwhelming it with traffic.

Homomorphic Cryptography: Homomorphic encryption is a type of encryption that allows you to perform computations on encrypted data without decrypting it.

Internet of Things (IoT): The Internet of Things (IoT) is a network of physical devices, vehicles, appliances, and other objects embedded with sensors, software, and network connectivity that allow them to collect and share data.

Multi-factor Authentication (MFA): Multi-factor authentication (MFA), sometimes called two-factor authentication (2FA), is a security system that requires users to provide two or more distinct verification factors to gain access to a resource.

Quantum Cryptography: Quantum cryptography is a type of encryption that leverages the principles of quantum mechanics to secure communications.

Symmetric Encryption: Symmetric encryption is a method of data security where the same secret key is used for both encrypting and decrypting data.

Chapter 6
Tokenization and Micropayments in Smart City Ecosystems

G. Sowmya
https://orcid.org/0000-0002-9275-7726
MLRIT, India

R. Sridevi
JNTUH, India

K. S. Sadasiva Rao
Sri Indu College of Engineering and Technology, India

ABSTRACT

This chapter explores the role of tokenization and micropayments as foundational tools in building scalable and inclusive smart city ecosystems. It examines how blockchain-based tokens can represent digital value and rights, enabling frictionless transactions across diverse urban services such as transportation, energy, and public utilities. The chapter also delves into the mechanisms that support real-time, low-cost micropayments, essential for machine-to-machine (M2M) interactions and citizen engagement in decentralized platforms. Furthermore, it addresses the underlying cryptographic principles, privacy concerns, regulatory challenges, and security implications associated with deploying token-based payment systems in a smart city context. Case studies and emerging use cases are presented to highlight real-world applications, and future directions are proposed to guide policymakers, technologists, and urban planners in leveraging tokenization to build resilient, transparent, and citizen-centric urban environments.

DOI: 10.4018/979-8-3373-3326-7.ch006

INTRODUCTION

Smart cities represent a forward-thinking model of urban development that leverages digital technology, data analytics, and interconnected systems to enhance the quality of life for citizens, optimize resource management, and streamline urban services. These cities employ a network of sensors, Internet of Things (IoT) devices, and real-time data platforms to enable more efficient transportation systems, intelligent energy grids, smart governance, and responsive public services. The foundation of smart cities lies in their ability to collect, analyze, and act upon data in a secure, scalable, and sustainable manner. However, achieving this level of coordination and service delivery requires an integrated financial infrastructure capable of facilitating high-frequency, low-cost transactions across a wide range of public and private stakeholders (Hernandez et al., 2023).

With the rise of digital platforms and interconnected services, smart cities are evolving into complex digital economies. In this context, value is exchanged not only between individuals and institutions, but also between devices and automated systems. Urban services such as pay-per-use mobility, decentralized energy sharing, digital identity verification, and participatory governance increasingly rely on seamless financial exchanges. Traditional financial systems often fall short in enabling micro-level, instant transactions due to limitations in scalability, speed, and cost. Consequently, there is a growing need for alternative digital payment infrastructures that are secure, efficient, and interoperable—paving the way for blockchain-based tokenization and micropayment systems.

Tokenization refers to the process of representing digital or physical assets as cryptographic tokens on a distributed ledger, enabling secure and programmable exchange of value. In smart city ecosystems, tokens can represent currency, service credits, access rights, or even reputation scores. When integrated with micropayment mechanisms, tokenization empowers new economic models such as machine-to-machine commerce, dynamic pricing of utilities, and incentive-based civic engagement. These technologies facilitate trustless, automated transactions at scale while minimizing intermediaries and overhead costs. Moreover, the programmable nature of smart contracts enables fine-grained control over access, usage, and rewards, reinforcing transparency and accountability in urban operations.

This chapter aims to explore the intersection of tokenization and micropayments within the context of smart city development. The objectives are fourfold:

To provide a foundational understanding of tokenization and micropayment technologies and their cryptographic underpinnings.

To analyze how these technologies are applied across various smart city use cases, including transportation, energy, governance, and digital identity.

To examine the security, privacy, and regulatory challenges associated with deploying token-based systems in urban environments.

To outline future directions, best practices, and policy recommendations for stakeholders aiming to implement secure and equitable token economies in smart cities.

FUNDAMENTALS OF TOKENIZATION

Definition and Purpose

Tokenization is the process of converting rights to an asset into a digital token that can be stored, transferred, and managed on a blockchain or distributed ledger system. This digital representation enables assets—tangible or intangible—to be programmable, divisible, and traceable in real-time (Jebbar, 2025). Within smart city ecosystems, tokenization serves multiple purposes: It facilitates digital transactions between machines and humans, enables granular access control to city services, and introduces economic incentives to drive citizen participation and sustainable behavior. By leveraging blockchain's immutable and transparent nature, tokenization ensures that asset ownership, usage rights, and transactions are verifiable and resistant to tampering or fraud (Freni et al., 2022).

Types of Tokens: Utility, Security, and Asset-backed

Token design varies depending on the function it is intended to serve within a system. The most common classifications include:

- Utility Tokens: These grant access to specific services or functions within a platform. In a smart city, utility tokens might be used to pay for bike-sharing, public Wi-Fi access, or smart parking. They are not designed as investments and are typically issued to encourage engagement or enable the use of decentralized applications.
- Security Tokens: These represent ownership in a real-world asset such as equity, bonds, or revenue shares, and are subject to financial regulations. In urban settings, security tokens could be used for fractional ownership of infrastructure projects or municipal bonds.
- Asset-backed Tokens: These are pegged to tangible or intangible assets, such as real estate, commodities, or fiat currencies (e.g., stablecoins). They serve as a bridge between the digital token economy and traditional asset class-

es, allowing for liquidity and simplified transfer of ownership (Di & Salzer, 2020).

Each type of token plays a unique role in creating economic and governance models within a smart city, and often multiple token types coexist to support different functions within an ecosystem.

Token Standards (ERC-20, ERC-721, etc.)

Token standards define the rules and functionalities for how tokens behave on blockchain platforms, ensuring interoperability and simplifying development. The most widely adopted standards are built on Ethereum but have been replicated across various blockchain networks:

- ERC-20: The most common standard for fungible tokens. These tokens are interchangeable and ideal for currencies, credits, and voting rights in smart city applications.
- ERC-721: A standard for non-fungible tokens (NFTs), where each token is unique. This standard is suitable for representing property titles, licenses, or identity credentials.
- ERC-1155: A multi-token standard that allows the creation of both fungible and non-fungible tokens within a single contract. It is particularly useful for complex systems that require multiple asset types, such as urban games or multi-service city passes.

These token standards streamline development, improve ecosystem compatibility, and enable composable applications across smart city platforms.

Cryptographic Underpinnings

Tokenization relies on robust cryptographic primitives to ensure security, authenticity, and privacy. Key mechanisms include:

- Public-Key Cryptography: Used for identity authentication and digital signatures, allowing only authorized entities to initiate or approve transactions.
- Hash Functions: Ensure data integrity and play a vital role in transaction verification and blockchain consensus mechanisms (Liu, 2024).
- Merkle Trees: Enable efficient and secure data verification, especially useful for handling large datasets like sensor logs or service usage histories (Rasha & Hammed, 2024).

- Zero-Knowledge Proofs (ZKPs): Allow validation of information without revealing the underlying data—important for privacy-preserving applications such as anonymous micropayments or decentralized identity systems.

These cryptographic techniques form the bedrock of secure tokenized ecosystems, enabling smart cities to manage vast quantities of sensitive, value-laden data with minimal risk.

MICROPAYMENTS: CONCEPT AND MECHANISMS

Understanding Micropayments

- Micropayments refer to financial transactions involving extremely small amounts of money, typically ranging from fractions of a cent to a few dollars. These transactions are crucial in smart city environments where services—such as accessing public transportation, renting shared devices, or paying for energy consumption—can be consumed in real-time and on a usage-based model. Traditional payment systems, due to high transaction fees and latency, are often impractical for such high-frequency, low-value payments. Blockchain-based micropayment systems, however, offer a decentralized and cost-effective alternative by enabling near-instantaneous settlement without intermediaries (Razzaq & Hammed, 2025). As smart cities evolve, micropayments are poised to become a foundational element in enabling machine-to-machine (M2M) commerce and real-time service billing (Almashaqbeh et al., 2020).

Payment Channels and Layer 2 Solutions

- To address blockchain scalability and reduce transaction costs, micropayments often leverage Layer 2 solutions—technologies built atop base-layer blockchains (Layer 1). Among these, payment channels and sidechains are the most prominent.
- Payment Channels (e.g., the Lightning Network for Bitcoin or state channels on Ethereum) allow two parties to conduct multiple off-chain transactions while only recording the opening and closing transactions on the main blockchain. This drastically reduces network congestion and fees, making real-time micropayments viable.

- Sidechains operate as independent blockchains pegged to a main chain, supporting faster and cheaper transactions while periodically anchoring to the main ledger for security (Sahoo et al., 2023).
- These solutions enable high-throughput, low-cost transactions ideal for smart city applications such as toll payments, digital vending, or per-second media consumption.

Use of Stablecoins and Cryptocurrencies

- While cryptocurrencies like Bitcoin and Ethereum enable permissionless micropayments, their price volatility can hinder usability in real-world commerce. To overcome this challenge, stablecoins—digital tokens pegged to stable assets like fiat currencies—are increasingly used in smart city ecosystems.
- Fiat-collateralized stablecoins (e.g., USDC, USDT) are backed by actual currency reserves.
- Crypto-collateralized and algorithmic stablecoins use decentralized mechanisms to maintain value stability (Ante et al., 2023).
- Stablecoins combine the benefits of cryptocurrency (speed, programmability, and borderless nature) with the price stability needed for practical micropayments. They allow service providers and users to transact with predictable value, crucial for tasks like ride payments, utility billing, or micro-donations in civic engagement platforms.

Privacy and Scalability Concerns

- Despite their advantages, micropayment systems face significant challenges, especially regarding privacy and scalability.
- Privacy: On public blockchains, transaction data is transparent and permanent, which can lead to user profiling and data leakage. Privacy-enhancing technologies such as ZKPs, ring signatures, and confidential transactions are increasingly being integrated to allow anonymous yet verifiable payments.
- Scalability: Handling thousands or millions of micropayments per second—especially from autonomous vehicles, IoT sensors, or smart meters—can overwhelm traditional blockchain networks. Layer 2 protocols, sharding, and rollups (e.g., ZK-rollups, Optimistic Rollups) offer scalable alternatives while preserving security.
- To achieve widespread adoption in smart city environments, micropayment systems must strike a balance between transparency for regulatory compliance and privacy for user protection, all while maintaining throughput sufficient to handle massive transaction volumes.

Comparative Analysis of Micropayment Technologies

A variety of technologies support micropayments in smart city ecosystems, each with its own strengths and limitations. Table 1 shows a detailed comparison report of micropayment technologies.

Table 1. Comparative analysis of micropayment technologies

Technology	Advantages	Limitations
Public Blockchains (e.g., Ethereum, Bitcoin)	Decentralized, transparent, widely adopted	High fees, low scalability, energy-intensive (for PoW chains)
Layer 2 Solutions (e.g., Lightning Network, State Channels)	Low fees, fast transactions, scalable for high frequency	Complex setup, liquidity management, delayed settlement on-chain
Sidechains (e.g., Polygon, xDai)	Faster and cheaper than main chains, customizable	Lower decentralization and security compared to Layer 1
Stablecoins (e.g., USDT, USDC)	Price-stable, ideal for everyday transactions	Centralization risk, regulatory scrutiny, reliance on collateral mechanisms
Feeless Protocols (e.g., IOTA)	No transaction fees, lightweight for IoT devices	Limited adoption, ongoing development, security model still maturing

TOKEN ECONOMY IN SMART CITIES

Incentivization Models Using Tokens

In smart cities, tokens are not just digital representations of value—they also act as mechanisms to influence behavior and foster participation in public systems. Incentivization models using tokens can encourage residents to make environmentally responsible choices, contribute to community initiatives, or share data voluntarily. For instance, tokens may be earned by using public transit instead of private cars, recycling waste, or reporting infrastructure issues via civic apps. These tokens can then be redeemed for discounts, access to city services, or even exchanged in local marketplaces.

By creating a gamified, reward-driven environment, token economies promote sustainable habits, enhance community engagement, and reduce administrative costs by automating reward distribution through smart contracts. Moreover, tokens align citizen interests with municipal goals, creating a participatory loop that strengthens urban governance (Drasch et al., 2020).

Urban Services Enabled by Tokenization

Tokenization is transforming how key urban services are delivered, priced, and consumed in smart cities. Below are major areas where tokenization is enabling innovative, decentralized service models:

a. Smart Transportation

Token-based systems allow for flexible, pay-per-use access to shared mobility options such as electric scooters, bicycles, and public transit. Users can pay with utility tokens or receive micro-rewards for carpooling, using low-traffic routes, or traveling during off-peak hours. Blockchain can also ensure transparent allocation of subsidies and reduce fare fraud.

b. Smart Energy Grids

Decentralized energy systems use tokens to facilitate peer-to-peer (P2P) energy trading, allowing households with solar panels to sell surplus energy directly to neighbors. Tokens can represent kilowatt-hours and be automatically traded via smart contracts. This reduces reliance on centralized utilities, optimizes grid load, and encourages renewable energy adoption.

c. Waste Management

Token incentives can be used to promote recycling and proper disposal. For example, smart bins can automatically issue tokens to users who correctly separate waste or return materials to collection centers. These tokens can be integrated into broader municipal reward systems or exchanged for utility credits. (Tian et al., 2022)

d. Peer-to-Peer Marketplaces

Tokens enable decentralized marketplaces for goods and services within a city. Citizens can trade excess food, rent tools, or offer local services without centralized intermediaries. Trust is maintained via token-based reputation systems and escrow smart contracts, while micropayments facilitate small, rapid transactions.

Digital Identity and Access Control

Digital identity is a cornerstone of smart city token economies, ensuring that services are personalized, secure, and compliant with privacy regulations. Token-based identity systems use decentralized identifiers (DIDs) and verifiable credentials to allow individuals to authenticate themselves without exposing sensitive personal information.

In practice, this means a resident could use a digital wallet to:

- Access public transport
- Enter secured buildings
- Prove age or residency for restricted services
- Vote in local elections

Tokens can act as access keys or proof of eligibility, enabling granular, programmable access control across city services. Combined with privacy-preserving technologies like zero-knowledge proofs, digital identity tokens empower citizens while minimizing surveillance risks (Glöckler et al., 2023).

SECURITY AND CRYPTOGRAPHIC CONSIDERATIONS

Blockchain and Distributed Ledger Technologies

At the heart of tokenization and micropayment systems lies blockchain—a form of distributed ledger technology (DLT) that ensures transparency, data integrity, and resilience against tampering. In a smart city context, blockchain provides a decentralized infrastructure that can:

- Log every token transaction immutably
- Ensure consensus across untrusted participants (e.g., multiple vendors or agencies)
- Reduce single points of failure common in traditional IT infrastructures

Public blockchains (e.g., Ethereum, Bitcoin) offer high transparency and decentralization, but may face performance bottlenecks. Private and permissioned blockchains (e.g., Hyperledger Fabric, Corda) are often more scalable and privacy-friendly for municipal use, enabling controlled access to data while maintaining auditability (Di Ciccio, 2023).

Smart Contract Vulnerabilities

Smart contracts, which automate token transactions and service delivery, introduce programmability but also expand the attack surface. Key vulnerabilities include:

- Reentrancy Attacks: Malicious contracts repeatedly call back into a vulnerable contract before previous executions complete, as seen in the historic DAO hack.
- Integer Overflows/Underflows: Improper handling of arithmetic operations can allow attackers to manipulate token balances (Chu et al., 2023).
- Logic Bugs: Flawed contract logic can lead to unintended consequences, such as irreversible token loss or privilege escalation.

To mitigate these risks, developers must adhere to best practices:

- Use audited libraries (e.g., OpenZeppelin).
- Employ formal verification where possible.
- Conduct rigorous security audits and testing, including fuzzing and penetration testing.

Zero-Knowledge Proofs and Privacy Enhancements

As smart city ecosystems collect and process vast amounts of sensitive data, privacy becomes a critical concern. ZKPs enable users to prove the validity of information without revealing the actual data. (Lavin et al., 2024). Applications include:

- Verifying eligibility for subsidies or services without exposing personal income or identity.
- Anonymous micropayments for public services.
- Private yet auditable transactions between IoT devices.

ZKPs, along with other privacy-enhancing technologies like ring signatures and homomorphic encryption, help strike a balance between user anonymity and regulatory transparency, ensuring compliance with frameworks such as GDPR.

Token Fraud Prevention and Secure Wallets

A secure token economy must address the risks of fraud, theft, and unauthorized access. Common threats include:

- Phishing and social engineering attacks targeting users' wallets.
- Malicious smart contracts that trick users into authorizing irreversible transfers.
- Rogue nodes in permissioned blockchains attempting to manipulate consensus.

Key countermeasures include:

- Multi-signature wallets and hardware wallets to protect private keys.
- Two-factor authentication (2FA) and biometric access controls (Houy et al., 2023).
- Token whitelisting/blacklisting to prevent interaction with known malicious contracts.
- Use of fraud detection algorithms powered by machine learning to identify abnormal transaction patterns.

ARCHITECTURE OF TOKEN-BASED MICROPAYMENT SYSTEMS

System Components and Roles

Figure 1 shows the architecture diagram of Token-Based Micropayment Systems, and the components of the diagram are explained below.

Figure 1. Architecture diagram

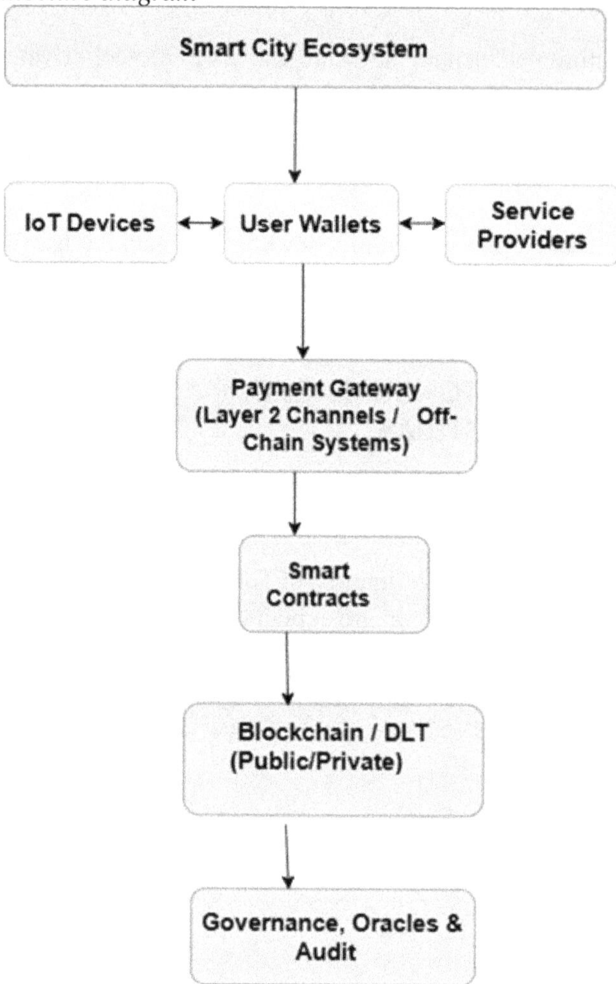

a. IoT Devices

Smart meters, public transport access points, parking sensors, EV chargers, etc., all embedded with microcontrollers and lightweight crypto wallets. These devices:

- Trigger token-based payments automatically.
- Collect and transmit service usage data securely.

b. User Wallets

Mobile apps or hardware wallets held by residents or users. They:

- Store private keys and tokens.
- Allow users to authorize transactions for services like transit, energy use, etc.
- Provide interfaces for monitoring usage, rewards, and balances.

c. Service Providers

Entities like public transport agencies, utilities, or municipal bodies that:

- Register services on the blockchain.
- Accept tokens in exchange for service.
- Interact with smart contracts for automated billing and fulfillment.

d. Payment Gateway (Layer 2 / Off-Chain)

Handles fast, low-cost micropayments by:

- Creating bidirectional channels between users and providers.
- Aggregating frequent micro-interactions before settling on-chain.
- Supporting real-time settlement with minimal latency.

e. Smart Contracts

Automate:

- Token issuance and distribution.
- Access control and usage limits.
- Escrow conditions and service-level enforcement.

f. Blockchain / DLT

Core ledger that:

- Stores immutable transaction records.
- Enforces consensus on state updates.
- Acts as the trusted backend for all token interactions.

g. Governance, Oracles & Audit Layer

- Governance: Token holders or designated parties propose and vote on policy changes.
- Oracles: Feed real-world data (e.g., energy rates, congestion metrics) into smart contracts.
- Audit: Regulatory and internal tools ensure compliance, transparency, and security.

Token Issuance and Distribution Mechanisms

Token creation and distribution must be governed by well-defined economic and policy frameworks to ensure fairness, scalability, and regulatory compliance. Common mechanisms include:

- Pre-minted Tokens: A fixed number of tokens is generated in advance and distributed based on predefined rules, often used for municipal credits or grant programs.
- Mint-on-Demand: Tokens are minted dynamically based on real-time demand or service usage (e.g., pay-as-you-go models in mobility or energy).
- Incentive-based Distribution: Tokens are earned by users through behaviors such as recycling, carpooling, or data sharing, creating a gamified incentive layer.
- Staking and Delegation: Users can lock tokens as collateral or delegate tokens to others, commonly used in governance or infrastructure maintenance systems.

Issuance logic is embedded within smart contracts, and transparent auditing mechanisms ensure public trust and accountability.

Transaction Validation and Governance

To maintain system integrity and trust, transactions must be validated securely and in real time, especially in a high-frequency micropayment environment. Mechanisms include:

- Consensus Protocols: Depending on the blockchain used, protocols like Proof of Stake (PoS), Practical Byzantine Fault Tolerance (PBFT), or Delegated PoS ensure transaction validity and agreement among network participants.
- Fee Structures: Micropayments require ultra-low fees. Layer 2 solutions or feeless models (e.g., IoTA) are often adopted to enable viable use cases.

- On-chain Governance: Enables token holders or designated stakeholders to vote on protocol upgrades, fee adjustments, or service integrations.
- Auditability: Every transaction can be cryptographically verified and traced, enabling real-time monitoring and compliance with financial regulations.

These governance models must be flexible enough to evolve with the smart city's growing demands, balancing decentralization with operational efficiency.

Integration with IoT Devices

IoT devices are at the core of smart city infrastructure, from autonomous vehicles to smart meters. Their integration with tokenized micropayment systems enables automated machine-to-machine (M2M) payments and decentralized service management. Key considerations include:

- Embedded Wallets: Devices are equipped with lightweight wallets to hold and transact tokens. These wallets may be hosted on secure chips or trusted execution environments (TEEs).
- Trigger-based Payments: IoT sensors can initiate transactions based on predefined conditions (e.g., an electric vehicle automatically paying for charging based on kWh consumed).
- Real-time Settlement: Low-latency communication protocols allow instant exchange of value without human intervention.
- Security Protocols: Authentication, encryption, and secure firmware updates are essential to protect IoT devices from token theft or network hijacking.

Integration standards such as W3C's Web of Things (WoT) and IETF IoT protocols (e.g., CoAP, MQTT) further streamline interoperability between devices, tokens, and distributed ledgers.

REAL-WORLD APPLICATIONS AND CASE STUDIES

As cities around the globe explore digital transformation, tokenization, and micropayments are increasingly becoming foundational tools in deploying secure, efficient, and participatory urban services. This section highlights real-world applications and case studies that demonstrate the integration of token-based systems into smart city functions.

Tokenized Urban Mobility Platforms

Case Example: TUMI Mobility Credits (Berlin, Germany)

The Transformative Urban Mobility Initiative (TUMI) piloted mobility credits in Berlin, where citizens received digital tokens in exchange for reducing car usage. These credits could be used for public transport, bike-sharing, or e-scooters. (Miron et al., 2025)

- Impact: Reduced traffic congestion, carbon emissions, and boosted use of sustainable transport.
- Technology Stack: Mobile app wallets, smart contracts for credit issuance, real-time IoT integration.

Tokenized Bike-Sharing

In Singapore and several European cities, decentralized bike-sharing systems use blockchain to:

- Charge riders per minute using utility tokens.
- Reward frequent users with tokens for discounts or service credits.
- Enable P2P rentals, where users can lend their bikes for a fee through smart contracts.

EV Charging Stations Platforms like Share&Charge use Ethereum-based tokens to automate EV charging payments. Users connect their digital wallets to charging stations and pay per kWh, while station owners earn tokens.

Decentralized Energy Trading

Case Example: Brooklyn Microgrid (New York, USA)

A pioneering peer-to-peer (P2P) energy marketplace where residents with solar panels trade excess electricity using blockchain-based smart contracts.

- Tokens represent kilowatt-hours (kWh) and are exchanged in real time.
- Benefits: Localized energy resilience, reduced dependency on centralized utilities, and direct economic incentives for clean energy producers (Tando et al., 2024).

Power Ledger (Australia)

Uses blockchain and tokenization to enable:

- Transparent billing across energy retailers and consumers.
- Settlement of energy trades through stablecoins or native tokens (POWR).
- Carbon credit trading on a shared ledger.

Smart Parking and Toll Systems

Case Example: Parksen (Netherlands)

Parksen provides smart parking solutions using IoT sensors and Ethereum smart contracts.

- Users pay per minute via tokens. (Fahim et al., 2021)
- Real-time parking data from sensors prevents overcharging and reduces idle driving time.

Toll Payment via Micropayments

In cities like Seoul and Singapore, blockchain-based toll systems:

- Allow real-time toll calculation based on route, time, and congestion.
- Deduct exact fees via automated micropayments from user wallets.
- Reduce fraud, eliminate cash handling, and improve traffic flow.

Public Engagement via Civic Tokens

Case Example: CityCoins (Miami & New York City, USA)

CityCoins allow citizens to support their city by mining a local token (e.g., $MIA for Miami), a portion of which goes directly to the city treasury (Nechesov & Ruponen, 2024).

- Citizens can vote on community initiatives, access local benefits, or earn staking rewards.
- Goal: Increase civic participation and create new funding models for public services.

Recycling Incentive Programs

Cities in South Korea and Sweden have experimented with recyclable return-for-token systems. Citizens deposit plastic, paper, or glass in smart bins and receive tokens in return. These can be redeemed for transit credits or local store discounts.

REGULATORY, ETHICAL, AND SOCIAL IMPLICATIONS

The deployment of tokenization and micropayment systems within smart cities brings not only technological innovation but also complex regulatory, ethical, and social challenges. Addressing these concerns is crucial for building systems that are secure, fair, and widely accepted by citizens.

Data Sovereignty and Citizen Privacy

Smart city token economies rely heavily on data generated by individuals, devices, and services. Ensuring data sovereignty means that citizens retain ownership and control over their personal data, including how it is collected, stored, and shared. Token systems must incorporate privacy-preserving techniques such as:

- Decentralized identity management to minimize centralized data silos.
- Use of zero-knowledge proofs to enable verification without revealing underlying data.
- Strict adherence to data minimization principles to limit unnecessary data collection.

Respecting privacy also involves transparency around data use and robust consent frameworks, especially given the sensitivity of location, health, and financial data often processed in these systems.

Compliance with Financial Regulations (e.g., AML/KYC)

Tokens that function as currency or represent assets fall under the scrutiny of financial regulators. Smart city implementations must comply with:

- Anti-Money Laundering (AML) regulations to prevent illicit transactions.
- Know Your Customer (KYC) rules to verify user identities.
- Taxation laws and reporting requirements for token transactions.

- Securities laws, particularly when tokens represent investments or profit-sharing.

Balancing regulatory compliance with user privacy and system usability is a delicate act. Solutions often involve permissioned blockchains with vetted participants, regulated digital identities, and cooperation with financial institutions.

Digital Divide and Inclusion Challenges

Token-based ecosystems risk excluding marginalized populations without access to smartphones, stable internet, or financial literacy. To foster digital inclusion, smart city initiatives must:

- Design user-friendly interfaces accessible to diverse demographics, including elderly and differently-abled users.
- Provide offline or low-bandwidth solutions for areas with poor connectivity.
- Implement education and outreach programs to build trust and competence in digital payments.
- Consider alternative access methods (e.g., NFC cards, SMS wallets) to bridge technological gaps.

Ensuring that token economies empower rather than alienate vulnerable communities is key to equitable urban development.

Token Governance and Community Trust

The decentralized nature of token economies necessitates clear and participatory governance frameworks to:

- Define rules for token issuance, usage, and burning.
- Manage dispute resolution and prevent abuse.
- Facilitate community voting and decision-making regarding system upgrades and policies.
- Maintain transparency about token supply, distribution, and economic incentives.

Without strong governance and communication, distrust may arise, undermining adoption. Incorporating mechanisms such as decentralized autonomous organizations (DAOs) or city-led oversight bodies can help balance decentralization with accountability (Polcumpally et al., 2024).

CHALLENGES AND FUTURE TRENDS

As tokenization and micropayment systems continue to evolve within smart city frameworks, several technical, operational, and strategic challenges remain. This section explores these challenges while highlighting emerging trends that could shape the future of secure and efficient urban digital economies.

Scalability and Interoperability Issues

One of the foremost technical challenges is scalability — the ability of blockchain networks and payment channels to handle massive transaction volumes generated by smart city applications without prohibitive costs or latency.

- Layer 1 blockchain limitations, such as throughput constraints and high gas fees, hinder large-scale adoption.
- Layer 2 solutions (e.g., payment channels, sidechains) mitigate these but introduce complexity in settlement finality.
- Interoperability between different blockchain platforms, token standards, and legacy payment systems is critical to avoid ecosystem fragmentation.
- Cross-platform bridges, atomic swaps, and interoperable protocols like Polkadot and Cosmos are emerging to address these gaps.

Balancing scalability with security and decentralization remains a key research and development focus.

Cross-border Micropayment Solutions

Smart cities increasingly operate within global and regional networks, requiring seamless cross-border micropayments that overcome issues like currency conversion, regulatory divergence, and latency.

- Stablecoins pegged to fiat currencies offer predictable value and reduce volatility in cross-border exchanges.
- Blockchain platforms supporting multi-currency transactions facilitate token swaps with low friction.
- Regulatory alignment between jurisdictions and global compliance frameworks remains essential to enable scalable, lawful cross-border payments.

Developing standardized protocols and global digital identity frameworks will further enhance these capabilities.

AI-Driven Automation in Tokenized Economies

Artificial Intelligence (AI) offers transformative potential in automating and optimizing token economies through:

- Dynamic pricing models that adjust token fees and incentives based on real-time demand and supply.
- Fraud detection and risk assessment by analyzing transaction patterns and user behaviors.
- Smart contract self-optimization and automatic dispute resolution through AI-enhanced decision-making.
- Personalized citizen engagement, tailoring token rewards and services to user preferences.

The convergence of AI and blockchain will create more adaptive, resilient, and efficient urban financial ecosystems.

Post-Quantum Cryptography Considerations

With the advent of quantum computing, traditional cryptographic schemes used in blockchain and token security may become vulnerable.

- Post-quantum cryptography (PQC) aims to develop quantum-resistant algorithms to safeguard digital signatures, hashing, and encryption.
- Smart cities adopting tokenization must plan migration paths for PQC integration to future-proof their systems.
- Hybrid approaches combining classical and quantum-resistant cryptography may be used during transition periods.

Early research and pilot deployments in PQC will be critical to maintaining trust and security in the long term.

FUTURE WORK AND CONCLUSION

As smart cities continue to evolve, future research should focus on enhancing cross-chain interoperability, developing robust governance frameworks, and ensuring post-quantum security for token-based systems. Real-world pilot studies are needed to evaluate long-term social, economic, and technical impacts, especially in diverse urban contexts. Additionally, integrating AI with tokenization and IoT can enable adaptive, data-driven services, while ethical frameworks must be established to ensure fairness, privacy, and digital inclusion. Harmonizing global regulatory standards will also be critical for the scalable and secure implementation of token economies in interconnected urban environments.

Tokenization and micropayments are key drivers in creating secure and efficient smart city ecosystems. They enable seamless digital transactions, promote sustainable urban services, and empower citizen participation. Despite challenges like scalability, privacy, and regulation, ongoing innovations in cryptography and AI offer promising solutions. With careful design and governance, these technologies can help build smarter, more inclusive, and resilient cities for the future.

REFERENCES

Almashaqbeh, G., Bishop, A., & Cappos, J. (2020). MicroCash: practical concurrent processing of micropayments. In Lecture notes in computer science (pp. 227–244). DOI: 10.1007/978-3-030-51280-4_13

Ante, L., Fiedler, I., Willruth, J. M., & Steinmetz, F. (2023). A Systematic literature review of Empirical research on stablecoins. *FinTech*, *2*(1), 34–47. DOI: 10.3390/fintech2010003

Chu, H., Zhang, P., Dong, H., Xiao, Y., Ji, S., & Li, W. (2023). A survey on smart contract vulnerabilities: Data sources, detection and repair. *Information and Software Technology*, *159*, 107221. DOI: 10.1016/j.infsof.2023.107221

Di Ciccio, C. (2023). Blockchain and distributed ledger technologies. In Cambridge University Press eBooks (pp. 11–34). DOI: 10.1017/9781009411783.003

Drasch, B. J., Fridgen, G., Manner-Romberg, T., Nolting, F. M., & Radszuwill, S. (2020). The token's secret: The two-faced financial incentive of the token economy. *Electronic Markets*, *30*(3), 557–567. DOI: 10.1007/s12525-020-00412-9

Fahim, A., Hasan, M., & Chowdhury, M. A. (2021). Smart parking systems: Comprehensive review based on various aspects. *Heliyon*, *7*(5), e07050. DOI: 10.1016/j.heliyon.2021.e07050 PMID: 34041396

Freni, P., Ferro, E., & Moncada, R. (2022). Tokenomics and blockchain tokens: A design-oriented morphological framework. *Blockchain Research and Applications*, *3*(1), 100069. DOI: 10.1016/j.bcra.2022.100069

Glöckler, J., Sedlmeir, J., Frank, M., & Fridgen, G. (2023). A Systematic review of identity and access management requirements in enterprises and potential contributions of Self-Sovereign Identity. *Business & Information Systems Engineering*, *66*(4), 421–440. DOI: 10.1007/s12599-023-00830-x

Hernandez, M. S., Sentosa, I., & Sharin, F. H. (2023). Ecosystem implementations in smart City through blockchain technology. *2023 3rd International Conference on Advance Computing and Innovative Technologies in Engineering (ICACITE)*, 1273–1278. DOI: 10.1109/ICACITE57410.2023.10182823

Houy, S., Schmid, P., & Bartel, A. (2023). Security Aspects of Cryptocurrency Wallets—A Systematic Literature Review. *ACM Computing Surveys*, *56*(1), 1–31. DOI: 10.1145/3596906

Jebbar, W. A. (2025). Optimization Solution Proposal for Smart Transaction Security of Smart Blockchain Contracts in E-Banking Applications. In *Sustainable Information Security in the Age of AI and Green Computing* (pp. 295–320). IGI Global Scientific Publishing.

Lavin, R., Liu, X., Mohanty, H., Norman, L., Zaarour, G., & Krishnamachari, B. (2024). A survey on the applications of Zero-Knowledge proofs. arXiv (Cornell University). /arxiv.2408.00243DOI: 10.48550

Liu, H. (2024). Employing cryptographic techniques for data security and privacy preservation. *Transactions on Computer Science and Intelligent Systems Research*, *5*, 35–39. DOI: 10.62051/58a35334

Miron, R., Hulea, M., Muresan, V., Clitan, I., & Rusu, A. (2025). Integrating Blockchain Technology into Mobility-as-a-Service Platforms for Smart Cities. *Smart Cities*, *8*(1), 9. DOI: 10.3390/smartcities8010009

Nechesov, A., & Ruponen, J. (2024). Empowering government efficiency through civic intelligence: Merging artificial intelligence and blockchain for smart citizen proposals. *Technologies*, *12*(12), 271. DOI: 10.3390/technologies12120271

Polcumpally, A. T., Pandey, K. K., Kumar, A., & Samadhiya, A. (2024). Blockchain governance and trust: A multi-sector thematic systematic review and exploration of future research directions. *Heliyon*, *10*(12), e32975. DOI: 10.1016/j.heliyon.2024.e32975 PMID: 38984295

Rasha, R., & Hammed, A. (2024). Maintaining security of patient data by employing private blockchain and fog computing technologies based on internet of medical things. *Informatica (Vilnius)*, *48*(12).

Razzaq, R., & Hammed, A. (2025). Combining Fog Computing and Blockchain Based on the Internet of Medical Things to Preserve Patient Information Privacy. In *Sustainable Information Security in the Age of AI and Green Computing* (pp. 525–546). IGI Global Scientific Publishing.

Sahoo, S. S., Hosmane, M. M., & Chaurasiya, V. K. (2023). A secure payment channel rebalancing model for layer-2 blockchain. *Internet of Things : Engineering Cyber Physical Human Systems*, *22*, 100822. DOI: 10.1016/j.iot.2023.100822

Tando, M. S., Gawusu, S., Yakubu, S., Kwabena, O. S., Donatus, D., & Abu, S. R. (2024). Decentralized energy trading with blockchain technology. In Elsevier eBooks (pp. 75–101). DOI: 10.1016/B978-0-443-23627-3.00004-1

Tian, Y., Wang, C., Asutosh, A., Woo, J., & Adriaens, P. (2022). Blockchain-enabled tokenization for sustainable and inclusive infrastructure investment. arXiv (Cornell University). /arxiv.2208.04709DOI: 10.48550

Chapter 7

Quantum Cryptography: The Future of Data Security in Smart Urban Environments

Nakul Pareek
https://orcid.org/0009-0002-4118-3440
Christ University, Delhi, India

Neha Saini
https://orcid.org/0009-0006-3174-1866
Christ University, Delhi, India

ABSTRACT

As cities adopt integrated IoT ecosystems and data-driven urban governance, traditional encryption faces the threat of obsolescence by quantum computing attacks. This chapter explores the application of quantum cryptography in protecting smart urban infrastructure, with a focus on quantum key distribution (QKD), post-quantum algorithms, and hybrid systems. Through an examination of deployments in smart grids, traffic management systems, and public health platforms, we illustrate how quantum-resistant protocols reduce threats of data breaches and spoofing attacks. There are special challenges: scaling QKD to millions of IoT devices will need new network architectures, and integrating with legacy systems will need phased "crypto-agility" plans. The chapter presents a model for incorporating quantum-safe practice into urban design, with an emphasis on inter-disciplinary collaboration among cryptographers, policymakers, and city administrators.

DOI: 10.4018/979-8-3373-3326-7.ch007

INTRODUCTION

The renovation of urban environments by digital technologies has radically changed the functioning, delivery of services, and relationship of cities with their residents. Smart cities are an integration of physical infrastructure with digital smarts, with interlinked ecosystems where networks, sensors, and computational systems collaborate to streamline city functions. These settings combine Internet of Things (IoT) devices, artificial intelligence systems, big data analytics, and next-generation communication networks to improve efficiency, sustainability, and quality of life for urban dwellers (Bibri & Krogstie, 2017).

But the pervasive digitization and interconnectivity that characterize smart cities also bring with them unprecedented cybersecurity risks. The attack surface of contemporary cities has grown exponentially, involving millions of interconnected devices, sophisticated network architectures, and enormous databases of sensitive citizen data. Classical cryptanalytic techniques, effective as they are against existing computational threats, are threatened with extinction by the rising quantum computing approach. Quantum computers, utilizing principles of quantum mechanics like superposition and entanglement, have the theoretical ability to weaken commonly used public-key cryptographic algorithms like Rivest, Shamir, Adleman (RSA), Elliptic Curve Cryptography (ECC), and Diffie-Hellman key exchange via Shor's algorithm (Shor, 1994). The quantum threat to cybersecurity is not just a theoretical one but an imminent one that requires proactive measures. Major technology firms and research organizations have shown substantial improvements in quantum computing potential, with companies such as IBM, Google, and IonQ attaining quantum advantage in certain computational problems. The timeframe for cryptographically significant quantum computers is unclear, but most experts agree that they can be made available within the next 10-20 years. This timeline generates an imperative of existential urgency for smart cities to start making the shift to quantum-safe cryptographic systems before their existing security infrastructure is compromised.

The incorporation of quantum cryptography into smart city infrastructure is both a once-in-a-lifetime opportunity and a collection of daunting challenges. On the one hand, quantum-safe cryptographic technologies can offer unprecedented security assurances for vital urban infrastructure, safeguarding against both immediate and future cyber threats. Conversely, the deployment of quantum technologies involves enormous investments in dedicated hardware, infrastructure changes, and training the workforce. Additionally, the scalability, interoperability, and economy of quantum cryptographic solutions need to be carefully assessed within the scope of large-scale urban deployments. This chapter offers a thorough analysis of quantum cryptography as an enabling technology for securing smart urban ecosystems. We examine the particular cybersecurity issues of contemporary cities, compare and contrast several quantum cryptography technologies and their uses, and outline how quantum-safe solutions could be combined with new urban technologies. In addition, we consider the practical issues, ethical aspects, and policy environments required for productive quantum cryptography implementation. By using in-depth case studies and expert commentary, this chapter seeks to equip urban planners, policymakers, and tech professionals with the information necessary to steer cities through the process of becoming quantum-safe smart cities.

CYBERSECURITY CHALLENGES IN SMART CITIES

Smart cities are exposed to a sophisticated and dynamic threat environment that is substantially different from the usual cybersecurity threat. The interconnected character of city infrastructure provides cascading vulnerabilities where a security compromise in one area can spread quickly to impact several key infrastructure elements. It is crucial to comprehend these challenges to design effective quantum cryptographic solutions that meet the particular requirements of urban settings. The large-scale deployment of IoT devices is one of the biggest security concerns in smart cities. An average smart city deployment can involve hundreds of thousands, and even millions of, interconnected devices with varying sizes from environmental sensors and traffic cameras to smart meters and autonomous vehicles. Most IoT devices are developed with limited computing power and poor security features to contain costs and reduce power consumption. These devices may use weak authentication methods, utilize default passwords, or not encrypt at all (Rasha et al., 2025). The Mirai botnet attack in 2016 proved the catastrophic impact of hacked IoT devices, where hundreds of thousands of unprotected cameras and routers were enlisted into a gargantuan distributed denial-of-service (DDoS) attack that knocked out major internet services worldwide (Antonakakis et al., 2017).

The problem of IoT security is exacerbated by the heterogeneity of smart city device ecosystems. Devices from varied vendors might employ incompatible security protocols, rendering it hard to roll out a uniform security policy throughout the urban landscape. Moreover, numerous IoT devices are equipped with confined update capabilities, rendering them insecure for extended periods after deployment against newly discovered security vulnerabilities. The extended lifespans of city infrastructure components result in security vulnerabilities remaining unaddressed for years or decades. Vulnerabilities in network infrastructure represent another key challenge to smart city cybersecurity. Contemporary city communication infrastructure is based on a technologically intricate combination of technologies such as 4G/5G cellular networks, Wi-Fi, fiber optic communications, and satellite communications. All of these technologies have specific security issues and possible attack vectors.

Wireless communications are most susceptible to eavesdropping, signal jamming, and man-in-the-middle attacks. The use of 5G networks in smart cities has added dimensions of complexity due to the technology's reliance on software-defined networking and network function virtualization, creating new attack surfaces for cybercriminals (Ahmad et al., 2018).

Critical infrastructure networks such as energy grids, water treatment plants, and transportation networks are vulnerable to advanced cyber threats that can have serious implications for public safety and financial stability. The 2015 cyberattack on the power grid in Ukraine showed how cyber adversaries can utilize advanced malware to destabilize electrical infrastructure, leaving hundreds of thousands of citizens without electricity. Such attacks have also been carried out against water treatment plants, and the 2021 attack on Oldsmar, Florida, demonstrated how hackers were trying to adjust chemical levels in the water supply to hazardous levels. Challenges for data privacy and protection are especially pronounced in smart cities because of the large amount of information being collected and processed about citizens. Smart city infrastructure collects data about citizen movement patterns, energy consumption, health information, and everyday activities constantly. This data generates rich digital dossiers that would be vulnerable to exploitation for surveillance, discriminatory, or commercial use if not adequately safeguarded. The General Data Protection Regulation of the European Union and equivalent privacy frameworks elsewhere in the world require stringent data protection requirements, but the requirements become difficult to meet as data passes through various linked systems with different security capabilities. These complex cybersecurity issues point to the pressing requirement for next-generation security products that are capable of meeting existing and emerging threats. Quantum cryptography provides potential solutions for a number of these challenges by establishing security certifications based on physical principles instead of computational conjectures. Nevertheless, the successful deployment of quantum cryptographic measures in smart cities demands that proper attention be given to the unique threat environment and operational circumstances of cities.

QUANTUM CRYPTOGRAPHY TECHNOLOGIES

Quantum cryptography is a groundbreaking paradigm shift in information security, harnessing the counterintuitive nature of quantum mechanics to provide security levels theoretically unattainable with traditional cryptographic methods. Quantum cryptography is based not on computational complexity assumptions, like traditional cryptographic schemes, but rather on the physical laws themselves, which means it is resistant to improvements in classical and quantum computing power.

Quantum Key Distribution

Quantum Key Distribution (QKD) is the most developed and most commonly used quantum cryptographic technology. The theoretical underpinnings of QKD were laid by Stephen Wiesner's quantum conjugate coding in the 1970s, but the first practical QKD protocol was presented by Charles Bennett and Gilles Brassard in 1984, the BB84 protocol (Bennett & Brassard, 1984). This protocol allows two parties, usually referred to as Alice and Bob, to agree on a common secret key with information-theoretic security guarantees.

The BB84 protocol works by placing information in the quantum state of photons, most commonly their polarization characteristics. Alice polarizes photons in one of four distinct polarization states: horizontal (0°), vertical (90°), diagonal (45°), or anti-diagonal (135°). There are two complementary bases, which these states are partitioned into: the rectilinear basis (horizontal and vertical) and the diagonal basis (diagonal and anti-diagonal). For each photon, Alice randomly chooses a bit value (0 or 1) and a basis and sends the encoded photons to Bob via a quantum channel, which is usually an optical fiber or free-space optical link. Bob receives the photons and randomly selects a measurement basis for each of them. Since the principle of complementarity in quantum mechanics, Bob will measure accurately the photons only when he uses the same basis that Alice employed for the encoding. When Bob incorrectly employs a different basis, he gets random outcomes. Following the phase of quantum transmission, Alice and Bob engage in classical communication to exchange their basis choices without divulging the true bit values. They exclude measurements where they employed different bases and keep only those where their bases were identical, creating the raw key material.

The security of QKD protocols is based on the quantum no-cloning theorem, which claims that arbitrary quantum states cannot be perfectly cloned, and the measurement postulate, which claims that quantum measurements inescapably disturb quantum states. Any eavesdropping (classically known as Eve) attempt to intercept and measure the quantum-transmitted photons will necessarily introduce detectable errors in the communication. Alice and Bob can identify eavesdropping by comparing a subset of their key bits via the classical channel and measuring the quantum bit error rate (QBER). If the QBER is above a chosen threshold, they terminate the protocol and try again at key distribution. Practical QKD systems have come a long way since the initial BB84 protocol. The SARG04 protocol, introduced by Scarani, Acín, Ribordy, and Gisin in 2004, provides better performance when operating in high-loss environments by adjusting the information reconciliation step. The decoy state approach, presented by Lo, Ma, and Chen in 2005, responds to security loopholes in practical QKD systems using weak coherent light sources instead of ideal single-photon sources. This approach randomly fluctuates Alice's transmitted pulse intensity, and thus, it becomes possible to detect photon-number-splitting attacks and other implementation-dependent security attacks.

Continuous-variable QKD is another method that encodes information on the quadrature amplitudes of coherent light states instead of discrete polarizations of photons. This method has a higher detector efficiency and compatibility with commercial telecommunications equipment, but needs advanced error correction and privacy amplification methods to be secure (Weedbrook et al., 2012). Recent technological breakthroughs in QKD have been aimed at resolving real-world deployment issues. Measurement-device-independent QKD eliminates the security risks related to flawed detectors by keeping all measurement devices outside of trusted parties' control. Twin-field QKD enables much higher transmission lengths using quantum interference effects, potentially supporting metropolitan-scale QKD networks without the need for middleman trusted nodes.

Post-Quantum Cryptographic Algorithms

Although QKD offers end-to-end security for key distribution, its implementation demands bespoke quantum hardware and is bound by transmission distance and infrastructural demands. Post-quantum cryptography (PQC) provides an alternative strategy through the construction of classical cryptographic schemes that are provably secure against both classical and quantum cryptanalysis. These schemes may be instantiated with standard computer hardware and incorporated into current communication protocols and systems. The quantum threat to existing cryptographic systems is well-documented and particular. Shor's algorithm, which was constructed by Peter Shor in 1994, gives an efficient quantum algorithm for factoring large integers and the computation of discrete logarithms. This would compromise the RSA, ECC, and Diffie-Hellman protocols that underpin contemporary public-key cryptography. Grover's algorithm, found by Lov Grover in 1996, gives a quadratic speedup for searching unordered databases, in effect reducing the security level of symmetric cryptographic functions and hash functions by half.

As a countermeasure to the quantum attack, the National Institute of Standards and Technology (NIST) launched Post-Quantum Cryptography Standardization in 2016 to find and standardize quantum-proof cryptographic algorithms. Following several rounds of review by cryptographic professionals from across the globe, NIST picked four algorithms for standardization in 2022: CRYSTALS-Kyber for key encapsulation, and CRYSTALS-Dilithium, FALCON, and SPHINCS+ for digital signatures.

Lattice-based cryptography is the mathematical basis for many of the most prominent post-quantum algorithms, such as CRYSTALS-Kyber and CRYSTALS-Dilithium. These algorithms are secured by problems in lattices in high dimensions, including the Learning with Errors (LWE) problem and Ring-LWE problem. Lattice-based algorithms have very good performance metrics, with key generation, encryption, and decryption functions that are efficient computationally and designed for use in resource-limited devices. The security of lattice-based cryptography has been extensively studied, and no efficient quantum algorithms are known for solving the underlying mathematical problems. Hash-based signatures, exemplified by the SPHINCS+ algorithm, provide digital signature capabilities based on the security of cryptographic hash functions. These algorithms are highly conservative from a security perspective, as they rely only on the existence of secure hash functions, which are fundamental building blocks in cryptography. Hash-based signatures have comparatively bigger signature sizes than conventional algorithms, but they provide high security assurances and are well suited to settings where signature verification is more common than signature generation.

Code-based cryptography algorithms get their security from error-correcting codes and decoding problems of random linear codes. Code-based algorithms trace their history back to the 1970s and even earlier, with some proposals existing even then. Although code-based algorithms generally use larger key sizes compared to other post-quantum methods, they provide efficient encryption and decryption operations and have survived decades of cryptanalysis. Multivariate cryptography relies on the hardness of solving multivariate polynomial systems over finite fields. Such algorithms allow for compact signatures and low-cost verification, which makes them appealing for environments with limited resources. Yet most multivariate schemes have been shattered by algebraic attacks, so careful security examination and cautious parameter choices must be made.

Isogeny-based cryptography, represented in the NIST process by the SIKE algorithm, relies on the hardness of computing isogenies between supersingular elliptic curves. Although these algorithms provide tight key sizes, the SIKE algorithm was recently broken in 2022, making it essential to have diversified cryptographic methods and ongoing security efforts.

Hybrid Encryption Systems

Hybrid cryptographic systems bring together quantum and classical cryptographic technologies to take advantage of the strengths of both methods without reproducing their specific disadvantages. They are especially valuable for deployment in smart cities, where backward compatibility, scalability, and economic cost need to be balanced against the requirements of security. The general idea of hybrid quantum-classical encryption is to employ QKD to safely deliver cryptographic keys, which are in turn employed with classical symmetric encryption schemes to encrypt data transmission. This method offers the information-theoretic security assurance of

QKD for key delivery but uses the efficiency and maturity of classical encryption for securing bulk data. The hybrid method is especially useful since symmetric encryption algorithms with key sizes large enough are quantum-proof if the keys are securely stored.

Crypto-agility is an important design principle for hybrid systems that would allow organizations to evolve their cryptographic implementations as new threats and technologies arise. Crypto-agile systems are made with modular architectures whereby cryptographic algorithms can be replaced or upgraded without total system redesign. This would be important for smart cities, which have to run critical infrastructure for decades while keeping up with changing security needs. The use of post-quantum algorithms with classic cryptographic systems is another key type of hybrid encryption. In the period between migration to post-quantum cryptography, numerous organizations use hybrid classical/post-quantum systems that combine traditional and quantum-resistant algorithms. This provides defense against both existing classical attacks and potential future quantum attacks while enabling step-by-step transition to entirely post-quantum systems.

APPLICATIONS IN URBAN INFRASTRUCTURE

The deployment of quantum cryptography in smart city infrastructure needs to carefully take into consideration certain use cases, performance needs, and integration complexities. Every area of urban infrastructure offers particular opportunities and limitations for the deployment of quantum cryptography, and these must be approached with customized strategies to adapt to domain-level security needs without compromising operational efficacy and cost.

Securing IoT Networks

Smart city Internet of Things networks contain millions of interconnected devices gathering, processing, and sending huge volumes of data regarding urban functions and citizens' behavior. The networks contain air quality sensors and noise sensors for monitoring the environment, smart streetlights with adjustable brightness depending on pedestrian flow, sensors in water distribution systems measuring water quality, waste collection sensors that determine optimal collection routes, and traffic systems monitoring and controlling signal timing and incidents.

The security problem for IoT networks is especially dire owing to the resource limitations of each device and the size of deployments. Conventional cryptographic technologies tend to fail to achieve proper security for IoT devices because of restricted computation resources, memory availability, and power constraints. Numerous IoT devices lack the ability to carry the computational cost of computationally expensive cryptographic techniques, and hence, lightweight encryption schemes are adopted that can be susceptible to breach.

Quantum cryptography provides a number of ways to protect IoT networks in smart cities. For high-value IoT applications like the monitoring of critical infrastructures or public safety networks, QKD can deliver ultimate security for key distribution between central management systems and IoT gateways. Although single IoT devices lack the capability to implement QKD, hierarchical security architectures can employ QKD for securing communication between IoT gateways or concentrators that later employ classical cryptography to communicate with individual devices.

Energy Grid Protection

Smart energy grids are an essential infrastructure that needs the best level of cybersecurity protection because of their critical role in urban operations and potential for cascading failures. Advanced smart grids have incorporated renewable sources of energy, energy storage facilities, demand response systems, and sophisticated monitoring and control systems that maximize energy distribution and use. The security of these systems is more important than ever since successful exploitation could lead to large-scale power disruptions, economic dislocation, and public safety threats. The Korea Electric Power Corporation (KEPCO) quantum cryptography deployment is an all-encompassing example of the potential of quantum technologies to secure smart grid operations. Starting in 2020, KEPCO deployed a hybrid QKD-classical encryption system to secure communications between electrical substations throughout South Korea. The system employs QKD to share encryption keys between key control centers and large substations, while classical encryption with quantum-safe key distribution secures communications to smaller distribution facilities and smart meters.

The KEPCO deployment illustrates a number of the most important advantages of quantum cryptography for energy grid security. The QKD system offers information-theoretic security for sensitive control communications, preventing grid operations from being manipulated even by an unlimited-computation adversary. The hybrid solution is compatible with current grid infrastructure and protects against both present and future threats from malicious attacks. Smart grid monitoring and control systems demand low-latency communications that are problematic for some quantum cryptographic solutions. The KEPCO system overcomes this by applying QKD to key distribution and sporadic key refreshing, while it uses fast symmetric encryption algorithms for real-time data transfer. It brings the security advantages of quantum cryptography without imposing unacceptable latency for time-sensitive grid activities.

Transportation Systems

Smart transportation systems in cities involve a sophisticated network of networked vehicles, traffic management infrastructure, public transport networks, and mobility services that need cutting-edge cybersecurity defenses. The safety-critical character of the transportation system makes cybersecurity especially critical, since a successful attack could lead to traffic accidents, service failures, or privacy breaches harming millions of citizens on a daily basis. Autonomous car security introduces specific challenges that can be addressed by quantum cryptography. Autonomous vehicles need to securely communicate with other vehicles (V2V), infrastructure networks (V2I), and cloud services (V2C) to drive safely and efficiently. Such communications involve real-time exchange of position, velocity, and intent data between vehicles, timing of traffic signals and road conditions from infrastructure systems, and software patches and map updates from cloud services (Hallem & Hammed, 2024).

Hyundai Motor Company deployed post-quantum cryptographic algorithms within its autonomous vehicle test fleet to secure V2X (Vehicle-to-Everything) communications from quantum attacks in the future. The solution employs lattice-based encryption algorithms with efficient operation that is appropriate for real-time vehicular communication while maintaining long-term security. The deployment highlights how vehicular systems are implemented by integrating quantum-safe cryptography without compromising safety and performance demands.

Public transit networks, buses, trains, and light rail systems all produce and depend on enormous volumes of data for scheduling, maintenance, and passenger services. The Singapore Mass Rapid Transit (MRT) system has put in place quantum-safe cryptography protocols to secure passenger information, operational communication, and maintenance systems. The deployments involve the use of hybrid quantum-classical encryption methods that offer ultimate security for vital operations while also being compatible with current transport infrastructure. Mobility-as-a-Service (MaaS) systems combining different means of transport into integrated services need robust privacy safeguards for user information and safe payments. MaaS platforms gather extensive data on user travel behaviors, likes, and payments that need safeguarding against present as well as future cyber threats. Quantum-resistant cryptographic protocols ensure that such sensitive data remains secure even against future improvements in computational power. The merging of quantum cryptography with intelligent transportation systems has to be done with sensitive balancing of performance demands and operational limitations. Automobiles tend to have stringent latency needs for vehicular safety applications, which require efficient cryptographic solutions that do not interfere with real-time operation. Algorithms like CRYSTALS-Kyber and CRYSTALS-Dilithium, which are post-quantum, have been tuned to such applications, and they offer reasonable performance at the cost of quantum-resistant security.

Healthcare Systems

Smart city healthcare systems incorporate electronic health records, telemedicine platforms, wearable health monitoring devices, and AI-based diagnostic tools that need strong privacy protections and security standards. Healthcare data is among the most sensitive data gathered in smart cities, and quantum-safe cryptographic protection becomes crucial for preserving patient privacy and regulatory compliance. The Boston Brigham and Women's Hospital has deployed QKD technology to secure electronic patient health records and telemedicine communications. The system employs quantum key distribution to encrypt communications between the hospital's central data center and remote clinics, so that patient information being sent for telemedicine consultation cannot be intercepted or tampered with. The deployment of quantum cryptography shows how ultimate privacy security for healthcare communications can be achieved without impairing the real-time response needed for medical applications. Wearable medical monitoring devices pose special challenges to quantum cryptographic deployment because of their limited processing capacity and power reserves. Such devices continuously gather sensitive biometric information, such as heart rate, blood pressure, sleep patterns, and activity level, which has to be securely transmitted to healthcare professionals and personal health record systems. The University of Singapore has created light post-quantum cryptographic protocols for wearable health devices that offer quantum-resistant security with minimal computational overhead and power.

Telemedicine platforms have seen explosive growth, especially after the COVID-19 pandemic, generating new security needs for remote healthcare provisioning. Telemedicine platforms need to secure video communications, diagnostic data exchanges, and electronic prescribing while allowing healthcare professionals to access relevant patient data in real-time. Kaiser Permanente's health system has adopted hybrid quantum-classical encryption for its telemedicine platform, employing QKD-based key distribution and classical encryption for real-time video communications. The convergence of healthcare systems and smart city infrastructure introduces new security needs that quantum cryptography is capable of solving. Emergency response systems that automatically alert healthcare providers to accidents or medical emergencies identified by smart city sensors need secure communication to guarantee accurate medical information transmission and patient privacy. The emergency medical services system in Amsterdam employs post-quantum cryptographic protocols to safeguard communications between emergency sensors, dispatch systems, and medical providers.

INTEGRATION WITH NEXT-GENERATION TECHNOLOGIES

Synergies between quantum cryptography and other next-generation technologies offer the potential to transform the operations of smart cities, solving multifaceted security and operational issues. Sophisticated architectural strategies are needed to take advantage of each technology's unique strengths while ensuring system coherence and performance.

Quantum Cryptography and Artificial Intelligence

The combination of quantum cryptography and artificial intelligence platforms in smart cities responds to core security and privacy concerns while facilitating advanced AI functionality. AI platforms need access to immense amounts of data to train and function, typically involving sensitive citizen data that is to be shielded from unauthorized use and privacy breaches. Quantum cryptographic technologies offer a means of protecting AI platforms while facilitating privacy-preserving computation and secure multi-party learning. Federated learning is a specific use case in which quantum cryptography is enhancing security in AI systems. In federated learning systems, artificial intelligence models are trained on multiple distributed datasets without raw data centralization, maintaining privacy while facilitating collaborative learning. Helsinki has developed a federated learning system for traffic optimization that employs post-quantum cryptographic protocols for securing communications among distributed nodes of learning. The system enables traffic data from various city districts to be used in the training of AI models without disclosing raw traffic patterns, safeguarding the privacy of citizens while enhancing city-wide traffic management.

Quantum cryptographic protocol-based secure multi-party computation (SMC) lets multiple organizations compute functions together over their private data without disclosing the underlying information. The feature is especially useful in smart city applications where multiple parties must collaborate without compromising data privacy. The European Union uses quantum-resistant SMC protocols in its GDPR compliance monitoring system to monitor privacy compliance across member states without divulging sensitive citizen data to unauthorized entities. Homomorphic encryption, complemented with quantum-safe cryptographic foundations, allows AI algorithms to process encrypted information without decryption. This feature enables smart cities to utilize cloud-based AI services while maintaining full control over sensitive information. The Toronto Smart City program has used quantum-safe homomorphic encryption for its predictive policing algorithms, enabling AI models to process crime patterns and forecast potential occurrences while keeping all citizen data encrypted during the computation.

The safeguarding of AI models themselves is another key use for quantum cryptography in smart cities. AI models, especially deep learning networks, are intellectual property that has to be safeguarded against stealing and adversarial attacks. Quantum-safe digital signature schemes can verify AI model updates and guard against unauthorized changes, while quantum key distribution can encrypt the exchange of model parameters between development and operational settings. Adversarial machine learning attacks, where an adversary inputs data to deceive AI systems, represent a major threat to smart city use cases. Quantum cryptographic protocols can offer authenticated input verification mechanisms that guarantee AI systems receive valid data. The Singapore Smart Nation program has used quantum-safe input verification on its AI-driven urban planning systems to block malicious players from injecting false data that will skew urban development decisions.

Quantum Cryptography and Blockchain

The alignment of quantum cryptography and blockchain technology resolves some of the basic security flaws in distributed ledger systems while introducing new use cases for smart city government and services. Conventional blockchain systems rely on cryptographic hash functions and digital signatures that are susceptible to quantum attacks, so the incorporation of quantum-resistant cryptographic algorithms becomes a prerequisite for long-term blockchain security. Estonia's e-Residency blockchain platform presents an extensive example of quantum-resistant blockchain deployment for smart city administration (Wid et al., 2024). The platform employs post-quantum digital signature schemes for transaction validation and quantum-resistant hash functions for block generation, making the blockchain quantum-resistant to future quantum attacks. The deployment has allowed more than 100,000 foreign e-residents to securely access Estonian digital services, showcasing the scalability and usability of quantum-resistant blockchain technology.

Quantum-safe smart contracts that automate city governance and service delivery processes need quantum-safe cryptographic underpinnings to validate and enforce over the long term. Zug, Switzerland, has adopted quantum-safe smart contracts for citizen services such as voting, authentication, and municipal service delivery. The platform utilizes lattice-based cryptographic schemes, ensuring smart contract execution to be tamper-proof and legally enforceable as quantum computing abilities evolve. Decentralized identity management networks based on blockchain technology for citizen authentication and identification gain considerably from quantum cryptographic upgrades. Such systems have to offer long-duration identity verification that holds good for decades, and hence, quantum-resistant cryptographic algorithms become inevitable. Amsterdam has implemented a quantum-resistant blockchain identity solution where citizens can have sovereign control over their digital identities with the assurance that identity verification will not be compromised by any future quantum attack.

Quantum Cryptography and 6G Networks

The advent of sixth-generation (6G) wireless networks in smart cities provides unprecedented opportunities to integrate quantum cryptography and meet new security requirements for ultra-high-speed, low-latency communications. 6G networks are anticipated to enable terahertz frequency communication, massive IoT connectivity, and integrated sensing and communications features that demand sophisticated security architectures. The extremely low latency demands of 6G networks supporting applications with sub-millisecond latency requirements pose special challenges for the implementation of quantum cryptography. Conventional QKD systems can add unacceptably high latency for real-time applications, and therefore, optimized quantum key distribution protocols and hardware implementations are needed. NTT Docomo developed high-speed QKD systems especially tailored for 6G networks that deliver more than 1 Gbps of key distribution speed and still provide quantum security assurances.

Terahertz frequency communication in 6G networks provides vast bandwidth capacity but introduces new security risks with their propagation behaviors and vulnerability to eavesdropping. Quantum cryptographic protocols can be used to give quantum-secured communication as a service capability for terahertz communications through mechanisms that make it possible to detect immediately any effort to intercept communications. The University of Tokyo has successfully implemented quantum-enhanced terahertz communication systems that integrate terahertz frequencies' high bandwidth capacity with quantum cryptography's ultimate security assurances.

Quantum Cryptography and IoT Integration

The massive scale of IoT deployments anticipated in smart cities, potentially involving billions of connected devices, creates unique opportunities and challenges for quantum cryptographic implementation. While individual IoT devices may lack the computational resources to support quantum cryptographic operations directly, hierarchical security architectures can extend quantum-safe protection throughout IoT ecosystems.

Swarm robotics applications in smart cities, where large numbers of autonomous robots collaborate to perform tasks such as environmental monitoring, infrastructure maintenance, and emergency response, require secure coordination mechanisms that can scale to thousands of participating devices. The Swiss Federal Institute of Technology (ETH Zurich) has developed quantum-safe swarm coordination protocols that use post-quantum cryptographic algorithms to secure inter-robot communications while maintaining the real-time responsiveness required for collaborative robotics applications. Table 1 provides a comparison between quantum cryptographic technologies.

Table 1. A comparative overview of quantum cryptographic technologies, highlighting their strengths and limitations across smart city applications

Technology	Security Basis	Key Advantages	Primary Limitations	Smart City Applications
Quantum Key Distribution (QKD)	Quantum mechanics (no-cloning theorem)	Information-theoretic security, immediate eavesdropping detection	Distance limitations, specialized hardware requirements	Critical infrastructure communications, government networks
Post-Quantum Cryptography	Mathematical complexity (lattice problems, hash functions)	Standard hardware compatibility, network protocol integration	Larger key sizes, computational overhead	IoT devices, mobile communications, legacy system integration
Hybrid Quantum-Classical	Combined quantum and classical approaches	Backward compatibility, scalable deployment	Implementation complexity, key management challenges	Enterprise networks, gradual migration scenarios

CHALLENGES AND ETHICAL ISSUES

Implementation of quantum cryptography in smart cities poses complex challenges across technical, economic, ethical, and governance aspects. It is essential to comprehend and manage such challenges for the effective implementation and acceptance of quantum-safe technology in urban spaces.

Technical and Scalability Challenges

The scalability of quantum cryptography technology is among the most important challenges in widespread deployment in smart cities. Presently, QKD systems are subject to intrinsic limitations in terms of transmission distance, generally being around 100 kilometers in the case of terrestrial fiber-optic implementations because of photon loss and decoherence effects. Satellite-based QKD can increase such distances dramatically, but the infrastructure cost and complexity are enormous and make city-wide deployment difficult.

Exponential management complexity grows with the size of quantum cryptographic implementations. Smart cities can demand secure communication among millions of devices and thousands of infrastructure nodes, posing key management challenges that dwarf ordinary cryptographic systems. The alignment of quantum key distribution, classical key backup systems, and hybrid encryption methods demands advanced key management infrastructures that can preserve security and offer reliable operation.

Network latency issues are paramount for real-time smart city use cases that are not allowed to incur the extra processing latencies added by quantum cryptographic computations. Emergency response systems, autonomous vehicle coordination, and industrial control systems need ultra-low latency communications that can be incompatible with some quantum cryptographic schemes. Quantum cryptographic protocols must be optimized for low-latency applications through continuous research and development.

Privacy and Data Protection

The use of quantum cryptography in smart cities poses significant privacy issues that go beyond technical security solutions to include data governance, citizen rights, and regulatory compliance. While quantum cryptographic technologies offer greater technical security for data, their usage must also be supported with end-to-end privacy frameworks that cater to citizens' concerns and comply with regulations. Consent management of quantum-encrypted smart city infrastructure needs to give citizens meaningful control over their personal information while acknowledging the technical restraints of quantum cryptographic implementation. Citizens ought to know how quantum cryptographic technologies safeguard their information and ought to be able to opt out of data gathering wherever feasible. The irreversible character of certain quantum cryptographic computations can make data deletion rights necessitated by privacy laws like GDPR difficult.

Transparency needs for algorithmic transparency can oppose the security advantages of quantum cryptographic systems. While citizens are entitled to know the impact automated decision-making systems have on them, divulging detailed information regarding quantum cryptographic implementations might expose them to threats. Finding an equilibrium between transparency demands and security demands needs precise consideration of what information can be made public without degrading system security.

Regulatory and Governance Frameworks

The regulatory environment for quantum cryptography in smart cities is multifaceted and dynamic, with several levels of government regulation, international standards, and industry guidelines. Cities are required to navigate this dynamic regulatory framework while being compliant with current laws and preparing for future regulatory changes. Table 2 describes current challenges and their evolving solutions in deploying quantum cryptography. Export control laws regulating quantum technologies differ substantially among jurisdictions and can impact cities' capacity to utilize some quantum cryptographic systems. The United States, the European Union, and other jurisdictions have export controls on quantum technologies that can restrict global cooperation and technology exchange. Cities intending quantum cryptographic deployments need to take into careful consideration export control ramifications, especially for systems involving international vendors or border-to-border communications.

Cybersecurity standards increasingly acknowledge the significance of quantum-safe cryptographic technologies and could require their implementation for use in critical infrastructure. The U.S. National Security Memorandum on Improving Cybersecurity for Critical Infrastructure Control Systems actually calls out for quantum-safe cryptographic transitions, imposing regulatory pressure on the early implementation of quantum cryptographic technology within smart city infrastructure. Standards development in the area of quantum cryptography is an ongoing process with several organizations collaborating to define technical standards, security assessment, and certification procedures. The International Organization for Standardization (ISO), International Telecommunication Union (ITU), and national standards organizations are creating holistic standards frameworks that will regulate quantum cryptographic deployments in smart cities.

Table 2. Current challenges and their evolving solutions in deploying quantum cryptography

Challenge	Impact	Current Solutions	Future Developments
Distance limitations	Restricts QKD to metropolitan scale	Trusted node networks, satellite QKD	Quantum repeaters, improved detectors
Key management complexity	Scalability issues for large networks	Hierarchical architectures, hybrid systems	Automated key management, AI optimization
Hardware costs	High deployment barriers	Public-private partnerships, phased rollout	Mass production, integrated photonics
Environmental sensitivity	Reliability concerns in urban settings	Robust enclosures, error correction	Self-calibrating systems, adaptive protocols

CASE STUDIES

Real-world deployments of quantum cryptography in smart cities give a true picture of the opportunities and challenges presented by quantum cryptography as well as lessons learned from actual experience. Such case studies reflect the state of quantum cryptographic technology at present and point to successful approaches and areas of improvement.

Tokyo's QKD Pilot Project

Tokyo's Quantum Key Distribution pilot project is a historic deployment of quantum cryptography in city infrastructure, illustrating the practical applicability of quantum-safe solutions for use in large-scale metropolitan settings. Launched in 2020 by the Tokyo Metropolitan Government together with NTT Corporation and the National Institute of Information and Communications Technology (NICT), the project seeks to protect key communications infrastructure from existing and future cyber threats. The deployment includes a wide-area QKD network linking central government buildings, financial organizations, and strategic infrastructure components throughout the metropolitan region of Tokyo. The network employs both fiber-optic and free-space optical quantum communications links to establish flexible connection opportunities that can be dynamic enough to conform to the intricacies of the metropolitan setting. The fiber-optic links make use of available telecommunications infrastructure whenever available, while free-space optical connections establish backup connectivity and support for areas where it is impossible to install fiber.

Among the key successes of the Tokyo pilot is the integration of QKD into mainstream enterprise network infrastructure. The experiment shows the way quantum key distribution can be integrated perfectly into traditional network systems without the need for total replacement of legacy equipment. The deployment relies on hybrid quantum-classical encryption methods wherein QKD generates cryptographic keys for symmetric encryption methods, balancing the highest level of security provided by quantum cryptography with the efficiency and compatibility of classical encryption techniques. The project has reached many key performance and reliability milestones. The QKD network dynamically maintains key generation rates of over 1 Mbps with distances up to 50 kilometers, allowing for adequate cryptographic material for safeguarding high-bandwidth communications. The system reflects 99.9% uptime reliability, adhering to the high availability requirements for critical infrastructure use. The implementation also features advanced monitoring and alerting systems that offer real-time insight into quantum channel quality and security status.

The economic study of the Tokyo pilot gives us some insight into the cost-effectiveness of quantum cryptography deployment. The initial infrastructure costs were estimated to be around $50 million, consisting of dedicated quantum hardware, network infrastructure upgrades, and system integration costs. However, the project showcases considerable cost savings through hybrid architectures that make use of existing infrastructure and phased deployment techniques, allowing step-by-step extension of quantum-safe capabilities. Lessons from the Tokyo implementation highlight the significance of stakeholder coordination and incremental deployment strategies. The accomplishment of the project is based on intimate collaboration among government agencies, telecommunications vendors, technology suppliers, and academic institutions. The collaborative framework facilitated knowledge sharing, risk management, and coordinated problem-solving that cut deployment schedules and lessened implementation difficulties. The Tokyo pilot has laid a foundation for more extensive adoption of quantum cryptography across Japan's smart city projects. The pilot project is a testing ground for creating best practices, training technical staff, and proving the viability of quantum-safe technologies to other cities and organizations. Expansion plans in the future involve expanding the QKD network to other cities and combining quantum cryptographic functions with emerging technologies like 5G networks and IoT platforms.

China's Micius Satellite Network

China's Micius satellite is a groundbreaking milestone in the quantum communication capabilities of the globe, illustrating the viability of satellite-based quantum key distribution for secure intercontinental communications. The Micius satellite was launched in August 2016 as part of China's ambitious program of quantum communication research and has already established quantum-encrypted links between the ground stations that are thousands of kilometers apart, transcending the distance limitations that bound QKD implementations on the ground.

The satellite flies at a height of around 500 kilometers in a sun-synchronous orbit, offering the best coverage for quantum communication experiments. The spacecraft is equipped with advanced quantum communication systems such as single-photon emitters, beam steering mechanisms, and high-precision pointing systems that allow quantum key distribution between the satellite and the ground stations with high accuracy. The system can support quantum communication connections with ground stations while moving at orbital speeds of over 7 kilometers per second. One of the greatest successes of the Micius satellite mission is demonstrating intercontinental quantum key distribution between Austria and China. In 2017, the satellite successfully enabled a quantum-encrypted video conference between researchers in Beijing and Vienna by establishing cryptographic keys via satellite-mediated QKD and applying these keys to encrypt the video communication. This experiment confirmed that quantum cryptography via satellites can offer viable security solutions for continent-spanning and ocean-crossing communications.

The technological performance of the Micius satellite has surpassed initial expectations in a number of important aspects. The system delivers quantum key generation rates of a few kilobits per second during overhead passages, which is enough to protect various kinds of communications. The satellite retains quantum communication links even under unfavorable atmospheric conditions, proving the reliability of the quantum communication protocols and the implementations in hardware.

Security assessment of Micius satellite operations verifies the inherent security benefits of quantum cryptography while finding special challenges faced by satellite-based applications. The quantum communication links from satellites to ground offer information-theoretic security promises similar to ground-based QKD systems, where any eavesdropping will inevitably be detected by quantum bit error rate monitoring. But satellite implementation poses extra security issues due to the space environment, orbital dynamics, and ground station security. The potential of the Micius satellite to support smart city applications is deep and extensive. QKD over satellites can deliver quantum-safe communications to cities that have no terrestrial quantum communication infrastructure, making it possible to build global networks of quantum-secured smart cities. The technology holds the greatest value in international collaborations, cross-border information exchanges, and global supply chain security applications that demand maximum cryptographic protection. Future applications founded on the Micius satellite experience include concepts for quantum communication satellite constellations that might offer constant worldwide coverage for quantum key distribution. Such constellations would break the existing restriction of periodic overhead passes and make possible real-time quantum-safe communications between any two points on Earth. Many nations and corporations are working on equivalent satellite-based quantum communication networks, leading towards a future global quantum communication infrastructure.

DISCUSSION

The examination of quantum cryptography use in smart cities provides a nuanced map of opportunity, challenges, and compromises that need to be approached deftly in order to support successful deployment. Discussion of the results necessitates consideration of the relative advantages and disadvantages of various quantum cryptographic methods, the appropriateness of these methods to different smart city uses, and the general implications for technology uptake in cities.

Security Architecture Implications

Application of quantum cryptography in smart cities requires substantial reappraisals of security architecture design principles and practices. Perimeter defense- and centralized security control-based traditional security architectures might not be effective in quantum-safe smart city environments demanding distributed security features and defense-in-depth methodologies.

Zero-trust models of security best align with quantum cryptographic potential because they presuppose that no communications channel or system element can be inherently trusted. Quantum cryptographic technologies offer the kinds of verification and authentication mechanisms required to fully take advantage of zero-trust architectures, while the decentralized nature of smart city infrastructure necessitates zero-trust strategies for end-to-end security. Threat modeling for quantum-safe smart cities must consider both current cybersecurity threats and future quantum-enabled attacks. The long operational lifespans of urban infrastructure mean that security architectures implemented today must remain effective against threats that may emerge decades in the future. This forward-looking approach to threat modeling necessitates conservative security assumptions and flexible architectural designs that can adapt to evolving threat landscapes.

Future Research Directions

The fast-changing character of quantum technologies and their use in smart cities provides many areas of future research that can overcome existing limitations and support novel applications. Critical research directions are the creation of more effective quantum cryptographic protocols, better integration techniques, and better performance optimization methods. Studies on optimizing post-quantum cryptographic algorithms by minimizing their computation overhead and resource needs could make them much more resource-friendly for IoT devices with limited resources and real-time applications. Investigations on applying specialized hardware and algorithm-hardware co-design could bring dramatic improvements in performance that would make quantum-safe cryptography much easier to deploy on a large-scale basis. Interdisciplinary research that integrates quantum cryptography with other new technologies like artificial intelligence, blockchain, and edge computing has the potential to unlock new applications and possibilities that are not possible with each technology in isolation. The convergence technologies can deliver solutions to smart city challenges that are complex and require the collective capabilities of several next-generation technologies.

Architecture for integrating quantum cryptography into a smart-city network, as shown in Figure 1. A metro QKD backbone links core/cloud facilities to access nodes; hybrid classical/quantum gateways relay keys to the edge; and IoT devices communicate over post-quantum-protected tunnels, enabling phased migration from conventional to quantum-safe security.

Comparative security lifespan (2000–2040) of classical public-key cryptography, post-quantum cryptography (PQC), and quantum key distribution (QKD), as shown in Figure 2. The timeline marks the anticipated vulnerability window for classical algorithms and the projected maturation of PQC and QKD solutions.

Figure 1. Quantum cryptography integration architecture for smart cities

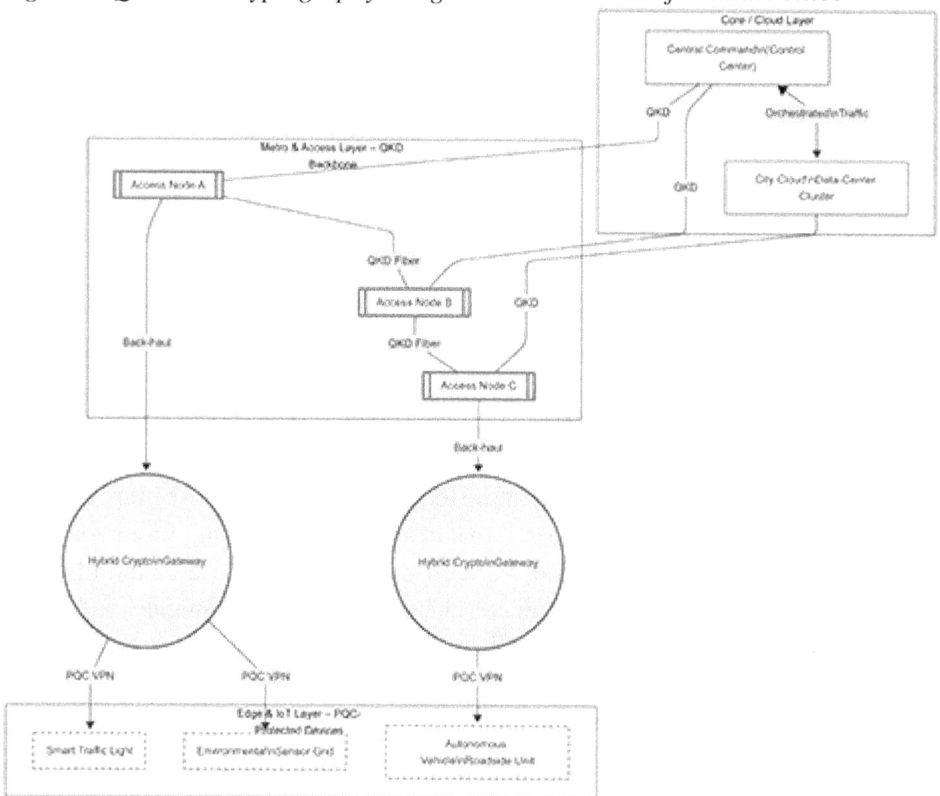

Figure 2. Comparative security timeline for classical vs. quantum cryptographic approaches

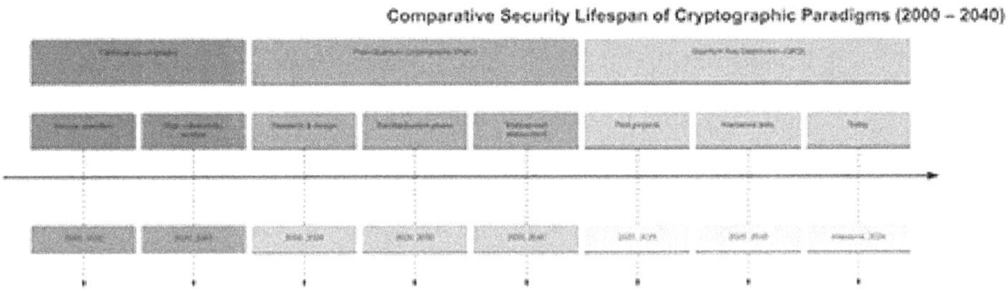

A cost-benefit matrix is for quantum-cryptography initiatives. Each option is plotted by relative implementation cost (x-axis) and security/operational benefit (y-axis), grouping actions into four decision quadrants: Invest Now, Strategic Opportunity, Monitor, and Defer/Reassess, as shown in Figure 3.

Figure 3. Cost-benefit analysis framework for quantum cryptography deployment

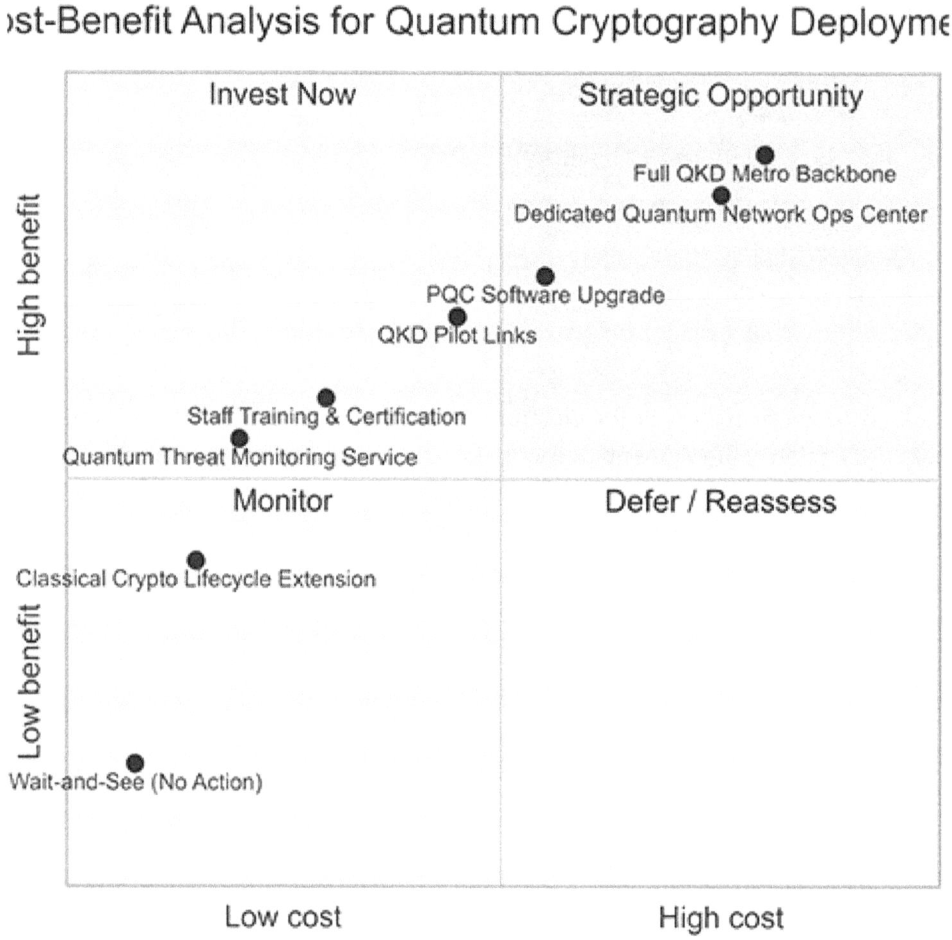

GLOBAL POLICY AND COOPERATION

Emergence and application of quantum cryptography in smart cities demand levels of global cooperation, coordination of policies, and standards building that are unprecedented. The globality of cybersecurity threats, the interconnected nature of urban systems in the contemporary era, and the intricacy of quantum technologies demand cooperative solutions that extend beyond conventional organization and national borders.

International Standards and Frameworks

The International Organization for Standardization (ISO) has formed Technical Committee 307 (ISO/TC 307) solely to deal with blockchain and distributed ledger technologies, and concurrent committees are preparing quantum cryptography standards that will regulate smart city deployments. The ISO 23053 standard for quantum key distribution sets the ground-level framework for evaluation and certification of QKD systems, while work continues on ISO 23554 to cover security specifications for QKD networks. The International Telecommunication Union (ITU) has created recommendation ITU-T Y.3800 that gives an overview of quantum key distribution networks, such as architectural considerations, security requirements, and performance metrics for use in smart city deployments. More ITU recommendations cover detailed aspects of quantum cryptographic implementations, such as network management, interoperability, and service definitions.

The European Telecommunications Standards Institute (ETSI) has set up the Industry Specification Group on Quantum Key Distribution (ISG QKD) to produce technical specifications and standards for quantum cryptographic systems. ETSI specifications include QKD system components, interfaces, protocols, and security evaluation methodologies that offer pragmatic guidance for smart city deployment. NIST's Post-Quantum Cryptography Standardization is the most extensive attempt at standardizing quantum-resistant algorithms for mass deployment. The NIST standards form the basis for post-quantum cryptographic implementations in smart cities, where they provide interoperability and security across various vendors and applications. The standardization process has entailed widespread international collaboration among cryptographic experts from academia, industry, and governments around the globe.

Regional Initiatives and Programs

The European Union's EuroQCI program has the goal of creating a secure quantum communication network covering all member states of the EU by 2027. The EuroQCI program will integrate terrestrial fiber-optic QKD networks with satellite quantum communications to enable end-to-end coverage for government, critical infrastructure, and commercial use. Smart cities in Europe will be among the prime beneficiaries of capabilities from EuroQCI, with various pilot programs already showing real-world applications. The United States National Quantum Initiative Act of 2018 created a unified federal program to jump-start research and development on quantum, including quantum cryptography technologies for the protection of critical infrastructure. The initiative allocates funds for research on quantum technology, workforce development, and international cooperation activities supporting smart city deployment of quantum cryptography.

China's huge investments in quantum technology R&D and infrastructure have paid off with the world's first functioning quantum communication satellite (Micius) and large-scale terrestrial QKD networks between major cities. The Chinese solution illustrates the feasibility of national-scale quantum communication infrastructure capable of powering smart city applications throughout a whole country. Asia-Pacific Economic Cooperation (APEC) has created working groups on quantum technology policy coordination and standards development, acknowledging the role of regional collaboration in the adoption of quantum technology. APEC programs respond to trade facilitation, technology transfer, and regulatory harmonization concerns that impact the deployment of quantum cryptography in smart cities in the Asia-Pacific region.

Regulatory Harmonization Efforts

Export control management of quantum technologies involves cooperation among nations to match legitimate security interests with the necessity for technological cooperation and commerce. The Wassenaar Arrangement and other multilateral export control regimes are engaged in crafting coordinated frameworks for controlling quantum technology while avoiding proliferation dangers and facilitating useful applications such as secure smart city cyberdefense. Table 3 introduces key international initiatives, their scope, and relevance to smart city quantum cryptography deployments. Alignment of privacy regulation across various jurisdictions is imperative for smart cities that cross national borders or manage global data flows. The European GDPR, the United States' California Consumer Privacy Act (CCPA), and equivalent privacy mechanisms globally develop intricate compliance needs that need to be tackled in quantum cryptography implementations.

Cybersecurity rule convergence activities try to design harmonized methods to meet quantum-resistant cryptographic needs in various nations and regions. The EU Network and Information Security (NIS) Directive, U.S. cybersecurity guidelines, and comparable rules globally are becoming more adaptive to counter quantum threats and could require the implementation of quantum-safe cryptography for key infrastructure.

Table 3. Summarizes key international initiatives, their scope, and relevance to smart city quantum cryptography deployments

Initiative	Geographic Scope	Focus Areas	Timeline	Smart City Relevance
EuroQCI	European Union	QKD infrastructure, standards	2019–2027	Government services, critical infrastructure
U.S. National Quantum Initiative	United States	Research, workforce development	2018–2023	Federal systems, critical infrastructure
China Quantum Communication Network	China	National QKD backbone	2016–ongoing	Urban communications, government services
NIST PQC Standardization	Global	Algorithm standards	2016–2024	All cryptographic applications
ITU-T Quantum Recommendations	Global	Technical standards	2018–ongoing	Telecommunications, network infrastructure

CONCLUSION AND RECOMMENDATIONS

The detailed examination of quantum cryptography use in smart city settings discloses a revolutionary technology with unmatched security potential, but also imposing implementation challenges and opportunities. While cities globally face mounting cybersecurity threats and the specter of a quantum computing revolution, quantum cryptography stands as a critical part of tomorrow's urban digital infrastructure.

Strategic Recommendations for Smart Cities

Based on the detailed analysis of quantum cryptography technologies, applications, and challenges, the following strategic recommendations act as guidance for cities contemplating the adoption of quantum-safe technology:

Immediate Actions (2024-2025)

Cities must start by undertaking a thorough risk analysis that analyzes existing cryptographic vulnerabilities and determines key infrastructure elements needing quantum-proof protection. Such analysis must take into account long infrastructure operational life spans and the possible timeline for quantum attacks against existing cryptographic systems. These applications should be prioritized: sensitive citizen data, control of critical infrastructure, and high-value financial transactions. The creation of quantum-resistant migration plans is a critical first step that needs to start now. They need to encompass technology assessment metrics, roll-out schedules, budgeting, and stakeholder coordination processes. Cities need to make crypto-agility a priority in new system procurements and infrastructure investment so future quantum-resistant changes can be facilitated without needing full system re-replacement.

Workforce development and training initiatives must be put in place to develop in-house talent for the evaluation, deployment, and management of quantum cryptography. These initiatives must incorporate technical training for information technology staff, policy-making for officials, and awareness training for citizens and stakeholders. Academic collaborations, industry associations, and other cities can be sources of useful knowledge sharing and capacity development.

Medium-Term Implementation (2025-2028)

Development of pilot projects must target high-value applications that can illustrate quantum cryptography advantages while creating organizational experience and technical competency. Suggested pilot applications are critical infrastructure communications, sensitive government services, and high-security healthcare systems. These pilots must have extensive evaluation metrics, lessons learned documentation, and scalability planning for future growth.

Post-quantum cryptography adoption needs to start with applications that will gain from near-term deployment on the current hardware infrastructure. Algorithms standardized by NIST need to be fast-tracked for their security verification and industry uptake. Post-quantum and classical cryptographic techniques combined in hybrid forms can offer high security with backward compatibility and performance profiles. Quantum key distribution infrastructure planning must start with feasibility analyses and vendor assessments for high-priority uses. Municipalities may opt for collaboration with telecommunications companies and technology vendors to split the cost of the infrastructure and utilize existing fiber-optic backbones. Satellite-based QKD solutions should be considered for long-distance communication or backup connectivity applications.

Policy and Governance Recommendations

Quantum cryptography regulatory frameworks must be established with the collaboration of national governments, industry associations, and international standards organizations. Such frameworks will need to cover security needs, protections of privacy, interoperability standards, and certification procedures for quantum cryptographic systems. Cities must push for enabling policies that facilitate the adoption of quantum technology while promoting responsible implementation and public safety.

Public consultation and transparency efforts must inform citizens regarding quantum cryptography advantages and mitigate privacy, surveillance, and technology sophistication concerns. Public consultations, privacy-impact assessments, and regular communication around deployments of quantum-safe technology must be included in such efforts. Citizen trust and acceptance are key to the successful uptake of quantum cryptography in democratic states. Economic incentive programs should be explored to encourage quantum cryptography adoption and accelerate technology maturation. These programs may include public-private partnerships, tax incentives for quantum technology investments, shared infrastructure development, and collaborative procurement initiatives. Economic incentives can help overcome cost barriers and demonstrate the government's commitment to quantum-safe technology development.

Research and Development Priorities

Optimization of technology research must aim at lowering costs, enhancing performance, and making quantum cryptographic systems more user-friendly for smart city use. Top areas of focus are integrated photonics for the miniaturization of QKD hardware, algorithm optimization for constrained devices, and network architecture advancements for scalability and dependability. University-industry collaborations can expedite the research while maintaining practical applicability. Interdisciplinary studies integrating quantum cryptography with other breakthrough technologies should identify new uses and functionalities that solve profound smart city problems. Some of the most relevant areas are quantum-resistant artificial intelligence, blockchain-based integration, edge computing utilization, and autonomous system protection. These studies need to address not just the technical possibilities but also the economic feasibility and social acceptance.

Security certification and evaluation schemes must set stringent test practices and validation procedures for quantum cryptographic technology employed in smart cities. The programs must cover both theoretical security characteristics and implementation-oriented vulnerabilities. International cooperation in security evaluation can guarantee common standards and recognition of results across borders. The future of smart cities relies more and more on the trust and security of their digital infrastructure. Quantum cryptography lays the technological basis to secure city digital systems against both existing and future cyber threats. Although challenges are enormous, quantum-safe technologies' advantages make investments and efforts worthwhile for effective implementation. Cities that initiate quantum-safe migration now will be best prepared to safeguard their citizens, infrastructure, and services in the quantum future ahead.

The path to quantum-safe smart cities needs dedicated effort, teamwork, and flexible strategies that will change with evolving technology and shifting threat profiles. Through the implementation of the suggestions in this analysis and deriving lessons from pioneer experiences, cities are able to transition to quantum-safe digital platforms while harnessing the greatest quantum cryptographic technology benefits to citizens and stakeholders.

REFERENCES

Ahmad, I., Kumar, T., Liyanage, M., Okwuibe, J., Ylianttila, M., & Gurtov, A. (2018). Overview of 5G security challenges and solutions. *IEEE Communications Standards Magazine*, *2*(1), 36–43. DOI: 10.1109/MCOMSTD.2018.1700063

Antonakakis, M., April, T., Bailey, M., Bernhard, M., Bursztein, E., Cochran, J., & Zhou, Y. (2017). *Understanding the Mirai botnet. In 26th USENIX Security Symposium*. USENIX Association., https://www.usenix.org/system/files/conference/usenixsecurity17/sec17-antonakakis.pdf

Bennett, C. H., & Brassard, G. (1984). Quantum cryptography: Public key distribution and coin tossing. In *Proceedings of the IEEE International Conference on Computers, Systems and Signal Processing* (pp. 175–179). IEEE.

Bibri, S. E., & Krogstie, J. (2017). Smart sustainable cities of the future: An extensive interdisciplinary literature review. *Sustainable Cities and Society*, *31*, 183–212. DOI: 10.1016/j.scs.2017.02.016

Grover, L. K. (1996). A fast quantum mechanical algorithm for database search. In *Proceedings of the Twenty-Eighth Annual ACM Symposium on Theory of Computing* (pp. 212–219). ACM. DOI: 10.1145/237814.237866

Hallem, R., & Hammed, A. (2024). Maintaining security of patient data by employing private blockchain and fog computing technologies based on internet of medical things. *Informatica (Vilnius)*, *48*(12).

Lo, H. K., Ma, X., & Chen, K. (2005). Decoy state quantum key distribution. *Physical Review Letters*, *94*(23), 230504. DOI: 10.1103/PhysRevLett.94.230504 PMID: 16090452

Rasha, R., Tahayur, D., & Jebbar, W. (2025). Sturdy Blockchain Combined with E-apps Repositories Based on Reliable Camouflaging and Integrating Mechanisms. *IJ Computer Network and Information Security*, *17*(3), 35–53. DOI: 10.5815/ijcnis.2025.03.03

Scarani, V., Acín, A., Ribordy, G., & Gisin, N. (2004). Quantum cryptography protocols robust against photon number splitting attacks for weak laser pulse implementations. *Physical Review Letters*, *92*(5), 057901. DOI: 10.1103/PhysRevLett.92.057901 PMID: 14995344

Shor, P. W. (1994). Algorithms for quantum computation: Discrete logarithms and factoring. In *Proceedings of the 35th Annual Symposium on Foundations of Computer Science* (pp. 124–134). IEEE. DOI: 10.1109/SFCS.1994.365700

U.S. National Institute of Standards and Technology. (2022). *Selected algorithms 2022: Post-quantum cryptography standardization* (NIST Special Publication 800-208). DOI: 10.6028/NIST.SP.800-208

Weedbrook, C., Pirandola, S., García-Patrón, R., Cerf, N. J., Ralph, T. C., Shapiro, J. H., & Lloyd, S. (2012). Gaussian quantum information. *Reviews of Modern Physics*, *84*(2), 621–669. DOI: 10.1103/RevModPhys.84.621

Wid, J., Razzaq, R., & Tahayur, D. (2024). Blockchain and cryptography framework of e-apps with big data. *Journal of Education for Pure Science*, *14*(3).

Yin, H. L., Chen, T. Y., Yu, Z. W., Liu, H., You, L. X., Zhou, Y. H., Chen, S.-J., Mao, Y., Huang, M.-Q., Zhang, W.-J., Chen, H., Li, M. J., Nolan, D., Zhou, F., Jiang, X., Wang, Z., Zhang, Q., Wang, X.-B., & Pan, J. W. (2016). Measurement-device-independent quantum key distribution over a 404 km optical fiber. *Physical Review Letters*, *117*(19), 190501. DOI: 10.1103/PhysRevLett.117.190501 PMID: 27858431

KEY TERMS AND DEFINITIONS

Crypto-Agility: The capacity of cryptographic systems to rapidly and effectively switch to new cryptographic algorithms or parameters in response to evolving threats or advancements in technology.

Digital Twin: A virtual copy of a physical object, system, or process that is regularly fed with real-time data. In smart cities, digital twins are employed to simulate and optimize urban structures, necessitating secure data exchange between physical sensors and virtual models that can be advantaged by quantum cryptographic security.

Hybrid Quantum-Classical Cryptography: Security solutions that bridge quantum cryptographic technologies (e.g., QKD) with classical cryptographic algorithms to deliver added security at the expense of retaining practical deployment features.

Information-Theoretic Security: A security level assured by mathematical proof instead of computational assumptions. Information-theoretic security holds true no matter the computational power at an attacker's disposal, and hence is not susceptible to improved computing technology such as quantum computers.

Lattice-Based Cryptography: A suite of post-quantum cryptographic algorithms whose security is derived from problems in lattices in high-dimensional mathematical structures. Lattice-based schemes, such as CRYSTALS-Kyber and CRYSTALS-Dilithium, provide nice performance properties and are among the strongest contenders for post-quantum cryptographic standardization.

Quantum Bit Error Rate (QBER): A metric of the rate of error in quantum key distribution networks, usually as a percentage of quantum bits sent that are received in error. QBER is utilized to identify eavesdropping and assess the quality of quantum communication channels.

Quantum cryptography: It is used in smart cities, demanding knowledge of technical terms cutting across quantum physics, cryptography, computer science, and urban technology fields.

Quantum No-Cloning Theorem: A fundamental principle of quantum mechanics stating that arbitrary quantum states cannot be perfectly copied. This theorem provides the theoretical foundation for QKD security by ensuring that eavesdroppers cannot make perfect copies of quantum-transmitted information without disturbing the original quantum states.

Quantum Supremacy: The milestone when quantum computers can solve certain computational tasks more quickly than the world's fastest classical computers.

Vehicle-to-Everything (V2X): Communication technologies that allow vehicles to talk with other vehicles (V2V), infrastructure systems (V2I), pedestrians (V2P), and cloud services (V2C).

Chapter 8
Protecting Data of Power Stations in Smart Cities Using Quantum-Resistant and Zero-Knowledge Proof

Mishall Hammed Al-Zubaidie
https://orcid.org/0000-0002-3149-9129
University of Thi-Qar, Iraq

Tuqa Ghani Tregi
https://orcid.org/0009-0003-4513-9751
University of Thi-Qar, Iraq

ABSTRACT

The rapid advancement of quantum computing poses significant challenges to conventional cryptography, necessitating the adoption of post-quantum cryptography (PQC) solutions. This chapter proposes a Post-Quantum Lattice Security (PQLS) system for protecting power plant data in smart cities. It integrates Kyber for secure key exchange, Falcon for quantum-resistant digital signatures, ZKP for efficient authentication without revealing sensitive data, and JSON-LD for standardizing the format of data received from different smart meters. To evaluate the security of the proposed framework, we analyze its resistance to various threats, such as side-channel and message recovery attacks. We measured key performance indicators. The results showed an average CPU utilization of 2.4592 MS, memory consumption averaging 1843.899 KB, an execution time of 2.45 MS, and a level averaging

DOI: 10.4018/979-8-3373-3326-7.ch008

66.27677. This demonstrates that our proposed system offers high security and efficiency, making it a practical solution for protecting electrical infrastructure in smart cities in the quantum era.

INTRODUCTION

The implementation of smart city mechanisms has become a hallmark of developed countries that aim to provide essential services to their citizens. However, there are some obstacles that hinder the progress and development of these smart cities and their practical implementation. This section highlights the importance of smart city development and explains the inadequacy of previous encryption methods in protecting smart city data. It also emphasizes the importance of implementing modern security techniques that keep pace with the evolution of smart cities. Therefore, this section includes the following subsections: Population growth and the emergence of smart cities, traditional encryption facing quantum computing threats, security techniques previously used in smart cities, and chapter objectives.

Population Growth and the Emergence of Smart Cities

Over the past 50 years, the global population has increased at an average annual pace of 1.2%. In 2007, the urban population surpassed the rural population for the first time. This ratio is projected to surpass 70% by 2050 (du Plessis, 2023). The 2013 United Nations World Economic and Social Survey estimates that Africa, Asia, and other emerging areas will comprise over 80% of the global urban population in the forthcoming years (Vučković & Adams, 2022). Despite the advantages of urbanization, it also brings challenges. Modern cities are dealing with major urbanization-related issues, such as privacy and the inappropriate use of technological resources, amid rapid technological developments and massive population growth (Awaad & Jebbar, 2014). These problems directly impact the quality of life, requiring innovative ideas to ensure the operational effectiveness and sustainability of cities. In this context, the concept of smart cities has become a technological solution that aims to integrate the IoT, Artificial Intelligence (AI), and big data analytics into infrastructure management, improving energy efficiency and achieving environmental sustainability (Razzaq & Al-Zubaidie, 2024a). Through integrated systems capable of monitoring data flow and controlling water and electricity usage, smart cities help create more sustainable and resilient urban environments capable of facing future challenges (Awaad & Jebbar, 2015). However, achieving this change requires the establishment of a robust and reliable digital infrastructure, as well as the adoption of robust cybersecurity policies to protect systems and data from cyberattacks. Security and encryption are, therefore, essential components of the success of these cities.

Traditional Encryption Facing Quantum Computing Threats

Though cybersecurity has advanced greatly, major challenges still exist in safeguarding smart city data against cyberattacks (Al-Zubaidie & Jebbar, 2024). The main obstacle is the poor application of contemporary cryptographic techniques in important infrastructure, so exposing systems to major vulnerabilities. Furthermore, undermining conventional data encryption methods is the fast development of quantum computing. Deciphering conventional techniques including Rivest–Shamir–Adleman (RSA) and Elliptic Curve Cryptography (ECC), quantum computers compromise important data in smart infrastructure (Tahayur & Al-Zubaidie, 2025). Post-quantum cryptography (PQC) has emerged as a possible answer to these problems meant to offer flexible security measures for improved processing capability (Sood, 2024). Nonetheless, the implementation of quantum-resistant cryptographic techniques encounters major challenges including major computational resource needs, effects on system efficiency, and fit with current infrastructure. Moreover, this study intends to investigate and assess quantum-resistant encryption methods by means of PQC algorithms in an experimental environment, quantifying their effects on security and operational performance in critical infrastructure, and investigating the difficulties of their application and integration with modern systems (Razzaq & Al-Zubaidie, 2024b).

The study aims to suggest a strong security model that might be a major post-quantum data protection advance. Given the growing security threats aiming at smart city infrastructure, it has become imperative to use strong and safe encryption solutions to guard data and systems from sophisticated attacks in view of developments in quantum computing. In this sense, safeguarding smart cities calls for a whole approach combining modern encryption techniques with advanced authentication systems to guarantee the integrity of digital communications and transactions (Mattsson et al., 2021).

Security Techniques Previously Used in Smart Cities

Protection of data in smart city contexts has long depended critically on conventional cryptography methods. Among the most often embraced are Blockchain for distributed trust and openness, Elliptic Curve Cryptography (ECC) for lightweight public key infrastructure, and Advanced Encryption Standard (AES) for symmetric encryption.

AES offers high-speed encryption and is computationally efficient, making it suitable for embedded IoT devices (El-Sofany et al., 2024). Its weakness, though, is in key management and its sensitivity to side-channel attacks. By contrast, ECC has been applied in smart grid communication systems and offers strong security with shorter key sizes than RSA (Joudah & Manaa, 2024). Still, its mathematical roots are now under danger under quantum algorithms such as Shor's method (Razzaq et al., 2024). Blockchain-based security systems have been installed to improve data immutability and traceability in smart infrastructure (Faberge & Bogoni, 2023), yet they suffer from latency, scalability issues, and regulatory concerns.

Notwithstanding these developments, the introduction of quantum computing challenges the fundamental ideas of conventional methods. Thus, the change towards PQC becomes essential to guarantee long-term resilience. Using Kyber, FALCON, and ZK-STARKs, each of which reflects a strategic response to known constraints in key exchange, digital signature, and zero-knowledge verification, respectively, our work builds on this need.

Chapter Objectives

The primary objectives are summarized below:

- Delivers a resilient key exchange mechanism using Kyber, hence mitigating the threat of quantum key analysis attacks.
- Utilizes a lightweight FALCON-based signature to minimize resource consumption for low-power devices.
- Validates digital signatures without disclosing them using Zero-Knowledge Proofs (ZKP), substantially decreasing processing and storage duration, hence augmenting the security of smart energy systems without compromising speed.

RELATED WORK

This section provides an overview of attempts to secure data and smart cities.

Egger et al. (2020) used the IEC 60870-5-104 asynchronous communication protocol. They investigated numerous approaches for identifying intrusions in power plant distribution substations. Applying the suggested techniques to a dataset comprising four separate assaults and regular running traffic helps one assess them.

The system has not, however, been tested on a sizable physical infrastructure, which could influence performance in various surroundings.

Rashid et al. (2020) proposed an intelligent model based on machine learning approaches to use Internet of Things (IoT) technologies to identify cyberattacks in settings of smart cities. The work evaluated performance using techniques including K-Nearest Neighbors (KNN) and Decision Trees using real-world data. The suggested system proved the efficiency of machine learning in safeguarding smart urban systems by attaining a high detection accuracy surpassing 93%. The study mostly aimed on lowering false positives in linked smart networks and enhancing early threat detection.

Ma (2021) presented scientific research that endeavors to examine and debate cybersecurity and smart cities, as well as to conduct a comprehensive review of the pertinent literature on security in this field. The four primary components of a smart city that were the focus of their research were smart infrastructure, smart structures, intelligent transportation systems, and smart healthcare. It specifically addresses the relationship between technology and smart cities, as well as a summary of two deep learning approaches and cybersecurity programs. Because the basis on small real-world datasets makes it challenging to extend the findings to many security contexts. Chen et al. (2021) suggested a post-quantum blockchain architecture suitable for smart cities and presented a new identity-based signature system meant to withstand quantum attacks. Their methodical, light-hearted cryptographic operations are suitable for limited resources. Still untested, though, are the framework's practical application and scalability in actual smart city infrastructures. Ismagilova et al. (2022) offered research examining some of the difficulties infrastructure connectivity in smart cities presents. The study is arranged around four important themes in smart city research: privacy and security of mobile devices and services; smart city infrastructure, energy systems, healthcare, operational challenges to smart cities, and blockchain technology deployment. Nonetheless, the small number of case studies led to the recommendations of the research not being thorough.

Ahmad et al. (2022) provided a study paper analyzing and investigating the primary obstacles preventing the successful implementation of artificial intelligence in human-centric applications, the hazards, future paths for research in these sectors, and how to close present gaps and create better solutions. AI judgments may, however, be biased, which would affect the accuracy and effectiveness of the applied cybersecurity systems. Jia et al. (2023) presented a sophisticated AI-powered defensive system meant to improve early attack detection in smart cities so strengthening cybersecurity. The paper presented the MDATA framework, which combines contextual analysis and deep learning to find intricate cyber threats aiming at smart infrastructure. Attaching a detection accuracy of 97.1%, the system exceeded several conventional models according to experimental findings. The paper stresses the strategic integration of artificial intelligence and dynamic threat analysis to create strong and flexible cybersecurity solutions for smart cities of next generation.

Faberge & Bogoni (2023) performed a thematic classification mostly on security and privacy concerns in authentication systems and key management for industrial Internet of Things (IoT) environments. Attacks and a framework for cryptographic technique-based protection of cloud learning systems from hacking. They first preprocessed the data and derived gray-scale covariance matrix (GLCM) features. They then classified attacks in cloud environments using a multi-convolutional neural network (M-CNN). They encrypted and decrypted data at last using a modified digital signature technique (MDSA). Consequently, the lack of thorough testing in actual surroundings could influence the practical relevance of this framework.

Jebbar & Al-Zubaidie (2024) suggested breaking out the system into several areas, each with unique standards and limitations. To authenticate the customer's identity, the smart contract checks adherence to these policies and tracks their application. The form of the request for electronic banking services was first decided upon using the two-stage commitment (2PC) process. Using the micro-segmentation concept, a discrete segment was generated by separating every type of electronic transaction operation; the segment was then compressed with the Zstd technique. The Yellow Sea Goat Algorithm (YSGA) was then employed to ascertain whether the smart contract's conditions were optimally satisfied. Nevertheless, the utilization of digital signatures to guarantee data integrity was not addressed. (Razzaq et al., 2024) introduced an innovative method for securing patient information (EASPI) that is based on blockchain and incorporates advanced encryption algorithms (AES), inverse word frequency analysis (TF-IDF), Lemplel-Ziv-Welch (LZW), decision tree models (DTM), and naive Bayes classifiers (NBC). The system was, however, computationally sophisticated. Tahayur & Al-Zubaidie (2024) proposed a security system that combines consortium blockchain blocks with Edwards 25519 (Ed25519) signatures to prevent block data tampering in the Internet of Things. They leveraged the Artificial Bee Colony (ABC) approach to preserve the unpredictable nature of Ed25519 signatures while identifying the optimal solution with Advanced Deep Learning (ADL) as a model for object tracking and evaluation in the optimizer system. Although the study used digital signatures, it did not address how they might address future quantum computing.

Walunj et al. (2025) examined the incorporation of cryptocurrency payment systems into Web 2.0 services, specifically emphasizing their utilization within data marketplaces, the Indian Urban Data Exchange (IUDX), and the Agricultural Data Exchange (ADeX) platforms. Primarily, they encounter regulatory obstacles in financial legislation, which impede their implementation. Sahu & Chandrakar (2025) proposed a secure consumer network model based on blockchain technology to harness green energy and meet the electricity demands of the Internet of Vehicles in smart cities. The Smart Parking Model (SPM) serves as a platform for customers and electric automobiles. Nonetheless, the scalability of blockchain technology and elevated latency in secure communication networks for automobiles persist as challenges. Gulzar & Mustafa (2025) introduced the deepCLG hybrid learning model designed to improve network intrusion detection systems (NIDS). The datasets first go through preprocessing and normalization. Then, a hybrid learning model called DeepCLG is formulated. It integrates convolutional neural network (CNN), long short-term memory (LSTM), and gated recurrent unit (GRU) with capsule network (CN). However, the hybrid model requires very high computing power. Table 1 describes existing studies and their limitations.

Table 1. Comparison of previous studies about smart city data protection

Researcher	Techniques/Algorithms	Study Benefit	Study Limitation
(Egger et al., 2020)	IEC 60870-5-104 protocol, intrusion detection techniques	Evaluated intrusion detection in power plant substations with real dataset testing.	Not tested on a large-scale physical infrastructure, affecting adaptability.
(Rashid et al., 2020)	KNN, Decision Trees	High detection accuracy (>93%) in identifying IoT-based cyberattacks; reduced false positives and improved early threat detection in smart networks.	Real-world applicability in complex, large-scale smart city networks not fully validated.
(Ma, 2021)	Deep learning, cybersecurity programs	Reviewed smart city security challenges and technologies, including AI approaches.	Findings are based on small real-world datasets, limiting generalization.
(Chen et al., 2021)	Post-Quantum Blockchain, Identity-Based Signatures	Introduced a quantum-resistant blockchain framework suitable for low-resource environments; future-proofing smart city security systems.	Practical implementation and scalability in real smart city environments remain untested.
(Ismagilova et al., 2022)	Blockchain, smart infrastructure security analysis	Examined infrastructure connectivity challenges in smart cities.	Few case studies limit the comprehensiveness of recommendations.
(Ahmad et al., 2022)	Artificial intelligence, cybersecurity frameworks	Analyzed AI applications and risks in cybersecurity for human-centric smart cities.	Potential bias in AI decision-making affecting accuracy and effectiveness.

continued on following page

Table 1. Continued

Researcher	Techniques/Algorithms	Study Benefit	Study Limitation
(Jia et al., 2023)	MDATA Framework (Deep Learning + Contextual Threat Analysis)	Achieved 97.1% detection accuracy; integrates AI for dynamic and context-aware cybersecurity; surpasses traditional methods.	Model complexity may pose implementation challenges; robustness in multi-domain smart cities not assessed.
(Faberge & Bogoni, 2023)	Authentication protocols, key management, cloud security	Classified privacy and security issues in IIoT and smart city environments.	Dependency on cloud infrastructure makes it vulnerable to cloud-based attacks.
(El-Sofany et al., 2024)	Multi-Convolutional Neural Network (M-CNN), Modified Digital Signature Algorithm (MDSA)	Developed a deep learning-based intrusion detection system and secure framework for cloud environments.	Lack of real-world testing, affecting practical applicability.
(Jebbar & Al-Zubaidie, 2024)	Micro-segmentation + Smart Contracts	High transaction security	The utilization of digital signatures to guarantee data integrity was not addressed.
(Razzaq et al., 2024)	Decentralized Computing + Private Blockchain	Privacy protection in IoMT	Computationally sophisticated.
(Tahayur & Al-Zubaidie, 2024)	Blockchain Search + E-signatures	Agricultural data integrity	Did not address how they might address future quantum computing.
(Walunj et al., 2025)	Crypto-based payment systems, blockchain	Examined secure cryptocurrency payments in Web 2.0 data marketplaces.	Regulatory obstacles hinder implementation in financial systems.
(Sahu & Chandrakar, 2025)	Blockchain-based secure communication, Smart Parking Model (SPM)	Proposed a secure consumer network model for green energy and electric vehicle management.	Scalability and high latency in blockchain-based secure communication.
(Gulzar & Mustafa, 2025)	DeepCLG hybrid model (CNN, LSTM, GRU, Capsule Networks)	Enhanced network intrusion detection systems with hybrid deep learning approach.	Requires very high computational power for implementation.

BACKGROUND

In this section, we will review the scientific background of the most important topics that we will address in the current study. To protect smart city data, it is crucial to provide robust security mechanisms. Relying on conventional encryption and signature methods will expose smart city data to various attacks that traditional security mechanisms cannot withstand. Therefore, smart cities should incorporate security mechanisms characterized by a high level of security and performance efficiency. This chapter focuses extensively on quantum technologies that provide high efficiency and significantly benefit the smart city environment. This section includes the following subsections: Post-quantum cryptography, lattice-based cryptography, JavaScript object notation for linked data, CRYSTALS-Kyber encryption, FALCON signatures, and zero-knowledge proof technology to support the protection of smart city data.

Post Quantum Cryptography

Encryption techniques that are resistant to attacks from quantum computers are referred to as post-quantum cryptography (Tregi & Al-Zubaidie, 2025). Conventional public-key cryptosystems, such as those that rely on integer factorization (e.g., RSA) and discrete logarithm problems (e.g., Digital Signature Algorithm, Diffie–Hellman), are vulnerable to quantum computation, particularly to Shor's method, which has the potential to resolve these issues with efficacy. In 1994, Peter Shor illustrated that these encryption techniques could be compromised by a quantum computer that was adequately advanced, thereby emphasizing this vulnerability (Joudah & Manaa, 2024). The National Institute of Standards and Technology (NIST) has initiated a process to standardize quantum-resistant encryption methods in response to this imminent peril. NIST designated Crystals-Kyber as the principal key encapsulation mechanism (KEM) for standardization in July 2022 (Iavich & Kuchukhidze, 2024a). A further evaluation and potential standardization of CrystalsKyber and four additional algorithms (cycle, traditional McEliece, HQC, and cycle) were selected for subsequent rounds (Alagic et al., 2022).

Lattice-Based Cryptography

LBC has surfaced as a highly promising approach in the realm of post-quantum cryptography, owing to its robust resistance against quantum attacks and its adaptability in various applications such as encryption, digital signatures, and key exchange mechanisms (Nonso Okika et al., 2025). In contrast to traditional cryptosystems that depend on factorization or discrete logarithm challenges, lattice cryptography is founded on complex lattice problems, including the shortest vector problem (SVP) and the learning-with-error (LWE) problem (Li et al., 2022). The strength lies in the fact that these mathematical problems still pose significant computational challenges, even with quantum computing. Nth-degree Truncated Polynomial Ring Unit (NTRU) is a prominent network encryption scheme known for its importance and longevity, as well as its strong resistance to quantum threats. Its development began in 1996, led by Jeffrey Hofstein, Gil Pifer, and Joseph Silverman (YULIA FATIN LESTARI, 2021).

JavaScript Object Notation for Linked Data

Built on JSON, an open standard offering both human- and machine-readable linked data, JSON-LD is JSON-LD was developed by the World Wide Web Consortium (W3C) to standardize data formats across many platforms and improve their interoperability (Plathe et al., 2024). This standard offers a means to show linked data such that several systems may interact with it more readily. It builds on conventional JSON but incorporates contextual information, so facilitating the standard and understandable linking of data from many sources. By connecting data from many sources consistently, it also enhances data integration between several applications (Chaerony Siffa et al., 2022). This standard helps unstructured data to be quickly converted into linked data, so enabling the creation of systems grounded on a consistent framework (Shyaa & Al-Zubaidie, 2023).

JSON-LD is an endeavor to develop a straightforward method for not only expressing Linked Data in JSON but also for incorporating semantics into existing JSON documents. It has been intended to be as straightforward, concise, and comprehensible as feasible. Additionally, the objective was to minimize the amount of effort required by developers to convert their plain old JSON to semantically rich JSON-LD. As a result, an entity-centric approach was implemented, as opposed to the triple-centric approach that is typically employed in traditional Semantic Web technologies. Although the initial versions [25] of JSON-LD appeared to be a more or less direct translation of Turtle to JSON, the syntax underwent a significant change in the most recent versions, enabling data to be serialized in a manner that is frequently indistinguishable from traditional JSON (Plathe et al., 2024).

CRYSTALS-Kyber

CRYSTALS-Kyber (Kyber) is an essential encapsulation technology used to withstand quantum attacks. Kyber is based on the complex challenges of lattice-based encryption, which is presently regarded as secure against quantum computing threats (YULIA FATIN LESTARI, 2021). Kyber functions as a Key Encapsulation Mechanism (KEM) and is employed to securely generate a shared encryption key between two parties. It was proposed as part of the NIST PQC post-quantum cryptography standard (Bandara et al., 2022) and is a component of the CRYSTALS (Cryptographic Suite for Algebraic Lattices) project. Kyber comprises three fundamental phases:

1. Key generation: In order to ensure the security of the communication, each party generates encrypted keys and subsequently generates a random matrix A from a finite mathematical field Zq. Then, a secret vector s and a minor noise vector e are selected. The equation t = A * s + e is used to calculate the public key pk. Algorithm 1 Explain Kyber key generation. It is worth noting that there are no external inputs as safe random value generators within the method provide keys at random.

```
Algorithm1: Kyber key generation
   Input: None
   Output: pk, sk
         A ← Sample_Matrix
         s, e ← Sample_Noise
         t ← A * s + e
         pk ← (A, t)
         sk ← s
         Return (pk, sk)
```

2. Key encapsulation: A shared key *K'* is chosen at random, then a random vector *r* is chosen, and noise *e1* and *e2* are added. The ciphertext $c = (u, v)$ is calculated from the equations: $u = A^T * r + e1$ and $v = t^T * r + e2 + Encode(K')$. Then *c* is sent to the other part, the final Shared key *K* is extracted using a hash function: $K = Hash(K')$. Algorithm 2 represents the PK encapsulation process to extract the ciphertext and the shared key (Iavich & Kuchukhidze, 2024b).

```
Algorithm 2: Kyber key encapsulation
   Input: pk
   Output: c, K
         r, e1, e2 ← Sample_Noise
         u ←AT * r + e1
         v ←tT * r + e2 + Encode(K')
         c ← (u, v)
         K ←Hash(K')
         Return (c, K)
```

3. Decapsulate the key: The receiver uses s to decrypt the key where $K' = Decode\ (v - s^T * u)$, and final key $K = Hash(K')$. Algorithm 3 shows the decryption of Kyber key capsule based on c,s (Iavich & Kuchukhidze, 2024b).

```
Algorithm 3: Kyber key decapsulate
    Input: c, s
    Output: K
1.          K' ← Decode (v - sT * u)
2.          K ← Hash(K')
3.          Return K
```

FALCON

One of the six-year NIST post-quantum cryptography standardizing competition winners, FALCON is a cryptographic signature system ending in 2022(Alagic et al., 2022). It runs under the famed Full-Domain-Hash (FDH) architecture first introduced by Gentry, Peikert, and Vaikuntanathan (GPV), which makes use of LBC, more especially, NTRU lattices by virtue of their features. It stands out among LBC systems with its very small signature sizes, attained by NTRU lattices' effective ring topology (Gaur et al., 2025). Reduced public key sizes and quicker calculations made possible by this structure greatly increase efficiency over unstructured lattice-based systems. In contrast to signature verification, which possesses a rather straightforward algorithmic framework and has been extensively explored for acceleration by several researchers' investigations into the acceleration of signature production are quite few (YULIA FATIN LESTARI, 2021). FALCON comprises three procedures: key generation, signature generation, and signature verification.

1. FALCON key generation: Keys are generated by sampling short polynomials f, g as a secret bases, then computing the public key polynomial $h = g f^{-1} mod\, q$. Algorithm 4 demonstrates the generation of the public key and the secret key *pk, sk,* in the falcon algorithm. Begins by generating four relatively short polynomials f, g, F, G using the *TpdGen* algorithm. These polynomials form a secret basis (trapdoor) for the NTRU polynomials. Then, *pk* is calculated by multiplying the polynomial g by the inverse polynomial f inside a special ring defined on the polynomial X^n+1, and the calculation is modulo prime number q. As for *sk* it is the set (f, g, F, G) (Farajzadeh & Chehreh Chelgani, 2022).

```
Algorithm 4: FALCON key generation
 Input: secret parameters (α, q).
Output: sk, pk
          Start
          R ← Zq[X]/(X n + 1),
          (f, g, F, G) ← TpdGen (R, α, q)
          h ← g * inverse(f) mod q
          sk ← (f, g, F, G)
          pk ← h
          return (sk, pk)
          End
```

2. FALCON signature: The message is signed by computing its hash with a random value (salt), then the secret key is used to create a brief signature on this output based on a length requirement. Algorithm 5 shows how to generate a digital signature using FALCON. A random value *r* is chosen, the hash is calculated for each attempt, and then a pair of very short vectors s_1, s_2 is generated using the secret key. The signature must be shorter than β, otherwise, the signature is returned and a new *r* is calculated (Castagna et al., 2024).

```
Algorithm 5: FALCON sign generation
 Input: sk, m \\ message.
Output: σ \\ signature
          Start
          repeat:
           r ← RandomSalt()
          c ← H (pk, r, m) mod q
          (s1, s2) ← PreSmp (sk, c)
          until (□ (s1, s2) □2< β)
          σ ← (r, s2)
          return σ
          End
```

3. FALCON verification: In this stage, c is reconstructed using the hashed message and r, then verify whether the calculated vector v meets the required base threshold and returns valid or invalid. Algorithm 6 shows how to verify a digital signature.

```
Algorithm 6: FALCON sign verification
 Input: σ
Output: valid, invalid
        Start
        c ← H (pk, r, m) mod q
         s1 ← (c - s2 * pk) mod q
        if || (s1, s2) ||2 ≤ β
        return "valid"
        else
        return "invalid"
        End
```

Zero-Knowledge Proof

Zero-knowledge scalable Transparent Argument of Knowledge (zk-STARKs) represents a significant advancement in cryptographic verification methods, as it enables a prover to verify the veracity of a statement without disclosing any additional information (Zhou et al., 2024). Goldwasser, Micali, and Rackoff introduced Zero-Knowledge Proofs (ZKPs) in 1985 [Goldwasser et al., 1985]. In this publication, they are expanded upon (Lavin et al., 2024). zk-STARKs have emerged as a more desirable alternative to zk-SNARKs due to their superior security against quantum attacks and increased transparency during the initial configuration. zk-STARKs Prover produces a non-interactive proof devoid of knowledge about the verification procedure (Kniep & Wattenhofer, 2024). Algorithm 7 starts by over a finite field F converting the input data x into a pylon poisson form f(x). This change lets one utilize algebraic methods for validation instead of directly handling basic arithmetic operations. The Fast Reed-Solomon Interactive (FRI) Oracle Proof technique is used to f(x), thereby improving efficiency and producing a low-degree poisson g(x). While maintaining the integrity of the original function, this lowers the proof's size and the computational cost. After that, the dedication to g(x) is generated using cryptographic hash algorithms, usually arranged in a Merkle tree to guarantee data integrity and stop unwanted alterations. By the Fiat-Shamir rule, zk-STARKs removes the necessity for a challenge produced by the verifier. Rather, hash the commitment C to produce a random challenge value r deterministically, hence rendering the proof non-interactive. The verifier constructs a cryptographic proof π using C, r, and f(x), thereby encapsulating the data required for verification. Then the proof π and the commitment C, which the verifier may utilize to independently confirm the validity of the proof devoid of direct contact with the verifier. This method guarantees scalability, post-quantum security, and efficiency, which qualifies zk-STARKs for use in smart cities aiming at maintaining anonymity (Kniep & Wattenhofer, 2024).

```
Algorithm7: NIZK-STARKs prover(x)
Input: x □ F
Output: π, C
          f(x) ← Arithmetize(x)
          g(x) ← FRI(f(x))
          C ← Commitment(g(x))
          r ← Hash(C)
          π ← Generate_Proof(C, r, f(x))
          Return (π, C)
Algorithm 8: NIZK-STARKs verifier (π, C, parameters)
Input: π, C, params
Output: "Valid" or "Invalid"
          r ← Hash(C)
          C' ← Verify_Proof (π, r, Parameters)
          Return "Valid" if C' = C, else "Invalid"
```

Algorithm 8 independently validates the proof π by regenerating the challenge r using the Fiat-Shamir heuristic. It then reconstructs the commitment C' from the proof and checks if it matches C. If they are equal, the proof is accepted as valid; otherwise, it is rejected to ensure noninteractive verification.

PROPOSING A QUANTUM THREAT-RESISTANT SECURITY SYSTEM

This section introduces our proposed Post-Quantum Lattice Security (PQLS) system, which employs post-quantum technologies to safeguard the data of smart power plants in a secure and adaptable manner.

The system is comprised of four primary components: ZK-STARKs, which are used to verify user identity and electronic payment information without disclosing any private information; Kyber, which facilitates secure key exchange between smart meters and central servers; FALCON, which is used to sign data to ensure its integrity before transmission; and JSON-LD, which standardizes the format of data received from various smart meters. This design, which commences with data collection at smart meters, offers comprehensive data protection by securing data during transmission and verifying its authenticity using ZK-STARKs prior to processing. This enables the system to effectively address both traditional and quantum threats. Our proposed system's total approach is depicted in Figure 1.

Key Exchange Mechanism

In smart cities, it is imperative to ensure the secure interchange of data between central power grid servers and smart meters. Traditional key exchange mechanisms, such as RSA and Diffie-Hellman, are known to be susceptible to quantum attacks, rendering them inappropriate for long-term security in infrastructure. Conversely, sensitive electricity consumption data is consistently transmitted to grid control centers from smart meters. We suggest that Kyber be employed to generate a shared encryption key between smart meters and grid servers in the electric station in order to address this challenge. FALCON is employed to encrypt the signature with this shared key, and ZK-STARKs are employed to verify zero-knowledge proofs. Kyber facilitates the establishment of a secure shared key between the smart meter and the server, thereby preventing the direct transmission of the secret key over the network. The key exchange procedure is divided into three primary stages:

1. Public and secret keys are generated by the smart meter. The public key is transmitted to the server by PK, while the private key is retained by SK.
2. The server constructs and encapsulates a shared key K using the public key of the smart meter and then transmits the encapsulated key back to the meter.

The K is decapsulated by the smart meter using the SK.

Figure 1. Post-quantum lattice security system

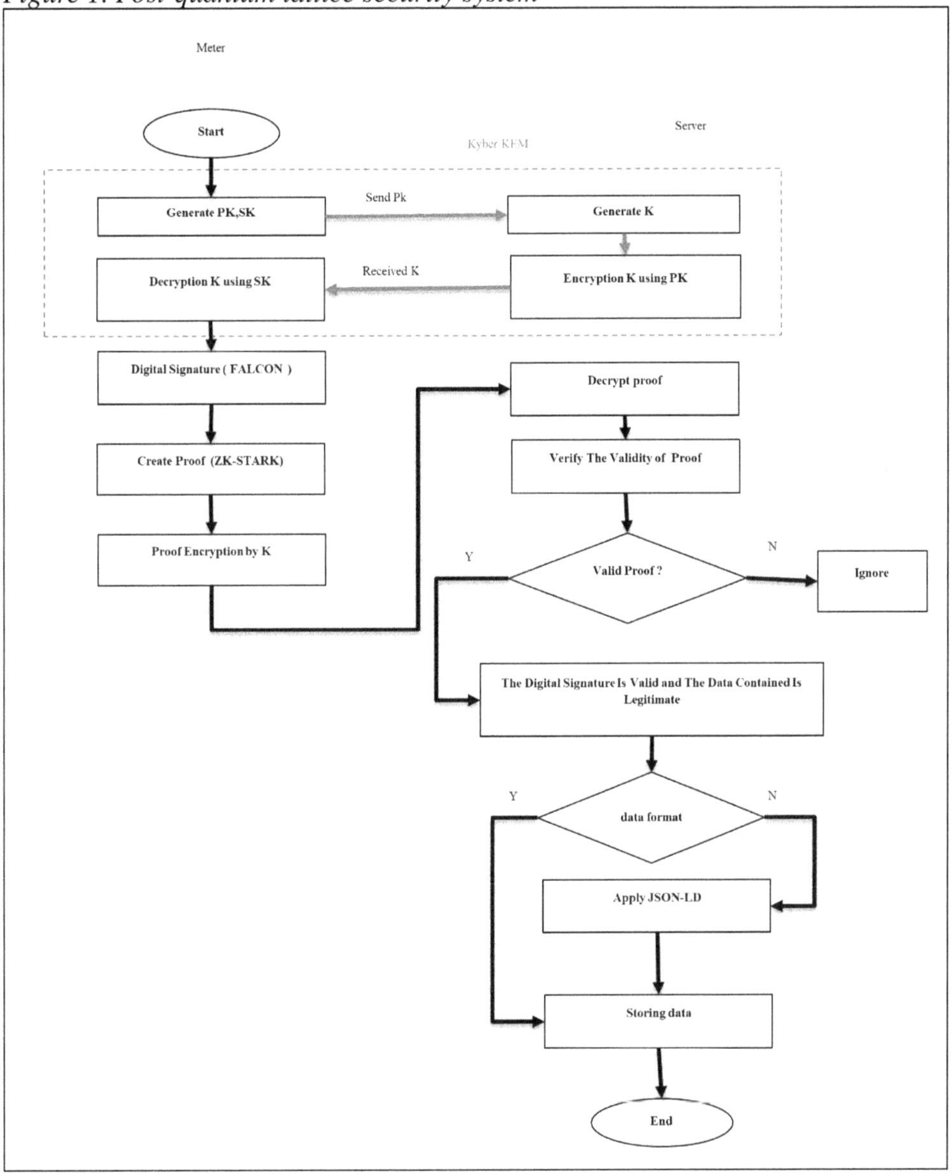


```
Algorithm 9: Kyber keys exchange
        Input: []
        Output: K
        Began
        (PK, SK) ← Kyber.KeyGen()
```

```
Store SK securely in SmartMeter
Send PK to Server
(ciphertext, K_server) ← Kyber.Encapsulate(PK)
Send (ciphertext) to SmartMeter
K_meter ← Kyber.Decapsulate(ciphertext, SK)
If K_meter == K_server Then Key Exchange Successful and Secure Communication Established
Else Key Exchange Failed
End
```

Algorithm 9 illustrates the key exchange process between the smart meter and the server.

Ensure Data Integrity Using FALCON

The transmission of electricity consumption data between smart meters and servers at the power facility in smart grids is contingent upon the preservation of data integrity. It is imperative that the data is sourced from a reliable source and has not been altered. This enhances the dependability of energy management, invoicing, and load-balancing systems in smart cities. We have incorporated FALCON into the system to ensure the long-term security of smart city infrastructure by providing a lightweight, quantum-resistant digital signature mechanism. This is necessary to accomplish this level of security. FALCON guarantees that energy data can only be signed by genuine smart meters and that power grid servers can verify the authenticity of the received data. A ZKP technique is employed to generate a proof of FALCON signature and refrain from transmitting the signature, as FALCON signatures must remain confidential. This mitigates replay attacks and unauthorized eavesdropping. The FALCON mechanism of our proposed system is as follows: Each smart meter digitally signs its energy consumption reports prior to transmitting them to the server, which is responsible for verifying the signature to ensure that the data originates from a valid smart meter. The validity of these signatures is subsequently verified by the server prior to executing any action without the signature being visible or being exposed by ZK-STARK. Algorithm 10 illustrates the process of signing data using FALCON.

```
Algorithm 10: FALCON Signature
Input: FALCON_SK, data
Output: σ \\ signature
Began
σ← FALCON.Sign(FALCON_Sk, data)
```

```
Return σ
End
```

Proofing Digital Signature Without Revealing

ZK-STARKs enable the verification of digital signatures without disclosing them, thereby ensuring the security of data from smart power plants. The legitimacy of the signature σ is established through the application of a mathematical proof that is derived from the transformation of the verification process into a polynomial representation rather than sharing it with other parties. The verification process is facilitated by ZK-STARKs. This is achieved by generating evidence that allows for the substantiation of the signature without direct observation. Furthermore, the evidence is encrypted with the shared key generated by Kyber KEM, which adds an additional layer of security. The signature can be verified by the individual who possesses the shared key. The ZK-STARK-Prove procedure is only implemented when data must be transmitted, as smart meters may have restricted processing capabilities. The computational demand on smart meters can be reduced by utilizing central servers for verification.

```
Algorithm 11: ZK_STARK_Generate proof
Input:  K, m, σ, FALCON_PK
Output: π \\ proof
    Began
    Verify_FALCON(m, σ, FALCON_PK) □ A * FALCON_Sk ≡ u
(mod q)
    P(x) = 1  if Verify_FALCON(m, σ, pk) holds
    P(x) = 0  otherwise
    r = H(K || m)
    FRI_Proof = FRI_Test(P(x))
    π = (H, FRI_Proof, Challenge_Values)
    π' = Encrypt(π, SK)
    RETURN π'
     End
```

Algorithm 11 demonstrates generating a zero-knowledge proof without the need to transmit sensitive data over communication channels. It starts with inputs K (shared key generated from Kyber KEM), m, σ, FALCON_PK and then defines the FALCON signature verification equation as $A * s \quad u \ (mod\ q)$ where A is a public matrix of the FALCON lattice structure and u represents generated signature value, q Prime modulus for modular arithmetic. Next, we enter the second stage, which converts the verification into polynomial form $P(x)$ so that the proof can be constructed and verified quickly, where $P(x)$ is a polynomial over a finite field Fq. Then, Fiat-Shamir challenges by computing a random challenge: $r = H(K \| m)$. By applying the FRI protocol for low-degree verification, generate proof for the low-degree check: *FRI_Proof = FRI_Test (P(x)).* After creating the ZK-STARK proof: $\pi = (H, FRI\_Proof, Challenge\_Values)$, the proof is encrypted using K: $\pi' = Encrypt(\pi, K)$.

```
Algorithm 12: ZK_STARK verify signature
Input: SK, m, π', FALCON_PK
Output: TRUE if the signature is valid, FALSE otherwise
        Began
        π = Decrypt(π', K)
        Extract (H, FRI_Proof, Challenge_Values) from π
        H' = MerkleRoot(H(P(x_i))
        IF H' ≠ H THEN RETURN FALSE
        IF FRI_Verify(FRI_Proof) = FALSE Then Return FALSE
        r' = H(K || m)
        IF r' ≠ Challenge_Values Then Return FALSE
        End
```

Algorithm 12 shows the process of verifying this proof after decrypting it without revealing sensitive data.

JSON-LD

JSON-LD's suggested function is to standardize and organize the data sent by diverse smart meters, guaranteeing consistent interpretation among several network components. Leveraging JSON-LD helps the system create a consistent semantic environment, facilitating correct data flow across many servers and devices and effective interoperability. Furthermore, it improves compliance with current web standards and helps data integration, therefore simplifying the processing and validation processes and keeping flexibility and clarity inside the smart-city data management system.

```
Algorithm 13: PQLS _Smart_Meter
Input: Sensor data
Output: π', data
        Began
```

```
(PK, SK) ← Kyber.KeyGen()
(FALCON_PK, FALCON_SK) ← FALCON.KeyGen()
data ← Read_Sensor()
σ ← FALCON.Sign(data, FALCON_SK)
π ← ZKSTARK.Generate(σ, data, FALCON_SK)
π' ← Kyber.Encrypt(π, PK)
Transmit (data, π') to Server
End
Algorithm 14: PQLS _Server
Input: π', data
Output: Accept, Reject
. Begin
2. Receive (data, π')
3. π ← Kyber.Decrypt(π', SK)
4. data_LD ← JSON-LD.Normalize(data)
5. Valid ← ZKSTARK.Verify(π, data_LD, FALCON_PK)
6. If Valid: Accept(data_LD)
7. Else: Reject(data_LD)
End
```

Algorithms 13 and 14 illustrate how PQLS takes a robust approach to ensuring the security of data sent from smart meters to the central server in a smart city power plant.

ANALYSIS OF PROTECTION PROCEDURES

To evaluate the proposed system, it is important to test its security both theoretically and practically (using simulation tools). This chapter applies a specific set of attacks, including: side-channel attacks, message recovery attacks, signature leakage attacks, forgery attacks, statistical dissection attacks, and anonymous identity attacks. The following security analyses demonstrate the proposed system's ability to withstand the attacks described in this chapter. In this part, we test the Scyther verification tool and analyze attacks to illustrate security analysis.

Analysis of Threats

1. **Side-channel attack:** It analyzes data to obtain secret keys using indirect information. Since the signature is authenticated without revealing the secret key in

our proposed system, ZKP helps conceal the verification procedures, reducing the possibility of this information being misused.

2. **Message recovery attack:** With this kind of assault, the assailant tries to get a ciphertext by means of protocol analysis for key exchange. Kyber is unique as it employs homomorphic encryption (IND-CCA2 safe), so the ciphertext cannot provide any information about the communication for an assailant.
3. **Signature leakage attack:** It aims at sensitive data leaks from digital signatures so that an assailant may produce fake signatures. The PQLS system employs ZKP to stop any sensitive data from being leaked, so the verification procedure does not show the signature itself.
4. **Forgery attack:** It aims to generate forged digital signatures acceptable to the system. The FALCON algorithm is designed to be resistant to forgery attacks, including existential forgery under chosen message attack (EUF-CMA).
5. **Statistical dissection attack:** It analyzes statistical patterns in encrypted data to extract sensitive information. PQLS, which is primarily based on Kyber and FALCON, uses lattice cryptography, a cryptographic system known for its resistance to statistical analysis due to its complex mathematical structure.
6. **Anonymous identity attack:** It targets users who rely on anonymity techniques. ZKP protects user identity by verifying signatures without revealing sensitive information.

Scyther's Analysis of Security

Scyther is a valuable instrument for verifying cryptographic protocols (Razaq, 2024). Thanks to its sophisticated capabilities, this application establishes the benchmark for rapid attack monitoring and verification. Its users can conduct unfettered verification or identify assaults. It is unique among protocol analysis tools in that it integrates the benefits of abstraction-based methods (unrestricted validation) or argument proving with model checking (attack identification and termination). Additionally, this tool provides cutting-edge capabilities that are not found in other applications, including comprehensive profiling and assault selection (Al-Zubaidie & Muhajjar, 2024). It may serve as a backend for analytic programs via Python interface methods, or it may function as a command line interface and graphical user interface. To verify the confidentiality and validity of data and identify information breaches, Scyther evaluates security specifications for various protocols. This information can be utilized in processes that involve the transmission and reception of information between SMeter and SERVER, as well as between companies or organizations. To verify signatures and specific signatures, this tool utilizes qualities that adhere to security standards, including Weakagree, Nisynch, Alive, and Niagree. Utilizing its instruments, we evaluate the efficacy of our proposed methodology. To ready our protocol roles for analysis, we implemented the Security Protocols Describing Linguistics (SPDL) feature of the program (Al-Zubaidie & Shyaa, 2023). In this instance, we employ a sequence of commands to communicate with the SMeter and SERVER. To facilitate communication between entities and confirm security requirements, we have implemented simulations of our proposed protocol between the role events. Weakagree, Nisynch, Niagree, and Alive are the events that have been tested. We can evaluate e-farming requests and identify potential security vulnerabilities or attacks by employing the send () and rec () commands. The findings indicate that our protocol satisfies the necessary security standards. Protocol security is achieved through the use of digital signatures, which guarantee the confidentiality and availability of information for all parties. This data contract is specifically associated with commitment. For instance, in our proposed protocol, SMeter and SERVER consent to the exchange of a specific set of data, and the information from the cultivator and farmer is exchanged in the following manner: The proposed method can be employed to obtain a non-injectable agreement. The integrity of the message between the parties can be guaranteed through this approach. Nisynch: The proposed protocol is designed to be resistant to attacks by providing a non-synchronization guarantee. Figures 2 and 3 show for the proposed PQLS results using Scyther.

Figure 2. An explanation of the designated role within the suggested scheme

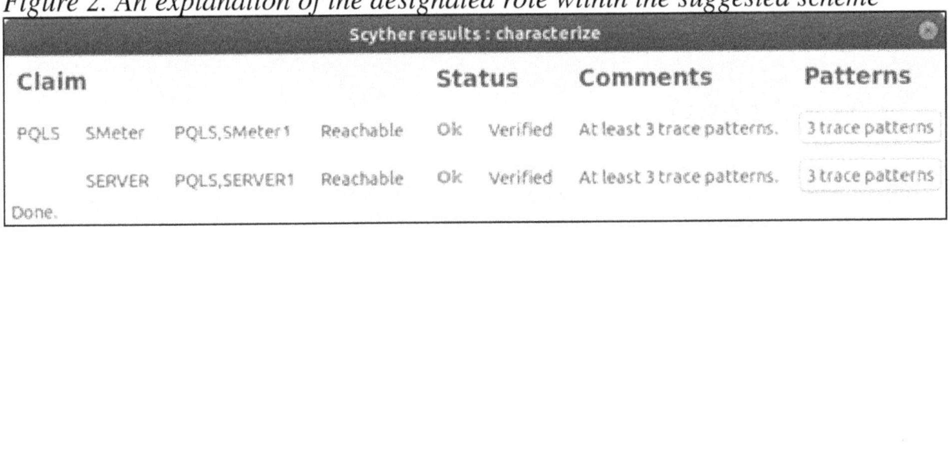

Figure 3. Using the Scyther tool to confirm the recommended security protocol

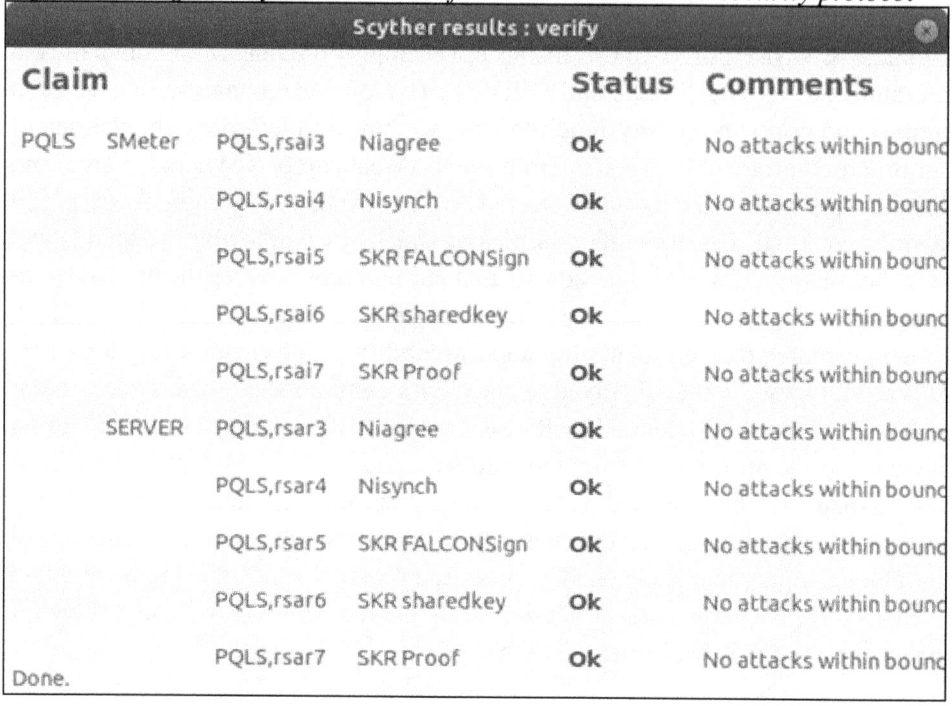

EXPERIMENT RESULTS

This section presents the experimental findings for assessing the performance of Kyber, FALCON, and zk-STARK based on important security and efficiency parameters, including randomness, determinism, stability, scalability, complexity, completeness, and traceability. The algorithms referenced were run up to 50 times using the configuration elements presented in Table 2.

Table 2. Configuration table for the experimental environment

Configuration Items	Configuration Details
OS	Ubuntu 18.04.6 LTS
CPU	11th Gen Intel(R) Core (TM) i5-1135G7 CPU
RAM	and 8.00 MB
Disk capacity	512GB, SSD

continued on following page

Table 2. Continued

Configuration Items	Configuration Details
Development environment	Eclipse IDE 2023-06 (4.28)
Programming Language Version	Java, OpenJDK 11.0.19

Resource Metrics

1. CPU Utilization: In the context of carrying out security activities, this term refers to the amount of processing power that the system consumes.

$$CPU\ Utilization = \frac{Time\ CPU\ is\ actively\ processing\ tasks}{Total\ available\ CPU\ time} \tag{1}$$

Our CPU use shows (in milliseconds) as follows: Kyber recorded 0.838 milliseconds; FALCON recorded 0.3894 milliseconds; ZK-STARK recorded 0.6348 milliseconds; JSON-LD consumed 0.597 milliseconds; and the PQLS approach overall recorded 2.4592 milliseconds, as shown in Figure 4.

Figure 4. CPU utilization for PQLS system

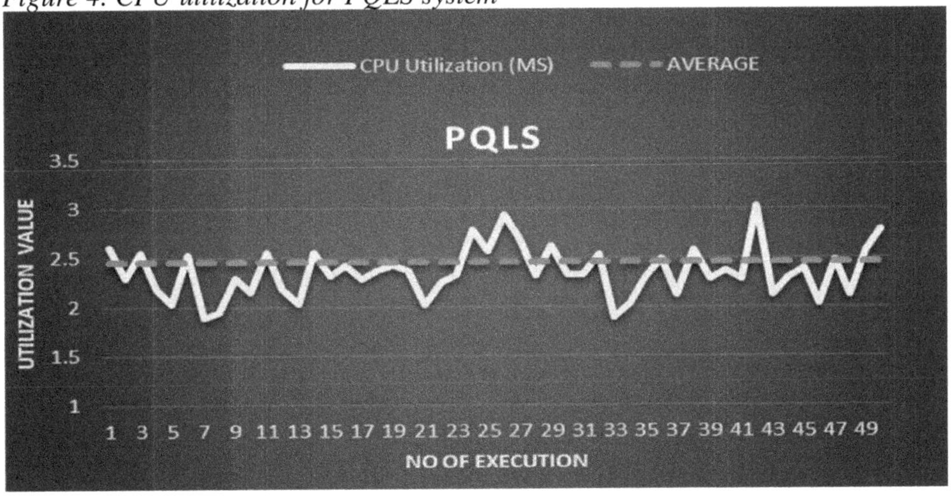

2. Memory Usage: Specifies the amount of RAM the system relies on for security operations. It measures the amount of data temporarily stored in memory while a particular technique or algorithm is being executed.

$$Memory\ Usage = \frac{Memory\ in\ Use}{Total\ Available\ Memory} \tag{2}$$

Figure 5. Memory usage for PQLS system

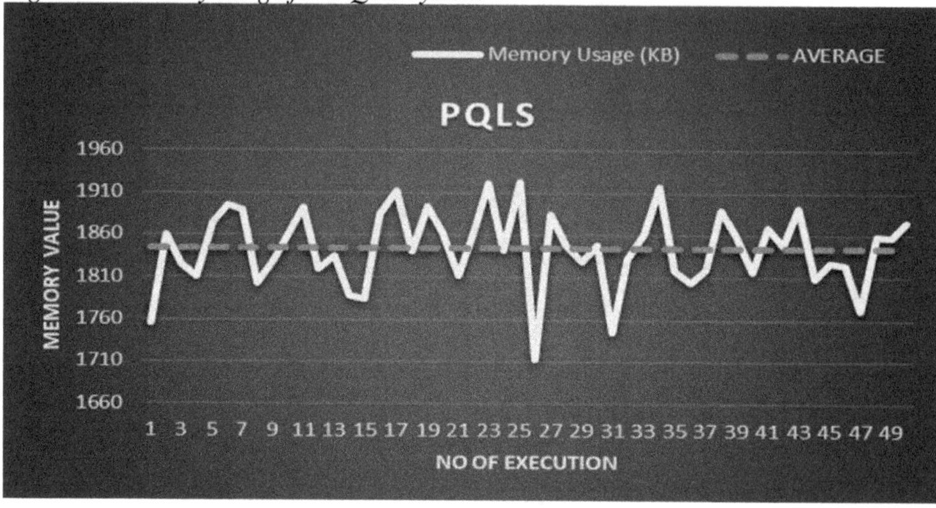

The following shows the memory use results for every method or tool: Kyber recorded 1712.810 KB, the greatest memory utilization. By comparison, with 40.589 KB and 40.487 KB, respectively, FALCON and JSON-LD displayed notably less memory use. ZK-STARK used little 50.013 KB for RAM. Reflecting the total resource needs of the combined algorithms, the integrated PQLS technique's overall memory consumption came out as 1843.899 KB, as shown in Figure 5.

3. Execution Time: It is the time taken to execute a specific process within the operating system.

$$Execution\ Time = End\ Time - Start\ Time \tag{3}$$

Figure 6. Execution time for FALCON and JSON-LD, ZK-STARK

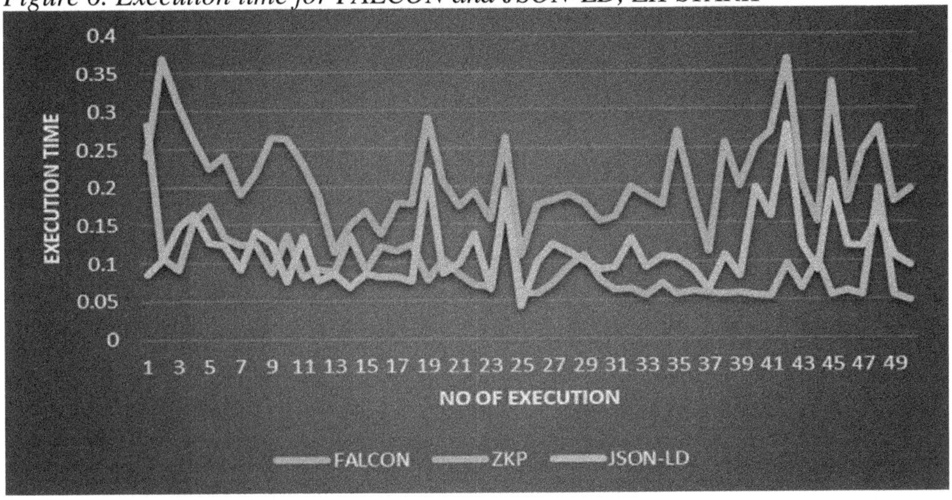

Figure 7. Execution time for Kyber

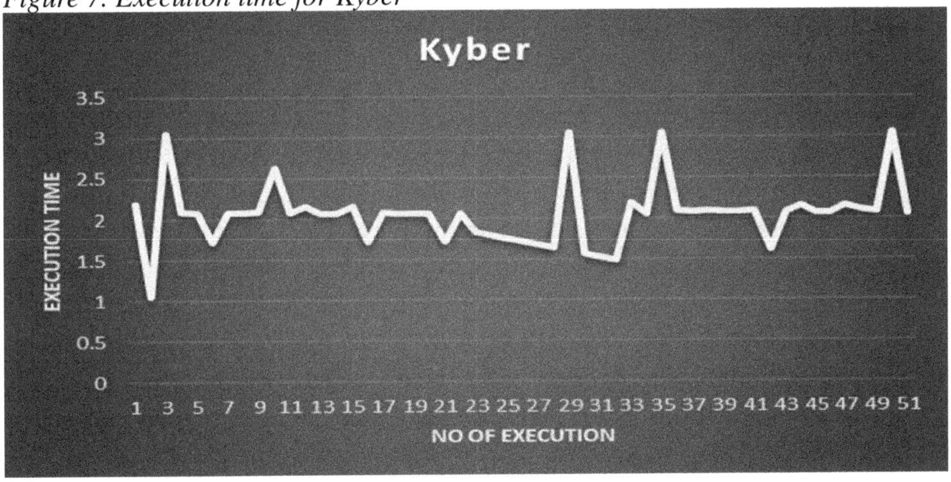

The efficiency of algorithm execution is a key factor in improving the performance of intelligent systems. In this analysis, the performance of Kyber, FALCON, ZKP, JSON-LD, and PQLS was measured over 50 executions to measure the average execution time. The results showed a significant variation in execution time, with FALCON (0.21 ms), ZKP (0.09 ms), and JSON-LD (0.11 ms) recording the lowest average execution time, reflecting their high efficiency and data processing speed. Kyber (2.04 ms) achieved a balance between performance and efficiency, making it a suitable choice for applications that require speed with a high level of security. Meanwhile, the overall PQLS system recorded an average execution time of 2.47 ms, as shown in Figures 6, 7, and 8.

Figure 8. Execution time for PQLS System

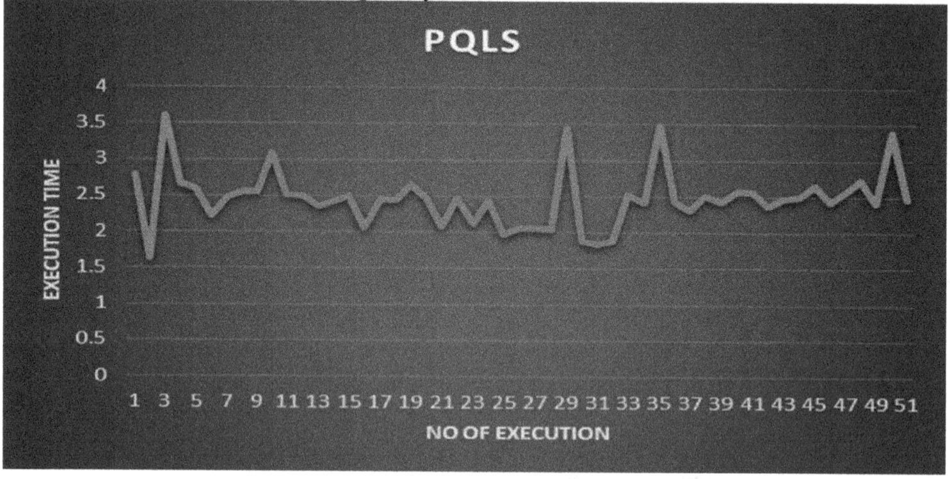

4. Computational Complexity: When its constituent elements interact in numerous ways and comply with local laws, a system or model is expected to demonstrate complex behavior, which includes nonlinearity, unpredictability, collective dynamics, hierarchy, and emergence. The phrase is typically employed to describe an object that possesses a multitude of components that interact with one another in a variety of ways to create a higher order of emergence that exceeds the sum of its elements. Complex Systems Theory's primary objective is to analyze these intricate interactions across a variety of scales. Our proposed system is composed of numerous layers. The computational complexity of our proposed system was 66.27677.

Table 3. Resource metrics results in PQLS system

Algorithm/Technique	CPU Utilization (MS)	Memory Usage (KB)	Execution Time (MS)	Complexity
Kyber	0.838	1712.810	2.04	1.8
FALCON	0.3894	40.589	0.21	0.37677
ZK-STARK	0.6348	50.013	0.09	64.0
JSON-LD	0.597	40.487	0.11	0.1
PQLS	2.4592	1843.899	2.45	66.27677

Table 3 shows the average results obtained for each of the memory consumption, execution time, UPS utilization, and computational complexity.

Table 4. Comparing the results of our proposal with other studies

Reference	Execution Time (ms)	Memory Usage (kB)
(Abu Al-Haija & Zein-Sabatto, 2020)	1	40960–61440
(Assa-Agyei & Olajide, 2023)	37–2218	-
(Sharmila & Nagapadma, 2023)	210	34816
PQLS	2.45	1843.899

Table 4 comparises of the proposed PQLS system with selected recent studies based on standardized performance metrics. PQLS shows competitive execution time (2.45 ms) and low memory usage (1843.899 kB), outperforming deep learning-based and classical systems in efficiency for constrained environments. Three post-quantum cryptographic technologies essential for smart infrastructure security CRYSTALS-Kyber, FALCON, and ZK-STARKs are compared in Table 5.

Table 5. Comparative overview of Kyber, FALCON, and ZK-STARKs

Feature	CRYSTALS-Kyber	FALCON	ZK-STARKs
Category	Key Encapsulation Mechanism (KEM)	Digital Signature Scheme	Zero-Knowledge Proof System
NIST Status	Finalist – Standardized (FIPS 203)	Finalist – Standardized (FIPS 204)	Not standardized (under academic use)
Security Basis	Lattice-based (Module-LWE)	Lattice-based (NTRU)	Polynomial IOP + STARK assumptions
Size	Public key: ~800 B Signature:1500 B	Signature: ~666 B (at NIST L1)	Proof size: ~100–300 KB

continued on following page

Table 5. Continued

Feature	CRYSTALS-Kyber	FALCON	ZK-STARKs
Performance	Fast, efficient in key exchange	Compact, efficient but floating-point sensitive	Requires more computation and memory
Quantum Resistance	Yes	Yes	Yes
Usage in PQLS system	Secure key exchange between devices	Signing meter data	Private verification of digital signatures
Advantages	Efficient, small ciphertext size	Short signatures, strong security	Verifiable, transparent, and non-interactive

From secure key exchange to data signing and private verification, every technology provides quantum-resistant guarantees and plays a different function within the PQLS system.

Recent benchmarking studies demonstrate that Kyber and FALCON offer superior performance in constrained environments, which led to their standardization by NIST in Federal Information Processing Standards (FIPS 203 and 204) (Gharavi et al., 2024) . While FALCON offers ultra-short signatures but requires floating-point accuracy, Kyber offers fast key exchange using small ciphertexts. Though not standardized, ZK-STARKs are extensively used in privacy-centric blockchain systems and allow transparent and scalable privacy-preserving computations (Fernández-Caramès & Fraga-Lamas, 2020),(Policharla et al., 2023) . STARK-based systems offer compelling quantum resistance and verifiability.

CONCLUSION

We propose a PQLS system for protecting smart power plant data by integrating FALCON digital signatures, Kyber key exchange, and ZK-STARKs for zero-knowledge verification. Our approach ensures computational efficiency while simultaneously protecting against quantum threats. Kyber enables secure and tamper-resistant key exchange between smart meters and central servers, eliminating the risks associated with traditional key distribution systems. FALCON also offers strong, light digital signatures to guarantee data integrity. Moreover, by allowing signature verification without disclosing the real signature, ZK-STARKs reduces the possibility of recursive attacks, so enhancing privacy. JSON-LD plays an important role in standardizing data formats before storage, ensuring consistency of information according to certain standards, and making it easier to retrieve and detect anomalies. This approach is suitable for real-time applications in smart grid environments due to its strong security against quantum hacks, as demonstrated by theoretical and experimental analysis. Future research will expand the concept to include additional smart city infrastructure.

FUTURE ENHANCEMENTS

The present work provides several directions for next validation and improvement. First, the suggested PQLS system can be expanded to incorporate alternative post-quantum schemes such CRYSTALS-Dilithium and Classic McEliece, so enabling relative benchmarking in terms of security, key size, and computational load. Second, by means of recursive proof composition or **Poisson** commitment strategies, optimization of ZK-STARK proof size can lower memory overhead and enhance real-time applicability: Third, applying the framework on hardware accelerators like RISC-V and FPGAs might help to lower energy consumption in smart meters with limited resources. Fourth, depending on traffic profiling or anomaly detection, dynamic key rotation policies may support Last but not least, pilot projects on actual municipal infrastructure would confirm system resilience under several operational environments and open the road for regulatory alignment with criteria like European Telecommunications Standards Institute (ETSI EN 303 645) and National Institute of Standards and Technology – Internal Report 8425 (NIST-IR 8425).

REFERENCES

Abu Al-Haija, Q., & Zein-Sabatto, S. (2020). An Efficient Deep-Learning-Based Detection and Classification System for Cyber-Attacks in IoT Communication Networks. *Electronics (Basel)*, *9*(12), 12. Advance online publication. DOI: 10.3390/electronics9122152

Ahmad, K., Maabreh, M., Ghaly, M., Khan, K., Qadir, J., & Al-Fuqaha, A. (2022). Developing future human-centered smart cities: Critical analysis of smart city security, Data management, and Ethical challenges. *Computer Science Review*, *43*, 100452. DOI: 10.1016/j.cosrev.2021.100452

Al-Zubaidie, M., & Jebbar, W. A. (2024). Providing Security for Flash Loan System Using Cryptocurrency Wallets Supported by XSalsa20 in a Blockchain Environment. *Applied Sciences (Basel, Switzerland)*, *14*(14), 6361. DOI: 10.3390/app14146361

Al-Zubaidie, M., & Muhajjar, R. A. (2024). Integrating Trustworthy Mechanisms to Support Data and Information Security in Health Sensors. *Procedia Computer Science*, *237*, 43–52. DOI: 10.1016/j.procs.2024.05.078

Al-Zubaidie, M., & Shyaa, G. S. (2023). Applying Detection Leakage on Hybrid Cryptography to Secure Transaction Information in E-Commerce Apps. *Future Internet*, *15*(8), 262. DOI: 10.3390/fi15080262

Alagic, G., Apon, D., Cooper, D., Dang, Q., Dang, T., Kelsey, J., Lichtinger, J., Liu, Y.-K., Miller, C., Moody, D., Peralta, R., Perlner, R., Robinson, A., & Smith-Tone, D. (2022). *Status report on the third round of the NIST Post-Quantum Cryptography Standardization process* (No. NIST IR 8413; p. NIST IR 8413). National Institute of Standards and Technology (U.S.). DOI: 10.6028/NIST.IR.8413

Assa-Agyei, K., & Olajide, F. (2023). A Comparative Study of Twofish, Blowfish, and Advanced Encryption Standard for Secured Data Transmission. *International Journal of Advanced Computer Science and Applications*, *14*(3). Advance online publication. DOI: 10.14569/IJACSA.2023.0140344

Awaad, M. H., & Jebbar, W. A. (2014). Prolong the lifetime of WSN by determining a correlation nodes in the same zone and searching for the best not the closest CH. *International Journal of Modern Education and Computer Science*, *6*(11), 31. DOI: 10.5815/ijmecs.2014.11.04

Awaad, M. H., & Jebbar, W. A. (2015). Extending the WSN lifetime by Dividing the Network Area into a Specific Zones. *International Journal of Computer Network and Information Security*, *7*(2), 33–39. DOI: 10.5815/ijcnis.2015.02.04

Bandara, H., Herath, Y., Weerasundara, T., & Alawatugoda, J. (2022). On Advances of Lattice-Based Cryptographic Schemes and Their Implementations. *Cryptography*, *6*(4), 56. DOI: 10.3390/cryptography6040056

Castagna, F., Montano, L., Lombardi, R., Pagano, A., Gigliotti, A., Bava, R., Lupia, C., Costagliola, A., Giordano, A., Palma, E., Britti, D., & Liguori, G. (2024). Understanding Environmental Contamination through the Lens of the Peregrine FALCON (Falco peregrinus). *Environments (Basel, Switzerland)*, *11*(12), 264. DOI: 10.3390/environments11120264

Chen, J., Gan, W., Hu, M., & Chen, C.-M. (2021). On the construction of a post-quantum blockchain for smart city. *Journal of Information Security and Applications*, *58*, 102780. DOI: 10.1016/j.jisa.2021.102780

du Plessis, A. (2023). Water Resources from a Global Perspective. In du Plessis, A. (Ed.), *South Africa's Water Predicament: Freshwater's Unceasing Decline* (pp. 1–25). Springer International Publishing., DOI: 10.1007/978-3-031-24019-5_1

Egger, M., Eibl, G., & Engel, D. (2020). Comparison of approaches for intrusion detection in substations using the IEC 60870-5-104 protocol. *Energy Informatics*, *3*(S1), 15. DOI: 10.1186/s42162-020-00118-4

El-Sofany, H., El-Seoud, S. A., Karam, O. H., Bouallegue, B., & Ahmed, A. M. (2024). A proposed secure framework for protecting cloud-based educational systems from hacking. *Egyptian Informatics Journal*, *27*, 100505. DOI: 10.1016/j.eij.2024.100505

Farajzadeh, S., & Chehreh Chelgani, S. (2022). Gravity separation by falcon concentrator- an over review. *Separation Science and Technology*, *57*(13), 2145–2164. DOI: 10.1080/01496395.2022.2028836

Fernández-Caramès, T. M., & Fraga-Lamas, P. (2020). Towards Post-Quantum Blockchain: A Review on Blockchain Cryptography Resistant to Quantum Computing Attacks. *IEEE Access : Practical Innovations, Open Solutions*, *8*, 21091–21116. DOI: 10.1109/ACCESS.2020.2968985

Gaur, A. S., Sharan, H. O., & Dudhagara, C. (2025). Research trends in blockchain and digital twins. *Digital Twins for Smart Cities and Villages*, 561–580.

Gharavi, H., Granjal, J., & Monteiro, E. (2024). Post-Quantum Blockchain Security for the Internet of Things: Survey and Research Directions. *IEEE Communications Surveys and Tutorials*, *26*(3), 1748–1774. DOI: 10.1109/COMST.2024.3355222

Gulzar, Q., & Mustafa, K. (2025). Enhancing network security in industrial IoT environments: A DeepCLG hybrid learning model for cyberattack detection. *International Journal of Machine Learning and Cybernetics*, *16*(7-8), 4797–4815. Advance online publication. DOI: 10.1007/s13042-025-02544-w

Iavich, M., & Kuchukhidze, T. (2024a). Investigating CRYSTALS-Kyber Vulnerabilities: Attack Analysis and Mitigation. *Cryptography*, *8*(2), 15. DOI: 10.3390/cryptography8020015

Ismagilova, E., Hughes, L., Rana, N. P., & Dwivedi, Y. K. (2022). Security, Privacy and Risks within Smart Cities: Literature Review and Development of a Smart City Interaction Framework. *Information Systems Frontiers*, *24*(2), 393–414. DOI: 10.1007/s10796-020-10044-1 PMID: 32837262

Jebbar, W. A., & Al-Zubaidie, M. (2024). Transaction-Based Blockchain Systems Security Improvement Employing Micro-Segmentation Controlled by Smart Contracts and Detection of Saddle Goatfish. *SN Computer Science*, *5*(7), 898. DOI: 10.1007/s42979-024-03239-9

Jia, Y., Gu, Z., Du, L., Long, Y., Wang, Y., Li, J., & Zhang, Y. (2023). Artificial intelligence enabled cyber security defense for smart cities: A novel attack detection framework based on the MDATA model. *Knowledge-Based Systems*, *276*, 110781. DOI: 10.1016/j.knosys.2023.110781

Joudah, R. H., & Manaa, M. E. (2024). A New Approach to Improving the Security of the 5G-AKA Using Crystals-Kyber Post-Quantum Technologies and ASCON Algorithm. *International Journal of Safety and Security Engineering*, *14*(6), 1729–1742. DOI: 10.18280/ijsse.140608

Kniep, Q., & Wattenhofer, R. (2024). *Tyche: Collateral-Free Coalition-Resistant Multiparty Lotteries with Arbitrary Payouts* (Version 1). arXiv. DOI: 10.48550/ARXIV.2409.03464

Lavin, R., Liu, X., Mohanty, H., Norman, L., Zaarour, G., & Krishnamachari, B. (2024). *A Survey on the Applications of Zero-Knowledge Proofs* (Version 1). arXiv. DOI: 10.48550/ARXIV.2408.00243

Li, Y., Ng, K. S., & Purcell, M. (2022). *A Tutorial Introduction to Lattice-based Cryptography and Homomorphic Encryption* (No. arXiv:2208.08125). arXiv. https://doi.org//arXiv.2208.08125DOI: 10.48550

Ma, C. (2021). Smart city and cyber-security; technologies used, leading challenges and future recommendations. *Energy Reports*, *7*, 7999–8012. DOI: 10.1016/j.egyr.2021.08.124

Mattsson, J. P., Smeets, B., & Thormarker, E. (2021). *Quantum-Resistant Cryptography* (No. arXiv:2112.00399). arXiv. https://doi.org//arXiv.2112.00399DOI: 10.48550

Okika, N., Nwatuzie, G. A., & Olarinoye, H. S. ugustine A. Nwaka, Emmanuel Igba, & Roland Dunee. (2025). *Assessing the Vulnerability of Traditional and Post-Quantum Cryptographic Systems through Penetration Testing and Strengthening Cyber Defenses with Zero Trust Security in the Era of Quantum Computing*. DOI: 10.5281/ZENODO.14959440

Policharla, G.-V., Westerbaan, B., Faz-Hernández, A., & Wood, C. A. (2023). *Post-Quantum Privacy Pass via Post-Quantum Anonymous Credentials* (No. 2023/414). Cryptology ePrint Archive. https://eprint.iacr.org/2023/414

Rashid, M. M., Kamruzzaman, J., Hassan, M. M., Imam, T., & Gordon, S. (2020). Cyberattacks Detection in IoT-Based Smart City Applications Using Machine Learning Techniques. *International Journal of Environmental Research and Public Health, 17*(24), 24. Advance online publication. DOI: 10.3390/ijerph17249347 PMID: 33327468

Razzaq, R. H., & Al-Zubaidie, M. (2024a). Maintaining Security of Patient Data by Employing Private Blockchain and Fog Computing Technologies based on Internet of Medical Things. *Informatica (Vilnius), 48*(12), 12. Advance online publication. DOI: 10.31449/inf.v48i12.6047

Razzaq, R. H., & Al-Zubaidie, M. (2024b). Formulating an Advanced Security Protocol for Internet of Medical Things based on Blockchain and Fog Computing Technologies. *Iraqi Journal for Computer Science and Mathematics, 5*(3). Advance online publication. DOI: 10.52866/ijcsm.2024.05.03.046

Razzaq, R. H., Al-Zubaidie, M., & Atiyah, R. G. (2024). Intermediary Decentralized Computing and Private Blockchain Mechanisms for Privacy Preservation in the Internet of Medical Things. *Mesopotamian Journal of CyberSecurity, 4*(3), 152–165. DOI: 10.58496/MJCS/2024/020

Sahu, B. L., & Chandrakar, P. (2025). Blockchain-oriented secure communication and smart parking model for internet of electric vehicles in smart cities. *Peer-to-Peer Networking and Applications, 18*(1), 51. DOI: 10.1007/s12083-024-01872-y

Sharmila, B. S., & Nagapadma, R. (2023). Quantized autoencoder (QAE) intrusion detection system for anomaly detection in resource-constrained IoT devices using RT-IoT2022 dataset. *Cybersecurity, 6*(1), 41. DOI: 10.1186/s42400-023-00178-5

Shyaa, G. S., & Al-Zubaidie, M. (2023). Utilizing trusted lightweight ciphers to support electronic-commerce transaction cryptography. *Applied Sciences (Basel, Switzerland), 13*(12), 7085. DOI: 10.3390/app13127085

Sood, N. (2024). *Cryptography in Post Quantum Computing Era* (SSRN Scholarly Paper No. 4705470). Social Science Research Network. DOI: 10.2139/ssrn.4705470

Tahayur, D. H., & Al-Zubaidie, M. (2024). Enhancing Electronic Agriculture Data Security with a Blockchain-Based Search Method and E-Signatures. *Mesopotamian Journal of CyberSecurity, 4*(3), 3. Advance online publication. DOI: 10.58496/MJCS/2024/012

Tahayur, D. H., & Al-Zubaidie, M. (2025). Establishing an optimized searching approach with e-signatures based on blockchain for electronic agriculture applications. *AIP Conference Proceedings, 3264*(1), 030001. DOI: 10.1063/5.0258784

Tregi, T. G., & Al-Zubaidie, M. (2025). Enhancing Traffic Data Security in Smart Cities Using Optimized Quantum-Based Digital Signatures and Privacy-Preserving Techniques. *Mesopotamian Journal of CyberSecurity, 5*(1), 1. Advance online publication. DOI: 10.58496/MJCS/2025/017

Vučković, M., & Adams, A. M. (2022). Population and Health Policies in Urban Areas. In May, J. F., & Goldstone, J. A. (Eds.), *International Handbook of Population Policies* (pp. 397–429). Springer International Publishing., DOI: 10.1007/978-3-031-02040-7_18

Walunj, V., Rajaraman, V., Dutta, J., & Sharma, A. (2025). Integrating Crypto-Based Payment Systems for Data Marketplaces: Enhancing Efficiency, Security, and User Autonomy. In Patil, V. T., Krishnan, R., & Shyamasundar, R. K. (Eds.), *Information Systems Security* (Vol. 15416, pp. 443–452). Springer Nature Switzerland., DOI: 10.1007/978-3-031-80020-7_25

Yulia Fatin Lestari, N. 16610033. (2021). *Sistem Kriptografi Ntru Pada Proses Pengamanan Data Rahasia* [Skripsi, Fakultas Sains Dan Teknologi]. https://digilib.uin-suka.ac.id/id/eprint/43711/

Zhou, L., Diro, A., Saini, A., Kaisar, S., & Hiep, P. C. (2024). Leveraging zero knowledge proofs for blockchain-based identity sharing: A survey of advancements, challenges and opportunities. *Journal of Information Security and Applications, 80*, 103678. DOI: 10.1016/j.jisa.2023.103678

KEY TERMS AND DEFINITIONS

FALCON Digital Signature: A post-quantum cryptographic signature scheme known for its efficiency and small signature sizes. FALCON ensures data authenticity and integrity even in a quantum computing environment.

JSON-LD: A lightweight linked data format used to organize and standardize data, facilitating interoperability between different systems. It is used to format smart meter data in a machine-readable manner.

Kyber Key Exchange: Created for safe key exchange, a post-quantum key encapsulating mechanism (KEM) Kyber makes ensuring gadgets communicate encrypted, therefore resisting quantum assaults.

Post-Quantum Cryptography (PQC): Discipline of cryptography dedicated to create security systems resistant to dangers posed by quantum computers. It comprises methods including Kyber, FALCON.

Zero-knowledge proofs (ZKPs): A cryptographic method whereby one party may prove knowledge of a value to another without revealing the value itself. A type of ZKP that increase scalability and transparency are zero-knowledge scalable transparent arguments of knowledge, or ZK-STARKs.

Chapter 9
Blockchain Technology as a Foundation for Smart City Security: Enhancing Trust and Resilience

R. Siva Subramanian
https://orcid.org/0000-0002-7509-9223
RMK College of Engineering and Technology, India

B. Yuvasri
RMK College of Engineering and Technology, India

K. Sudha
RMD Engineering College, India

ABSTRACT

The rapid development of smart cities has introduced new security challenges, necessitating advanced solutions to ensure trust, resilience, and data integrity. Blockchain technology provides a decentralized and tamper-resistant framework to enhance smart city security, enabling secure identity management, cybersecurity, critical infrastructure protection, and transparent financial transactions. This chapter explores blockchain's role in smart city security, highlighting key applications, challenges, and future research directions. While blockchain enhances security, scalability, interoperability, regulatory concerns, and high implementation costs pose significant challenges. Advancements in quantum-resistant cryptography, AI-driven security models, and decentralized governance are expected to shape the future of blockchain-enabled smart cities. By addressing these challenges, blockchain can provide a secure and transparent foundation for smart city ecosystems, ensuring long-term sustainability and efficiency.

DOI: 10.4018/979-8-3373-3326-7.ch009

INTRODUCTION

Overview of Smart City Security Challenges

Smart cities apply the use of IoT, AI, and cloud to support various functions of city life through the use of information technology and big data analytics, among others (Chataut et al., 2023). These technologies help in resource management, traffic control, monitoring, and enhancing the quality of services to the public. However, as smart cities are made more and more interconnected, they become very susceptible to cyber threats and security issues. IoT is a network of devices and sensors, and, hence, produces a huge volume of data that, if not secured, can easily be manipulated (Abadía et al., 2022). Vulnerabilities in smart grid, transportation, healthcare, and administration applications may affect the functionality of a city and citizens' privacy. The last one that is closely related to the previous one is data privacy. Smart cities monitor their citizens through surveillance cameras, smart meters, and other biometric identification methods to gather data about them. The main risks associated with the breach of this data include identity theft, unauthorized surveillance, and loss of public confidence. These threats are not easily addressed by traditional measures of cybersecurity, for instance, centralized security approaches. Centralized databases are known to have a single point of failure and, therefore, are easily attacked. Many new forms of cyber threats are emerging, and therefore, smart cities require strong and sustainable security systems that are capable of protecting data, transactions, and the infrastructure.

The Role of Blockchain in Enhancing Trust, Security, and Resilience

Blockchain technology is an effective solution for a smart city since it provides decentralization, immutability, and transparency in the system (Singh & Singh, 2023). Compared to the conventional security models, blockchain decentralizes the data and distributes it among the nodes in the P2P network, which means that no single entity can have complete control over the system. This decentralization helps to reduce the vulnerability of hacking of data and other unlawful amendments. The nature of the blockchain is such that it cannot be changed once information has been entered, which makes the information it contains reliable and authentic. Another very important use case scenario of smart city security is identity management, where blockchain can be effectively applied. The current traditional methods of identity management are insecure for they can easily be forged, have cases of identity theft, and at times, unauthorized access (Trivedi, 2023).

Digital identities based on blockchain ensure that citizens have SSI, enabling them to control their information and have limited access to their data. Also, the use of blockchain provides for secure communication between IoT devices so that no third-party intrusions can be made, and data integrity is ensured (Jebbar, 2025). Smart contracts are self-executing contracts with programmed conditions and, therefore, increase security through automated functions like access to information, control of access, and payments. In addition, blockchain plays an important role in the enhancement of the smart city's reliability in key areas such as energy, transportation, and emergency management. For instance, blockchain can provide smart grids security through direct trading of energy between consumers and producers and by decentralization, which decreases the vulnerability to hackers. Likewise, in transport, blockchain can ensure that vehicles are able to communicate with other vehicles in a secure and tamperproof way, thereby minimizing transport system cyber threats (Tahayur, 2025). The integration of blockchain with AI and IoT enhances its security capabilities by analyzing the deviations from a standardized average and responding to them immediately.

Benefits of Decentralized and Tamper-Resistant Architectures

The decentralized structure achieved by blockchain brings about improved security, accuracy, and effectiveness when managing a smart city. A major advantage of decentralization is the absence of bottlenecks and centralized control, which are considered to be major vulnerabilities. Unlike most data processing systems, which have a central point from where all the data processing, archiving, and security is controlled, decentralized computer networks have various processing nodes, which make them less vulnerable to hacking. In any case, the functionality of the system is maintained, and the malicious nodes cannot take over the network (Yamini et al., 2025). Another benefit of blockchain technology is that it has the capability of producing records that cannot be altered. Every single transaction or data input that is entered into the blockchain is secured by an encrypted code and is connected to the preceding block. It means that data cannot be changed once it is recorded without changing the following blocks; this makes it very hard for the attackers to change the information. Specifically, such mechanisms are highly effective for protecting the records of the government, the registries of land, and the databases of law enforcement agencies in smart cities (Ponmalar et al., 2025).

Transparency is one more advantage of applying blockchain. Public blockchains enable the citizens, government, and other organizations to check the transactions occurring in the network in real-time. Such openness ensures that smart city governance is transparent and people have faith in its leadership. For instance, through blockchain, one can be able to make procurement more transparent by eliminating fraud and corruption in the city. Likewise, the use of blockchain technology in voting systems can increase electoral democracy due to the transparency and decentralization of the records of votes. Also, blockchain facilitates the integration of various smart city systems with each other (Razzaq, 2025). Most smart city services are developed in isolation, thus creating duplication of services, and the infrastructure is insecure. Blockchain thus offers a single platform of interconnecting various systems in such a way that may allow data sharing and aggregation across different organizations and entities. This is especially crucial in emergency response networks wherein information sharing is critical between the police, hospitals, and disaster management departments (Babu et al., 2024).

Chapter Objectives

As such, a general question is asked to know the role of blockchain as an underlying security for smart cities in this survey. It will also give a review on the use of blockchain technology in the development of smart cities' infrastructure, in ensuring the security of citizen data, and in building confidence in the governance of smart cities. In the chapter, the focus will be on the most promising application areas of blockchain in smart city security, including identification, cybersecurity, protection of critical infrastructure, secure digital transactions, supply chain security, and law enforcement. In addition, factors that have inhibited the use of blockchain in smart city security will also be explored, such as scalability, energy consumption, regulation, and compatibility. Smart cities are a part of the future that can be built using blockchain technology; however, their implementation has certain technical and policymaking issues that should be considered. In the conclusion section of this chapter, the future research areas will include the scalability of blockchain, AI in conjunction with blockchain security, quantum-proof cryptography, and the use of DAOs in the management of cities. Thus, this survey will give a comprehensive outlook of how blockchain technology can improve the security and reliability of smart cities. The present book will be useful for researchers, policymakers, and city planners who are eager to apply blockchain technology in the construction of safe, open, and effective urban environments. Blockchain will be a significant factor in smart cities as they grow in the future, as it will help to fight against cyber threats, maintain data accuracy, and increase the level of trust between all the interested parties.

FUNDAMENTALS OF BLOCKCHAIN TECHNOLOGY FOR SMART CITIES

Core Principles of Blockchain: Decentralization, Transparency, and Immutability

In conjunction, blockchain technology has three pillars on which it is founded, which include decentralization, transparency, and immutability, which make it a vital solution in improving security and trusted smart cities. It erases the need for a central body to oversee the exchange of information or even conduct the transactions. In the conventional smart city model, databases and authorities are responsible for records and management of citizens, infrastructures, and cybersecurity. Nevertheless, the system that is used in the smart city case is centralized, which presents a number of single points of failure and is protected against cyberattacks insufficiently. Blockchain, however, stores data in a distributed manner in a decentralized network so that no single party has full control. This technology, called DLT, is secure against such alterations, increases the stability against cyber risks, and offers a sound foundation for data integrity (Waghmare et al., 2023).

Immutability helps in making all the records that are stored in the blockchain easily accessible to any authorized member. Public blockchains are fully transparent and thus enable stakeholders like the government, companies, and the public to cross-check on the transactions in real-time. This feature is especially useful in governance since blockchain can be applied in voting systems, transparency in procurement, and compliance. For example, the use of smart contracts through blockchain technology can help eliminate corrupt bidding in the provision of public infrastructure. Immutability refers to the irreversible nature of blockchain records (Wid et al., 2024). The major characteristic of the blockchain is that information that is stored in it cannot be modified or removed. This is done through what is known as a cryptographic hash, which helps to add the new block to the chain of records while ensuring that it is secure. In smart cities, there is paramount importance in the integrity of records such as property, legal, or police records. It offers protection against fraud, alteration of important information, and loss, which increases trust and security in the digital structures within urban cities (Swarnalatha & Prabu, 2022).

Blockchain Consensus Mechanisms

Consensus algorithms are the processes adopted to authorize operations and decentralize the management of the blockchain. There are several consensus algorithms that are available, each with unique features that include security, effectiveness, and scalability, thus making their choice important in smart city applications. Proof of

Work (PoW) is the first and probably the most popular consensus algorithm, which is used in Bitcoin and many other cryptocurrencies. It involves the use of network members, termed miners, who are tasked with validating transactions through certain algorithms before entering the blockchain technology. However, PoW is very secure, which is a great disadvantage for smart city applications since it consumes a lot of energy. This is a significant improvement to the energy issue that PoW faces by allowing a validator to propose a new block depending on the quantity of coins owned and willing to risk being locked in a staking pool.

In comparison with PoW, PoS is much more energy-saving and has a higher speed of transaction confirmation, which makes it suitable for implementing smart city applications such as identification, payments, and data protection. Thus, more developments of it, like the Delegated Proof of Stake (DPoS), work in a way that the token holders elect a few validators who, in turn, validate transactions. Practical Byzantine Fault Tolerance, or PBFT, is a consensus mechanism that is suitable for high-speed and low-latency applications. In contrast to PoW and PoS, PBFT does not use techniques of solving computational riddles or owning stakes, but works on the basis of consensus between several responsible nodes making messages. PBFT is best for private and consortium blockchains where a number of known participants, such as government departments, work in harmony to handle smart city systems. This mechanism is especially useful for smart grids, secure management of patients' data, and IoT device synchronization in smart cities. Two other consensus methods are Proof of Authority (PoA) and Directed Acyclic Graphs (DAGs), which are also beneficial for smart cities as they solve issues of security, scalability, and efficiency. Choosing the right consensus model is therefore crucial to make blockchain applications in smart cities secure as well as capable of handling high throughput for a large number of transactions (Verma et al., 2023).

Smart Contracts and Their Role in Automating City Governance

Smart contracts are digital contracts that are written into code and reside on the distributed ledger to execute a certain decision when certain conditions are fulfilled. Such contracts also remove brokers who, in most cases, act as middlemen and make governance more efficient, cheaper, and transparent. In smart cities, there are numerous possibilities of using smart contracts for the following:

Automation of services: Some of the possible applications of smart contracts are within the sphere of public service, for example, tax collection, payment for utilities, calculation of social benefits, and so on. For instance, in a blockchain system, the tax can be automatically charged and recorded when a transaction is made to minimize fraud and mistakes that are normally made by hand.

Real estate transactions: title deeds and property deeds can be safely executed using the blockchain and smart contracts. This makes sure that all the ownership records are not interfered with and that transactions are done effectively without involving third parties.

Traffic management and fines: Penalties for traffic laws can also be managed through smart contracts by integrating them with IoT devices for surveillance. In case a vehicle is involved in an infraction of a traffic rule, an appropriate penalty can be levied by the smart contract, and the record of the same can be registered on the blockchain to ensure that the fine is paid on time.

Honest and fair bidding: Governments can make procurement platforms that are based on blockchain to enable honest bidding for the infrastructure projects. Smart contracts can help in the fulfilment of contracts, monitoring of progress, and the release of funds can only be done once specific conditions have been met.

The use of smart contracts in the management of municipalities can improve the delivery of services, lessen administrative procedures, and decrease corruption in city management.

Integration of Blockchain with IoT, AI, and Cybersecurity Frameworks

The smart cities are built based on IoT devices and AI, their analytics, and cybersecurity features for managing the city's facilities (Jain & Mitra, 2025). Blockchain is used to provide a secure and interoperable environment for these technologies to work efficiently.

Blockchain and IoT: Since IoT devices collect and transmit large amounts of data, they are at risk of cyberattacks, including data leakage, unauthorized access, and tampering of the devices. Blockchain also helps in solving IoT security issues through the implementation of identity management, secure data transfer, and an audit trail. Firstly, the smart city applications – the connected traffic light signals, surveillance cameras, the smart meters, and many others – can be protected from hackers, and the malicious attacks on the city's tactile infrastructures can be prevented by the use of the blockchain. Also, microtransactions based on blockchain provide for decentralized trading of electricity in smart grids, and people can sell and purchase electricity (Saini et al., 2023).

AI and Blockchain: AI helps smart cities to gain information for decision-making in traffic management, security, and energy usage, among others. But AI models come with the need to train on big data sets, which is a major issue with data privacy and even data falsification. Blockchain also brings accountability into the AI decision-making process by providing traceability of the AI actions. For example, in the use of predictive policing, blockchain can guarantee that the data on which

AI makes crime prediction will not be biased, and the data cannot be manipulated (Maheshwaran et al., 2024).

Blockchain and Cybersecurity: With the rising threat level in smart cities, blockchain enhances cybersecurity by offering better protection to data, identity, and access. PKI can be improved through the use of blockchain by decentralizing identity management, thus avoiding a single point of attack that is vulnerable to hackers. It also defends essential facilities to the degree that it logs security occurrences in a blockchain to facilitate prompt threat identification and remediation (Sriram et al., 2023).

Incorporation of smart cities can use IoT, AI, cybersecurity, and Blockchain technologies to construct a responsive, secure, and proficient urban environment that can command public confidence, secure data, and guarantee the soundness of city functionality. The fundamental principles of blockchain—decentralization, transparency, and immutability make it a powerful foundation for smart city security. The advanced consensus mechanisms, smart contracts, and integration with future technologies make the blockchain increase trust, effectiveness, and anti-susceptibility in urban governance. In the future, cities and smart cities, especially when using digital infrastructure, it is crucial to adopt blockchain technology to overcome cybersecurity threats and to provide secure transactions for the development of sustainable and secure cities.

BLOCKCHAIN APPLICATIONS IN SMART CITY SECURITY

Secure Identity Management and Authentication

One of the most important components of smart city security is identity management since people, companies, and government agencies need to be provided access to digital services. The traditional identity management systems include the use of centralized databases, which can easily be hacked, leading to identity theft and unauthorized access. Decentralized identity (DID) or even self-sovereign identity (SSI) is another area of cryptocurrency application where, as per the title of the study, cryptocurrency identity management, which incorporates decentralized identity or self-sovereign identity. DID provided users with complete authority to manage their digital identity without the intervention of a controlling body. In contrast to the government or corporate database, blockchain makes sure that users keep their credentials on a distributed ledger. This method increases security since it minimizes single points of failure, and hackers cannot easily gain access to identity information. SSI is a concept where an individual owns their data and only gives selected parts of that data to service providers without having to reveal all the information. This approach is quite useful in e-governance, healthcare, and financial services where identity authentication is necessary. It can also be applied to the context of government identification, which would allow only authorized citizens to vote, receive benefits, or securely communicate with the government. Figure 1 shows blockchain applications in smart city security.

Figure 1. Blockchain applications in smart city security

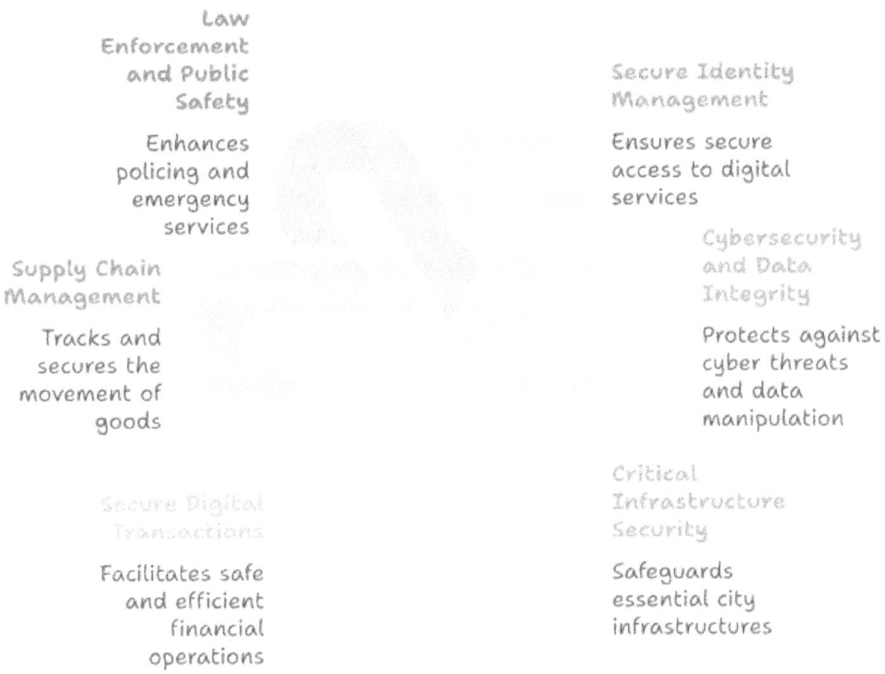

Cybersecurity and Data Integrity

Issues such as data leaks, various hacking or ransomware assaults, and unauthorized alteration of data remain some of the critical concerns for smart cities. It should also be noted that the traditional security measures are based on the concept of centralized control, which is often affected by hacking and data manipulation. Blockchain technology helps in increasing security in the cybersecurity approach since it offers a decentralized and tamper-proof record. Data security is one of the most significant advantages of using blockchain technology in the field of cybersecurity. Since the data on the blockchain is stored in the nodes, it is very difficult for attackers to manipulate or delete the records. This makes blockchain a convenient solution for safekeeping such data as citizen records, medical histories, and financial operations. Also, the integration of smart cities' intrusion detection and prevention systems (IDPS) using blockchain technology can improve their security by providing real-time monitoring of traffic flow in the network. The data collected through blockchain can be analyzed by artificial intelligence and machine learning to identify threats, recognize security threats, and initiate an appropriate response in case of threat occurrences. These characteristics make blockchain a useful tool in protecting against cyberattacks, as well as ensuring the safety of communication networks and the validity of transactions in smart cities.

Critical Infrastructure Security

Smart cities are networks of communication, power, transportation, and service infrastructures that are vulnerable to cyber-attacks and operational disruptions. Blockchain technology, on the other hand, provides a very strong security platform for these critical infrastructures as they can be monitored in real time and security threats dealt with automatically, and records are also unalterable. In power grids, blockchain helps in managing decentralized systems of energy trading and tracking of energy usage in real-time. This also helps in ensuring the energy supply chain and minimizes the vulnerability of hacking attacks on the central grid control systems. Indeed, smart contracts in the context of blockchain technology can be used to address the issue of the distribution of power and guarantee its delivery by supplying electricity in an efficient and secure manner. Security is another area that smart cities apply to transportation networks through the use of blockchain. It can also be used to protect V2I and V2V connections so that traffic information and automatic vehicle guidance systems can be protected from unauthorized changes. Also, the implementation of blockchain technology can improve public transport security through ticketing, tracking the movement of the transport fleet, and preventing fraudulent transactions. Some of the IoT devices are used in public utility services like water supply and sewage systems, fire alarms, and other emergency services. Blockchain enables IoT to maintain the safety of the data and prevent changes by other entities that are not allowed to do so; only authorized updates are made. This level of security is very important in avoiding cyber-criminal attacks on public services that are cardinal to city functioning.

Secure Digital Transactions and Smart Payments

Smart cities also require secure digital transactions for government, citizens, and the IoT-based financial systems of the city. The application of blockchain technology in digital transactions reduces the risk of fraud and offers a secure way of conducting transactions since there is no need for the involvement of third-party service providers. The e-governance platforms, which are based on blockchain technology, enable citizens to pay for government services like taxes, utility bills, and business registrations securely. Smart contracts are used in such transactions where payment is made contingent on certain conditions being met through automation. This cuts on time wastage, eradicates corruption, and increases the level of trust between the people and the government agencies. Micropayments are important in smart cities, especially in services that involve the Internet of Things, such as toll payments, smart parking, and public transportation. In conventional payment methods, there are charges attached to the transaction through the middlemen. Cryptocurrencies and stablecoins used in micropayment solutions offer instant funds transfers with favorable fees and no requirement for third-party validation. For instance, smart parking can incorporate blockchain in order to enable cars to pay for parking through the use of smart contracts, depending on the amount of time spent in the parking lot, without the need for human intervention.

It also helps in the provision of a safe form of digital money for the financially excluded population. Those who do not have a bank account have the option of using blockchain-based mobile wallets for the storage and transfer of funds for economic activity.

Supply Chain and Asset Management in Smart Cities

Adequate supply chain management is important in the development of smart cities to meet the needs of the communities in terms of the supply of goods and other materials, such as infrastructure needs and other emergency essentials. Blockchain, as a technology, has the capability of creating a clear and secure record of assets, fighting against fraud, and enhancing the supply chain. It can be seen that through the implementation of the blockchain, smart cities will be able to effectively track the movement of goods from the manufacturers to the end user in real time. Every single transaction, production, shipment, and delivery is done on the blockchain so that the supply chain data is safe and cannot be altered. This is especially crucial for food chains, drugs, and suppliers of other essential components, as well as infrastructural projects. For instance, in smart city healthcare systems, blockchain can help in tracking the authenticity of some medicines to prevent counterfeit drugs from being sold in the market. There are also the so-called digital twins, which represent the digital copy of physical assets, and can also be linked to blockchain for better infrastructure management. The digital twin that will be developed on the basis of the blockchain can contain actual information about buildings, roads, state, and performance of utilities that can be used for analysis of maintenance needs in their condition. This makes city planning easier and also helps in the proper management of public structures.

Blockchain for Law Enforcement and Public Safety

Police forces and other law enforcement agencies in smart cities need reliable and unchangeable database systems to store criminals' records, evidence, and trials. Blockchain is used in this case to improve public safety since the information collected by the police cannot be altered, hidden, or deleted, and it can only be accessed by authorized personnel. The first area of using blockchain in policing is the prevention of crime through the storage of evidence, which cannot be changed. The traditional methods of managing evidence can be manipulated, and the information contained in them lost, thus affecting criminal investigations. Through the use of blockchain technology, it is possible for law enforcement agencies to record the evidence on a blockchain ledger, hence making the forensic data, video footage, and case files tamper-proof and easily accessible by the court. It is also important to note that smart contracts may also be used for legal and security purposes. For instance, smart contracts that are based on blockchain technology can self-apply a set of rules, for example, the traffic rules, licenses for certain businesses, and environmental laws. Penalties can be automatically assigned by using blockchain in tracking the violation cases of the law enforcement agencies. Also, it is noteworthy that the use of blockchain can also help improve emergency services, as it will be possible to ensure the protection of communication between law enforcement agencies, emergency medical services, and disaster response teams. Blockchain guarantees that the data exchange in real-time will remain secure, so that cyber threats that may hinder emergency services will not occur.

Blockchain technology can support smart city security by solving some of the challenges that include identity, security, infrastructure, monetary, supply chain, and policing. It can also be concluded that the smart city elements, such as decentralised, immutable, and transparent systems of functioning, can increase the levels of trust, resiliency, and effectiveness in security management practices in smart cities. It is evident that as more and more companies embrace blockchain, the integration with new technologies such as IoT and AI will enhance smart city security systems and create a more secure and sustainable environment for citizens.

CHALLENGES AND LIMITATIONS OF BLOCKCHAIN IN SMART CITY SECURITY

One of the opportunities that may be provided through the use of blockchain technology is the reliability of smart cities. Nevertheless, the use of blockchain in smart city security has some drawbacks and limitations as follows. The problems associated with these issues include the scalability of the grid, the interoperability of the grid, legal issues, and the economics of the grid. It is imperative to overcome these challenges in order to enhance the usage of blockchain security solutions in smart cities.

Scalability and Energy Consumption Concerns

Another problem that is closely related to the use of blockchain technology in the context of smart city security is the issue of scalability. The public blockchain that particularly relies on the PoW is known to have a major problem in handling transactions in a short span of time. Smart cities produce huge amounts of data daily, consisting of surveillance feeds, IoT sensors, citizens' activities, and criminal records, among others. The current systems, like Bitcoin and Ethereum, for instance, have some issues concerning the number of transactions that can be processed, more so within a short period needed for handling smart city data. The scalability issue comes from the fact that blockchain is based on distributed ledger technology, and each transaction should be processed and recorded by many nodes. Due to this verification, the number of transactions rises, so does the delay time for each transaction, making it hard to process a large amount of data in smart cities. Improvement of this necessarily involves the application of layer-2 scaling, such as the Lightning network, Plasma, among others, a concept that is still in the development stage and has not fully been incorporated in smart city applications. Another important problem that is also connected with the concept of scalability is the matter of high energy consumption inherent to modern blockchain networks, especially those that are based on PoW. Mining in the PoW-based blockchains demands a lot of computational power, which results in high energy usage and environmental impacts. The problem arises when a smart city aims at sustainable energy use, and an energy-hungry blockchain system is implemented. Altogether, the PoS and DPoS algorithms are more energy-friendly compared to PoW, but the level of security and decentralization they provide might vary.

Interoperability with Existing Smart City Infrastructure

Smart cities use several technologies such as IoT, intelligent analytics, cloud computing, and conventional databases, among others. To incorporate blockchain into smart city security, it has to be compatible with these existing technologies. However, most of the current blockchain platforms are fashion in their own and this hinders their compatibility with centralized and legacy systems. These are the issues of interoperability because each blockchain network is built with a unique protocol, consensus algorithm, and programming language for smart contracts. For instance, a smart city may have a permissioned ledger for the government and a permissionless ledger for citizens' services. Integrating these blockchains with others and legacy databases is not easy because there are no well-defined standards for communication and middleware. However, there are more problems that arise when integrating blockchain with IoT infrastructure. The problem with developing blockchain-based security for many IoT devices used in smart cities is that they have small memories and processing power. Traditional blockchain solutions like IoTA's Tangle and Hyperledger Fabric are also currently being considered to implement in solving this problem, but the problem of high adoption rates still persists. There is, therefore, the possibility that smart city administrators may have a challenge in implementing blockchain solutions that interoperate with other systems. Figure 2 shows the challenges and limitations of blockchain in smart city security.

Figure 2. Challenges and limitations of blockchain in smart city security

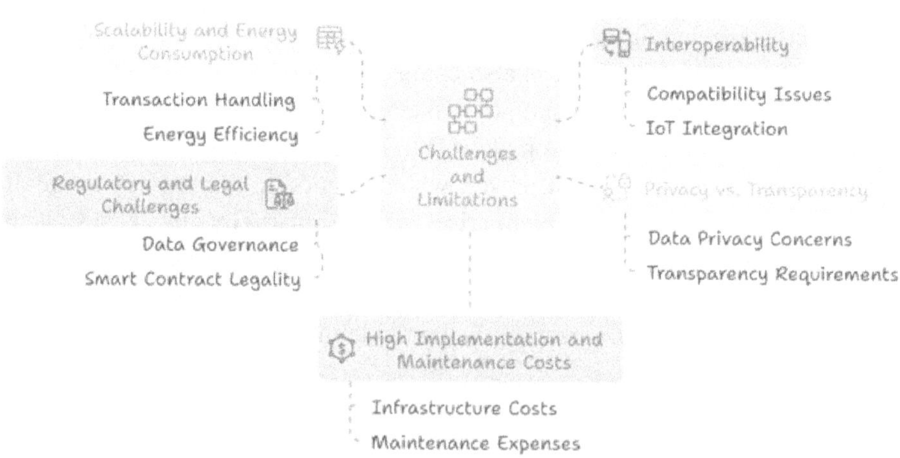

Privacy vs. Transparency Trade-offs in Blockchain Networks

Some of the key characteristics of blockchain are openness, non-adjustability, and decentralization. The former are useful in securing smart city systems as well as improving the credibility of the systems, but the latter is a major concern, especially when handling personal information belonging to the citizens. It is a fact that many smart cities collect and process large and sensitive data about individuals, such as biometrics, health records, payments, and video surveillance. If such data is to be stored on a public blockchain, the data will be available to all the participants in the network, which is a major issue of privacy. One of the major issues that needs to be addressed when implementing blockchain in smart cities includes the privacy vs. transparency dilemma. On the one hand, they are transparent, and this guarantees that there is no fraud since they can be used in government services. However, it has the disadvantage of compromising the security of the information in question, hence leading to violations of data privacy. In response to this challenge, solutions based on blockchain and privacy are being worked on, which include: Zero-knowledge proofs (ZKPs), Homomorphic encryption, and secure multi-party computation (SMPC). These cryptographic techniques make it possible to confirm transactions without disclosing the details of the transactions, thus making blockchain personal. However, the above-mentioned privacy-oriented solutions add more computational overhead and may affect the performance of blockchain systems. Moreover, rules with regard to data protection, like the GDPR, contain strict requirements regarding user data and the right to erasure. However, since blockchain is a permanent ledger, erasing personal data from the blockchain is almost impossible, which may pose a problem in compliance with the laws of privacy. The key issue that has been observed while implementing smart city security on the blockchain is the conflict between the decentralized and transparent nature of the blockchain and the requirement for privacy.

Regulatory and Legal Challenges in Blockchain Adoption

The growth of blockchain technology in smart cities is still limited mainly due to the lack of proper legislation and legal guidelines. Because blockchain works on decentralized and cross-border platforms, it becomes extremely difficult to give legal jurisdiction, legal obligations, and compliance. Currently, governments and policymakers are trying to define the correct regulatory measures for blockchain-based security applications, and that is why smart city planners and technology developers are still in doubt. Data governance is one of the most important regulatory issues that has been of interest in the recent past. This means that governments must ensure that smart city security solutions based on blockchain technology take into consideration the legal requirements of data protection laws in the country and the international ones. Nonetheless, due to the differences in the rules and policies of each country concerning data localization, financial operations, and identity, it is difficult to develop an effective model for the governance of blockchains. Smart contracts, which are self-executing and self-enforceable digital contracts on the blockchain, also pose legal challenges. Smart contracts increase the level of security and effectiveness of contracts, but do not have a legal basis. Regarding disputes or contract breaches, there is no clear way to determine which legal body should intervene since traditional legal systems cannot address self-enforcing smart contracts. However, the fear of other unlawful activities like money laundering and cybercrime has made some governments put restrictions on the use of blockchain for any form of financial transactions. Laws and regulations regarding the use of cryptocurrencies and the governance of blockchains may hinder the integration of blockchain in smart city security. It means that the unclear legislation might be seen by the city administrators as a reason not to invest in blockchain solutions because of non-compliance risks.

High Implementation and Maintenance Costs

Integrating blockchain solutions in smart cities also involves a large amount of money for the development of infrastructure and subsequent maintenance. Unlike conventional security systems, Blockchain networks call for special hardware, high-speed internet connections, and highly qualified personnel to implement and maintain the systems. The first cost of implementation of blockchain technology is the creation of specialized blockchain solutions, as well as the connection of smart city systems to blockchain, and personnel familiarization with blockchain processes. Public blockchain networks, being decentralized, have a concept of transaction fees, which are also known as gas fees for each operation, and which can accumulate rather quickly. Both private and consortium blockchains have lower transaction costs, but they have specific dedicated resources for network validation and management. Also, the blockchain security requires constant software upgrades, security checks, and network surveillance, among others. Currently, blockchain technology is still under development, and therefore, smart city administrators must ensure that they continuously carry out research and development to be in a position to adapt to any new development or vulnerability that might arise. If there is no funding, it may be a challenge for many cities to adopt blockchain security solutions in the larger market.

Despite the potential benefits of blockchain technology in improving smart city security, there are some drawbacks and limitations associated with this technology. Before blockchain can be implemented in smart city security, several challenges, such as scalability, interoperability, privacy, legal concerns, and cost, must be considered. To overcome these challenges, there is a need for cooperation between the government, technology firms, and researchers to deploy effective, secure, and cheap blockchain solutions. Thus, certain aspects such as scalability innovations, improved compliance requirements, and privacy preservation will determine the further development of the smart city security systems based on the blockchain.

FUTURE TRENDS AND RESEARCH DIRECTIONS

It has become apparent that as smart cities develop more layers of sophistication, the question of how to incorporate blockchain into their security becomes an important point of study and development. The development prospects are concealed by such disadvantages of the blockchain as its high decentralization, transparency, and increased security. To overcome these challenges, there is a need to scale, enhance cryptography, and implement advanced security using artificial intelligence, decentralized governance, and regulation. This section discusses the future trends and research areas that will define the development of blockchain technology in the security of smart cities.

Advances in Blockchain Scalability and Energy-Efficient Consensus Mechanisms

The major issue that blockchain is facing as an enabler of smart cities is scalability. Most, especially those that are based on the Proof of Work consensus algorithm, have issues such as slow transaction rates and high computational expenses. In the future, new scalability solutions will be decisive for the possibility of blockchain's application in large-scale urban settings, as shown in Figure 3. There are several measures being pursued in an attempt to increase the scalability of blockchain technology. For instance, Sharding is when the chain is split into different partitions, known as shards, so that several transactions can be processed concurrently instead of being processed in a sequential manner. Ethereum 2.0 is one of the most significant blockchain projects that utilizes Sharding to enhance the TPS of the platform. Layer-2 scaling is another possible solution that implies executing many transactions off-chain, but keeping them on-chain occasionally during the settlement process. The Lightning Network, together with Plasma, is considered the Layer-2 solution that presented as having the potential to enhance blockchain's transaction speed for use in smart cities. Another important area of research is energy consumption and management, as the problem of energy scalability is also crucial. The PoW uses a lot of computational power in the consensus and is not feasible for smart cities that want to run on renewable energy. Other models like PoS, DPoS, and PoA are less demanding in terms of energy consumption as they do not require the mining processes. There are also some combined consensus mechanisms under investigation to achieve the best of both worlds in terms of security and energy consumption. Thus, integration of PoS with BFT might allow not only faster and more efficient transaction validation, but also secure it as well. In addition, studies are being done on new structures of Blockchain, like the DAGs (Directed Acyclic Graph) that do not include mining and allow the transactions to be validated in parallel.

Figure 3. Future trends and research directions

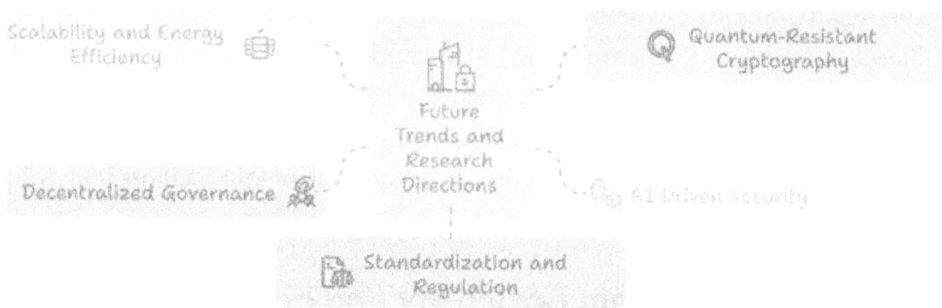

Integration of Quantum-Resistant Cryptography for Smart City Security

The new quantum technology is therefore a threat to most of the cryptographic key models used in blockchain networks. RSA and ECC are the two widely used encryption algorithms that are at risk of being beaten by quantum computers. Blockchain is expected to play a crucial role in the management of identity, finance, and protection of infrastructure in smart cities, and thus, there is a need for quantum-resistant cryptography. Post-quantum cryptography, or PQC, can be understood as a new, august research field that deals with the advancement of cryptography techniques that are resistant to quantum attacks. Lattice-based cryptography, hash-based cryptography, and multivariate polynomial cryptography are among the cryptographic techniques that have considerable potential for solving blockchain quantum security. This is why researchers are constantly trying to implement such cryptographic methods into blockchain networks for better security in the future. The other method is quantum key distribution (QKD), in which the principle of quantum mechanics is used to generate a secure key for encrypting messages. The combination of QKD with blockchain shall make smart cities secure not only critical infrastructures, financial strategies, and government networks. However, there are still a number of challenges for the practical application of QKD-based blockchain systems, which are related to the current state of quantum networking and infrastructure.

AI-Driven Blockchain Security and Threat Prediction Models

AI is becoming a significant factor in the improvement of blockchain security, especially in smart city systems. Artificial intelligence-based security models can process big data, identify various irregularities, and anticipate cyber threats in real-time; they can be effectively used to enhance security for blockchain systems. The first category is AI for fraud detection in blockchain transactions. Through the use of machine learning on the data contained in the blockchain, researchers can easily detect anomalies and even insider threats with the aim of combating financial fraud. RNNs and transformer-based architectures are being used to learn fraud and unauthorized access anomalies in Decentralized networks. One of the other significant areas of AI application in blockchain security is an intelligent intrusion detection system. Smart cities' networks can be constantly supervised by AI-based IDS, as well as the detection of attacks and responses to threats. Currently, threat detection and prevention can be enhanced through combining the AI technology with the blockchain deployment to form a strongly protective framework. AI is also being applied to improving the efficiency of the consensus mechanism of blockchain. It gives the functionality of Adaptive consensus, where consensus validation mechanisms are enhanced through Artificial intelligence to use less energy and are more efficient in their performance. This is because future studies in this field may result in a fully autonomous blockchain network capable of adapting to threats by changing the secure parameters in response to the threat analysis.

Role of Decentralized Autonomous Organizations (DAOs) in City Governance

Smart city governance through decentralized autonomous organizations (DAOs) is a new trend in the development of modern society. DAOs are autonomous organizations managed by code; this means that they are not controlled by any individual or group of people. In the context of smart city security, DAOs can provide a way to decentralize the decision-making processes within the smart city by involving the citizens, businesses, and government agencies. For instance, DAOs can be applied to organize the maintenance of urban facilities, distribute security measures, and regulate the processes of identification in the digital space. Policy-making as well as decision-making on the most important security concerns can be made by consensus through token-based voting systems. Another strength of DAOs is that they help in increasing accountability and minimizing bureaucratic procedures. Due to the fact that all the transactions and decisions are recorded on the blockchain, which cannot be altered, DAOs are transparent and secure. However, there are still many issues that need further investigation, including the security issues of smart contracts, legal issues of regulation, and the ways to govern disputes in decentralized systems.

Standardization Efforts and Regulatory Frameworks for Blockchain Adoption

The use of blockchain technology in smart city security is not well adopted due to the absence of standardization and legislation on blockchain technology. The main problem associated with blockchain adoption at the moment is that there are no standards for blockchains established across different jurisdictions to guarantee a common code of conduct, legal permissibility, and mutual compatibility. ITU and ISO are the two major organizations across the world that are focusing on setting up blockchain standards in terms of data protection, identity, and smart contracts. These standards are to establish a guideline on how blockchain can be implemented in a smart city to ensure compatibility between various platforms and service providers. In terms of governance, governments and policymakers are in the process of considering legal and policy issues of data privacy, financial policies, and cybersecurity. For example, the European Union's GDPR hinders blockchain implementation because it cannot be changed in any way. More research is needed to develop a blockchain that meets the privacy requirements of the country and retains its security elements. There are other areas of regulation that are also important, and one of them is the regulation of blockchain-based identity systems. The governments have to ensure that the decentralized identity management systems are in compliance with the national security standards and identification verification standards. Some of the topics, like SSI and DID, are being discussed as solutions for building a blockchain identity that will be compliant with the regulations.

With the development of blockchain technology, it is expected that it will greatly contribute to improving the security of smart cities. The development of new layering, quantum cryptography, artificial intelligence technologies, and sovereignty of the new-generation blockchain security will define further development. Nevertheless, the issues of regulation, interoperability, and energy consumption can be solved only with the help of collective efforts of governments, researchers, and industry participants. Thus, the given challenges can be solved by utilizing blockchain as the basis for developing safe, stable, and credible smart cities.

CONCLUSION

Blockchain technology has been found to be a revolutionary solution when it comes to the security of smart cities through decentralization, transparency, and integrity of data. This chapter explored its fundamental principles, key applications, challenges, and future research directions. It is used for identification and authorization, defending critical assets, performing secure payments, providing supply chain visibility, and aiding law enforcement through the use of blockchain technology. In this sense, smart contracts and decentralized networks in smart cities improve trust and strengthen cooperation. However, the following challenges have been observed to limit its widespread adoption. It is found that an inherent problem related to using, scalability, and high energy consumption makes it even difficult, and that due to interoperability challenges, integrating them with the existing smart city infrastructure is complicated. Also, another challenge to the implementation is legal and regulatory issues, as well as privacy and security issues. Solving these problems, it is necessary to develop new approaches to energy-efficient consensus, establish clear standards, and optimize the system of governance. In the next steps, the development of the use of blockchain in smart city security will be associated with new trends such as the integration of AI for threat prediction, quantum-resistant encryption, and DAOs. Blockchain with AI and IoT integration will only enhance cybersecurity and promote the efficient running of the city. The governments, researchers, and policymakers should come up with policies that enhance the security of the blockchain and, at the same time, protect the privacy of the users. In summary, it is evident that blockchain is a suitable environment for smart city security, but its potential is yet to be fully explored due to the need for further development of technology and legislation. This chapter aims to identify current limitations and challenges towards the development of smart cities through blockchain technology and proposes possible solutions towards the improvement of urban life in the future digital society.

REFERENCES

Abadía, J. J. P., Walther, C., Osman, A., & Smarsly, K. (2022). A systematic survey of Internet of Things frameworks for smart city applications. *Sustainable Cities and Society*, *83*, 103949. DOI: 10.1016/j.scs.2022.103949

Babu, A. A., Jebamalar, G. B., Kumar, P., & Nalini, M. (2024, December). Blockchain Technology: Evolution and Future Prospects. In *2024 International Conference on Sustainable Communication Networks and Application (ICSCNA)* (pp. 381-387). IEEE. DOI: 10.1109/ICSCNA63714.2024.10864089

Chataut, R., Phoummalayvane, A., & Akl, R. (2023). Unleashing the power of IoT: A comprehensive review of IoT applications and future prospects in healthcare, agriculture, smart homes, smart cities, and industry 4.0. *Sensors (Basel)*, *23*(16), 7194. DOI: 10.3390/s23167194 PMID: 37631731

Jain, V., & Mitra, A. (2025). Optimizing Real-Time Traffic Management Using Blockchain-Enabled VANET: Enhancing Efficiency and Security in Smart Cities. In *Leveraging VANETs and Blockchain Technology for Urban Mobility* (pp. 289-314). IGI Global Scientific Publishing.

Jebbar, W. A. (2025). Optimization Solution Proposal for Smart Transaction Security of Smart Blockchain Contracts in E-Banking Applications. In *Sustainable Information Security in the Age of AI and Green Computing* (pp. 295–320). IGI Global Scientific Publishing.

Maheshwaran, T., Muthumarilakshmi, S., Suganya, K., Maheswari, B., & Girija, P. (2024). Securing E-Commerce Strategies with Cloud, Blockchain, AI, and ML. In *Strategies for E-Commerce Data Security: Cloud, Blockchain, AI, and Machine Learning* (pp. 470-500). IGI Global.

Ponmalar, A., Muthuram, A., Therasa, M., Priya, V., Sathya, V., Subha, S., & Subramanian, R. S. (2025). Convergence of Advanced Technologies for Sustainable Development and Smart Cities. In *AI and Green Technology Applications in Society* (pp. 189–218). IGI Global Scientific Publishing.

Razzaq, R. (2025). Combining Fog Computing and Blockchain Based on the Internet of Medical Things to Preserve Patient Information Privacy. In *Sustainable Information Security in the Age of AI and Green Computing* (pp. 525–546). IGI Global Scientific Publishing.

Saini, K., Mummoorthy, A., Chandrika, R., & Gowri Ganesh, N. S. (Eds.). (2023). *AI, IoT, and Blockchain Breakthroughs in E-governance*. IGI Global. DOI: 10.4018/978-1-6684-7697-0

Singh, P., & Singh, N. (2023). Blockchain with IoT and AI: A review of agriculture and healthcare. *Research Anthology on Convergence of Blockchain, Internet of Things, and Security*, 1315-1330.

Sriram, V. P., Sanyal, S., Laddunuri, M. M., Subramanian, M., Bose, V., Booshan, B., & Thangam, D. (2023). Enhancing cybersecurity through blockchain technology. In *Handbook of Research on Cybersecurity Issues and Challenges for Business and FinTech Applications* (pp. 208–224). IGI Global.

Swarnalatha, P., & Prabu, S. (Eds.). (2022). *Blockchain Technologies for Sustainable Development in Smart Cities*. IGI Global. DOI: 10.4018/978-1-7998-9274-8

Tahayur, D. H. (2025). Security Cooperation in the Protection Concerns of Agriculture Data Using Efficient Signatures and Artificial Bee Colony Manner. In *Sustainable Information Security in the Age of AI and Green Computing* (pp. 439–460). IGI Global Scientific Publishing.

Trivedi, S. (2023). Convention of Blockchain in financial services: a state-of-the-art literature review. *Revolutionizing Financial Services and Markets through FinTech and Blockchain*, 237-250.

Verma, A., Singh, A., Sethi, P., Jain, V., Chawla, C., Bhargava, A., & Gupta, A. (2023). Applications of Data Security and Blockchain in Smart City Identity Management. In *Handbook of Research on Data-Driven Mathematical Modeling in Smart Cities* (pp. 154–174). IGI Global. DOI: 10.4018/978-1-6684-6408-3.ch009

Waghmare, G., Sundram, S., Kumar, B., Raman, M. S., Yagnam, N., Motekar, H. S., & Kaushik, D. (2023). Blockchain in Supply Chain Management Prevailing in Smart Cities: Prospects and Approaches. In *Handbook of Research on Data-Driven Mathematical Modeling in Smart Cities* (pp. 117-137). IGI Global.

Wid, J., Razzaq, R., & Duaa, T. (2024). Blockchain and cryptography framework of e-apps with big data. *Journal of Education for Pure Science*, *14*(3).

Yamini, B., Dinesh, M. G., Gracious, L. A., & Subramanian, R. S. (2025). Exploring Blockchain Technology: Concepts, Features, and Industry Transformations. In *Blockchain Applications for the Energy and Utilities Industry* (pp. 305-322). IGI Global Scientific Publishing.

Chapter 10
Blockchain-Driven Cybersecurity Architectures for Smart Cities

Koduri Sreelakshmi
Department of ECE, GMR Institute of Technology, Rajam, India

Rajesh V. Argiddi
https://orcid.org/0000-0002-4227-2384
Department of Computer Science and Engineering, Walchand Institute of Technology, Solapur, India

Syeda Meraj Bilfaqih
https://orcid.org/0000-0001-9865-1263
Department of computer Science, King Khalid University, Gregar, Saudi Arabia

Sanya Yadv
https://orcid.org/0000-0002-4892-6617
School of Law, Bennett University, Greater Noida, India

D. Ramya
https://orcid.org/0000-0002-7970-3483
Department of English, Kongu Engineering College, Perundurai, Indonesia

M. Sudha
https://orcid.org/0009-0000-0343-4451
SaiSriram Engineering College, India

ABSTRACT

This chapter invites the integration of blockchain technology and cryptographic consensus methods to increase cybersecurity in smart city ecosystems. As the urban environment becomes more and more connected by IoT and data-based infrastructure, the need for safe, transparent, and elastic systems is important. Blockchain provides decentralized trust, tamper-proof records, and strong control, which is important for protecting complex services such as energy grids, traffic systems, and

DOI: 10.4018/979-8-3373-3326-7.ch010

public safety networks. This chapter evaluates the applicable challenges in cases of various consensus models and smart cities, illuminating the challenges and future directions to protect the urban structures of the upcoming pay general.

INTRODUCTION

The rapid development of digital techniques and the spread of the Internet of Things (IoT) devices transformed the urban environment into each other and data - based smart cities. This digitally gives the powerful cities the benefit of real-time data collection, analysis, and auto tomatoes to enhance urban efficiency, durability, governance, and quality of life. From intelligent transport systems and smart grids to e-governance platforms and connected public structures, smart cities promise to revolutionize and manage urban centers. However, this increasing interconnectivity and data Reliance simultaneously highlight these systems in a wide range of cyber safety risks and privacy weaknesses. The complexity of smart city ecosystems presents a unique cybersecurity challenge - the traditional central security models are proving to be inadequate in view of the demand for dynamic, decentralized, and interactive digital infrastructures (Kumar & Rasool, 2023).

As smart cities develop, the volume and sensitivity of the data produced from billions of connected sensors, civilian devices, and municipal systems. Cyberattacks on urban structures, such as traffic signal tampering, ransomware attacks on public health databases, and the critical energy grid, show serious consequences of already inadequate cyber safety. Moreover, centralized architects operating in the traditionally smart city network often represent an issue of failure, making them very sensitive to system-wide settlement. In this regard, blockchain technology emerges as an attractive example to reconsider cybersecurity architectures in smart cities (Rathod et al., 2023).

Blockchain provides a transformative foundation to strengthen cyber safety at both the architectural and operational levels, both in a decentralized, cryptographically secure, and tamper-resistant digital system. It provides a strong structure to protect data transactions without depend on the dependence on the moderators of the internal features, including immutability, distributed consensus, transparent Audit detection trails, and peer-to-peer trust-centralized mediators. As a result, blockchain can address issues of many pressure security and privacy in smart cities, including secure identification management, reliable data protection, elastic communication channels, and automatic controls (Hammed and Jebbar, 2025). By decentralizing data governance and strengthening system-level transparency, blockchain technologies can significantly increase trust and liability in public and private digital services operating in smart city ecosystems (Ahakonye et al., 2024).

The integration of blockchain with smart city infrastructure, however, is not without complexity. The multidisciplinary nature of smart cities requires both technically possible and socially acceptable solutions for blockchain architects, blockchain architectures, in information, urban planning, data expression, policy, and man-centered designs. Implementing blockchain in this regard requires not only reconfiguration of technical stacks, but also a regulatory, moral, and operational framework. For example, personal identifiable information (PII) in the blockchain environment must be carefully balanced between the mandatory disorder and "right to forget" by data protection law, such as the General Data Protection Regulation (GDPR). Similarly, the scalability limitations of blockchain, especially in public and non-permitted types, must be taken into account to support the high transaction throughput and low delays required by real-time smart city services (Balasaheb & Kumar, 2024).

In recent years, some pilot projects and research initiatives have explored the application of blockchain in smart city domains. These include blockchain-based smart grid systems, secure digital identity for civil services, Temper-proof land registries, and decentralized voting platforms for decentralized energy trade. These case chairs have shown both the promise and the blockchain's limits in practical urban contexts. Importantly, they indicate the need for hybrid architectural models that combine the power of blockchain with complementary technologies such as the same computing, artificial intelligence (AI), and secure multi-party computation. For example, the conversion of blockchain with AI-driven threat investigation provides an active approach to reducing cyber threats in real-time, increasing the conditions of urban systems (Soni et al., 2024).

This chapter aims to take a comprehensive examination of blockchain-based cybersecurity architectures corresponding to smart cities. By referring to the unique threatening landscape for urban digital infrastructures, it illuminates the weaknesses associated with IoT, centralized control systems, and data silos. This chapter focuses on the main principles and technical underpinnings of blockchain, emphasizing their relevance in reducing these weaknesses. Various architectural models are invented, including layered frameworks that integrate blockchain into application levels of vision, network, and smart city systems. To manage blockchain to enhance cybersecurity and trust, special attention is paid to the use of many urban areas - energy, mobility, public health, waste management, and governance cases (Maurya et al., 2025).

Furthermore, this chapter investigates technical challenges and ideas of operations, such as the trade-off of modulation, energy room efficiency, and consensus algorithm, which must pay attention to large-scale blockchain deployment in smart cities. Moral and regulatory effects are also discussed, with data sovereignty, models of regime, and a focus on compliance with international cybersecurity standards

(Shayea et al., 2025). Finally, this chapter ends with a visible view on the role of blockchain in the future urban elasticity strategy, emphasizing the importance of interdependent cooperation, open norms, and agile regime to promote safe, transparent, and citizen-centered smart cities (Pothireddy, 2025).

Hence, this chapter argues that a blockchain, when integrated, can serve as the foundation of confidence in the developed landscape of cyber safety and smart cities. It represents the blockchain not as a panacea but as a strategic component of the comprehensive, layered security architecture, which must be adaptive, incorporated, and elastic in the always-changing, cyber-threatening environment (Saad & Mustafa, 2025; Wimal et al., 2025). With the onset of worldwide aspiring digital transformation traveling, the intention and frameworks presented in this chapter, including the inevitable and reliable urban digital ecosystems, including blockchain technologies, are aimed at leading the empowered and trusted urban digital ecosystems.

Chapter Objectives

This chapter aims to explore the integration of blockchain technology in cybersecurity architectures for smart cities. It strives to identify the main weaknesses in current urban digital infrastructures and show how blockchain can improve data integrity, access control, and trust in each other's connected systems. This chapter also presents Architectural models, practical use cases, and implementation challenges, including scalability, regulatory compliance, and interoperability. By evaluating both technical and policy parameters, this chapter provides strategic guidance to stakeholders adopting elastic, decentralized cybersecurity solutions that align with the growing demand for smart cities. The goal is to report a safe, durable, and civil-focused urban innovation.

Figure 1. Smart city ecosystem-threat landscape

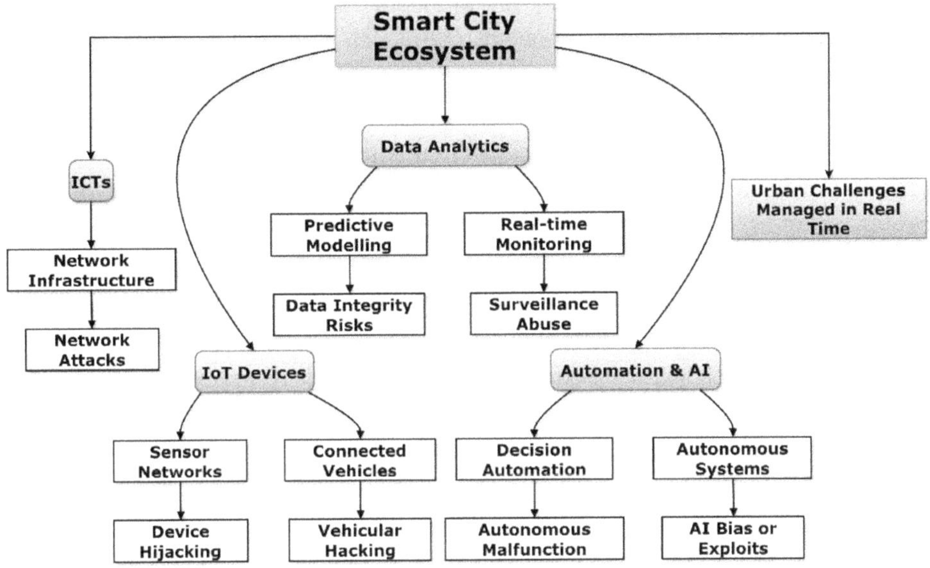

SMART CITY ECOSYSTEM: THREAT LANDSCAPE

The emergence of smart cities represents an instance shift in urban development, which is created by the conversion of information and communication techniques (ICTs), IoT, data analytics, and automation. These innovations enable the city administration to allocate resources, improve civil services, and react to urban challenges in real time. However, the growing dependence on each other's digital infrastructure also introduces a complex and developing threatening landscape. As the number of endpoints increases rapidly in smart cities, the surface area for cyberattacks increases. This department investigates cyber safety challenges in the IoT-based environment and outlines the primary attack vectors and weaknesses compromising urban systems (Anwar & Ali, 2022). Figure 1 illustrates the core technological components of a smart city.

Cybersecurity Challenges in IoT-Driven Environments

The rear of any smart city is its IoT ecosystem, which includes various and distributed devices - such as sensors, actuators, meters, cameras, and embedded systems - transport, energy zones, water management, healthcare, and law enforcement. While these devices enable seamless data storage and real-time response, they often lack adequate calculation power, memory, and embedded security protocols. This creates a low-knit fruit view for cyber opponents (Muheden et al., 2024).

Lack of standardization in IOT device manufacturing is one of the most challenging. Many devices are made by vendors who prefer security costs and speed-to-market. As a result, devices are sent with hardcoded credentials, unknown firmware, or unsafe communication protocols. Moreover, the life cycle of these devices - ranging from secure deployment to software updates - is often ignored by vendors and municipal IT departments, leaving the devices vulnerable for an extended period. Another challenge is the intense scale and sexuality of the IoT network in smart cities. A variety of communication standards, platforms, and data formats leads to inefficiency issues, making it difficult to apply similar security policies. These pieces not only weaken the security posture but also complicate the threat of investigations and phenomena.

Complicating the security landscape is the absence of central inspection. Many smart city functions are governed by various agencies, each with its own security standards and levels of risk tolerance. This silly approach hinders an integrated defense strategy, which allows attackers to absorb weak links in the ecosystem. Additionally, real-time data flow requirements impose a barrier to encryption and authentication methods, potentially compromising integrity in favor of the confidentiality and influence of data. The dynamic and mobile nature of certain IoT components - such as connected vehicles, drones, and mobile sensors - strips the second layer of complexity. These devices often change networks and locations, making them more difficult to monitor and secure. This dynamic atmosphere creates the opportunity for attackers to disrupt the corrupt code and network continuity.

Finally, the use of cloud and edge computing in smart city infrastructure, while enhancing scalability and low-latency operations, represents new attack surfaces. Incorrect cloud storage, insufficient controls and policies, and weaknesses in API can expand the potential influence of cyber infiltration, expanding sensitive data and services to unauthorized access in certain cases.

Attack Vectors and Vulnerabilities in Urban Systems

Smart cities are susceptible to a wide array of attack vectors that target both digital and physical dimensions of urban infrastructure. This attack vector can be widely classified into data-centered, network-centered, and service-centered threats (Anisetti et al., 2020; Nanayakkara et al., 2024).

i. **Data-Centric Attacks**: These include data intercept, tampering, and individually identifiable information (PII) and unauthorized access of sensitive municipal records. Attackers will exploit poor encryption protocols or insecure data in transit to manipulate information or steal. For example, unauthorized access to health or surveillance data can lead to breach of privacy, blackmail, or reputational damage to public bodies.

ii. **Network-Centric Attacks**: Attacks of network-level threats, such as delivered refusal service attacks, can disrupt smart city services through excessive systems. These attacks are particularly dangerous when they target critical structural facilities such as emergency response systems or public utilities. Routing attack, man-in-the-middle (MITM) functions, and signal jamming can further compromise data flow and operational continuity in the city network.

iii. **Device-Level Exploits**: IoT devices in traffic lights, parking meters, surveillance cameras, or streetlights can be hijacked using default credentials or unpaid firmware. Once compromised, these devices can serve as entrance points for widespread network infiltration or enter a botnet.

iv. **Application-Level Threats**: Smart city applications, including e-governance portals, mobile citizen apps, and cloud-based dashboards, can be vulnerable to software bugs, insecure APIs, and improper access controls. Attackers may exploit these weaknesses to escalate privileges, inject malicious scripts, or corrupt service logic—leading to systemic failures or misinformation campaigns.

v. **Insider Threats and Human Error**: A significant proportion of cyber incidents in smart cities arises from internal actors or unintentional errors. Poor password hygiene, lack of cybersecurity training, and misconfigured access privileges can enable threat actors to bypass technical controls. Public employees or contractors with privileged access may intentionally or unintentionally expose sensitive systems to risk.

vi. **Physical Attacks on Infrastructure**: Many IoT devices are installed in a public or outdoor environment, making them susceptible to physical tampering, theft, or vandalism. Devices lacking tamper-proof casing or secure installation processes can be easily compromised to replace data, device configuration, or deploy malware.

vii. **Supply Chain Vulnerabilities**: Smart City Infrastructures depend very much on third-party vendors for hardware, Software, and cloud services. The compromising supplier may represent malicious code or weaknesses during a settlement or deployment. An example of a SolarWinds attack is how opponents can infiltrate critical systems through a reliable supply chain.

The cyber safety landscape of smart cities is very complex, characterized by connected devices, wide data flow, and involvement of various stakeholders. The number of attack vectors and weaknesses needs to be relocated from reactive to active security architects (Anwar & Ali, 2022; Nanayakkara et al., 2024). Addressing these risks requires a holistic, layered, and decentralized security strategy that combines advanced technologies such as strong standards, secure-by-design principles, real-time threat intelligence, and blockchain. Cities can really protect their digital futures while ensuring public trust and reliability of public confidence and service through a multi-leisure and forward-looking approach.

FOUNDATIONS OF BLOCKCHAIN TECHNOLOGY

Blockchain technology emerged as a groundbreaking innovation in digital recordkeeping and trust management, redefining how data is stored, shared, and validated in distributed systems. At its origin, blockchain is a decentralized, cryptographically secure ledger that enables multiple participants to maintain a shared record of transactions without the need for central rights. This distributed nature offers significant benefits for transparency, elasticity, and protection, which are critically valuable for complex, data-intensive ecosystems such as smart cities. It is necessary to understand the basic components of blockchain technology to appreciate its transformative potential in cybersecurity architecture and system integrity (Wimal et al., 2025). Figure 2 illustrates the Blockchain Technology for visualizing the key components and principles.

Figure 2. Foundations of blockchain technology for visualizing the key components and principles

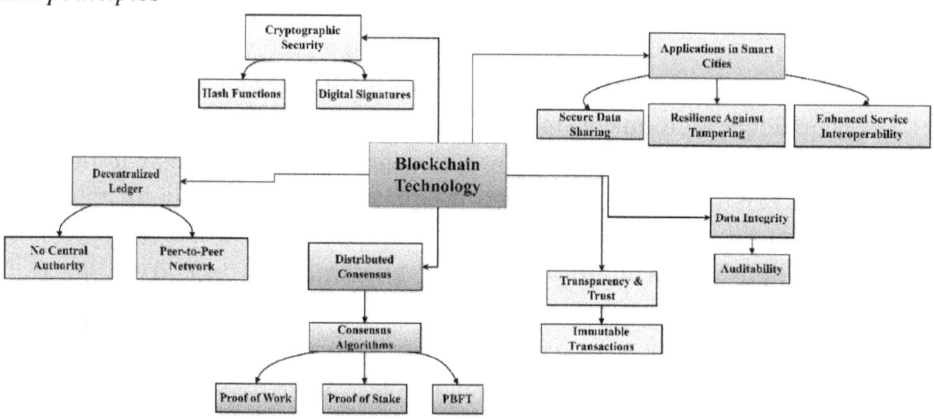

Key Components: Blocks, Hashes, Consensus

The most basic structural element of the blockchain is the block, which acts as a data container. Each block has a unique identifier called a batch of valid transactions, a timestamp, a cryptographic hash of the previous block, and a nonce. Cryptographic hash serves a dual purpose: it acts as a unique digital fingerprint of block content and connects the block to its predecessor, creating a real estate chain of data blocks. Any change in the block data will produce a completely different hash, immediately invalidating all subsequent blocks - so strengthen the data and integrity (Rathod et al., 2023; Wimal et al., 2025).

The consensus system is a protocol that determines how the contract between the nodes is delivered before the new block is attached to the chain. Various blockchain platforms use various consensus algorithms such as Proof of Work (POW), Proof of Stake (POS), Delegated Proof of Stake (DPO), and Practical Byzantine Fault Tolerance (PBFT). These algorithms are designed to prevent double costs, ensure the legality of transactions, and prevent malicious artists from compromising the network. The choice of a consensus algorithm plays a crucial role in defining a blockchain system, defining energy efficiency, and security posture.

Public vs. Private vs. Consortium Blockchains

Blockchain networks can be classified into public, private, and consortium blockchains, corresponding to different cases and governance models of each use. Public blockchains are permitted and open to anyone who wants to join, validate transactions, or participate in consensus. Examples include Bitcoin and Ethereum. This platform provides maximum decentralization and transparency, but often at the cost of low transaction throughput and high energy consumption. Public blockchains are especially useful in scenarios that demand openness and trust in anonymous participants, but may not be suitable for data-sensitive applications in smart cities due to privacy and compliance concerns (Pothireddy, 2025).

On the contrary, private blockchains are a permission system controlled by an organization. Access is restricted to authorized participants, and generally, a faster, more efficient protocol is the consensus. While private blockchains provide high performance and data privacy, they represent central control points, potentially limiting transparency and elasticity. Consortium blockchains hold a balance between the two; a group of trusted organizations - such as government agencies, utility providers, and technical partners - allows the network to operate collectively. These blockchains are ideal for smart city implementations where data sharing is required across institutional boundaries but must be done within a reliable and regulatory structure. They support the cooperative regime, maintaining the degree of decentralization and mutual responsibility.

The most radical aspect of the blockchain is support for smart contracts-self-protective agreements encoded in software that automatically apply predefined terms and conditions. Smart contracts eliminate the need for mediators by enabling the programmable, when a certain criterion is completed. For example, a smart agreement can be used to automate utilization billing on the basis of real-time consumption data or to trigger maintenance requests when a sensor threshold is violated. These agreements are transparent, tamper-proof, and on-chain, can be cited, greatly enhance operational efficiency, and reduce the risk of fraud or misconduct. In the context of smart cities, the smart contract facilitates seamless interaction between various urban services, such as energy trade, decentralized identification verification, or the cost of dynamic congestion in transport systems.

Smart Contracts and Decentralized Applications (dApps)

Construction on a smart contract, decentralized applications (dApps) are user-facing software that runs at the top of a blockchain network. Unlike traditional applications that depend on centralized servers, dApps operate on a distributed infrastructure and contract directly with a smart contract. This architecture offers many benefits: lower risk of server downtime, resistance to censorship, and transparent data flow (Anwar & Ali, 2022; Emmanuel et al., n.d.; Nanayakkara et al., 2024). dApps can be avoided in numerous smart city scenes, from participating governance platforms and civilian engagement equipment to protect voting systems and decentralized environmental monitoring dashboards. Consistency with their composable nature and blockchain protocols makes dApps very convenient to develop urban needs, enabling city organizers and developers to quickly deploy innovative, trusted applications that increase civil services and civilian connections.

In summary, the basic principles of blockchain include a strong structural design for creating the basic principles, cryptographic security, decentralization, unanimous validity, and program Macy-protected, transparent, and efficient systems. Smart contracts and DAPS provide a comprehensive toolkit to address many confident and security challenges faced by blockchain smart cities, by flexible data structures, flexible governance models or automation, by smart cities. As cities continue to adopt a digital transformation initiative by integrating blockchain into their operational fabric, they also promote innovation, elasticity, and civil trust. However, to fully realize its potential, its deployment should be strategically arranged with technical capabilities, policy structures, and long-term urban development goals.

Figure 3. Integration of blockchain into smart city systems

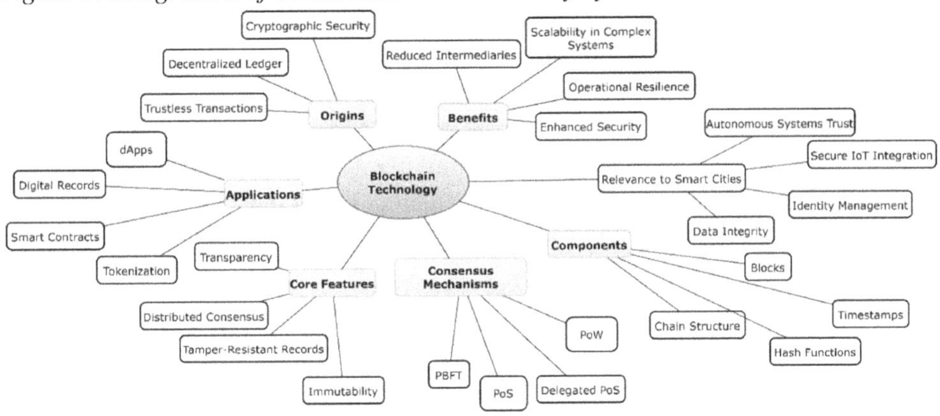

INTEGRATION OF BLOCKCHAIN INTO SMART CITY SYSTEMS

The integration of blockchain technology in smart city systems represents a strategic move towards creating safe, transparent, and elastic urban structures. Cities rely on more and more complex digital ecosystems, with large quantities of data, connected devices, and autonomous decisions. The need for trusted, real-time data exchange and secure system interaction becomes highest. Blockchain, with its cryptographically safe, decentralized, and tamper-resistant architecture, provides a strong foundation to eliminate these demands in different layers of smart city functions. Its implementation facilitates enhanced data governance, privacy-saving identification framework, reliable control, and seamless service interoperability-fate-ready urban landscape (Rahman et al., 2022). The integration of blockchain into smart city systems is illustrated in Figure 3.

Data Integrity and Tamper-Proof Logs

One of the most attractive value proposals in smart cities lies in its ability to guarantee data integrity and to create Temper-Proof. Such urban systems produce and process a large amount of data - ranging from environmental sensors and traffic cameras to health records and civil services - this data is unflattering and findable. This is especially beneficial in scenarios where data proven and transparency are essential, such as supply chain tracking in city logistics, Audit detection trails at public costs, or gang of environmental compliance (Khawaja & Javidroozi, 2023).

Once the data is recorded on the blockchain, it cannot be deleted or corrected without a consensus from the network, making it very difficult to manipulate sensitive records for malicious artists or internal threats. Moreover, the distributed nature of the blockchain ensures that there is no unilateral control over any entity's data, which reduces the risk of central breach or unauthorized data change. In essence, the blockchain multi-stakeholder acts as a reliable third-party fertilizer for the urban environment where data reliability is non-negotiable (Wong et al., 2020).

Secure Identity and Access Management

Supplementing this is the ability of a safe identification and blockchain to enable access management (IAM), which is the foundation of smart city cybersecurity. Traditional IAM systems often depend on centralized servers and databases, which are susceptible to a single point of failure and are attractive targets for cybercrime. Blockchain introduces the concept of self-sovereign identification (SSI), where individuals and organizations maintain control over their digital identity through cryptographically secure means. This digital identity is stored on decentralized lagers and can be selected or verified selectively without disclosing unnecessary personal information, supporting privacy-by-design principles (Biswas & Muthukkumarasamy, 2016).

In smart cities, Blockchain-based IAMs can streamline and protect a wide range of potential-centered cases, such as resident boards, civil tests for government services, digital health passports, driver's license recognition, and school registration authentication. Moreover, it can support seamless cross-entity access for services, for example, allowing residents to use similar verification in the utility platform without transportation systems, healthcare networks, or redundant registration or rebuilding. Such systems drastically reduce the administrative overhead when improving both security and user experience.

Decentralized Authentication and Authorization

In conjunction with identification management, blockchain also strengthens decentralized authentication and authenticity methods that are required to manage control in the heterogeneous smart city network. Traditional authentication methods are usually based on control-based on user name-password compounds. These approaches are increasingly inadequate for dynamic and distributed environments such as IoT-based urban services. Blockchain introduces a decentralized trust model where authentication can be executed using public-private key cryptography, and authenticity decisions are governed by a smart agreement (Bhushan et al., 2020).

This smart contract complex can automate multi-party access workflow-asphalt, allowing emergency respondents to provide temporary giving access to surveillance feeds during an emergency, or allow the city's specific structural facilities for maintenance by certified contractors. Decentralized authentication is especially useful for resource-limited IoT devices, which often cannot support traditional security protocols. By giving the benefit of a blockchain, these devices can always safely test and communicate with each other without depending on the central server. This reduces peer-to-peer authentication delays, eliminates obstacles, and increases system elasticity against central rejection-service attacks or breach of credentials.

Interoperability Across Urban Services

Perhaps a blockchain has a role in enabling inter-functioning in urban services, which is a crucial requirement for the efficiency of a holistic and unified smart city. Urban ecosystems usually have siloed digital systems powered by various departments or private vendors, each with its own data standards, governance protocols, and policies. This fragmentation limits data sharing and operational compilation - two essential elements of smart city intelligence. Blockchain shared facilitates interchangeably by the design of a reliable data layer, which can cause accusations without compromising multiple stakeholders' data control or security (Bhushan et al., 2020; Esposito et al., 2021).

Using tokenization, consensus protocol, and permitted layers, blockchain can ensure that the data produced in one system (eg, smart energy grid) can be safely transmitted to the other (eg, sustainability analytics platform) and auditability is preserved. Interoperability is also enhanced by a certified smart agreement that encodes the rules and implementation logic, divided into jurisdictions and service providers. For example, smart contracts can synchronize real-time parking availability data of various providers in a unified platform through autonomous vehicles or civil applications. In a more advanced deployment, blockchain can facilitate machine-to-machine economic interactions, such as houses equipped with solar panels and a decentralized energy-of-the-art trading between the municipal grid by the inter-relevant smart contract (Biswas & Muthukkumarasamy, 2016a; Krishnamoorthy et al., 2022).

In conclusion, the integration of blockchain technology in smart city systems provides a multilayered approach to consider some of the most significant challenges of urban digital transformation. From ensuring data honesty and trackability, enabling secure and privacy identity identification management, from automation of access control, to the convenience of seamless interoperability between the systems, the blockchain establishes a trust infrastructure, and the design. However, more than technical readiness is required for successful implementation; It demands a thoughtful regime, regulatory arrangement, stakeholders' engagement, and scalability planning. As cities aim to be more intelligent, incorporated, and secure, the integration of blockchain will play an important role in shaping tomorrow's urban digital infrastructure - a smart city will promote patterns that are not only efficient and innovative but also fundamentally trusted.

Figure 4. Architectural models and frameworks for implementation of blockchain technology

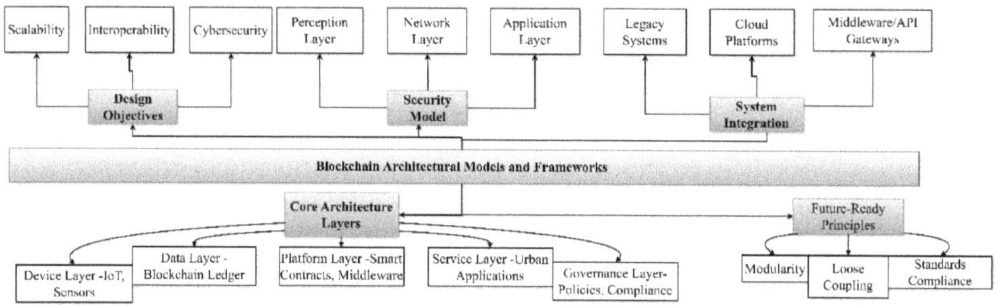

ARCHITECTURAL MODELS AND FRAMEWORKS

As the digital fabric of smart cities has been developed, the implementation of blockchain technology must be guided by well-structured architectural models that support scalability, interoperability, and strong cybersecurity. It is important to develop a consistent and flexible architecture to integrate blockchain into various urban services while maintaining compatibility with existing technical ecosystems and governance models (Tang et al., 2004). Architectural models and frameworks for the implementation of blockchain technology are depicted in Figure 4.

Blockchain-Enabled Smart City Reference Architecture

A blockchain-enabled Smart City reference architecture provides a blueprint that specifies how blockchain can be embedded in levels of data trust, system transparency, and operational coordination. At its origin, this architecture contains five key levels: device layers (IoT and Edge devices), data layer (blockchain-based data capture and validation), platform layer (smart contracts and middleware), service layers (urban service applications), and governance layers. In this structure,

Blockchain serves as a secure, decentralized data management platform that enables reliable interaction with stakeholders such as city officials, utility providers, transport agencies, healthcare organizations, and citizens (Leist & Zellner, 2006). By supporting tokenization, cryptographic scrutiny, and unchanging ledgers, blockchain ensures that each transaction includes data access, provision, or identification verification of service-it can be verified and temporarily resistant. This context can also be customized for domain-specific cases such as decentralized energy markets, smart mobility platforms, or e-governance portals, providing a flexible foundation for safe urban innovation.

Layered Security Model (Perception, Network, Application)

Complementing this reference structure is the layered protection model—a cybersecurity design paradigm that segments the smart city ecosystem into functional levels: belief, network, and application. At the belief layer, which encompasses sensors, actuators, and other IoT gadgets, blockchain may be used to authenticate gadgets and validate the integrity of information at the point of origin. Device identities may be securely registered at the blockchain, and all generated statistics can be hashed and timestamped before being transmitted to the network, thereby ensuring traceability and stopping forgery (De Vires, 2010; Mora et al., 2008). At the community layer, where verbal exchange between gadgets and systems happens, blockchain allows decentralized routing and stable peer-to-peer communications. It can also be integrated with software determined networking (SDN) and edge computing infrastructures to detect inconsistencies through smart contracts and run security policies. The use of blockchain as a delivered key management system can further strengthen the encryption and reduce the risks associated with the central certificate authorities. Proceeding at the application level, blockchain data privacy, control, and strengthens service-level integrity. Through the smart agreement, the application logic can be transparently and automatically applied, ensuring that urban service interactions ride-sharing payments, e-voting, or health data accesses, are pre-defined parameters. This layered approach to security enables cities to deploy blockchain in a modular and scalable fashion, targeting weaknesses at certain levels without overlaying the entire infrastructure.

Integration with Legacy Systems and Cloud Platforms

A significant challenge in the adoption of blockchain in smart cities is the integration with legacy systems and cloud platforms, which are deployed in urban IT operations. Many municipal services depend on long-lasting information systems and cloud-based applications that are not designed with decentralization or blockchain compatibility. To overcome this technical distance, the development of interoperability gateways, middleware solutions, and API levels requires the development of data exchange between blockchain networks and traditional databases or cloud services. A practical approach is to use hybrid architectures where sensitive or practical data is stored on-chain, while bulk data is operated in a secure cloud environment. In such systems, the blockchain anchors the complex metadata, acting as a source of truth, when taking advantage of the scalability and flexibility of cloud computing for storage. Software components such as blockchain oracles and integration platforms can be operated to ensure seamless and secure interaction between legacy API and decentralized applications (Cervantes et al., 2012; Ota & Gerz, 2011). Additionally, containerization and micro services can be used to accommodate legacy functions in a modern software environment that is compatible with blockchain workflow. This allows the IT to be preserved in the infrastructure while still enabling the adoption of blockchain-powered innovations.

In order to support effective integration and long-term operability, it is necessary to adopt architectural principles such as modularity, loose coupling, service abstractions, and adherence to standards. These principles enable the smart city platforms to be more involved, without the risk of systemic disturbances. The need for a cross-layer governance framework is just as important as the ownership of data in the system's blockchain components, accommodation rights, compliance, and performance. This framework must be adjusted with the best efforts of local rules, international standards, and the decentralized regime and data sovereignty.

Hence, the development of blockchain-enabled architectural models and frameworks is important for secure, scalable, and interoperable smart city ecosystems. Cities can create future-prepared digital infrastructure by forming multi-layered architectures aligned with blockchain with urban service domains, strengthening cyber safety by layered defense mechanisms, and ensuring compatibility with legacy systems and cloud environments. These models not only support operational elasticity and innovation but also promote public confidence and liability in a data-based urban environment.

USE CASES AND APPLICATIONS

Blockchain technology, when applicable strategically in terms of smart cities, provides many cases of transformative use in urban domains. The decentralized energy serves as the foundation of blockchain confidence, auto tomatoes, and operational elasticity, from securing the transparency in the public regime. Practical integration of blockchain not only reduces systemic risks in data-intensive services but also enhances citizen engagement, durability, and service efficiency. Some promising application fields highlight the utility of blockchain to increase smart city functions, especially in safe smart grid, intelligent transport, digital governance, and environmental management (Rotună et al., 2019).

Secure Smart Grids and Energy Management

Safe smart grid and energy are one of the most effective uses in the management, where blockchain enables decentralized, efficient, and transparent energy ecosystems. As cities transition to renewable energy, zones and distributed generation models, which struggle to maintain practical integrity and real-time coordination of ceiling solar panels, energy zoning collection systems, and electric vehicles, are traditional, central grid architects. Blockchain provides a distributed ledger mechanism through which energy can be safely recorded, tested, and traded in a peer-to-peer fashion. Smart Agreement can automatically automate energy transactions, micro-payments can be settled immediately, and apply dynamic pricing contracts based on supply-demand terms (Alnahari & Ariaratnam, 2022; Ghazal et al., 2022). For example, in the community solar network, blockchain energy can make a track to the product, allocate shares, and ensure fair returns through a third-party tokenized payment without mediation. In addition, the tamper-proof nature of the blockchain loggers improves the grid's IT detail ability and prevents fraudulent meter data manipulation. Utility companies can take advantage of the blockchain to create transparent billing systems, to meet demand for demand-responsive operations, and create data exchanges between edge devices, sensors, and control systems. In the context of a smart city, these capabilities reduce the elasticity of energy and carbon footprints and support the realization of civil empowerment in the energy value chain.

Blockchain for Intelligent Transportation Systems

Blockchain is set to revolutionize intelligent transport systems (ITS) by increasing confidence in data protection, operational coordination, and various stakeholders, including passengers, mobility providers, city organizers, and autonomous vehicle networks. Smart transportation infrastructure-chemical connected vehicles, traffic signals, toll booths, and public transport systems produce large volumes of real-time data that must be shared and reliably shared among agencies and platforms. By removing concerns about data tampering and unauthorized access, blockchain decentralized leaders can serve mobility transactions, vehicle telemetry, and sensor data in a stable and verified format. A crucial application is in the communication of safe vehicles, where blockchain can validate the identity of vehicles, authorize communication, and prevent spoofing or relay attacks threatening road safety (Li, 2018; Mohanta et al., 2018).

In the tolling and congestion pricing system, smart contracts can enable automatic fee deduction based on geofencing and consumption status, reduce human intervention, and improve operational transparency. Blockchain also supports the mobility-as-a-Service (MaaS) platform by integrating various transport providers into trust-based ecosystems where ride data, rental payment, and service-level contracts are transparently recorded and algorithmically applied. For autonomous vehicles, blockchain routes can provide a decentralized coordination framework for the convenience of secure data sharing for optimization, environmental sensing, and regulatory compliance. Collectively, these applications will forward the goal of a safer, more efficient, and interoperable urban mobility system.

Citizen Data Privacy and E-Governance

In the field of civil data privacy and e-governance, blockchain can play a key role in promoting digital trust and enhancing public sector responsibility. E-governance systems handle more and more sensitive personal data, with identity records and voting credentials up to health, land, and tax information. Traditional central reserves are susceptible to breaking, internal abuse, and administrative ambiguity. Blockchain introduces a decentralized and cryptographically secure data infrastructure where citizens can dominate their digital identity and control data sharing through verified credentials (Li, 2018; Mohanta et al., 2018). The Self-sovereign identity (SSI) Framework, which is built on a blockchain, allows individuals to present the government's documents in a privacy-saving way, which is required for a given transaction. This not only ensures GDPR-containing data minimization but also eliminates the risks of excessive exposure and data duplication. In the voting system, blockchain provides the possibility of transparent, tamper-proof, and auditable elections, enabling remote partnerships with end-to-end verification. Smart contracts can automate public service distribution processes such as licensing issues, subsidies distribution, or complaint redress, reducing bureaucratic overheads and reducing corruption opportunities. The public procurement system can be recorded on transparent ledgers to ensure the vendor's responsibility and fair competition. By embedding blockchain in the digital backbone of civil services, governments can create more participatory, secure, and efficient administrative ecosystems.

Waste Management and Environmental Monitoring

Another important area where blockchain can provide significant value is waste management and environmental inspection, especially to support real-time trackability, regulatory compliance, and sustainable behavior incentives. West management includes multiple actors in smart cities engaged in nervous agencies, private contractors, citizens, and recycling tracking, collection, disposal, and recycling operations. Blockchain can create an indefinite chain of custody for waste materials, ensuring that the waste on the original, storage time, transport routes, and the status of the process are verified and tamper-proof (Chang & Chang, 2018; Hakak et al., 2020). This prevents illegal dumping, incorrect reporting, or recyclable waste diversion, while enabling operations-based incentives for contractors and citizens. Smart contracts can automate service payment based on verified work completion or environmental influence metrics. For risky waste, blockchain disposal guarantees trackability during the life cycle, adheres to environmental rules, and reduces the risks of ecological contamination. Environmental monitoring systems, policies, and people can use blockchain to validate air and water quality sensor data by providing trusted insights. Community-based environmental report-based efforts can be more democratic and can increase urban elasticity by token-based awards. Integrating blockchain with IoT sensors and geographical information systems (GIS) creates a powerful tool to track pollution sources, apply environmental laws, and manage stability initiatives with transparency and liability.

In summary, blockchain applications in smart cities are not limited to theoretical models but are rapidly ripening into operational tools that protect data, automate processes, and configure various urban stakeholders through shared digital trusts. Managing the decentralized energy flows, orchestring safe transport systems, empowering citizens with privacy-saving regime equipment, or ensuring environmental transparency, providing a reliable and scalable foundation for the digital conversion of blockchain cities. Continuous integration of a smart urban framework will be necessary to create future secure, durable, and citizen-centered cities.

PERFORMANCE AND SCALABILITY CONSIDERATIONS

While blockchain technology offers attractive benefits to transparency, security, and decentralization, its deployment in smart city ecosystems demands precautionary evaluation of its deployment and scalability. Such urban infrastructures produce a large amount of data and require real-time response to various services, so blockchain systems must be optimized to meet strict operational requirements. In time-sensitive domains such as latency, throughput, and transaction costs, especially traffic control, emergency response, and energy distribution, can significantly affect the possibility of blockchain integration (Biswas & Muthukkumarasamy, 2016; Li, 2018). The performance and scalability considerations for blockchain deployment in smart city ecosystems are shown in Figure 5.

Figure 5. Performance and scalability considerations for blockchain deployment in smart city ecosystems

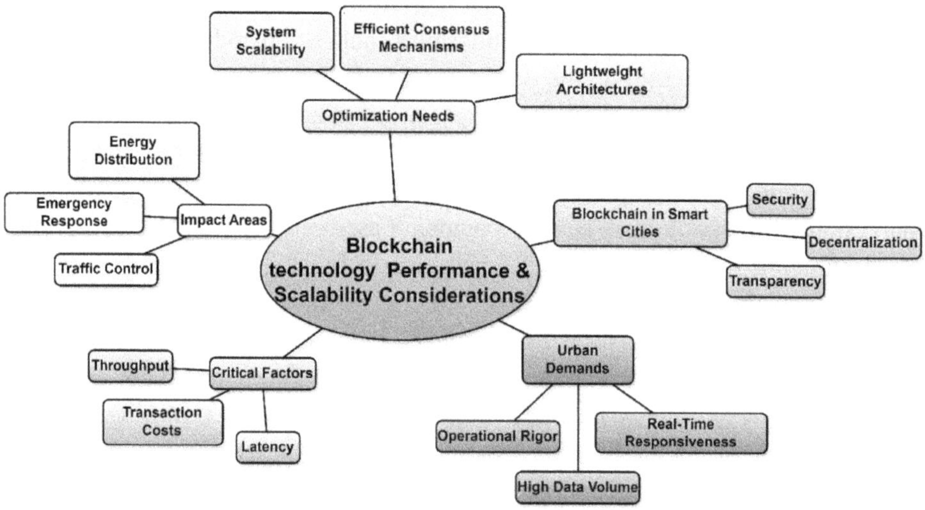

Latency, Throughput, and Transaction Costs

The time delay between starting and confirming a transaction on a latency, or blockchain, is a critical determinant of response. In many public blockchain networks, the latency can range from several seconds to several minutes due to complex consensus processes and network congestion. While this may be tolerated in cases of financial transactions or archival use, it is inappropriate for real-time applications such as autonomous vehicle coordination, instant control, or methods of dynamic prices (Ivanisevic et al., 2023; Sifah et al., 2020).

Throughput, defined as the number of transactions that can be processed by the network per second (TPS), also presents a challenge. Popular blockchains such as Bitcoin and Ethereum support only 7-30 TPS in their base layers, which are inadequate for typical high-frequency operations in smart cities. Moreover, transaction costs, often paid in the form of gas fees or network fees, can significantly fluctuate based on network loads, making the operational budget unpredictable. Since it is economically viable on public chains, high costs such as mobility services or micro-payments for sensor-to-sensor data exchanges can prevent frequent or low-value transactions.

Consensus Algorithm Trade-offs

To overcome these limitations, it is necessary to consider the underlying trade in various consensus algorithms, which serves as the spinal cord of the reliable scrutiny of the blockchain. Traditional Proof of Work (POW) provides high protection by the difficulty of calculating, but suffers from high latency, energy zoning consumption, and limited scalability, which makes it impractical for most smart city applications. On the other hand, the evidence of the stake (POS) and its types - such as the Delegated Proof of Stake (DPO) and the Bonded Proof of Stake (BPO) - significantly high throughput and low energy wheel costs, making them more suitable for the environment. Practical Byzantine Fault Tolerance (PBFT) and other unanimous consensus protocols used in permissioned blockchains, providing low-latency consensus with the final, allowing transactions almost immediately, which is ideal for applications such as smart metering, public safety, and health inspection (Rotună et al., 2019; Sifah et al., 2020).

However, these permitted systems usually sacrifice the degree of decentralization and openness in exchange for control and motion. The choice of a consensus method should be arranged with a specific trust model, the design of the stakeholder, and the requirements of the application operation.

Lightweight Blockchain for Resource-Constrained Devices

The emerging area of focus is the development of lightweight blockchain solutions ready for resource-limited devices such as embedded sensors, RFID tags, and IOT microcontrollers in smart cities. These devices often work with limited processing power, memory, and battery life, and cannot directly participate in complete blockchain operations such as mining or consensus recognition. To overcome this distance, solutions such as layer-2 protocols, seed chain, and chain computation structures allow data to be processed or collected from the main chain and later committed to the batch, reducing the load and network congestion (Rotună et al., 2019; Sifah et al., 2020).

Light client's easy payment verification nodes enable IoT devices to test transactions without downloading the entire blockchain, improving the energy efficiency while maintaining security. Additionally, blockchain frameworks such as IoT, Nano, and Hyperledger fabric, especially modular, lightweight unanimous options designed for IoT ecosystems, balance security and scalability without overburdening edge devices.

Hence, the successful implementation of the blockchain in smart city contexts depends not only on its security and transparency features, but also on its ability to deliver high performance and scalable operations corresponding to the urban environment. Optimizing for low delay, high throughput, and managed transaction costs, when appropriate consensus algorithms and lightweight implementation selection- an appropriate consensus that can support blockchain durable, real-time, data-intensive services. Addressing these technical challenges through architectural innovation and performance-aware design, it is important to unlock the full potential of blockchain in the upcoming phase of smart cities.

CHALLENGES AND FUTURE RESEARCH DIRECTIONS

Despite its changing probability, the integration of blockchain in smart city infrastructures presents many unresolved challenges that require further research and development. The most pressurized issues have limitations of scalability and interoperability, which hinder widespread adoption in heterogeneous urban systems. Such cities depend on thousands of sensors, devices, and digital platforms that produce real-time data; blockchain networks should be able to handle high throughput with minimal delay. However, most blockchain platforms, especially public ones, struggle to process their utility, limiting their utility in time-sensitive programs such as traffic control, energy wheel distribution, or emergency services (Xie et al., 2019). Moreover, interoperability between blockchain networks and blockchain and legacy systems is a significant barrier. Lack of certified protocol and data formats hinders the development of unified smart city ecosystems, enabling seamless cross-platform integration. Future research must focus on data exchange standards to remove cross-chain communication frameworks, blockchain-nonstick middleware, and this distance, and to ensure functional connection to various systems (Khalil et al., 2022; Rejeb et al., 2022).

Another crucial concern lies in security risks associated with smart contracts, which, despite their automation benefits, are susceptible to coding errors, logic errors, and vulnerabilities. Unlike traditional Software, once the blockchain is deployed, the smart contract is messy, perpetuating errors or weaknesses until the complex upgrade mechanisms are reduced. Past events, attacks, and functions of reentrancy exploits have shown that economic and operational losses can result from weak written contracts.

In the smart city application - where the contract can control the critical infrastructure, manage citizen data, or facilitate payment - such weaknesses can lead to serious consequences. To overcome these risks, strong formal verification techniques, a secure contract development framework, and real-time monitoring tools are needed that can detect inconsistencies in contractual behavior and prevent unnecessary execution ways (Pothireddy, 2025; Saad & Mustafa, 2025; Wimal et al., 2025).

The promising direction to overcome many of these challenges is the conversion of blockchain and artificial intelligence (AI) to enable active security methods. AI algorithms can analyze patterns in blockchain practice, detect inconsistencies, and predict potential attacks or system failures. Machine learning models can also increase the efficiency of consensus algorithms, OPTIM allocation in a blockchain-based IoT network, and guide smart contract testing and verification. The synergy between AI and Blockchain can further support adaptive security policies, automatic threat response, and intelligent identification verification in real time. However, this conversion also raises questions about confidence, transparency, and explanation in AI's decision, especially when applicable to crucial public systems. Future research should focus on the development of reliable, clear AI systems associated with blockchain to create secure, responsive, and intelligent smart city infrastructures developed with emerging threats and technological advances.

CONCLUSION

The integration of blockchain technology in smart city ecosystems presents a powerful opportunity to redefine the foundation of urban cybersecurity. As cities become more and more interconnected and data-based, the need for faith, transparency, and elasticity in digital infrastructures has never been more crucial. Blockchain provides a decentralized and compromised-resistant framework for data integrity, secure identification management, and authentication, and is capable of addressing major challenges such as interpretation in interactions.

This chapter investigates architectural principles, influence, and blockchain practical applications in areas such as smart energy grid, intelligent transport, digital governance, and environmental monitoring. It has also invented the limits of the existing blockchain platform in terms of consolidation with scalability, smart contract security, and the importance of research in the lightweight protocol, cross-chain framework, and AI-enhanced threat detection. While blockchain is not a therapeutic, its strategic deployment in smart cities can enable a protected, transparent, and civic-centered urban future connected with supporting policy, regime, and emerging technologies. Path forward not only includes technical innovation, but also cross-sector collaboration, standard development, and incorporated design thinking to ensure that digital transformation benefits all stakeholders. Ultimately, the blockchain represents more than the security level - it is a confident infrastructure that can increase responsibility, improve service distribution, and protect the digital rights of citizens in a world that is more and more connected.

REFERENCES

Ahakonye, L. A. C., Nwakanma, C. I., & Kim, D.-S. (2024). Tides of blockchain in IoT cybersecurity. *Sensors (Basel)*, *24*(10), 3111. DOI: 10.3390/s24103111 PMID: 38793962

Alnahari, M. S., & Ariaratnam, S. T. (2022). The application of blockchain technology to smart city infrastructure. *Smart Cities*, *5*(3), 979–993. DOI: 10.3390/smartcities5030049

Anisetti, M., Ardagna, C., Cremonini, M., Damiani, E., Sessa, J., & Costa, L. (2020). Security threat landscape. *White Paper Security Threats*.

Anwar, R. W., & Ali, S. (2022). Smart cities security threat landscape: A review. *Computer Information*, *41*(2), 405–423.

Balasaheb, B. P., & Kumar, M. S. (2024). Review of IoT-enabled Smart Cities: Cybersecurity Threat Detection Using Cloud Computing. *2024 15th International Conference on Computing Communication and Networking Technologies (ICCCNT)*, 1–11.

Bhushan, B., Khamparia, A., Sagayam, K. M., Sharma, S. K., Ahad, M. A., & Debnath, N. C. (2020). Blockchain for smart cities: A review of architectures, integration trends and future research directions. *Sustainable Cities and Society*, *61*, 102360. DOI: 10.1016/j.scs.2020.102360

Biswas, K., & Muthukkumarasamy, V. (2016). Securing smart cities using blockchain technology. *2016 IEEE 18th International Conference on High Performance Computing and Communications; IEEE 14th International Conference on Smart City; IEEE 2nd International Conference on Data Science and Systems (HPCC/SmartCity/DSS)*, 1392–1393.

Cervantes, H., Velasco-Elizondo, P., & Kazman, R. (2012). A principled way to use frameworks in architecture design. *IEEE Software*, *30*(2), 46–53. DOI: 10.1109/MS.2012.175

Chang, S. E., & Chang, C.-Y. (2018). Application of blockchain technology to smart city service: A case of ridesharing. *2018 IEEE International Conference on Internet of Things (iThings) and IEEE Green Computing and Communications (GreenCom) and IEEE Cyber, Physical and Social Computing (CPSCom) and IEEE Smart Data (SmartData)*, 664–671. DOI: 10.1109/Cybermatics_2018.2018.00134

De Vires, M. (2010). A framework for understanding and comparing enterprise architecture models. *Management Dynamics: Journal of the Southern African Institute for Management Scientists, 19*(2), 17–29.

Emmanuel, O., Aria, J., Jose, D., & Diego, C. (n.d.). *Cyber-Resilient Smart Cities: The Power of AI and Big Data in Defending Urban Landscapes.*

Esposito, C., Ficco, M., & Gupta, B. B. (2021). Blockchain-based authentication and authorization for smart city applications. *Information Processing & Management, 58*(2), 102468. DOI: 10.1016/j.ipm.2020.102468

Ghazal, T. M., Hasan, M. K., Alzoubi, H. M., Al Hmmadi, M., Al-Dmour, N. A., Islam, S., Kamran, R., & Mago, B. (2022). Securing smart cities using blockchain technology. *2022 1st International Conference on AI in Cybersecurity (ICAIC)*, 1–4.

Hakak, S., Khan, W. Z., Gilkar, G. A., Imran, M., & Guizani, N. (2020). Securing smart cities through blockchain technology: Architecture, requirements, and challenges. *IEEE Network, 34*(1), 8–14. DOI: 10.1109/MNET.001.1900178

Hammed, M., & Jebbar, W. A. (2025). Blockchain-Powered Dynamic Segmentation in Personal Health Record. *Mesopotamian Journal of CyberSecurity, 5*(3), 953–976.

Ivanisevic, S., Ivić, A., & Ćirić, Z. (2023). Blockchain implementation in smart cities–discussion on performance indicators. *Strategic Management-International Journal of Strategic Management and Decision Support Systems in Strategic Management, 28*(4).

Khalil, U., Malik, O. A., & Hussain, S. (2022). A blockchain footprint for authentication of IoT-enabled smart devices in smart cities: State-of-the-art advancements, challenges and future research directions. *IEEE Access : Practical Innovations, Open Solutions, 10*, 76805–76823. DOI: 10.1109/ACCESS.2022.3189998

Khawaja, S., & Javidroozi, V. (2023). Blockchain technology as an enabler for cross-sectoral systems integration for developing smart sustainable cities. *IET Smart Cities, 5*(3), 151–172. DOI: 10.1049/smc2.12059

Krishnamoorthy, R., Kamala, K., Soubache, I., Karthik, M. V., & Begum, M. A. (2022). Integration of blockchain and artificial intelligence in smart city perspectives. *Smart City Infrastructure: The Blockchain Perspective*, 77–112.

Kumar, S., & Rasool, M. (2023). *AI and Blockchain Fusion: Building Resilient Information Security Systems.*

Leist, S., & Zellner, G. (2006). Evaluation of current architecture frameworks. *Proceedings of the 2006 ACM Symposium on Applied Computing*, 1546–1553. DOI: 10.1145/1141277.1141635

Li, S. (2018). Application of blockchain technology in smart city infrastructure. *2018 IEEE International Conference on Smart Internet of Things (SmartIoT)*, 276–2766. DOI: 10.1109/SmartIoT.2018.00056

Maurya, V., Rishiwal, V., Yadav, M., Shiblee, M., Yadav, P., Agarwal, U., & Chaudhry, R. (2025). Blockchain-driven security for IoT networks: State-of-the-art, challenges and future directions. *Peer-to-Peer Networking and Applications*, *18*(1), 53. DOI: 10.1007/s12083-024-01812-w

Mohanta, B. K., Panda, S. S., & Jena, D. (2018). An overview of smart contract and use cases in blockchain technology. *2018 9th International Conference on Computing, Communication and Networking Technologies (ICCCNT)*, 1–4.

Mora, R., Bédard, C., & Rivard, H. (2008). A geometric modelling framework for conceptual structural design from early digital architectural models. *Advanced Engineering Informatics*, *22*(2), 254–270. DOI: 10.1016/j.aei.2007.03.003

Muheden, K., Mohammed, M., & Bilal, N. (2024). Exploring the Landscape of Smart Cities: A Comprehensive Review of IoT and Cyber-Physical Systems. *The Indonesian Journal of Computer Science*, *13*(2). Advance online publication. DOI: 10.33022/ijcs.v13i2.3843

Nanayakkara, N., Nanayakkara, G., Karunanayaka, K., Kumara, C., & Karunanayake, N. (2024). Smart Cities, Secure Data: Navigating the Evolving Landscape of Data Protection Challenges. In *Data Protection: The Wake of AI and Machine Learning* (pp. 251–285). Springer.

Ota, D., & Gerz, M. (2011). *Benefits and challenges of architecture frameworks.*

Pothireddy, N. K. R. (2025). Network Security Threat Detection in IoT-Enabled Smart Cities. *Authorea Preprints*. DOI: 10.22541/au.174352871.10041922/v1

Rahman, M. S., Chamikara, M., Khalil, I., & Bouras, A. (2022). Blockchain-of-blockchains: An interoperable blockchain platform for ensuring IoT data integrity in smart city. *Journal of Industrial Information Integration*, *30*, 100408. DOI: 10.1016/j.jii.2022.100408

Rathod, T., Jadav, N. K., Tanwar, S., Sharma, R., Tolba, A., Raboaca, M. S., Marina, V., & Said, W. (2023). Blockchain-driven intelligent scheme for IoT-based public safety system beyond 5G networks. *Sensors (Basel)*, *23*(2), 969. DOI: 10.3390/s23020969 PMID: 36679767

Rejeb, A., Rejeb, K., Simske, S. J., & Keogh, J. G. (2022). Blockchain technology in the smart city: A bibliometric review. *Quality & Quantity*, *56*(5), 2875–2906. DOI: 10.1007/s11135-021-01251-2 PMID: 34629554

Rotună, C., GHEORGHI Ă, A., Zamfiroiu, A., & SMADA ANAGRAMA, D. (2019). Smart City Ecosystem Using Blockchain Technology. *Informatica Economica, 23*(4).

Saad, J., & Mustafa, F. (2025). *AI Manipulation Meets Quantum Decryption: A SOC-Driven Cybersecurity Blueprint for IoT-Powered Smart Cities and Self-Driving Ecosystems*.

Shayea, G. G., Tameemi, H. A., Khaleel, Y. L., Habeeb, M. A., Hussein, N. A. H. K., & Albahri, A. S. (2025). A Systematic review of metaverse cybersecurity: Frameworks, challenges, and strategic approaches in a quantum-driven era. *Mesopotamian Journal of CyberSecurity*, *5*(2), 770–803.

Sifah, E. B., Xia, H., Cobblah, C. N. A., Xia, Q., Gao, J., & Du, X. (2020). BEMPAS: A decentralized employee performance assessment system based on blockchain for smart city governance. *IEEE Access : Practical Innovations, Open Solutions*, *8*, 99528–99539. DOI: 10.1109/ACCESS.2020.2997650

Soni, T., Kaur, R., Gupta, D., Sharma, A., & Gupta, G. (2024). Opportunities and Challenges of Data-Driven Cybersecurity for Smart Cities: Blockchain-Driven Approach. *Sustainable Mobility: Policies, Challenges and Advancements*, 223–236.

Tang, A., Han, J., & Chen, P. (2004). A comparative analysis of architecture frameworks. *11th Asia-Pacific Software Engineering Conference*, 640–647. DOI: 10.1109/APSEC.2004.2

Wimal, K., Cullen, G., & Donovan, J. (2025). Blockchain-Driven Smart Cities: Review of Key Applications and Emerging Trends. *2025 2nd International Conference on Advanced Innovations in Smart Cities (ICAISC)*, 1–8.

Wong, P., Chia, F., Kiu, M., & Lou, E. (2020). The potential of integrating blockchain technology into smart sustainable city development. *IOP Conference Series. Earth and Environmental Science*, *463*(1), 012020. DOI: 10.1088/1755-1315/463/1/012020

Xie, J., Tang, H., Huang, T., Yu, F. R., Xie, R., Liu, J., & Liu, Y. (2019). A survey of blockchain technology applied to smart cities: Research issues and challenges. *IEEE Communications Surveys and Tutorials*, *21*(3), 2794–2830. DOI: 10.1109/COMST.2019.2899617

Compilation of References

Abadía, J. J. P., Walther, C., Osman, A., & Smarsly, K. (2022). A systematic survey of Internet of Things frameworks for smart city applications. *Sustainable Cities and Society*, *83*, 103949. DOI: 10.1016/j.scs.2022.103949

Abdelkader, S., Amissah, J., Kinga, S., Mugerwa, G., Emmanuel, E., Mansour, D.-E. A., Bajaj, M., Blazek, V., & Prokop, L. (2024). Securing modern power systems: Implementing comprehensive strategies to enhance resilience and reliability against cyber-attacks. *Results in Engineering*, *23*, 102647. DOI: 10.1016/j.rineng.2024.102647

Abiodun, O. I., Abiodun, E. O., Alawida, M., Alkhawaldeh, R. S., & Arshad, H. (2021). A Review on the Security of the Internet of Things: Challenges and Solutions. *Wireless Personal Communications*, *119*(3), 2603–2637. DOI: 10.1007/s11277-021-08348-9

Abu Al-Haija, Q., & Zein-Sabatto, S. (2020). An Efficient Deep-Learning-Based Detection and Classification System for Cyber-Attacks in IoT Communication Networks. *Electronics (Basel)*, *9*(12), 12. Advance online publication. DOI: 10.3390/electronics9122152

Achuthan, K., Sankaran, S., Roy, S., & Raman, R. (2025). Integrating sustainability into cybersecurity: Insights from machine learning based topic modeling. *Discover Sustainability*, *6*(1), 44. DOI: 10.1007/s43621-024-00754-w

Acosta Llano, E., Hurmelinna-Laukkanen, P., & Haapanen, L. (2025). Blockchain for the circular economy, implications for public governance. *International Journal of Public Sector Management*, *38*(1), 30–52. DOI: 10.1108/IJPSM-12-2023-0365

Adeodato, R., & Pournouri, S. (2020). *Secure Implementation of E-Governance: A Case Study About Estonia*., DOI: 10.1007/978-3-030-35746-7_18

Aggarwal, T., Kumar, S., Singh, S. K., Gupta, B. B., Nedjah, N., & Castiglione, A. (2024). *Zero Knowledge Proofs and Their Applications in Cryptography*., DOI: 10.4018/979-8-3693-5330-1.ch003

Ahakonye, L. A. C., Nwakanma, C. I., & Kim, D.-S. (2024). Tides of blockchain in IoT cybersecurity. *Sensors (Basel)*, *24*(10), 3111. DOI: 10.3390/s24103111 PMID: 38793962

Ahmad, A. Y. A. B., Verma, N., Sarhan, N. M., Awwad, E. M., Arora, A., & Nyangaresi, V. O. (2024). An IoT and blockchain-based secure and transparent supply chain management framework in smart cities using an optimal queue model. *IEEE Access : Practical Innovations, Open Solutions*, *12*, 51752–51771. DOI: 10.1109/ACCESS.2024.3376605

Ahmad, I., Kumar, T., Liyanage, M., Okwuibe, J., Ylianttila, M., & Gurtov, A. (2018). Overview of 5G security challenges and solutions. *IEEE Communications Standards Magazine*, *2*(1), 36–43. DOI: 10.1109/MCOMSTD.2018.1700063

Ahmad, K., Maabreh, M., Ghaly, M., Khan, K., Qadir, J., & Al-Fuqaha, A. (2022). Developing future human-centered smart cities: Critical analysis of smart city security, Data management, and Ethical challenges. *Computer Science Review*, *43*, 100452. DOI: 10.1016/j.cosrev.2021.100452

Ahmad, S., & Mir, A. H. (2021). Scalability, Consistency, Reliability and Security in SDN Controllers: A Survey of Diverse SDN Controllers. *Journal of Network and Systems Management*, *29*(1), 9. DOI: 10.1007/s10922-020-09575-4

Ahmed, S., Alshater, M. M., El Ammari, A., & Hammami, H. (2022). Artificial intelligence and machine learning in finance: A bibliometric review. *Research in International Business and Finance*, *61*, 101646. DOI: 10.1016/j.ribaf.2022.101646

Ahuja, B., Doriya, R., Salunke, S., Hashmi, M. F., & Gupta, A. (2023). IoT-Based Multi-Dimensional Chaos Mapping System for Secure and Fast Transmission of Visual Data in Smart Cities. *IEEE Access : Practical Innovations, Open Solutions*, *11*, 104930–104945. DOI: 10.1109/ACCESS.2023.3318014

Akhmetbek, Y., & Špaček, D. (2021). Opportunities and barriers of using blockchain in public administration: The case of real estate registration in Kazakhstan. NISP. *J. Public Adm. Policy*, *14*(2), 41–64. DOI: 10.2478/nispa-2021-0014

Alagic, G., Apon, D., Cooper, D., Dang, Q., Dang, T., Kelsey, J., Lichtinger, J., Liu, Y.-K., Miller, C., Moody, D., Peralta, R., Perlner, R., Robinson, A., & Smith-Tone, D. (2022). *Status report on the third round of the NIST Post-Quantum Cryptography Standardization process* (No. NIST IR 8413; p. NIST IR 8413). National Institute of Standards and Technology (U.S.). DOI: 10.6028/NIST.IR.8413

Alam, T. (2022). Blockchain cities: The futuristic cities driven by Blockchain, big data and internet of things. *GeoJournal*, *87*(6), 5383–5412. DOI: 10.1007/s10708-021-10508-0

Al-Badi, A., Sharma, S. K., Jain, V., & Khan, A. I. (2020). Investigating emerging technologies role in smart cities' solutions. In *IFIP Advances in Information and Communication Technology* (pp. 230–241). Springer International Publishing.

Alenezi, M. N., Alabdulrazzaq, H., Alhatlani, H. M., & Alobaid, F. A. (2024). On the performance of AES algorithm variants. *International Journal of Information and Computer Security*, *23*(3), 322–337. DOI: 10.1504/IJICS.2024.138494

Alharbi, E., Alsulami, G., Aljohani, S., Alharbi, W., & Albaradei, S. (2025). Real-time detection and monitoring of public littering behavior using deep learning for a sustainable environment. *Scientific Reports*, *15*(1), 3000. DOI: 10.1038/s41598-024-77118-x

Alkhabet, M. M., & Ismail, M. (2023). Security algorithms for distributed storage system for E-health application over wireless body area network. *Journal of Ambient Intelligence and Humanized Computing*, *14*(12), 15781–15792. DOI: 10.1007/s12652-020-02733-1

Alkhudhayr, H. (2025). Internet of things based parking slot detection and occupancy classification for smart city traffic management. *Engineering Applications of Artificial Intelligence*, *152*, 110802. DOI: 10.1016/j.engappai.2025.110802

Almashaqbeh, G., Bishop, A., & Cappos, J. (2020). MicroCash: practical concurrent processing of micropayments. In Lecture notes in computer science (pp. 227–244). DOI: 10.1007/978-3-030-51280-4_13

Almihat, M. G. M., & Munda, J. L. (2025). The Role of Smart Grid Technologies in Urban and Sustainable Energy Planning. *Energies*, *18*(7), 1618. DOI: 10.3390/en18071618

Almutairi, B. (2024). *Integrating AI.* Blockchain, and Cloud Computing for Enhanced E-Government Solutions., DOI: 10.4018/979-8-3693-7678-2.ch011

Alnahari, M. S., & Ariaratnam, S. T. (2022). The application of blockchain technology to smart city infrastructure. *Smart Cities*, *5*(3), 979–993. DOI: 10.3390/smartcities5030049

Alva, P., Mosteiro-Romero, M., Pei, W., Bartolini, A., Yuan, C., & Stouffs, R. (2023). Bottom-up approach for creating an urban digital twin platform and use cases. CAADRIA Proceedings. DOI: 10.52842/conf.caadria.2023.1.605

Alzahrani, N. M., & Alfouzan, F. A. (2022). Augmented Reality (AR) and cyber-security for smart cities-A systematic literature review. *Sensors (Basel)*, *22*(7), 2792. DOI: 10.3390/s22072792 PMID: 35408406

Al-Zubaidie, M., & Jebbar, W. A. (2024). Providing Security for Flash Loan System Using Cryptocurrency Wallets Supported by XSalsa20 in a Blockchain Environment. *Applied Sciences (Basel, Switzerland)*, *14*(14), 6361. DOI: 10.3390/app14146361

Al-Zubaidie, M., & Muhajjar, R. A. (2024). Integrating Trustworthy Mechanisms to Support Data and Information Security in Health Sensors. *Procedia Computer Science*, *237*, 43–52. DOI: 10.1016/j.procs.2024.05.078

Al-Zubaidie, M., & Shyaa, G. S. (2023). Applying Detection Leakage on Hybrid Cryptography to Secure Transaction Information in E-Commerce Apps. *Future Internet*, *15*(8), 262. DOI: 10.3390/fi15080262

Ananda Mohan, P. V. (2023). Hash-based Digital Signatures- A tutorial review. *2023 IEEE International Conference on Public Key Infrastructure and Its Applications (PKIA)*, 1–8. DOI: 10.1109/PKIA58446.2023.10262777

Anisetti, M., Ardagna, C., Cremonini, M., Damiani, E., Sessa, J., & Costa, L. (2020). Security threat landscape. *White Paper Security Threats*.

Ante, L., Fiedler, I., Willruth, J. M., & Steinmetz, F. (2023). A Systematic literature review of Empirical research on stablecoins. *FinTech*, *2*(1), 34–47. DOI: 10.3390/fintech2010003

Anthony Jnr, B., Abbas Petersen, S., Helfert, M., & Guo, H. (2021). Digital transformation with enterprise architecture for smarter cities: A qualitative research approach. *Digit. Pol. Regul. Gov.*, *23*(4), 355–376. DOI: 10.1108/DPRG-04-2020-0044

Antonakakis, M., April, T., Bailey, M., Bernhard, M., Bursztein, E., Cochran, J., & Zhou, Y. (2017). *Understanding the Mirai botnet. In 26th USENIX Security Symposium*. USENIX Association., https://www.usenix.org/system/files/conference/usenixsecurity17/sec17-antonakakis.pdf

Anwar, R. W., & Ali, S. (2022). Smart cities security threat landscape: A review. *Computer Information*, *41*(2), 405–423.

Asha, S., Baddur, K., & Jaya Singh Dhas, L. (2025). High speed wireless communication technologies including 5G and beyond for reliable smart city IoT networks. In IoT Architectures and AI-Enabled Smart City Solutions for Sustainable Urban Development (pp. 102–132). RADemics Research Institute.

Assa-Agyei, K., & Olajide, F. (2023). A Comparative Study of Twofish, Blowfish, and Advanced Encryption Standard for Secured Data Transmission. *International Journal of Advanced Computer Science and Applications*, *14*(3). Advance online publication. DOI: 10.14569/IJACSA.2023.0140344

Awaad, M. H., & Jebbar, W. A. (2014). Prolong the lifetime of WSN by determining a correlation nodes in the same zone and searching for the best not the closest CH. *International Journal of Modern Education and Computer Science*, *6*(11), 31. DOI: 10.5815/ijmecs.2014.11.04

Awaad, M. H., & Jebbar, W. A. (2015). Extending the WSN lifetime by Dividing the Network Area into a Specific Zones. *International Journal of Computer Network and Information Security*, *7*(2), 33–39. DOI: 10.5815/ijcnis.2015.02.04

Aydeger, A., Zeydan, E., Yadav, A. K., Hemachandra, K. T., & Liyanage, M. (2024). Towards a Quantum-Resilient Future: Strategies for Transitioning to Post-Quantum Cryptography. *2024 15th International Conference on Network of the Future (NoF)*, 195–203. DOI: 10.1109/NoF62948.2024.10741441

Babu, A. A., Jebamalar, G. B., Kumar, P., & Nalini, M. (2024, December). Blockchain Technology: Evolution and Future Prospects. In *2024 International Conference on Sustainable Communication Networks and Application (ICSCNA)* (pp. 381-387). IEEE. DOI: 10.1109/ICSCNA63714.2024.10864089

Bakirci, M. (2025). Internet of Things-enabled unmanned aerial vehicles for real-time traffic mobility analysis in smart cities. *Computers & Electrical Engineering*, *123*, 110313. DOI: 10.1016/j.compeleceng.2025.110313

Balasaheb, B. P., & Kumar, M. S. (2024). Review of IoT-enabled Smart Cities: Cybersecurity Threat Detection Using Cloud Computing. *2024 15th International Conference on Computing Communication and Networking Technologies (ICCCNT)*, 1–11.

Balogun, A. A., & Olorunmade, G. (2023). Blockchain technology adoption against corruption in emerging economies. In Advances in Finance, Accounting, and Economics (pp. 22–36). IGI Global. DOI: 10.4018/979-8-3693-0770-0.ch002

Bandara, E., Liang, X., Foytik, P., Shetty, S., Hall, C., Bowden, D., Ranasinghe, N., & De Zoysa, K. (2021). A blockchain empowered and privacy preserving digital contact tracing platform. *Information Processing & Management*, *58*(4), 102572. DOI: 10.1016/j.ipm.2021.102572

Bandara, H., Herath, Y., Weerasundara, T., & Alawatugoda, J. (2022). On Advances of Lattice-Based Cryptographic Schemes and Their Implementations. *Cryptography*, *6*(4), 56. DOI: 10.3390/cryptography6040056

Banoth, R., & Regar, R. (2023). Asymmetric Key Cryptography. In *Classical and Modern Cryptography for Beginners* (pp. 109–165). Springer Nature Switzerland., DOI: 10.1007/978-3-031-32959-3_4

Baroudi, S., & Benghida, S. (2022). Blockchain in Dubai: Toward a Sustainable Digital Future. In *Contemporary Research in Accounting and Finance* (pp. 253–271). Springer Nature Singapore. DOI: 10.1007/978-981-16-8267-4_11

Barrett, B. F. D., DeWit, A., & Yarime, M. (2021). Japanese smart cities and communities: Integrating technological and institutional innovation for Society 5.0. In *Smart Cities for Technological and Social Innovation* (pp. 73–94). Elsevier., DOI: 10.1016/B978-0-12-818886-6.00005-8

Bennett, C. H., & Brassard, G. (1984). Quantum cryptography: Public key distribution and coin tossing. In *Proceedings of the IEEE International Conference on Computers, Systems and Signal Processing* (pp. 175–179). IEEE.

Bharany, S., Kaur, K., Badotra, S., Rani, S., Kavita, , Wozniak, M., Shafi, J., & Ijaz, M. F. (2022). Efficient middleware for the portability of paas services consuming applications among heterogeneous clouds. *Sensors (Basel)*, *22*(13), 5013. DOI: 10.3390/s22135013

Bhat, M. I., & Giri, K. J. (2021). *Impact of Computational Power on Cryptography*., DOI: 10.1007/978-981-15-8711-5_4

Bhushan, B., Khamparia, A., Sagayam, K. M., Sharma, S. K., Ahad, M. A., & Debnath, N. C. (2020). Blockchain for smart cities: A review of architectures, integration trends and future research directions. *Sustainable Cities and Society*, *61*, 102360. DOI: 10.1016/j.scs.2020.102360

Bibri, S. E., & Krogstie, J. (2017). Smart sustainable cities of the future: An extensive interdisciplinary literature review. *Sustainable Cities and Society*, *31*, 183–212. DOI: 10.1016/j.scs.2017.02.016

Bibri, S. E., & Krogstie, J. (2020). The emerging data–driven Smart City and its innovative applied solutions for sustainability: The cases of London and Barcelona. *Energy Informatics*, *3*(1), 5. DOI: 10.1186/s42162-020-00108-6

Biswas, K., & Muthukkumarasamy, V. (2016). Securing smart cities using blockchain technology. *2016 IEEE 18th International Conference on High Performance Computing and Communications; IEEE 14th International Conference on Smart City; IEEE 2nd International Conference on Data Science and Systems (HPCC/SmartCity/DSS)*, 1392–1393.

Biswas, S., Goswami, R. S., & Reddy, K. H. K. (2024). Advancing quantum steganography: A secure IoT communication with reversible decoding and customized encryption technique for smart cities. *Cluster Computing*, *27*(7), 9395–9414. DOI: 10.1007/s10586-024-04429-z

Bodkhe, U., Tanwar, S., Parekh, K., Khanpara, P., Tyagi, S., Kumar, N., & Alazab, M. (2020). Blockchain for Industry 4.0: A Comprehensive Review. *IEEE Access : Practical Innovations, Open Solutions*, *8*, 79764–79800. DOI: 10.1109/ACCESS.2020.2988579

Bourbon, B., & Murimi, R. (2024). Decentralization, blockchains, and the development of smart communities in economically challenging environments. *Ledger*, *9*, 30–50. DOI: 10.5195/ledger.2024.302

Cao, J., Wang, X., Chen, G., Tu, W., Shen, X., Zhao, T., & Li, Q. (2025). Disentangling the hourly dynamics of mixed urban function: A multimodal fusion perspective using dynamic graphs. *Information Fusion*, *117*, 102832. DOI: 10.1016/j.inffus.2024.102832

Castagna, F., Montano, L., Lombardi, R., Pagano, A., Gigliotti, A., Bava, R., Lupia, C., Costagliola, A., Giordano, A., Palma, E., Britti, D., & Liguori, G. (2024). Understanding Environmental Contamination through the Lens of the Peregrine FALCON (Falco peregrinus). *Environments (Basel, Switzerland)*, *11*(12), 264. DOI: 10.3390/environments11120264

Cengiz, B., Adam, I. Y., Ozdem, M., & Das, R. (2025). A survey on data fusion approaches in IoT-based smart cities: Smart applications, taxonomies, challenges, and future research directions. *Information Fusion*, *121*, 103102. DOI: 10.1016/j.inffus.2025.103102

Cervantes, H., Velasco-Elizondo, P., & Kazman, R. (2012). A principled way to use frameworks in architecture design. *IEEE Software*, *30*(2), 46–53. DOI: 10.1109/MS.2012.175

Chalhoub, G., Kraemer, M. J., Nthala, N., & Flechais, I. (2021). "It did not give me an option to decline": A Longitudinal Analysis of the User Experience of Security and Privacy in Smart Home Products. *Proceedings of the 2021 CHI Conference on Human Factors in Computing Systems*, 1–16. DOI: 10.1145/3411764.3445691

Chang, S. E., & Chang, C.-Y. (2018). Application of blockchain technology to smart city service: A case of ridesharing. *2018 IEEE International Conference on Internet of Things (iThings) and IEEE Green Computing and Communications (GreenCom) and IEEE Cyber, Physical and Social Computing (CPSCom) and IEEE Smart Data (SmartData)*, 664–671. DOI: 10.1109/Cybermatics_2018.2018.00134

Chataut, R., Phoummalayvane, A., & Akl, R. (2023). Unleashing the power of IoT: A comprehensive review of IoT applications and future prospects in healthcare, agriculture, smart homes, smart cities, and industry 4.0. *Sensors (Basel)*, *23*(16), 7194. DOI: 10.3390/s23167194 PMID: 37631731

Chen, J., Gan, W., Hu, M., & Chen, C.-M. (2021). On the construction of a post-quantum blockchain for smart city. *Journal of Information Security and Applications*, *58*, 102780. DOI: 10.1016/j.jisa.2021.102780

Chu, H., Zhang, P., Dong, H., Xiao, Y., Ji, S., & Li, W. (2023). A survey on smart contract vulnerabilities: Data sources, detection and repair. *Information and Software Technology*, *159*, 107221. DOI: 10.1016/j.infsof.2023.107221

Das, S., & Das, A. (2023). Future perspective of quantum cryptography for smart cities of the 21st century. In Advances in Systems Analysis, Software Engineering, and High Performance Computing (pp. 326–342). IGI Global.

De Vires, M. (2010). A framework for understanding and comparing enterprise architecture models. *Management Dynamics: Journal of the Southern African Institute for Management Scientists*, *19*(2), 17–29.

Demertzi, V., Demertzis, S., & Demertzis, K. (2023). An Overview of Cyber Threats, Attacks and Countermeasures on the Primary Domains of Smart Cities. *Applied Sciences (Basel, Switzerland)*, *13*(2), 790. DOI: 10.3390/app13020790

Demirbaga, Ü., Aujla, G. S., Jindal, A., & Kalyon, O. (2024). Cloud Computing for Big Data Analytics. In *Big Data Analytics* (pp. 43–77). Springer Nature Switzerland., DOI: 10.1007/978-3-031-55639-5_4

Dey, J., & Dutta, R. (2023). Progress in Multivariate Cryptography: Systematic Review, Challenges, and Research Directions. *ACM Computing Surveys*, *55*(12), 1–34. DOI: 10.1145/3571071

Di Ciccio, C. (2023). Blockchain and distributed ledger technologies. In Cambridge University Press eBooks (pp. 11–34). DOI: 10.1017/9781009411783.003

Diaz-Sanchez, D., Marin-Lopez, A., Mendoza, F. A., Cabarcos, P. A., & Sherratt, R. S. (2019). TLS/PKI Challenges and Certificate Pinning Techniques for IoT and M2M Secure Communications. *IEEE Communications Surveys and Tutorials*, *21*(4), 3502–3531. DOI: 10.1109/COMST.2019.2914453

Djenna, A., Harous, S., & Saidouni, D. E. (2021). Internet of Things Meet Internet of Threats: New Concern Cyber Security Issues of Critical Cyber Infrastructure. *Applied Sciences (Basel, Switzerland)*, *11*(10), 4580. DOI: 10.3390/app11104580

Drasch, B. J., Fridgen, G., Manner-Romberg, T., Nolting, F. M., & Radszuwill, S. (2020). The token's secret: The two-faced financial incentive of the token economy. *Electronic Markets*, *30*(3), 557–567. DOI: 10.1007/s12525-020-00412-9

du Plessis, A. (2023). Water Resources from a Global Perspective. In du Plessis, A. (Ed.), *South Africa's Water Predicament: Freshwater's Unceasing Decline* (pp. 1–25). Springer International Publishing., DOI: 10.1007/978-3-031-24019-5_1

Dwivedi, Y. K., Hughes, L., Ismagilova, E., Aarts, G., Coombs, C., Crick, T., & Williams, M. D. (2021). Artificial Intelligence (AI): Multidisciplinary perspectives on emerging challenges, opportunities, and agenda for research, practice and policy. *International Journal of Information Management*, *57*, 101994. DOI: 10.1016/j.ijinfomgt.2019.08.002

Dziundziuk, B., & Dziundziuk, V. (2025). Methodology for integrating blockchain into digital governance systems: Analysis of challenges, benefits, and opportunities for society. *Science & Public Policy*, scaf022. DOI: 10.1093/scipol/scaf022

Egger, M., Eibl, G., & Engel, D. (2020). Comparison of approaches for intrusion detection in substations using the IEC 60870-5-104 protocol. *Energy Informatics*, *3*(S1), 15. DOI: 10.1186/s42162-020-00118-4

Elassy, M., Al-Hattab, M., Takruri, M., & Badawi, S. (2024). Intelligent transportation systems for sustainable smart cities. *Transportation Engineering*, *16*, 100252. DOI: 10.1016/j.treng.2024.100252

El-Sofany, H., El-Seoud, S. A., Karam, O. H., Bouallegue, B., & Ahmed, A. M. (2024). A proposed secure framework for protecting cloud-based educational systems from hacking. *Egyptian Informatics Journal*, *27*, 100505. DOI: 10.1016/j.eij.2024.100505

Emmanuel, O., Aria, J., Jose, D., & Diego, C. (n.d.). *Cyber-Resilient Smart Cities: The Power of AI and Big Data in Defending Urban Landscapes.*

Ertane Baş, E., Emeç, Ş., & Yiğit, V. (2025). Simulation of Renewable Energy Systems with Alternative Energy Scenarios in Turkey's Electrical Energy Planning. *Sustainability (Basel)*, *17*(6), 2665. DOI: 10.3390/su17062665

Esposito, C., Ficco, M., & Gupta, B. B. (2021). Blockchain-based authentication and authorization for smart city applications. *Information Processing & Management*, *58*(2), 102468. DOI: 10.1016/j.ipm.2020.102468

Fahim, A., Hasan, M., & Chowdhury, M. A. (2021). Smart parking systems: Comprehensive review based on various aspects. *Heliyon*, *7*(5), e07050. DOI: 10.1016/j.heliyon.2021.e07050 PMID: 34041396

Fang, Y., Shan, Z., & Wang, W. (2021). Modeling and key technologies of a data-driven smart city system. *IEEE Access : Practical Innovations, Open Solutions*, *9*, 91244–91258. DOI: 10.1109/ACCESS.2021.3091716

Farajzadeh, S., & Chehreh Chelgani, S. (2022). Gravity separation by falcon concentrator- an over review. *Separation Science and Technology*, *57*(13), 2145–2164. DOI: 10.1080/01496395.2022.2028836

Fathalla, E., & Azab, M. (2024). Beyond Classical Cryptography: A Systematic Review of Post-Quantum Hash-Based Signature Schemes, Security, and Optimizations. *IEEE Access : Practical Innovations, Open Solutions*, *12*, 175969–175987. DOI: 10.1109/ACCESS.2024.3485602

Fei, N., Lu, Z., Gao, Y., Yang, G., Huo, Y., Wen, J., & Wen, J. R. (2022). Towards artificial general intelligence via a multimodal foundation model. *Nature Communications*, *13*(1), 3094. DOI: 10.1038/s41467-022-30761-2

Fernández-Caramès, T. M., & Fraga-Lamas, P. (2020). Towards Post-Quantum Blockchain: A Review on Blockchain Cryptography Resistant to Quantum Computing Attacks. *IEEE Access : Practical Innovations, Open Solutions*, *8*, 21091–21116. DOI: 10.1109/ACCESS.2020.2968985

Figueiredo, B. J. R. Costa Rogério Lu\'\is de C and Santos, L., & Rabadão, C. (2022). Cybersecurity and privacy in smart cities for citizen welfare. In Smart Cities, Citizen Welfare, and the Implementation of Sustainable Development Goals (pp. 197–221). IGI Global.

Firmansyah, B., & Bansal, R. (2024). *Standardization and Regulatory Challenges in Modern Cryptography*., DOI: 10.4018/979-8-3693-3824-7.ch006

Freni, P., Ferro, E., & Moncada, R. (2022). Tokenomics and blockchain tokens: A design-oriented morphological framework. *Blockchain Research and Applications*, *3*(1), 100069. DOI: 10.1016/j.bcra.2022.100069

G, V., & Vinothiyalakshmi, P. (2023). Secure Electronic Banking Transaction using Double Sanction Security Algorithm in Cyber Security. *2023 International Conference on Research Methodologies in Knowledge Management, Artificial Intelligence and Telecommunication Engineering (RMKMATE)*, 1–5. DOI: 10.1109/RMKMATE59243.2023.10369665

Garba, A., Chen, Z., Guan, Z., & Srivastava, G. (2021). LightLedger: A Novel Blockchain-Based Domain Certificate Authentication and Validation Scheme. *IEEE Transactions on Network Science and Engineering*, *8*(2), 1698–1710. DOI: 10.1109/TNSE.2021.3069128

Gaur, A. S., Sharan, H. O., & Dudhagara, C. (2025). Research trends in blockchain and digital twins. *Digital Twins for Smart Cities and Villages*, 561–580.

Gharavi, H., Granjal, J., & Monteiro, E. (2024). Post-Quantum Blockchain Security for the Internet of Things: Survey and Research Directions. *IEEE Communications Surveys and Tutorials*, *26*(3), 1748–1774. DOI: 10.1109/COMST.2024.3355222

Ghazal, T. M., Hasan, M. K., Alzoubi, H. M., Al Hmmadi, M., Al-Dmour, N. A., Islam, S., Kamran, R., & Mago, B. (2022). Securing smart cities using blockchain technology. *2022 1st International Conference on AI in Cybersecurity (ICAIC)*, 1–4.

Glöckler, J., Sedlmeir, J., Frank, M., & Fridgen, G. (2023). A Systematic review of identity and access management requirements in enterprises and potential contributions of Self-Sovereign Identity. *Business & Information Systems Engineering*, *66*(4), 421–440. DOI: 10.1007/s12599-023-00830-x

Gong, Y., Chang, X., Mišić, J., Mišić, V. B., Wang, J., & Zhu, H. (2024). Practical solutions in fully homomorphic encryption: A survey analyzing existing acceleration methods. *Cybersecurity*, *7*(1), 5. DOI: 10.1186/s42400-023-00187-4

Grover, L. K. (1996). A fast quantum mechanical algorithm for database search. In *Proceedings of the Twenty-Eighth Annual ACM Symposium on Theory of Computing* (pp. 212–219). ACM. DOI: 10.1145/237814.237866

Gulzar, Q., & Mustafa, K. (2025). Enhancing network security in industrial IoT environments: A DeepCLG hybrid learning model for cyberattack detection. *International Journal of Machine Learning and Cybernetics*, *16*(7-8), 4797–4815. Advance online publication. DOI: 10.1007/s13042-025-02544-w

Habib, M. Y., Qureshi, H. A., Khan, S. A., Mansoor, Z., & Chishti, A. R. (2023). *Cybersecurity and Smart Cities: Current Status and Future*. Chapter presented at the 2023 IEEE International Conference on Emerging Trends in Engineering, Sciences and Technology (ICES&T). DOI: 10.1109/ICEST56843.2023.10138843

Hakak, S., Khan, W. Z., Gilkar, G. A., Imran, M., & Guizani, N. (2020). Securing smart cities through blockchain technology: Architecture, requirements, and challenges. *IEEE Network*, *34*(1), 8–14. DOI: 10.1109/MNET.001.1900178

Halak, B., Yilmaz, Y., & Shiu, D. (2022). Comparative Analysis of Energy Costs of Asymmetric vs Symmetric Encryption-Based Security Applications. *IEEE Access : Practical Innovations, Open Solutions*, *10*, 76707–76719. DOI: 10.1109/ACCESS.2022.3192970

Hammed, M., & Jebbar, W. A. (2025). Blockchain-Powered Dynamic Segmentation in Personal Health Record. *Mesopotamian Journal of CyberSecurity*, *5*(3), 953–976.

Hazra, R., Chatterjee, P., Singh, Y., Podder, G., & Das, T. (2024). *Data Encryption and Secure Communication Protocols*., DOI: 10.4018/979-8-3693-6557-1.ch022

Hemminghaus, C., Bauer, J., & Wolsing, K. (2021). SIGMAR: Ensuring Integrity and Authenticity of Maritime Systems using Digital Signatures. *2021 International Symposium on Networks, Computers and Communications (ISNCC)*, 1–6. DOI: 10.1109/ISNCC52172.2021.9615738

Herath, H. M. S. S., Herath, H. M. K. K. M. B., Madhusanka, B. G. D. A., & Guruge, L. G. P. K. (2024). Data Protection Challenges in the Processing of Sensitive Data. In *Data Protection* (pp. 155–179). Springer Nature Switzerland., DOI: 10.1007/978-3-031-76473-8_8

Hernandez, M. S., Sentosa, I., & Sharin, F. H. (2023). Ecosystem implementations in smart City through blockchain technology. *2023 3rd International Conference on Advance Computing and Innovative Technologies in Engineering (ICACITE)*, 1273–1278. DOI: 10.1109/ICACITE57410.2023.10182823

Höglund, J., Lindemer, S., Furuhed, M., & Raza, S. (2020). PKI4IoT: Towards public key infrastructure for the Internet of Things. *Computers & Security*, *89*, 101658. DOI: 10.1016/j.cose.2019.101658

Hossain Faruk, M. J., Alam, F., Islam, M., & Rahman, A. (2024). Transforming online voting: A novel system utilizing blockchain and biometric verification for enhanced security, privacy, and transparency. *Cluster Computing*, *27*(4), 4015–4034. DOI: 10.1007/s10586-023-04261-x

Houy, S., Schmid, P., & Bartel, A. (2023). Security Aspects of Cryptocurrency Wallets—A Systematic Literature Review. *ACM Computing Surveys*, *56*(1), 1–31. DOI: 10.1145/3596906

Hwang, G. J., Xie, H., Wah, B. W., & Gašević, D. (2020). Vision, challenges, roles and research issues of Artificial Intelligence in Education. *Computers and Education: Artificial Intelligence*, *1*, 100001. DOI: 10.1016/j.caeai.2020.100001

Iavich, M., & Kuchukhidze, T. (2024a). Investigating CRYSTALS-Kyber Vulnerabilities: Attack Analysis and Mitigation. *Cryptography*, *8*(2), 15. DOI: 10.3390/cryptography8020015

Irshad, R. R., Hussain, S., Hussain, I., Ahmad, I., Yousif, A., Alwayle, I. M., & Badr, M. M. (2023). An intelligent buffalo-based secure edge-enabled computing platform for heterogeneous IoT network in smart cities. *IEEE Access : Practical Innovations, Open Solutions*, *11*, 69282–69294. DOI: 10.1109/ACCESS.2023.3288815

Ismagilova, E., Hughes, L., Rana, N. P., & Dwivedi, Y. K. (2022). Security, Privacy and Risks Within Smart Cities: Literature Review and Development of a Smart City Interaction Framework. *Information Systems Frontiers*, *24*(2), 393–414. DOI: 10.1007/s10796-020-10044-1

Ismail, A. I., Ismail, M. A. H., & Johari, S. (2025). Smart cities implementing IoT applications for security technologies and future recommendations. *Ijirss*, *8*(3), 1376–1387. DOI: 10.53894/ijirss.v8i3.6802

ITGovernanceUK. (2020). List of data breaches and cyber attacks in January 2020. *ITGovernanceUK*. Retrieved from https://www.itgovernance.co.uk/blog/list-of-data-breaches-and-cyber-attacks-in-january-2020-1-5-billion-records-breached

Ivanisevic, S., Ivić, A., & Ćirić, Z. (2023). Blockchain implementation in smart cities–discussion on performance indicators. *Strategic Management-International Journal of Strategic Management and Decision Support Systems in Strategic Management, 28*(4).

Jain, V., & Mitra, A. (2025). Optimizing Real-Time Traffic Management Using Blockchain-Enabled VANET: Enhancing Efficiency and Security in Smart Cities. In *Leveraging VANETs and Blockchain Technology for Urban Mobility* (pp. 289-314). IGI Global Scientific Publishing.

Javaid, M., Haleem, A., Singh, R. P., & Suman, R. (2023). Towards insighting cybersecurity for healthcare domains: A comprehensive review of recent practices and trends. *Cyber Security and Applications*, *1*, 100016. DOI: 10.1016/j.csa.2023.100016

Javed, M. A., Alkhathami, M., AlMohimeed, A., & Almujalli, A. (2024). Secure Multi-hop assisted IoT communications in Smart cities. *IEEE Access : Practical Innovations, Open Solutions*.

Jebbar, W. A. (2025). Optimization Solution Proposal for Smart Transaction Security of Smart Blockchain Contracts in E-Banking Applications. In *Sustainable Information Security in the Age of AI and Green Computing* (pp. 295–320). IGI Global Scientific Publishing.

Jebbar, W. A., & Al-Zubaidie, M. (2024). Transaction-Based Blockchain Systems Security Improvement Employing Micro-Segmentation Controlled by Smart Contracts and Detection of Saddle Goatfish. *SN Computer Science*, *5*(7), 898. DOI: 10.1007/s42979-024-03239-9

Jebbar, W., Razzaq, R., & Tahayur, D. (2024). Blockchain and cryptography framework of e-apps with big data. *Journal of Education for Pure Science*, *14*(3).

Jia, Y., Gu, Z., Du, L., Long, Y., Wang, Y., Li, J., & Zhang, Y. (2023). Artificial intelligence enabled cyber security defense for smart cities: A novel attack detection framework based on the MDATA model. *Knowledge-Based Systems*, *276*, 110781. DOI: 10.1016/j.knosys.2023.110781

Jnr., B. A., Sylva, W., & Watat Josue Kuika and Misra, S. (2023). A framework for standardization of distributed ledger technologies for interoperable data integration and alignment in sustainable smart cities. J. Knowl. Econ., 15(3), 12053–12096.

Johri, S., Mehta, K. J. S., Shukla, P. K., Podile, V., & Singh, D. P. (2022). The Impact of Block Chain in Accounting and Auditing Domain - A Critical Approach for Enhanced Efficiency and Transparency. *2022 2nd International Conference on Advance Computing and Innovative Technologies in Engineering (ICACITE)*, 1628–1632. DOI: 10.1109/ICACITE53722.2022.9823420

Jørgensen, B. N., & Ma, Z. G. (2025). Digital Twin of the European Electricity Grid: A Review of Regulatory Barriers, Technological Challenges, and Economic Opportunities. *Applied Sciences (Basel, Switzerland)*, *15*(12), 6475. DOI: 10.3390/app15126475

Joshi, H. P., & Sulaiman, S. A. (2024). Revolutionizing Smart City Communication: A Secure Framework Using Modern Security Technologies. *Asian American Research Letters Journal*, *1*(10), 48–64.

Joudah, R. H., & Manaa, M. E. (2024). A New Approach to Improving the Security of the 5G-AKA Using Crystals-Kyber Post-Quantum Technologies and ASCON Algorithm. *International Journal of Safety and Security Engineering*, *14*(6), 1729–1742. DOI: 10.18280/ijsse.140608

Joysoyal, R., Uddin, S. S., Islam, T., Sarker, S. K., Li, L., Ahsan, F., Bhatti, U. A., & Zafir, E. I. (2024). Blockchain for sustainable city transformation: A review on Bangladesh. *Engineering Reports*, *6*(9), e12948. Advance online publication. DOI: 10.1002/eng2.12948

Kahanda, G., Patel, V., Parikh, M., Ippolito, M., Solanki, M., & Ahmed, S. (2023). *The Future Era of Quantum Computing*., DOI: 10.1007/978-3-031-20160-8_27

Kálmán, M. (2024). Mosaics from the legal regulation of blockchain technology. In *Collection Regional Law Review* (pp. 215–223). Institute of Comparative Law. DOI: 10.56461/iup_rlrc.2024.5.ch17

Kamble, A., Jiet, M. M., & Puri, C. (2024). Homomorphic Encryption and its Applications in Multi-Cloud Security. *2024 International Conference on Inventive Computation Technologies (ICICT)*, 1493–1499. DOI: 10.1109/ICICT60155.2024.10544773

Kaniadakis, A., & Foster, P. (2024). The role of fintech startups and big banks in shaping trust expectations from blockchain use in mainstream financial markets. *Technological Forecasting and Social Change*, *203*, 123376. DOI: 10.1016/j.techfore.2024.123376

Kannan, N., Sundar, R., Rammorthy, M., Haleem, S. L. A., & Manikandan, R. (2024). *Healthcare Data Encryption Based on Secure AI Model with Computational Analysis Using Machine Learning Algorithms*., DOI: 10.1007/978-3-031-75771-6_29

Karie, N. M., Sahri, N. M., Yang, W., Valli, C., & Kebande, V. R. (2021). A Review of Security Standards and Frameworks for IoT-Based Smart Environments. *IEEE Access : Practical Innovations, Open Solutions*, *9*, 121975–121995. DOI: 10.1109/ACCESS.2021.3109886

Khalil, U., Malik, O. A., & Hussain, S. (2022). A blockchain footprint for authentication of IoT-enabled smart devices in smart cities: State-of-the-art advancements, challenges and future research directions. *IEEE Access : Practical Innovations, Open Solutions*, *10*, 76805–76823. DOI: 10.1109/ACCESS.2022.3189998

Khan, A. A., Laghari, A. A., Alroobaea, R., Baqasah, A. M., Alsafyani, M., Bacarra, R., & Alsayaydeh, J. A. J. (2024). Secure remote sensing data with blockchain distributed ledger technology: A solution for smart cities. *IEEE Access : Practical Innovations, Open Solutions*, *12*, 69383–69396. DOI: 10.1109/ACCESS.2024.3401591

Khan, H. U., Sohail, M., Nazir, S., Hussain, T., Shah, B., & Ali, F. (2023). Role of authentication factors in Fin-tech mobile transaction security. *Journal of Big Data*, *10*(1), 138. DOI: 10.1186/s40537-023-00807-3

Khan, M. A., Javaid, S., Mohsan, S. A. H., Tanveer, M., & Ullah, I. (2024). Future-Proofing Security for UAVs With Post-Quantum Cryptography: A Review. *IEEE Open Journal of the Communications Society*, *5*, 6849–6871. DOI: 10.1109/OJCOMS.2024.3486649

Khan, M. A., Siddiqui, M. S., Rahmani, M. K. I., & Husain, S. (2022). Investigation of big data analytics for sustainable smart city development: An emerging country. *IEEE Access : Practical Innovations, Open Solutions*, *10*, 16028–16036. DOI: 10.1109/ACCESS.2021.3115987

Khan, S., Luo, F., Zhang, Z., Rahim, M. A., Ahmad, M., & Wu, K. (2022). Survey on Issues and Recent Advances in Vehicular Public-Key Infrastructure (VPKI). *IEEE Communications Surveys and Tutorials*, *24*(3), 1574–1601. DOI: 10.1109/COMST.2022.3178081

Khan, T., Rahman, S. M., & Hasan, M. M. (2020). Barriers to Growth of Renewable Energy Technology in Bangladesh. *Proceedings of the International Conference on Computing Advancements*, 1–6. DOI: 10.1145/3377049.3377086

Khawaja, S., & Javidroozi, V. (2023). Blockchain technology as an enabler for cross-sectoral systems integration for developing smart sustainable cities. *IET Smart Cities*, *5*(3), 151–172. DOI: 10.1049/smc2.12059

Kim, J., Manna, A., Roy, A., & Moon, I. (2025). Clustered vehicle routing problem for waste collection with smart operational management approaches. *International Transactions in Operational Research*, *32*(2), 863–887. DOI: 10.1111/itor.13282

Kniep, Q., & Wattenhofer, R. (2024). *Tyche: Collateral-Free Coalition-Resistant Multiparty Lotteries with Arbitrary Payouts* (Version 1). arXiv. DOI: 10.48550/ARXIV.2409.03464

Krishna Pasupuleti, M. (2024). Blockchain for Transparent Governance: Securing Public Services in the digital era. In Blockchain in Government: Tools for Transparent Governance and Secure Public Services (pp. 146–173). National Education Services.

Krishna, B., Krishnan, S., & Sebastian, M. P. (2025). Understanding the process of building institutional trust among digital payment users through national cybersecurity commitment trustworthiness cues: A critical realist perspective. *Information Technology & People*, *38*(2), 714–756. DOI: 10.1108/ITP-05-2023-0434

Krishnamoorthy, R., Kamala, K., Soubache, I., Karthik, M. V., & Begum, M. A. (2022). Integration of blockchain and artificial intelligence in smart city perspectives. *Smart City Infrastructure: The Blockchain Perspective*, 77–112.

Kshetri, N. (2018). 1 Blockchain's roles in meeting key supply chain management objectives. *International Journal of Information Management*, *39*, 80–89. https://doi.org/https://doi.org/10.1016/j.ijinfomgt.2017.12.005. DOI: 10.1016/j.ijinfomgt.2017.12.005

Kumar, S., & Rasool, M. (2023). *AI and Blockchain Fusion: Building Resilient Information Security Systems.*

Kumaran, K. S., Khekare, G., Thanu Athitya, M., & Arulmozhivarman, A. (2025). Integrating blockchain, internet of things, and cloud for secure healthcare. *Indonesian Journal of Electrical Engineering and Computer Science*, *37*(2), 928–936. DOI: 10.11591/ijeecs.v37.i2.pp928-936

Kuvonchbek, R., Azamzade, A. K., Makhmudov, S., Bekzod, T., & Sarvar, M. (2024, December). Ensuring the Security of Transactions in Financial Information Networks Based on Modern Symmetric Cryptosystems in the Digital Economy. *In Conference on Internet of Things and Smart Spaces* (pp. 145-162). Cham: Springer Nature Switzerland. DOI: 10.1007/978-3-031-95299-9_13

Lavin, R., Liu, X., Mohanty, H., Norman, L., Zaarour, G., & Krishnamachari, B. (2024). *A Survey on the Applications of Zero-Knowledge Proofs* (Version 1). arXiv. DOI: 10.48550/ARXIV.2408.00243

Lavin, R., Liu, X., Mohanty, H., Norman, L., Zaarour, G., & Krishnamachari, B. (2024). A survey on the applications of Zero-Knowledge proofs. arXiv (Cornell University). /arxiv.2408.00243DOI: 10.48550

Lawelai, H., Purnomo, E. P., Nurmandi, A., Jovita, H., & Baulete, E. M. (2025). Cybersecurity policy on smart city infrastructure: a mapping of new threats and protections. J. Sci. Technol. Policy Manag.

Leist, S., & Zellner, G. (2006). Evaluation of current architecture frameworks. *Proceedings of the 2006 ACM Symposium on Applied Computing*, 1546–1553. DOI: 10.1145/1141277.1141635

Li, D., Cao, J., & Yao, Y. (2015). Big data in smart cities. *Science China. Information Sciences*, *58*(10), 1–12.

Limniotis, K. (2021). Cryptography as the Means to Protect Fundamental Human Rights. *Cryptography*, *5*(4), 34. DOI: 10.3390/cryptography5040034

Li, S. (2018). Application of blockchain technology in smart city infrastructure. *2018 IEEE International Conference on Smart Internet of Things (SmartIoT)*, 276–2766. DOI: 10.1109/SmartIoT.2018.00056

Li, S., Niu, K., & Wu, B. (2025). A blockchain-based secure data sharing scheme with efficient attribute revocation. *Journal of Systems Architecture*, *159*, 103309. DOI: 10.1016/j.sysarc.2024.103309

Liu, H. (2024). Employing cryptographic techniques for data security and privacy preservation. *Transactions on Computer Science and Intelligent Systems Research*, *5*, 35–39. DOI: 10.62051/58a35334

Lo, H. K., Ma, X., & Chen, K. (2005). Decoy state quantum key distribution. *Physical Review Letters*, *94*(23), 230504. DOI: 10.1103/PhysRevLett.94.230504 PMID: 16090452

Lucia, C., Zhiwei, G., & Michele, N. (2023). Biometrics for Industry 4.0: A survey of recent applications. *Journal of Ambient Intelligence and Humanized Computing*, *14*(8), 11239–11261. DOI: 10.1007/s12652-023-04632-7

Lykidis, I., Drosatos, G., & Rantos, K. (2021). The use of blockchain technology in e-government services. *Computers*, *10*(12), 168. DOI: 10.3390/computers10120168

Ma, C. (2021). Smart city and cyber-security; technologies used, leading challenges and future recommendations. *Energy Reports*, *7*, 7999–8012. DOI: 10.1016/j.egyr.2021.08.124

Maheshwaran, T., Muthumarilakshmi, S., Suganya, K., Maheswari, B., & Girija, P. (2024). Securing E-Commerce Strategies with Cloud, Blockchain, AI, and ML. In *Strategies for E-Commerce Data Security: Cloud, Blockchain, AI, and Machine Learning* (pp. 470-500). IGI Global.

Majeed, U., Khan, L. U., Yaqoob, I., Kazmi, S. M. A., Salah, K., & Hong, C. S. (2021). Blockchain for IoT-based smart cities: Recent advances, requirements, and future challenges. *Journal of Network and Computer Applications*, *181*, 103007. DOI: 10.1016/j.jnca.2021.103007

Mansoor, K., Afzal, M., Iqbal, W., & Abbas, Y. (2025). Securing the future: Exploring post-quantum cryptography for authentication and user privacy in IoT devices. *Cluster Computing*, *28*(2), 93. DOI: 10.1007/s10586-024-04799-4

Martinez, C., Bueti, C., Brékine, A., Grimm, C., & Ziegler, S. (2024). *IoT for SDGs*., DOI: 10.1007/978-3-031-39650-2_31

Masood, I., Daud, A., Wang, Y., Banjar, A., & Alharbey, R. (2024). A blockchain-based system for patient data privacy and security. *Multimedia Tools and Applications*, *83*(21), 60443–60467. DOI: 10.1007/s11042-023-17941-y

Matura, A., Singh, R. K., & Kumar, R. (2025). Decarbonizing road transport: A systematic literature review based on use case analysis. *Case Studies on Transport Policy, 101416*, 101416. Advance online publication. DOI: 10.1016/j.cstp.2025.101416

Maurya, V., Rishiwal, V., Yadav, M., Shiblee, M., Yadav, P., Agarwal, U., & Chaudhry, R. (2025). Blockchain-driven security for IoT networks: State-of-the-art, challenges and future directions. *Peer-to-Peer Networking and Applications*, *18*(1), 53. DOI: 10.1007/s12083-024-01812-w

Ma, Y., & Peng, Y. (2024). Design of Intelligent City Communication Network Based on Internet of Things. *Applied Mathematics and Nonlinear Sciences*, *9*(1), 1–15. DOI: 10.2478/amns-2024-1509

Minbaleev, A. V, & Evsikov, K. S. (2023). Regulation of quantum communications in the ``smart city'' information system. E3S Web Conf., 419, 1006.

Min, K. S. (2023). An exploratory research of anti-corruption policy using blockchain. *Korea Assoc Corruption Stud*, *28*(3), 5–26. DOI: 10.52663/kcsr.2023.28.3.5

Miron, R., Hulea, M., Muresan, V., Clitan, I., & Rusu, A. (2025). Integrating Blockchain Technology into Mobility-as-a-Service Platforms for Smart Cities. *Smart Cities*, *8*(1), 9. DOI: 10.3390/smartcities8010009

Mishra, H., & Maheshwari, P. (2021). Blockchain in Indian Public Distribution System: A conceptual framework to prevent leakage of the supplies and its enablers and disablers. *Journal of Global Operations and Strategic Sourcing*, *14*(2), 312–335. DOI: 10.1108/JGOSS-07-2020-0044

Mohanta, B. K., Panda, S. S., & Jena, D. (2018). An overview of smart contract and use cases in blockchain technology. *2018 9th International Conference on Computing, Communication and Networking Technologies (ICCCNT)*, 1–4.

Mora, R., Bédard, C., & Rivard, H. (2008). A geometric modelling framework for conceptual structural design from early digital architectural models. *Advanced Engineering Informatics*, *22*(2), 254–270. DOI: 10.1016/j.aei.2007.03.003

Mosca, M. (2018). Cybersecurity in an Era with Quantum Computers: Will We Be Ready? *IEEE Security and Privacy*, *16*(5), 38–41. DOI: 10.1109/MSP.2018.3761723

Mouha, N., & Celi, C. (2023). *A Vulnerability in Implementations of SHA-3, SHAKE, EdDSA, and Other NIST-Approved Algorithms* (pp. 3–28). DOI: 10.1007/978-3-031-30872-7_1

Mourtzis, D., Angelopoulos, J., & Panopoulos, N. (2023). The Future of the Human–Machine Interface (HMI) in Society 5.0. *Future Internet*, *15*(5), 162. DOI: 10.3390/fi15050162

Muheden, K., Mohammed, M., & Bilal, N. (2024). Exploring the Landscape of Smart Cities: A Comprehensive Review of IoT and Cyber-Physical Systems. *The Indonesian Journal of Computer Science*, *13*(2). Advance online publication. DOI: 10.33022/ijcs.v13i2.3843

Muniswamy, A., & Rathi, R. (2024). A detailed review on enhancing the security in Internet of Things-Based Smart City Environment using Machine learning algorithms. *IEEE Access : Practical Innovations, Open Solutions*, *12*, 120389–120413. DOI: 10.1109/ACCESS.2024.3450180

Munjal, K., & Bhatia, R. (2023). A systematic review of homomorphic encryption and its contributions in healthcare industry. *Complex & Intelligent Systems*, *9*(4), 3759–3786. DOI: 10.1007/s40747-022-00756-z

Munk, T. (2022). *The Rise of Politically Motivated Cyber Attacks*. Routledge., DOI: 10.4324/9781003126676

Murdoch, B. (2021). Privacy and artificial intelligence: Challenges for protecting health information in a new era. *BMC Medical Ethics*, *22*(1), 122. DOI: 10.1186/s12910-021-00687-3

Mustafa, G., Rafiq, W., Jhamat, N., Arshad, Z., & Rana, F. A. (2025). Blockchain-based governance models in e-government: A comprehensive framework for legal, technical, ethical and security considerations. *International Journal of Law and Management*, *67*(1), 37–55. DOI: 10.1108/IJLMA-08-2023-0172

Nanayakkara, N. D. G. T., Nanayakkara, G. A. S. Y., Karunanayaka, K. M. C. M., Kumara, C. P. T. K., & Karunanayake, N. (2024). Smart Cities, Secure Data: Navigating the Evolving Landscape of Data Protection Challenges. In *Data Protection* (pp. 251–285). Springer Nature Switzerland. DOI: 10.1007/978-3-031-76473-8_11

Nanayakkara, N., Nanayakkara, G., Karunanayaka, K., Kumara, C., & Karunanayake, N. (2024). Smart Cities, Secure Data: Navigating the Evolving Landscape of Data Protection Challenges. In *Data Protection: The Wake of AI and Machine Learning* (pp. 251–285). Springer.

Nechesov, A., & Ruponen, J. (2024). Empowering government efficiency through civic intelligence: Merging artificial intelligence and blockchain for smart citizen proposals. *Technologies*, *12*(12), 271. DOI: 10.3390/technologies12120271

Okika, N., Nwatuzie, G. A., & Olarinoye, H. S. ugustine A. Nwaka, Emmanuel Igba, & Roland Dunee. (2025). *Assessing the Vulnerability of Traditional and Post-Quantum Cryptographic Systems through Penetration Testing and Strengthening Cyber Defenses with Zero Trust Security in the Era of Quantum Computing*. DOI: 10.5281/ZENODO.14959440

Oliha, J. S., Biu, P. W., & Obi, O. C. (2024). Securing the smart city: A review of cybersecurity challenges and strategies. Eng. Sci. Technol. j., 5(2), 496–506.

Osman, A. M. S. (2019). A novel big data analytics framework for smart cities. *Future Generation Computer Systems*, *91*, 620–633. DOI: 10.1016/j.future.2018.06.046

Ota, D., & Gerz, M. (2011). *Benefits and challenges of architecture frameworks*.

Padma, A., & Ramaiah, M. (2024). Blockchain based an efficient and secure privacy preserved framework for smart cities. *IEEE Access : Practical Innovations, Open Solutions*, *12*, 21985–22002. DOI: 10.1109/ACCESS.2024.3364078

Pali, P., Pandey, D., & Yadav, M. (2025). *Enhancing Smart Transportation System: Blockchain Based Integrating Cloud Database Management System* (pp. 603–617). DOI: 10.1007/978-3-031-72617-0_31

Panahi Rizi, M. H., & Hosseini Seno, S. A. (2022). A systematic review of technologies and solutions to improve security and privacy protection of citizens in the smart city. *Internet of Things : Engineering Cyber Physical Human Systems*, *20*, 100584. DOI: 10.1016/j.iot.2022.100584

Pandey, S., Bhushan, B., & Hameed, A. A. (2024). Securing Healthcare 5.0: Zero-Knowledge Proof (ZKP) and Post Quantum Cryptography (PQC) Solutions for Medical Data Security. In *Soft Computing in Industry 5.0 for Sustainability* (pp. 339–355). Springer Nature Switzerland. DOI: 10.1007/978-3-031-69336-6_15

Parenti, C., Noori, N., & Janssen, M. (2022). A Smart Governance diffusion model for blockchain as an anti-corruption tool in Smart Cities. *Journal of Smart Cities and Society*, *1*(1), 71–92. DOI: 10.3233/SCS-210122

Patel, V., Department of Computer Engineering Silver Oak College of Engineering & Technology, S. O. U. and D. D. J. A., Khara, D. S., & Tivari, G. D. (2024). Examining the integration of responsible AI principles in Social Media Marketing for Digital Health: A theoretical analysis. INTERANTIONAL JOURNAL OF SCIENTIFIC RESEARCH IN ENGINEERING AND, 08(07), 1–13.

Periyasamy, G., Rangaswamy, E., & Nawaz, N. (2023). *Big Data Systems Architecture and Data Security Fundamentals—Case Study Approach for a Hospital in Singapore* (pp. 277–287). DOI: 10.1007/978-3-031-17746-0_23

Polcumpally, A. T., Pandey, K. K., Kumar, A., & Samadhiya, A. (2024). Blockchain governance and trust: A multi-sector thematic systematic review and exploration of future research directions. *Heliyon*, *10*(12), e32975. DOI: 10.1016/j.heliyon.2024.e32975 PMID: 38984295

Policharla, G.-V., Westerbaan, B., Faz-Hernández, A., & Wood, C. A. (2023). *Post-Quantum Privacy Pass via Post-Quantum Anonymous Credentials* (No. 2023/414). Cryptology ePrint Archive. https://eprint.iacr.org/2023/414

Ponmalar, A., Muthuram, A., Therasa, M., Priya, V., Sathya, V., Subha, S., & Subramanian, R. S. (2025). Convergence of Advanced Technologies for Sustainable Development and Smart Cities. In *AI and Green Technology Applications in Society* (pp. 189–218). IGI Global Scientific Publishing.

Popov, E., & Semyachkov, K. (2020). 7I-model for smart city development. *Archives of Business Research*, *8*(7), 143–157. DOI: 10.14738/abr.87.8615

Pothireddy, N. K. R. (2025). Network Security Threat Detection in IoT-Enabled Smart Cities. *Authorea Preprints*. DOI: 10.22541/au.174352871.10041922/v1

Prateek, K., Maity, S., & Amin, R. (2023). An Unconditionally Secured Privacy-Preserving Authentication Scheme for Smart Metering Infrastructure in Smart Grid. *IEEE Transactions on Network Science and Engineering*, *10*(2), 1085–1095. DOI: 10.1109/TNSE.2022.3226902

Quelhas Poças, M. (2025). *Public Sector Blockchain Use Cases for Societal Development.*, DOI: 10.1007/978-3-031-85936-6_6

Quiles-Rodriguez, J., Palau, R., & Mateo-Sanz, J. M. (2025). How Artificial Intelligence-Assisted Colour Lighting Can Improve Learning: Evidence from Recent Classrooms Studies. *Applied Sciences (Basel, Switzerland)*, *15*(7), 3657. Advance online publication. DOI: 10.3390/app15073657

Ragab, M., Ashary, E. B., Alghamdi, B. M., Aboalela, R., Alsaadi, N., Maghrabi, L. A., & Allehaibi, K. H. (2025). Advanced artificial intelligence with federated learning framework for privacy-preserving cyberthreat detection in IoT-assisted sustainable smart cities. *Scientific Reports*, *15*(1), 4470. DOI: 10.1038/s41598-025-88843-2

Rahaman, M., Arya, V., Orozco, S. M., & Pappachan, P. (2024). *Secure Multi-Party Computation (SMPC).* Protocols and Privacy., DOI: 10.4018/979-8-3693-5330-1.ch008

Rahman, M. S., Chamikara, M., Khalil, I., & Bouras, A. (2022). Blockchain-of-blockchains: An interoperable blockchain platform for ensuring IoT data integrity in smart city. *Journal of Industrial Information Integration*, *30*, 100408. DOI: 10.1016/j.jii.2022.100408

Rahouti, M., Drid, H., Hamouid, K., Massmi, K., & Mehenna, S. E. (2025). Brave-sdn: Blockchain-reliant authentication for versatile east–west bound in distributed sdns. *International Journal of Information Security*, *24*(1), 1–15. DOI: 10.1007/s10207-024-00962-5

Rajabpour Sanati, S., Zebardast, M., Jamshidi, R., & Sadeghi, M. E. (2024). Designing and localizing a novel cybersecurity model according to smart city digital infrastructure components (A Case Study of GreenWeb Co.). International Journal of Innovation in Management. *Economics and Social Sciences*, *4*(3), 1–18.

Rajawat, A. S., Bedi, P., Goyal, S. B., Shaw, R. N., Ghosh, A., & Aggarwal, S. (2022). *AI and Blockchain for Healthcare Data Security in Smart Cities*., DOI: 10.1007/978-981-16-7498-3_12

Rasha, R., & Hammed, A. (2024). Maintaining security of patient data by employing private blockchain and fog computing technologies based on internet of medical things. *Informatica (Vilnius)*, *48*(12).

Rasha, R., Tahayur, D., & Jebbar, W. (2025). Sturdy Blockchain Combined with E-apps Repositories Based on Reliable Camouflaging and Integrating Mechanisms. *IJ Computer Network and Information Security*, *17*(3), 35–53. DOI: 10.5815/ijcnis.2025.03.03

Rashid, M. M., Kamruzzaman, J., Hassan, M. M., Imam, T., & Gordon, S. (2020). Cyberattacks Detection in IoT-Based Smart City Applications Using Machine Learning Techniques. *International Journal of Environmental Research and Public Health*, *17*(24), 24. Advance online publication. DOI: 10.3390/ijerph17249347 PMID: 33327468

Rasool, R. U., Ahmad, H. F., Rafique, W., Qayyum, A., & Qadir, J. (2022). Security and privacy of internet of medical things: A contemporary review in the age of surveillance, botnets, and adversarial ML. *Journal of Network and Computer Applications*, *201*, 103332. DOI: 10.1016/j.jnca.2022.103332

Rathod, T., Jadav, N. K., Tanwar, S., Sharma, R., Tolba, A., Raboaca, M. S., Marina, V., & Said, W. (2023). Blockchain-driven intelligent scheme for IoT-based public safety system beyond 5G networks. *Sensors (Basel)*, *23*(2), 969. DOI: 10.3390/s23020969 PMID: 36679767

Ravi, P., Chattopadhyay, A., D'Anvers, J. P., & Baksi, A. (2024). Side-channel and Fault-injection attacks over Lattice-based Post-quantum Schemes (Kyber, Dilithium): Survey and New Results. *ACM Transactions on Embedded Computing Systems*, *23*(2), 1–54. DOI: 10.1145/3603170

Razzaq, R. H., & Al-Zubaidie, M. (2024a). Maintaining Security of Patient Data by Employing Private Blockchain and Fog Computing Technologies based on Internet of Medical Things. *Informatica (Vilnius)*, *48*(12), 12. Advance online publication. DOI: 10.31449/inf.v48i12.6047

Razzaq, R. H., & Al-Zubaidie, M. (2024b). Formulating an Advanced Security Protocol for Internet of Medical Things based on Blockchain and Fog Computing Technologies. *Iraqi Journal for Computer Science and Mathematics*, *5*(3). Advance online publication. DOI: 10.52866/ijcsm.2024.05.03.046

Razzaq, R. H., Al-Zubaidie, M., & Atiyah, R. G. (2024). Intermediary Decentralized Computing and Private Blockchain Mechanisms for Privacy Preservation in the Internet of Medical Things. *Mesopotamian Journal of CyberSecurity*, *4*(3), 152–165. DOI: 10.58496/MJCS/2024/020

Rejeb, A., Rejeb, K., Simske, S. J., & Keogh, J. G. (2022). Blockchain technology in the smart city: A bibliometric review. *Quality & Quantity*, *56*(5), 2875–2906. DOI: 10.1007/s11135-021-01251-2 PMID: 34629554

Ren, Y., Chen, L., Bai, Y., Ye, J., & Zhao, Y. (2025). Blockchain-based cross-domain query integrity verification mechanism for outsourced database. *Computer Standards & Interfaces*, *92*, 103926. DOI: 10.1016/j.csi.2024.103926

Reshma, S., Goyal, V., Kokila, R., Vibha, K., & Indirani, S. (2025). AI Tools for the Software Development of Real-Time Communication Systems. In *Modern Insights on Smart and Secure Software Development* (pp. 139–172). IGI Global., DOI: 10.4018/979-8-3693-9851-7.ch005

Riki, R., Widyarto, S., Kahar, S., & Hariyanto, S. (2020). Smart city comprehension in community development. Proceedings of the Proceedings of the Third Workshop on Multidisciplinary and Its Applications, WMA-3 2019, 11-14 December 2019, Medan, Indonesia. DOI: 10.4108/eai.11-12-2019.2290864

Rishiwal, V., Agarwal, U., Alotaibi, A., Tanwar, S., Yadav, P., & Yadav, M. (2024). Exploring secure V2X communication networks for human-Centric security and privacy in Smart cities. *IEEE Access : Practical Innovations, Open Solutions*, *12*, 138763–138788. DOI: 10.1109/ACCESS.2024.3467002

Robinson, L., Ragnedda, M., & Schulz, J. (2020). Digital inequalities: Contextualizing problems and solutions. *Journal of Information. Communication and Ethics in Society*, *18*(3), 323–327. DOI: 10.1108/JICES-05-2020-0064

Rotună, C., GHEORGHI Ă, A., Zamfiroiu, A., & SMADA ANAGRAMA, D. (2019). Smart City Ecosystem Using Blockchain Technology. *Informatica Economica, 23*(4).

Russell, S., & Norvig, P. (2020). Artificial Intelligence: A Modern Approach. *Pearson*. ISBN 10: 1-292-40113-3. Available in http://lib.ysu.am/disciplines_bk/efdd4d1d4c2087fe1cbe03d9ced67f34.pdf

Saad, J., & Mustafa, F. (2025). *AI Manipulation Meets Quantum Decryption: A SOC-Driven Cybersecurity Blueprint for IoT-Powered Smart Cities and Self-Driving Ecosystems*.

Sadhya, D., & Sahu, T. (2024). A critical survey of the security and privacy aspects of the Aadhaar framework. *Computers & Security*, *140*, 103782. DOI: 10.1016/j.cose.2024.103782

Sahoo, A. K, I. K. A., & Rajagopal, S. M. (2024). Comparative Study of Cryptographic Algorithms in Post Quantum Computing Landscape. *2024 5th International Conference on Data Intelligence and Cognitive Informatics (ICDICI)*, 36–40. DOI: 10.1109/ICDICI62993.2024.10810828

Sahoo, S. S., Hosmane, M. M., & Chaurasiya, V. K. (2023). A secure payment channel rebalancing model for layer-2 blockchain. *Internet of Things : Engineering Cyber Physical Human Systems*, *22*, 100822. DOI: 10.1016/j.iot.2023.100822

Sahu, B. L., & Chandrakar, P. (2025). Blockchain-oriented secure communication and smart parking model for internet of electric vehicles in smart cities. *Peer-to-Peer Networking and Applications*, *18*(1), 51. DOI: 10.1007/s12083-024-01872-y

Saini, K., Mummoorthy, A., Chandrika, R., & Gowri Ganesh, N. S. (Eds.). (2023). *AI, IoT, and Blockchain Breakthroughs in E-governance*. IGI Global. DOI: 10.4018/978-1-6684-7697-0

Saleem, M., Farooq, M. S., Shahzad, T., Hassan, A., Abbas, S., Ali, T., & Khan, M. A. (2024). Secure and transparent mobility in smart cities: Revolutionizing AVNs to predict traffic congestion using MapReduce, Private Blockchain and XAI. *IEEE Access : Practical Innovations, Open Solutions*, *12*, 131541–131555. DOI: 10.1109/ACCESS.2024.3458983

Sanada, K., & Zappa, M. (2025). Japan's international cooperation on smart city development in Asia: International effort beneath the smart rhetoric in India and in Thailand. *Research in Globalization*, *10*, 100270. DOI: 10.1016/j.resglo.2025.100270

Sanaj, M. S., & Prathap, P. J. (2020). Nature inspired chaotic squirrel search algorithm (CSSA) for multi objective task scheduling in an IAAS cloud computing atmosphere. *Engineering Science and Technology, an International Journal, 23*(4), 891–902. DOI: 10.1016/j.jestch.2019.11.002

Sarker, I. H. (2022). Smart City Data Science: Towards data-driven smart cities with open research issues. *Internet of Things : Engineering Cyber Physical Human Systems, 19*, 100528. DOI: 10.1016/j.iot.2022.100528

Scarani, V., Acín, A., Ribordy, G., & Gisin, N. (2004). Quantum cryptography protocols robust against photon number splitting attacks for weak laser pulse implementations. *Physical Review Letters, 92*(5), 057901. DOI: 10.1103/PhysRevLett.92.057901 PMID: 14995344

Schumacher, L. V. (2024). Central Bank Digital Currencies (CBDCs): Exploring Characteristics, Risks and Benefits. In *Decoding Digital Assets* (pp. 81–157). Springer Nature Switzerland. DOI: 10.1007/978-3-031-54601-3_12

Sefati, S. S., Craciunescu, R., Arasteh, B., Halunga, S., Fratu, O., & Tal, I. (2024). Cybersecurity in a scalable smart city framework using blockchain and federated learning for internet of things (IoT). *Smart Cities, 7*(5), 2802–2841. DOI: 10.3390/smartcities7050109

Shafik, W. (2024). *Shaping the Next Generation Smart City Ecosystem: An Investigation on the Requirements*. Applications, Architecture, Security and Privacy, and Open Research Questions., DOI: 10.1007/978-3-031-59846-3_1

Shafik, W. (2025). *Generative Adversarial Networks: Security*. Privacy, and Ethical Considerations., DOI: 10.1007/978-3-031-76710-4_5

Shang, F., & Deng, X. (2025). A data sharing scheme based on blockchain for privacy protection certification of Internet of Vehicles. *Vehicular Communications, 51*, 100864. DOI: 10.1016/j.vehcom.2024.100864

Sharma, H., Kumar, P., & Sharma, K. (2025). Advanced Security for IoT and Smart Devices. In *Emerging Threats and Countermeasures in Cybersecurity* (pp. 191–216). Wiley., DOI: 10.1002/9781394230600.ch10

Sharma, P., Agrawal, A., Bhatia, V., Prakash, S., & Mishra, A. K. (2021). Quantum Key Distribution Secured Optical Networks: A Survey. *IEEE Open Journal of the Communications Society, 2*, 2049–2083. DOI: 10.1109/OJCOMS.2021.3106659

Sharma, S., & Shrestha, S. (2024). Integrating HCI principles in AI: A review of human-Centered Artificial Intelligence applications and challenges. *J. Fut. Artif. Intell. Tech., 1*(3), 309–317. DOI: 10.62411/faith.3048-3719-47

Sharma, T., Kumar, M. R., Kaushal, S., Chaudhary, D., & Saleem, K. (2023). Privacy aware post quantum secure ant colony optimization ad hoc on-demand distance vector routing in intent based internet of vehicles for 5G smart cities. *IEEE Access : Practical Innovations, Open Solutions*, *11*, 110391–110399. DOI: 10.1109/ACCESS.2023.3311515

Sharmila, B. S., & Nagapadma, R. (2023). Quantized autoencoder (QAE) intrusion detection system for anomaly detection in resource-constrained IoT devices using RT-IoT2022 dataset. *Cybersecurity*, *6*(1), 41. DOI: 10.1186/s42400-023-00178-5

Shin, D., & Ibahrine, M. (2020). The socio-technical assemblages of blockchain system: How blockchains are framed and how the framing reflects societal contexts. *Digital Policy. Regulation & Governance*, *22*(3), 245–263. DOI: 10.1108/DPRG-11-2019-0095

Shneiderman, B. (2020). Bridging the Gap Between Ethics and Practice. *ACM Transactions on Interactive Intelligent Systems*, *10*(4), 1–31. DOI: 10.1145/3419764

Shor, P. W. (1994). Algorithms for quantum computation: Discrete logarithms and factoring. In *Proceedings of the 35th Annual Symposium on Foundations of Computer Science* (pp. 124–134). IEEE. DOI: 10.1109/SFCS.1994.365700

Shuaib, M., Alam, S., Ahmed, R., Qamar, S., Nasir, M. S., & Alam, M. S. (2022). Current Status, Requirements, and Challenges of Blockchain Application in Land Registry. *International Journal of Information Retrieval Research*, *12*(2), 1–20. DOI: 10.4018/IJIRR.299934

Shyaa, G. S., & Al-Zubaidie, M. (2023). Utilizing trusted lightweight ciphers to support electronic-commerce transaction cryptography. *Applied Sciences (Basel, Switzerland)*, *13*(12), 7085. DOI: 10.3390/app13127085

Sifah, E. B., Xia, H., Cobblah, C. N. A., Xia, Q., Gao, J., & Du, X. (2020). BEMPAS: A decentralized employee performance assessment system based on blockchain for smart city governance. *IEEE Access : Practical Innovations, Open Solutions*, *8*, 99528–99539. DOI: 10.1109/ACCESS.2020.2997650

Sindhuja, M., Alice, K., Nancy, A. M., & Vinoth, N. A. S. (2024). Cybersecurity Strategies for Smart Cities. In Advances in Geospatial Technologies (pp. 77–98). IGI Global. DOI: 10.4018/979-8-3693-8104-5.ch004

Singh, P., & Singh, N. (2023). Blockchain with IoT and AI: A review of agriculture and healthcare. *Research Anthology on Convergence of Blockchain, Internet of Things, and Security*, 1315-1330.

Singh, S., Sharma, P. K., Moon, S. Y., & Park, J. H. (2024). Advanced lightweight encryption algorithms for IoT devices: Survey, challenges and solutions. *Journal of Ambient Intelligence and Humanized Computing*, *15*(2), 1625–1642. DOI: 10.1007/s12652-017-0494-4

Singun, A. (2025). Unveiling the barriers to digital transformation in higher education institutions: A systematic literature review. *Discover Education*, *4*(1), 37. DOI: 10.1007/s44217-025-00430-9

Song, Y., Liu, J., Zhang, W., & Li, J. (2023). Blockchain's role in e-commerce sellers' decision-making on information disclosure under competition. *Annals of Operations Research*, *329*(1–2), 1009–1048. DOI: 10.1007/s10479-021-04276-w

Soni, T., Kaur, R., Gupta, D., Sharma, A., & Gupta, G. (2024). Opportunities and Challenges of Data-Driven Cybersecurity for Smart Cities: Blockchain-Driven Approach. *Sustainable Mobility: Policies, Challenges and Advancements*, 223–236.

Sood, N. (2024). *Cryptography in Post Quantum Computing Era* (SSRN Scholarly Paper No. 4705470). Social Science Research Network. DOI: 10.2139/ssrn.4705470

Sriram, V. P., Sanyal, S., Laddunuri, M. M., Subramanian, M., Bose, V., Booshan, B., & Thangam, D. (2023). Enhancing cybersecurity through blockchain technology. In *Handbook of Research on Cybersecurity Issues and Challenges for Business and FinTech Applications* (pp. 208–224). IGI Global.

StraitsTimes. (2024). Singapore is world's 5th smartest city. Retrieved April 3, 2025, from https://www.straitstimes.com/singapore/singapore-is-5th-smartest-city-in-the-world-top-in-asia-global-index

Suleski, T., Ahmed, M., Yang, W., & Wang, E. (2023). A review of multi-factor authentication in the Internet of Healthcare Things. *Digital Health*, *9*, 20552076231177144. Advance online publication. DOI: 10.1177/20552076231177144

Sultana, S. S., & Sangeetha, J. (2022). *Internet of Things: Security Mechanisms* (pp. 581–595). DOI: 10.1007/978-981-16-8862-1_38

Sun, C.-C., Sebastian Cardenas, D. J., Hahn, A., & Liu, C.-C. (2021). Intrusion Detection for Cybersecurity of Smart Meters. *IEEE Transactions on Smart Grid*, *12*(1), 612–622. DOI: 10.1109/TSG.2020.3010230

Sung, C. S., & Park, J. Y. (2021). Understanding of blockchain-based identity management system adoption in the public sector. *Journal of Enterprise Information Management*, *34*(5), 1481–1505. DOI: 10.1108/JEIM-12-2020-0532

Susilowati, A. P. E., Rachmawati, R., & Rijanta, R. (2025). Smart village concept in Indonesia: ICT as determining factor. *Heliyon*, *11*(1), e41657. Advance online publication. DOI: 10.1016/j.heliyon.2025.e41657

Swarnalatha, P., & Prabu, S. (Eds.). (2022). *Blockchain Technologies for Sustainable Development in Smart Cities*. IGI Global. DOI: 10.4018/978-1-7998-9274-8

Tahayur, D. H., & Al-Zubaidie, M. (2024). Enhancing Electronic Agriculture Data Security with a Blockchain-Based Search Method and E-Signatures. *Mesopotamian Journal of CyberSecurity*, *4*(3), 3. Advance online publication. DOI: 10.58496/MJCS/2024/012

Tahayur, D. H., & Al-Zubaidie, M. (2025). Establishing an optimized searching approach with e-signatures based on blockchain for electronic agriculture applications. *AIP Conference Proceedings*, *3264*(1), 030001. DOI: 10.1063/5.0258784

Tameemi, H. A., Shayea, G. G., Khaleel, Y. L., Habeeb, M. A., Hussein, N. A. H. K., & Albahri, A. S. (2025). A Systematic review of metaverse cybersecurity: Frameworks, challenges, and strategic approaches in a quantum-driven era. *Mesopotamian Journal of CyberSecurity*, *5*(2), 770–803. DOI: 10.58496/MJCS/2025/045

Tando, M. S., Gawusu, S., Yakubu, S., Kwabena, O. S., Donatus, D., & Abu, S. R. (2024). Decentralized energy trading with blockchain technology. In Elsevier eBooks (pp. 75–101). DOI: 10.1016/B978-0-443-23627-3.00004-1

Tang, A., Han, J., & Chen, P. (2004). A comparative analysis of architecture frameworks. *11th Asia-Pacific Software Engineering Conference*, 640–647. DOI: 10.1109/APSEC.2004.2

Tan, T. M., Salo, J., Alejandro, T. G. B., Tan, G. W. H., Ooi, K. B., & Dwivedi, Y. K. (2024). Guest editorial: A blockchain-based approach to marketing in the sharing economy. *Journal of Business Research*, *177*, 114639. DOI: 10.1016/j.jbusres.2024.114639

Toh, C. K. (2020). Security for smart cities. *IET Smart Cities*, *2*(2), 95–104. DOI: 10.1049/iet-smc.2020.0001

Tregi, T. G., & Al-Zubaidie, M. (2025). Enhancing Traffic Data Security in Smart Cities Using Optimized Quantum-Based Digital Signatures and Privacy-Preserving Techniques. *Mesopotamian Journal of CyberSecurity*, *5*(1), 1. Advance online publication. DOI: 10.58496/MJCS/2025/017

Trivedi, S. (2023). Convention of Blockchain in financial services: a state-of-the-art literature review. *Revolutionizing Financial Services and Markets through FinTech and Blockchain*, 237-250.

Troitiño, D. R., Mazur, V., & Kerikmäe, T. (2024). E-governance and integration in the European union. *Internet of Things : Engineering Cyber Physical Human Systems, 27,* 101321. DOI: 10.1016/j.iot.2024.101321

Tshuma, S., Masengu, R., & Dube, M. (2024). *Security and Privacy Challenges in Digital Marketing*., DOI: 10.4018/979-8-3693-2165-2.ch018

Tyagi, A. K., & Seranmadevi, R. (2024). Blockchain for Enhancing Security and Privacy in the Smart Healthcare. In *Digital Twin and Blockchain for Smart Cities* (pp. 343–370). Wiley., DOI: 10.1002/9781394303564.ch16

U.S. National Institute of Standards and Technology. (2022). *Selected algorithms 2022: Post-quantum cryptography standardization* (NIST Special Publication 800-208). DOI: 10.6028/NIST.SP.800-208

Ugbedeojo, M., Adebiyi, M. O., Aroba, O. J., & Adebiyi, A. A. (2024). RSA and Elliptic Curve Encryption System. *International Journal of Information Security and Privacy, 18*(1), 1–27. DOI: 10.4018/IJISP.340728

Ullah, A., Anwar, S. M., Li, J., Nadeem, L., Mahmood, T., Rehman, A., & Saba, T. (2024). Smart cities: The role of Internet of Things and machine learning in realizing a data-centric smart environment. *Complex & Intelligent Systems, 10*(1), 1607–1637. DOI: 10.1007/s40747-023-01175-4

UN. (2022). World Population Prospects 2022: Summary of Results. Retrieved April 3, 2025, from https://www.un.org/development/desa/pd/content/World-Population-Prospects-2022

UN. (2025). Adapting Humanitarian Action to an Urban World. Retrieved from https://unhabitat.org/sites/default/files/download-manager-files/Global Alliance for Urban Crises WHS Brief - Final.pdf

Uzun, E., Yagemann, C., Chung, S., Kolesnikov, V., & Lee, W. (2021). Cryptographic Key Derivation from Biometric Inferences for Remote Authentication. *Proceedings of the 2021 ACM Asia Conference on Computer and Communications Security,* 629–643. DOI: 10.1145/3433210.3437512

Vasani, V., Prateek, K., Amin, R., Maity, S., & Dwivedi, A. D. (2024). Embracing the quantum frontier: Investigating quantum communication, cryptography, applications and future directions. *Journal of Industrial Information Integration, 39,* 100594. DOI: 10.1016/j.jii.2024.100594

Vempati, S. (2024a). Securing smart cities: A cybersecurity perspective on integrating IoT, AI, and Machine Learning for digital twin creation. *J. Electr. Syst., 20*(3), 1420–1429. DOI: 10.52783/jes.3548

Verma, A., Singh, A., Sethi, P., Jain, V., Chawla, C., Bhargava, A., & Gupta, A. (2023). Applications of Data Security and Blockchain in Smart City Identity Management. In *Handbook of Research on Data-Driven Mathematical Modeling in Smart Cities* (pp. 154–174). IGI Global. DOI: 10.4018/978-1-6684-6408-3.ch009

Vignesh, R., Pabitha, C., Shamritha, V., & Prathija, A. (2025, January). Integrated Road Safety System for Real-Time Waterlogging Detection and Traffic Management Using Google Maps API. *In 2025 International Conference on Multi-Agent Systems for Collaborative Intelligence (ICMSCI)* (pp. 1165-1170). IEEE. DOI: 10.1109/ICMSCI62561.2025.10894697

Vijayalakshmi, D., Krithiga, S., Gangisetty, T., Dayana, R., & Vadivukkarasi, K. (2024). *Encryption Protocols and Security for 5G* (pp. 78–112). DOI: 10.4018/979-8-3693-2786-9.ch004

Vishnu, C. R., Chatterjee, P., Maddali, S. P., & Akenroye, T. O. (2025). Characterizing the critical success factors influencing blockchain technology adoption in Indian public distribution system: An exploratory approach. *Benchmarking*, *32*(4), 1410–1433. DOI: 10.1108/BIJ-07-2023-0466

Vučković, M., & Adams, A. M. (2022). Population and Health Policies in Urban Areas. In May, J. F., & Goldstone, J. A. (Eds.), *International Handbook of Population Policies* (pp. 397–429). Springer International Publishing., DOI: 10.1007/978-3-031-02040-7_18

Waghmare, G., Sundram, S., Kumar, B., Raman, M. S., Yagnam, N., Motekar, H. S., & Kaushik, D. (2023). Blockchain in Supply Chain Management Prevailing in Smart Cities: Prospects and Approaches. In *Handbook of Research on Data-Driven Mathematical Modeling in Smart Cities* (pp. 117-137). IGI Global.

Walunj, V., Rajaraman, V., Dutta, J., & Sharma, A. (2025). Integrating Crypto-Based Payment Systems for Data Marketplaces: Enhancing Efficiency, Security, and User Autonomy. In Patil, V. T., Krishnan, R., & Shyamasundar, R. K. (Eds.), *Information Systems Security* (Vol. 15416, pp. 443–452). Springer Nature Switzerland., DOI: 10.1007/978-3-031-80020-7_25

Wang, J., Nguyen, D. Q., Bonkalo, T., & Grebennikov, O. (2021). Smart governance of urban data. E3S Web Conf., 301, 5005.

Wang, H., Kang, X., Li, T., Lei, Z., Chu, C.-K., & Wang, H. (2023). An Overview of Trust Standards for Communication Networks and Future Digital World. *IEEE Access : Practical Innovations, Open Solutions*, *11*, 42991–42998. DOI: 10.1109/ACCESS.2023.3270042

Ward, K., Abbruzzese, T., Bunnell, T., Cardullo, P., Chang, I. C. C., Miller, B., & Woods, O. (2025). A comparison of comparisons: Evidence from an international comparative study of 'smart cities'. *Environment and Planning C. Politics and Space, 23996544251320261*(7), 1217–1239. Advance online publication. DOI: 10.1177/23996544251320261

Weedbrook, C., Pirandola, S., García-Patrón, R., Cerf, N. J., Ralph, T. C., Shapiro, J. H., & Lloyd, S. (2012). Gaussian quantum information. *Reviews of Modern Physics, 84*(2), 621–669. DOI: 10.1103/RevModPhys.84.621

Widodo, A. M., Pappachan, P., Sekti, B. A., Anwar, N., Widayanti, R., Rahaman, M., & Bansal, R. (2024). Quantum-resistant cryptography. In *Innovations in Modern Cryptography* (pp. 100–130). IGI Global., DOI: 10.4018/979-8-3693-5330-1.ch005

Wimal, K., Cullen, G., & Donovan, J. (2025). Blockchain-Driven Smart Cities: Review of Key Applications and Emerging Trends. *2025 2nd International Conference on Advanced Innovations in Smart Cities (ICAISC)*, 1–8.

Wong, B. K. M., Voon, M. L., & Law, F. L. (2025). Preparing digital citizens for smart healthcare in the Asia-Pacific: Strategies, challenges, and opportunities. In *Digital Healthcare, Digital Transformation and Citizen Empowerment in Asia-Pacific and Europe for a Healthier Society* (pp. 539–560). Elsevier., DOI: 10.1016/B978-0-443-30168-1.00008-6

Wong, P., Chia, F., Kiu, M., & Lou, E. (2020). The potential of integrating blockchain technology into smart sustainable city development. *IOP Conference Series. Earth and Environmental Science, 463*(1), 012020. DOI: 10.1088/1755-1315/463/1/012020

Wu, Z., Xuan, S., Xie, J., Lin, C., & Lu, C. (2022). How to ensure the confidentiality of electronic medical records on the cloud: A technical perspective. *Computers in Biology and Medicine, 147*, 105726. DOI: 10.1016/j.compbiomed.2022.105726

Xenofontos, C., Zografopoulos, I., Konstantinou, C., Jolfaei, A., Khan, M. K., & Choo, K.-K. R. (2022). Consumer, Commercial, and Industrial IoT (In)Security: Attack Taxonomy and Case Studies. *IEEE Internet of Things Journal, 9*(1), 199–221. DOI: 10.1109/JIOT.2021.3079916

Xie, J., Tang, H., Huang, T., Yu, F. R., Xie, R., Liu, J., & Liu, Y. (2019). A survey of blockchain technology applied to smart cities: Research issues and challenges. *IEEE Communications Surveys and Tutorials, 21*(3), 2794–2830. DOI: 10.1109/COMST.2019.2899617

Yamini, B., Dinesh, M. G., Gracious, L. A., & Subramanian, R. S. (2025). Exploring Blockchain Technology: Concepts, Features, and Industry Transformations. In *Blockchain Applications for the Energy and Utilities Industry* (pp. 305-322). IGI Global Scientific Publishing.

Yin, H. L., Chen, T. Y., Yu, Z. W., Liu, H., You, L. X., Zhou, Y. H., Chen, S.-J., Mao, Y., Huang, M.-Q., Zhang, W.-J., Chen, H., Li, M. J., Nolan, D., Zhou, F., Jiang, X., Wang, Z., Zhang, Q., Wang, X.-B., & Pan, J. W. (2016). Measurement-device-independent quantum key distribution over a 404 km optical fiber. *Physical Review Letters, 117*(19), 190501. DOI: 10.1103/PhysRevLett.117.190501 PMID: 27858431

Yulia Fatin Lestari, N. 16610033. (2021). *Sistem Kriptografi Ntru Pada Proses Pengamanan Data Rahasia* [Skripsi, Fakultas Sains Dan Teknologi]. https://digilib.uin-suka.ac.id/id/eprint/43711/

Zafir, E. I., Akter, A., Islam, M. N., Hasib, S. A., Islam, T., Sarker, S. K., & Muyeen, S. M. (2024). Enhancing security of Internet of Robotic Things: A review of recent trends, practices, and recommendations with encryption and blockchain techniques. *Internet of Things : Engineering Cyber Physical Human Systems, 28*, 101357. DOI: 10.1016/j.iot.2024.101357

Zhang, R., Xue, R., & Liu, L. (2019). Security and Privacy on Blockchain. *ACM Computing Surveys, 52*(3), 1–34. Advance online publication. DOI: 10.1145/3316481

Zhou, L., Diro, A., Saini, A., Kaisar, S., & Hiep, P. C. (2024). Leveraging zero knowledge proofs for blockchain-based identity sharing: A survey of advancements, challenges and opportunities. *Journal of Information Security and Applications, 80*, 103678. DOI: 10.1016/j.jisa.2023.103678

Zhuang, Y., Cenci, J., & Zhang, J. (2024). Review of big data implementation and expectations in smart cities. *Buildings (Basel, Switzerland), 14*(12), 3717. DOI: 10.3390/buildings14123717

Zhuk, A. (2025). Beyond the blockchain hype: Addressing legal and regulatory challenges. *SN Social Sciences, 5*(2), 11. DOI: 10.1007/s43545-024-01044-y

About the Contributors

Mishall Al-Zubaidie (Member, IEEE) received a bachelor's degree in computer science from Basrah University, Iraq, in 2004, and a master's degree in the security of the wireless network from Basrah University, Iraq, in 2010. He received his Ph.D. degree from the School of Agricultural, Computational and Environmental Sciences, Faculty of Health, Engineering, and Sciences, University of Southern Queensland, Australia in 2020. He has authored many peer-reviewed research in different journals in the field of communications and network security. In addition, he provided review and evaluation services for more than 1100 research papers in various respected journals. His current research interests are communications and networks security including public-key algorithms, authorising users in electronic health record (EHR), electronic medical record (EMR), and both security, efficiency of the wireless sensor network of health systems, keys exchange/agreement algorithms in protecting patients' data/information and smart city security.

***

Yuvasri B is a faculty member in the Department of Computer Science and Engineering at R.M.K. College of Engineering and Technology, Tamil Nadu, India. She is actively involved in teaching and academic development in the field of computer science. Her interests include guiding students in innovative projects and contributing to research-oriented learning.

Most. Sharmin Ara Chowdhury is a research practitioner with a strong focus on key areas such as Artificial Intelligence, strategic innovation, management information systems, and sustainability. Her research explores the intersection of emerging technologies and organizational strategy. By aligning innovation with practical needs, she addresses real-world challenges through applied and impactful research. Sharmin's work bridges academic theory and professional practice, making significant contributions to the evolving landscape of digital transformation and sustainable development.

Md Mehedi Hasan Emon is a research practitioner in Business and Management, with specialized in Supply Chain Management, Digital Transformation, Marketing, Information Systems, and Educational Technology (Edutech). His work bridges a diverse range of domains including Artificial Intelligence in Business, Human-Computer Interaction, Cognitive Behaviour, E-commerce, and Smart Logistics. His research extensively explores the integration of emerging technologies in business ecosystems focusing on AI-driven innovation, behavioral responses to technology adoption, and digital marketing strategies. He has also contributed significantly to sustainability-focused fields such as GreenTech, Green Finance, Renewable Energy, and Blockchain-enabled financial innovation. Additionally, his work in Smart Cities and IoT adoption emphasizes the importance of user trust, security, and operational efficiency. Emon has authored numerous peer-reviewed publications on topics including AI adoption intention, supply chain visibility, digital learning acceptance, and crisis-resilient supply chains. Many of his studies adopt behavioral and cognitive perspectives to understand how professionals and consumers interact with technology highlighting the psychological and user-centric aspects of digital transformation. He has participated in several research initiatives funded by the University Grants Commission of Bangladesh and the European Union. His work aligns closely with the United Nations Sustainable Development Goals (SDGs), particularly in areas such as poverty reduction, access to quality education, clean and affordable energy, inclusive economic growth, sustainable industrialization, responsible consumption, climate resilience, and ocean sustainability. His work also reflects a commitment to reducing inequalities and fostering international partnerships for sustainable development. In addition to his research contributions, he serves as a peer reviewer for several high-impact academic journals and is widely recognized for promoting academic rigor and ethical scholarship. As a prolific author, he continues to shape the discourse on sustainability, innovation, and digital advancement through his research, writing, and knowledge dissemination.

G. Sowmya is an Assistant Professor in the Department of Computer Science and Engineering at MLRIT, Hyderabad, with over a decade of teaching experience. Currently pursuing a Ph.D. in CSE from JNTUH, her research focuses on the formal verification of smart contracts. Sowmya holds an M.Tech and B.Tech in CSE and has received the prestigious Prathibha Award for academic excellence. She has contributed to numerous international journals and conferences, authored several patents, and actively engages in various FDPs and certifications, particularly in

Blockchain, AI, and IoT. She has also conducted workshops and webinars on cutting-edge technologies such as blockchain and machine learning

Anorgul Ashirova is an Associate Professor working at the Department of General Professional Sciences, Mamun University, Khiva, Uzbekistan.

Sudha K is a faculty member in the Department of Computer Science and Business Systems at R.M.D. Engineering College, Tamil Nadu, India. She has academic and research interests spanning computer science, business systems, and interdisciplinary applications. She is actively engaged in teaching, research, and mentoring students in innovative and industry-oriented projects.

Ganesh Kumar K working as a Professor in the department of Information Technology, Velalar College of Engineering and Technology, Thindal, Erode, Tamilnadu, India. He has published 15 articles in various national and international level journals. He is an active review member in various reputed journal.

S. Rajalakshmi received her B.E – CSE from Periyar University, Salem in 2003, M.E – CSE from Anna University, Chennai in 2007and Ph.D. from Anna University, Chennai in 2012.she has 16years of Academic and 10 years of Research experience. Her main research areas are Data mining, Artificial Intelligence, Cloud Computing and Wireless Networks. She has published research articles 13 in SCI/ Scopus and 23 papers in refereed Journals. She has organized National and International Conferences and also acting as a Journal Editor and Reviewer in International Journal Engineering Science and Technology by Elsevier. Patent publications on "Intelligent customer segmentation using machine learning and deep learning programming" and "Pet Companion". She published three books related to CSE. She awarded for "Dr.APJ.Abdul Kalam Award for Scientific Excellence 2016" by Marina Labs and received Global Faculty Award 2022 for "Outstanding contributions to Education and for being role model to students" by AKS Educational Awards.

Zokir Mamadiyarov is a professor working in the Department of Finance and Tourism at Termez University of Economics and Service, Termez, Uzbekistan.

Gularam Masharipova is working at the Department of Social Science, Alfraganus University, Tashkent, Uzbekistan

Md. Mazid-Ul-Haque is working as an Assistant Professor in the Department of Computer Science at American International University- Bangladesh. He has completed both his Master of Science in Computer Science degree and Bachelor of Science in Computer Science and Engineering degree from American International

University- Bangladesh. He did his HSC at Notre Dame College, Dhaka. Previously, he worked as a Lecturer and as an Instructor in the Department of Computer Science at American International University- Bangladesh. His research interests include ML, Wireless Communication, WSN, etc. He was born in Kushtia. He has a strong passion and dedication for teaching and research work. He believes in hard work and sincerity for achieving life goals. Apart from teaching, his hobbies include playing football, traveling, watching movies, and reading newspapers.

Keerthana N V is an Assistant Professor with 8 Years of experience in teaching and 1-year experience in research (IUCAA LIGO Data Centre, Pune). Her area of interest is Network Security, Blockchain Security, and Machine Learning Algorithms. She is pursuing PhD at Anna University in Security in Blockchain. She has a working experience in High-Performance Computing (HTCondor) in LIGO INDIA Project. She has written many research articles in Network Security and assisted Scientists in analyzing Datasets in HTCondor.

Nakul Pareek has completed a Bachelor's degree in Computer Applications from Christ University, Delhi NCR, India. His areas of interest include quantum cryptography, cybersecurity, and emerging technologies in smart cities. He has completed internships in system administration and data analysis, gaining hands-on experience with IT systems and data-driven decision-making. He is passionate about research and aims to contribute to the field of secure and intelligent urban infrastructure.

Siva Subramanian R is affiliated with R M K College of Engineering and Technology, Puduvoyal, Tamil Nadu, India. His academic and research interests focus on emerging technologies in computer science and engineering. He has contributed to studies in areas such as artificial intelligence, machine learning, and blockchain applications. He is actively engaged in research that addresses real-world challenges through innovative digital solutions. With a commitment to academic excellence, he continues to explore advancements in technology for societal benefit.

Ravikumar R. Natarajan is an experienced academician with over 12+ years of teaching and research expertise across institutions in India, the UAE, and the Maldives. He currently serves as an Assistant Professor at Marwadi University, Rajkot, specializing in Machine Learning, Recommender Systems, and AI-driven applications in healthcare and security. He holds a Ph.D. in Machine Learning and Recommender Systems from Amity University, Jaipur, a Master of Engineering in CSE from VMRF University, Salem, and a Bachelor of Engineering in CSE from Anna University. He also has a MiniMBA from the Swiss eLearning Institute. Dr. Ravikumar has authored more than 8+ multiple SCIE/Scopus-indexed journal articles, 25+ IEEE/Springer conference papers, and co-authored a book on Artificial Intelligence. He has also published 9 patents and contributed 10+ book chapters in emerging domains such as Federated Learning, Blockchain, and Digital Twins for IGI Global, Wiley and Springer publisher. He actively mentors students through initiatives like the Research Activities Club (RAC) and Student Research Internship Training (SRIT), promoting innovation and research culture.

Kh. Mustafizur Rahman has done his B.Sc. From Department of Computer Science And Engineering and M.Eng. From Department of Information Systems Security, in Bangladesh. He has more than 12 years of working experience after completing studies in his regarding fields. He is currently working as a respected faculty of Department of Computer Science And Engineering in a renowned private university named "World University of Bangladesh". Before that he worked with a renowned multinational company named "Accenture" popularly known as Grameenphone IT Limited situated in Dhaka, Bangladesh. He has Four published International Journal Paper and Two conference paper. Currently working on another paper for publication. He is also looking forward for more and more studies and researches. His Current research focuses are on Data Science, Internet of Things, Cyber Security and Networking.

Aarthi S is a dedicated Assistant Professor in Computer Science with over six years of teaching experience. She is currently pursuing her Ph.D. at Marwadi University, Gujarat, and holds an M.Phil. and MCA from Bharathiar University, Tamil Nadu. Throughout her academic career, Aarthi has specialized in programming languages such as C++, Java, and C, and contributed to research in recommender systems and AI-related data privacy. She has published journal articles, contributed to book chapters, and actively participated in technical workshops. Known for her student mentorship and engagement in academic events, Aarthi remains committed to fostering innovation and excellence in computer science education.

Neha Saini is working as Assistant Professor in the School of Sciences. She is currently pursuing Doctor of Philosophy (Ph.D.) in Computer Science and Engineering from Amity University, Noida, India. Her research area for the Ph.D is Federated learning . Her current research interests include Machine Learning, cryptography and wireless sensor networks.She holds two master's degree, MCA from BTKIT Dwarahat Uttrakhand and M.Tech (CSE) From IIT Dhanbad. She has published research paper in various journals and also has one patent. She has 12 years of academic experience. She keeps updating herself with the latest knowledge of the subjects as Python,Machine Learning and Andriod Applicatios in her discipline and likes to interact with the students on contemporary issues and topics. She has served the institution as a member of various committees and also organized technical and cultural events.

Lal Tlan Sang is a dedicated Data Analyst currently working in the IT Department at TODA PVC Co., Ltd. With a strong background in data analytics and information systems, Lal specializes in transforming complex data into actionable insights that support strategic decision-making and enhance operational efficiency. At TODA PVC Co., Ltd., Lal manages data workflows, performs advanced data analyses, and develops visualizations and reports that help guide management in optimizing business processes. Holding a Bachelor's degree in Computer Science and an MBA in Business Analytics, Lal combines technical expertise with business acumen to effectively address real-world challenges. Passionate about leveraging data-driven approaches, Lal continuously hones skills in emerging technologies and analytical tools. Beyond professional responsibilities, Lal is committed to knowledge sharing and community development by organizing training sessions and workshops aimed at empowering youth and professionals in data IT skills.

Binastya Anggara Sekti has been a lecturer at the Faculty of Computer Science, Esa Unggul University, Jakarta, since 2016. He is actively involved in the Artificial Intelligence and Information Security Study Group. He holds a Bachelor's degree in Informatics Engineering from the Bandung Institute of Technology and a Master's degree in Information Systems Management from Trisakti University, Jakarta. Prior to entering academia, he accumulated over 25 years of professional experience as an IT practitioner in various companies across Jakarta. His work focused on developing data centers for internet service providers and delivering IT solutions for the manufacturing and oil & gas sectors. His research interests include artificial intelligence, cybersecurity, and the development of IT infrastructure.

Tuqa Ghani Treji received her bachelor's degree in computer science from the Department of Computer Science, College of Education for Pure Sciences, University of Thi-Qar, Iraq, in 2016. She is currently pursuing a master's degree in cybersecurity. Her research focuses on securing smart city data against quantum computing threats using quantum-resistant key exchange methods, digital signatures that ensure the integrity of big data in urban infrastructures, quantum encryption, quantum signatures, and exchange keys using quantum techniques.

Index

B

C

D

E

F

H

I

J

K

T

U

Z

www.ingramcontent.com/pod-product-compliance
Lightning Source LLC
LaVergne TN
LVHW081348300926
849161LV00008B/2094